Perspectives on the American Way of War

Perspectives on the American Way of War examines salient cases of American experience in irregular warfare, focusing upon the post-World War II era.

This book asks why recent misfires have emerged in irregular warfare from an institutional, professional, and academic context which regularly produces evidence that there is in fact no lack of understanding of both irregular challenges and correct responses. Expert contributors explore the reasoning behind the inability to achieve victory, however defined, and argue that what security professionals have failed to fully recognize, even today, is that what is at issue is not warfare suffused with politics but rather the very opposite, politics suffused with warfare.

Perspectives on the American Way of War will be of great interest to scholars of war and conflict studies, strategic and military studies, insurgency and counterinsurgency, and terrorism and counterterrorism. The book was originally published as a special issue of *Small Wars & Insurgencies*.

Thomas A. Marks is Distinguished Professor and MG Edward Lansdale Chair of Irregular Warfighting Strategy at the College of International Security Affairs (CISA) of the National Defense University (NDU) in Washington, DC. He assumed this position after 12 years as Chair of the War and Conflict Studies (WACS) Department at CISA.

Kirklin J. Bateman is Chair of the War and Conflict Studies (WACS) Department at the College of International Security Affairs (CISA) of the National Defense University (NDU) in Washington, DC. He assumed this position after previously serving as CISA Associate Dean of Curriculum Development.

Perspectives on the American Way of War

The U.S. Experience in Irregular Conflict

Edited by
Thomas A. Marks and Kirklin J. Bateman

LONDON AND NEW YORK

First published 2020
by Routledge
2 Park Square, Milton Park, Abingdon, Oxon, OX14 4RN

and by Routledge
52 Vanderbilt Avenue, New York, NY 10017

Routledge is an imprint of the Taylor & Francis Group, an informa business

© 2020 Taylor & Francis

All rights reserved. No part of this book may be reprinted or reproduced or utilised in any form or by any electronic, mechanical, or other means, now known or hereafter invented, including photocopying and recording, or in any information storage or retrieval system, without permission in writing from the publishers.

Trademark notice: Product or corporate names may be trademarks or registered trademarks, and are used only for identification and explanation without intent to infringe.

British Library Cataloguing in Publication Data
A catalogue record for this book is available from the British Library

ISBN13: 978-0-367-40688-2

Typeset in Myriad Pro
by Newgen Publishing UK

Publisher's Note
The publisher accepts responsibility for any inconsistencies that may have arisen during the conversion of this book from journal articles to book chapters, namely the inclusion of journal terminology.

Disclaimer
Every effort has been made to contact copyright holders for their permission to reprint material in this book. The publishers would be grateful to hear from any copyright holder who is not here acknowledged and will undertake to rectify any errors or omissions in future editions of this book.

Contents

Citation Information	vii
Notes on Contributors	ix

Introduction – Perspectives on the American way of war: the U.S. experience in irregular conflict   1
Thomas A. Marks and Kirklin J. Bateman

1 The Mexican War: frontier expansion and selective incursion   14
   Craig A. Deare

2 Birth of the Cold War: irregular warfare first blood in Greece   31
   Andrew Novo

3 Organizing for the 'gray zone' fight: early Cold War realities and the CIA's Directorate of Operations   62
   David P. Oakley

4 Counterinsurgency in Vietnam – schizophrenia until too late   81
   Rufus Phillips

5 Turning gangsters into allies: the American way of war in Northern Afghanistan   101
   Matthew P. Dearing

6 Iraq, 2003–2011: succeeding to fail   140
   Jeanne Godfroy and Liam Collins

7 The American way of war in Africa: the case of Niger   176
   LTC Joseph Guido

8 Too little, too late: protecting American soft networks in COIN/CT   200
   Steve Miska and Samuel Romano

9 Systems failure: the US way of irregular warfare   223
   David H. Ucko

   Index   255

Citation Information

The chapters in this book were originally published in *Small Wars & Insurgencies FSWI*, volume 30, issue 1 (February 2019). When citing this material, please use the original page numbering for each article, as follows:

Introduction
Perspectives on the American way of war: the U.S. experience in irregular conflict
Thomas A. Marks and Kirklin J. Bateman
Small Wars & Insurgencies FSWI, volume 30, issue 1 (February 2019) pp. 1–13

Chapter 1
The Mexican War: frontier expansion and selective incursion
Craig A. Deare
Small Wars & Insurgencies FSWI, volume 30, issue 1 (February 2019) pp. 14–30

Chapter 2
Birth of the Cold War: irregular warfare first blood in Greece
Andrew Novo
Small Wars & Insurgencies FSWI, volume 30, issue 1 (February 2019) pp. 31–61

Chapter 3
Organizing for the 'gray zone' fight: early Cold War realities and the CIA's Directorate of Operations
David P. Oakley
Small Wars & Insurgencies FSWI, volume 30, issue 1 (February 2019) pp. 62–80

Chapter 4
Counterinsurgency in Vietnam – schizophrenia until too late
Rufus Phillips
Small Wars & Insurgencies FSWI, volume 30, issue 1 (February 2019) pp. 81–100

Chapter 5
Turning gangsters into allies: the American way of war in Northern Afghanistan
Matthew P. Dearing

Chapter 6
Iraq, 2003–2011: succeeding to fail
Jeanne Godfroy and Liam Collins

Chapter 7
The American way of war in Africa: the case of Niger
LTC Joseph Guido

Chapter 8
Too little, too late: protecting American soft networks in COIN/CT
Steve Miska and Samuel Romano

Chapter 9
Systems failure: the US way of irregular warfare
David H. Ucko

For any permission-related enquiries please visit:
www.tandfonline.com/page/help/permissions

Notes on Contributors

Kirklin J. Bateman is the chair of the department of War and Conflict Studies (WACS), College of International Security Affairs (CISA) of the National Defense University (NDU) in Washington, DC, USA.

Liam Collins is the director of the department of Military Instruction at the United States Military Academy (USMA) in West Point, NY, USA.

Craig A. Deare is the chair of the department of Strategic Initiatives and Leadership (SIL), College of International Security Affairs (CISA), National Defense University, Washington, DC, USA.

Matthew P. Dearing is an assistant professor and the director of the South and Central Asia Security Studies Program at the College of International Security Affairs (CISA), National Defense University, Washington, DC, USA.

Jeanne Godfroy is a strategy and management consultant in the Army Reserves based in Las Vegas, Nevada, USA.

LTC Joseph Guido is a U.S. army sub-Saharan Africa foreign area officer (48J) currently working at the U.S. Army Africa Command in Vicenza, Italy.

Thomas A. Marks is Distinguished Professor and MG Edward Lansdale Chair of Irregular Warfighting Strategy at the College of International Security Affairs (CISA) of the National Defense University (NDU) in Washington, DC, USA.

Steve Miska is the CEO of SLC Consulting based in San Clemente, CA, USA.

Andrew Novo is an associate professor at the College of International Security Affairs (CISA), National Defense University, Washington, DC, USA.

David P. Oakley is an assistant professor at the College of International Security Affairs (CISA), National Defense University, Washington, DC, USA.

Rufus Phillips is the author of *Why Vietnam Matters: An Eyewitness Account of Lessons Not Learned* (Naval Institute Press, 2008). He spent much of 1954–1968 involved with counterinsurgency in Vietnam.

Samuel Romano is the lead researcher and a legal assistant at the Soft Networks Project (SPSN) based in Los Angeles, California, USA.

David H. Ucko is the director of the Combating Terrorism & Irregular Warfare (CTIW) Fellowship Program at the College of International Security Affairs (CISA), National Defense University, Washington, DC, USA.

Introduction – Perspectives on the American way of war
The U.S. experience in irregular conflict

Thomas A. Marks and Kirklin J. Bateman

> Strategically, adaptation to insurgent challenges invariably proves difficult. Not only must the precise nature of the threat be discerned, but adaptation must occur even as the conflict develops. Too often, focus is upon immediate, tactical quick-fixes rather than reform realized through correct strategy and operational art.
>
> *Counterinsurgency in Modern Warfare*[1]

Significantly, the passage above, which spoke to Colombia's successful effort, went on to observe that there were two salient features of the case. First, whatever the particulars of the insurgent threat, which in this instance was the criminally enabled Revolutionary Armed Forces of Colombia or FARC, the parameters of meeting an insurgency built upon terrorism remained 'classic' in their essence. Correct implementation by Bogotá, therefore, resulted in success as defined by the goals laid out for the project. Second, though the strategy and its implementation, especially in its operational art, were Colombian, the Americans played a consistent and important role. All the more puzzling, therefore, was Washington's 'partial success' experienced in Iraq and Afghanistan. Left unsaid was the obvious point: how could the United States demonstrate such a schizophrenic understanding of irregular warfare?

Therein lies the heart of this special volume: *Perspectives on the American Way of War: The U.S. Experience in Irregular Conflict*, with the theme emerging clearly in the contribution by Jeanne Godfroy and Liam Collins on Iraq, 2003–2011: 'Succeeding to Fail.' It would be difficult to craft a more apt description of recent American irregular efforts. Their tactical successes have at times reached the point of near-legend, even as their strategic drift if not outright failure has become an ongoing subject for both condemnation and speculation.[2] The former requires little explanation, but it is the latter that is intriguing, if for no other reason than the harsh reality that recent misfires have emerged from an institutional, professional, and academic context which regularly produces evidence that there is in fact no lack of understanding of both irregular challenges and correct responses.

Examining the past

It is difficult to note definitely in history when challenge to the existing order became a matter not merely to be crushed but to be explained and hence responded to in holistic fashion in order to preclude having to do it all over again. Certainly, the discussion was placed on the record, both extensively and in a fashion noteworthy for its acuity, as early as the American Revolution. Extensive material from that rebellion turned revolutionary war, predictably mainly in English but some also in German and French, highlighted the reality that revolt stemmed from a political opportunity structure that did not mediate grievances.[3] Such specific terminology did not emerge until the 1960s, when, ironically, the United States asked itself why its cities were exploding in riots; but the point was hammered home not only in painfully accurate assessment by Patriot theorists but in their powerful campaign of information warfare. Disseminated both at home and abroad, particularly in Britain itself, Patriot positions established a dominance that London proved quite incapable of countering. To do so would have required a comprehensive focus upon political rather than military response.[4] Turn the clock forward, and we find the United States substituting for the British.

Both London (then) and Washington (now) have mistaken violent challenge as necessitating violent response. The specialists for this – especially when matters grow beyond the local armed representatives of the state, the police – are found in the military. It is for this reason that violent politics so readily leads policymakers to summon their men at arms, whether the task at hand is containment or suppression. The soldiers, in turn, classify what they are about as warfare of an irregular type, because it is obviously not what they regularly do, which is to face their peer rivals. That certain facets of regular conflict may well be irregular (in fact, almost invariably are) has been recognized formally as early as Alexander the Great and later the Romans, doctrinally by the British (hence Americans) as early as the period of the Seven Years War and American Revolution.[5] What security studies professionals have failed to fully recognize, even today, is that what is at issue is not warfare suffused with politics but rather the very opposite, politics suffused with warfare. The two are far from the same.

The act of rebellion is always political, but it does not rise to the level of insurgency, as per the modern usage of the term, unless the rebels become aware of the structural issues at stake. Such knowledge makes clear that it is no longer sufficient to change personalities, replacing the bad with the good, instead to create a new-order. This order requires a strategy that removes in all its facets the power that sustains the old-order. It was no accident that the American Patriots deployed a sweeping propaganda effort alongside their steadily improving deployment of force. That force, in turn, was a hybrid of what was known: regular and irregular tactical forms deployed in operational art that consistently baffled the British. If the strategy was Fabian, the design of the project was offensive. Only the reality of its intangible nature provided suitable concealment. It struck at British tangible might to the extent necessary to free up the political space required for local and regional, hence national, domination of human terrain.

In contrast, the British did what ruling powers had always done when faced with the lowers charging at their superiors: they deployed tangible force, made all the more ineffective by tactical regularity, albeit the presence of certain irregular units.[6] This brings us to our subject in ways that are perhaps not immediately evident. It was, after all, a failure of the British to imagine new constructs of imperial association that doomed them to plunging forward in an all or nothing manner[7]; and it is just such terms of incorporation which, in the final analysis, separate nation- from empire-building. This distinction between the two lies not in the process of construction itself but rather in the end-state sought; respectively, to rule all as one through a single body of law in a unified polity, making no discrimination between the parts, or to maintain division so that the center can benefit from the exploitation of the periphery.

Reality can be messy indeed, but the process of post-Second World War decolonialization, in particular, has created a false picture of potentialities. Had any of the great empires sought actually to implement their ideologies and achieved success, we might well think differently of them. France and Algeria, for example, were not so far apart in geography but instead, as De Gaulle assessed, in their separate socio-cultural systems, with never the twain to meet. The same could be seen from Senegal to Indochina. America and the Caribbean were outliers in the British imperial approach, with London's actions in India being more typical. There, unlike the French in their verbiage, there was not even the pretense of one system for all. The same was true of the Netherlands. The Portuguese stood out among the late-imperial Europeans for their attempt, at least at the bitter end in Africa, to embrace integration. This assessment, though, is contested, and upheaval at home left reality a hypothetical. Japan's empire had been destroyed in the world war itself, while that of China had in some respects been given a new basis for renewal. Both these great East Asian empires are of interest here precisely because of their astonishing brutality in ensuring the construction of a certain imperial unity. Only the Chinese still, notably in Tibet and Xinjiang, and the Russians, wherever they are involved, have continued to behave as though no advance in consciousness has occurred as to what is permissible of an imperial ruling power.

If we turn, then, to classic texts of counterinsurgency, we see played out just that: how to incorporate those absorbed into the polity, be it intended as nation-state or empire. The French, for instance, claimed Algeria as a department of France but Indochina as a part of the empire. Similarly, the British saw settler-colonialists in North America and the Caribbean as fellow members of the British nation but Indians and Africans (regardless where they were) as something altogether apart (hence the riveting opening episode in the film *Gandhi*[8]). It was the French who led the way doctrinally, with the works of Joseph Gallieni and Hubert Lyautey the best known, even as it has been demonstrated they were in essence products of an approach pioneered by others.[9] This approach posited simply that incorporation through development in its socioeconomic sense was a more viable strategy for governance than privileging force. Considerable debate attends reality, but this is perhaps to miss the forest for the trees. Ultimately, it was the lack of a political exit strategy that doomed French governance abroad, not the specifics of their strategy.

Ironically, the superior characteristics of French ideology in the matter have been brushed aside in irregular war studies, because it was the post-World War II British who upended their own political beliefs and fought their wars of decolonization not to keep empire but to determine the terms of reference in what they left behind. Malaya, to cite only the most celebrated example, provided a counterinsurgency model only because the British admitted political defeat from the start by announcing their intention to grant the colony its independence. In contrast, they had every intention of staying in India, yet ultimately, faced with the sheer scope of the task, simply walked away, leaving behind a staggering human catastrophe largely of their own making. The Dutch were run out of the Netherlands East Indies (Indonesia); Portugal collapsed at home; Spain finally gifted to Morocco its last remaining slice of an empire which for more than three centuries had been unparalleled in extent and wealth in human history; and Japan had lost all through its lack of success in challenging its Western imperial rivals for the right to brutalize those resident in its own conquests, in the process fostering what now is three-quarters of a country of enmity in some cases, continued estrangement between Seoul and Tokyo being but one of the most prominent illustrations.

Only the Americans, with much less over which to contend, emerged less scarred. Indeed, in honoring its pre-war promise of independence to the Philippines, then remaining in truncated but ultimately salutary form to assist in quelling the so-called Huk Rebellion, Washington gained influence which was potent through some four post-World War II decades. That this was so stemmed from the emphasis of key personalities, notably Ed Lansdale (see below), upon utilizing wide-ranging, innovative approaches to support local impulse for self-governance. Lost in many discussions of the effort was its essence: a variety of political responses were implemented to deal with political challenges. Violence, for all its interesting tactical aspects, was only the enabling mechanism.

Back to the future

It is at this point that we return to this volume. Our intent is not simply to revisit well-trod ground, extracting lessons learned; instead to provide fresh examination of a transition and deepening of trends which have seen the United States increasingly diverge from the generally positive legacy illustrated by its involvement in the Huk Rebellion. The timing is certainly appropriate as the 2018 U.S. National Defense Strategy calls for the opposite, a shift from focusing on 'terrorism' as the primary concern for U.S. strategy to inter-state competition.[10] Allowing for the confusion of terminology – U.S. doctrine well understands the distinction between insurgency using terrorism as method and the divorce from purported social base which produces terrorism as logic – there remains the imperative to avoid normal American 'all or nothing' approach as some claim animates the document. As Frank Hoffman has correctly observed, 'The strategy does not overlook the various forms that warfare may take in the future. Peacetime competition, "gray zone" tactics, Small War or hybrid combinations are not dismissed.'[11]

Indeed, as Max Boot so adroitly argues in his 2002 work, *The Savage Wars of Peace: Small Wars and the Rise of American Power*, 'If you want to see what lies in store for the armed forces in the future, you could do worse that to cast your gaze back to the past.'[12] Irregular conflict is not going away, whatever our military proclivities. What needs to be sharpened is our understanding of the phenomenon.

At the strategic level, irregular warfare is a contest of governance but not in the manner so often portrayed. Rebellion erupts from the perception, more often than not grounded in reality, that the political opportunity structure – society's terms of incorporation and empowerment – is failing to deliver justice. This is true whether we are describing Filipinos, who sought redress by backing various communist efforts at establishing a new-order, or Nigerian Muslims who support Boko Haram, a violent radical Islamist option. The role played by tangible factors (greed and grievance) is of a piece with the intangible assessment that the existing order is failing to deliver.

Deliver what? Therein lies the rub. Simply because a particular end-state is desired does not make it proper, right, or just – the Islamic State has reminded all of *that* – but neither does it mean popular impulse, however misguided, can be wished away. Politicians are rarely at one with supporters, but they end up leaders, because they speak to the desires and aspirations of their potential followers. Coercion always plays a role in this process. We delude ourselves in not recognizing that it comes in any number of socio-economic-political forms. It is into this reality that the United States has in modern history intruded, increasingly not with political approaches buttressed by self-defense but with military power enjoined to keep politics in mind as it engages in 'warfighting.'

Irony therefore informs our title. The American way of war – which necessarily as per our particular strategic culture means the military's approach to warfighting, regardless of level under consideration – leads and often is nearly the entirety of modern U.S. experience in irregular conflict. The category is of our own analytical making. The conflicts under consideration are irregular only in the sense that the challengers to the existing order must engage in asymmetric approaches, from strategy to tactics. To do otherwise would be squarely and foolishly to face our regular warfighting finesse. This makes them, to our mind, irregular. We have proved more than adept at responding tactically. No longer is the SAS the stuff of legend and movies, not even Delta, rather SEALS and, more controversially, drone strikes. The end is remarkably the same, however: succeeding to fail.

To engage with this reality, we begin with Craig Deare on the Mexican War. A puzzling choice if considered in its normal position, as but a minor if interesting run-up to the Civil War, with key figures experiencing their first taste of major combat, the conflict in reality was a harbinger of challenges to come. The central question should be less why America won as why the national legacy of more than three centuries of successful Spanish military effort in North America lost. The answer lies in the unrealized nation-building that followed a revolutionary experience utterly unlike our own, despite ample effort to portray the Latin American wars of independence as but the southern branch of our own war of independence. Put directly, Latin American states would have been unlikely to emerge had Napoleon's invasion of Spain not decapitated the empire and thrust to the fore the latent questions of who was to govern and how. The decades of sorting out the matter meant a half-formed Mexico faced an expanding, assertive America, which was driven in its tactical particulars by innovative tactical leadership at the head of profoundly racist manpower. That the occupation which followed major combat provided salutary lessons learned in dealing with guerrillas rather than a Vietnam-like litany of quagmire eventuated from the conscious designs of military leadership steeped in the same Napoleonic dynamic that had produced our opponent. Winfield Scott, a student of history, saw the agony of the Spanish peninsula as a salutary admonition to achieve realizable objectives and depart rapidly before matters took on a negative life of their own as the local resistance forces mobilized. The United

States chose to leave issues of state-building and governance to the Mexicans themselves, while annexing the sparsely populated (by any measure, indigenous or settler population) half of 'Mexico,' in reality, a particular remnant of Spanish empire.

It was a wise move, The Philippine pacification is well known, as are the so-called Banana Wars, less so our next transitional case, that of American support for Greece as treated by Andrew Novo. As neither conquest nor expansion was sought, the way forward could build upon the salutary lessons gained in successful occupation and reconstruction of nations in Europe. Those lessons, while they put on display extensive and consistent application of American power, economic and social deployed behind a military shield, were in the final instance built upon local particulars that emphasized state strengths even as the opponent and his supporters committed fatal errors. Seen by contemporaries as but part of the larger effort to rebuild Europe and swept away in salience by the emerging communist threat in Asia, the case had little impact on American approach beyond the individual level.

At the institutional level, the post-World War II years thrust forward consideration of just who was to fight these new wars, proxy or locally-inspired. Though it was this bifurcation of inspiration that was to absorb decades of national effort and profoundly distort our decision-making with respect to irregular challenges, this was to come. In the moment, the issue was combat of a new variety. Thus, it was a new organization that entered this 'gray zone.' The means at hand, as detailed by Dave Oakley, was provided by the Central Intelligence Organization (CIA). This resulted, from the very beginning, in an organization torn between two missions, production of intelligence and clandestine warfighting (in the most kinetic sense). That American security agencies produced no strategic as opposed to operational lessons goes almost without saying.

Lessons are the topic with which Rufus Phillips deals in his revisiting of Vietnam, a subject he knows well, both operationally and academically. A member of what was often termed simply 'the Lansdale team,' he has already produced a much-lauded exploration of the Vietnam conflict.[13] Here, he revisits the essence of the Lansdale approach and why it could not be transferred from the Philippines to Vietnam. As Novo notes with Greece, the context is all-important. Lansdale, observes Phillips, understood that, but he was unable to get the system to do likewise. What was required was a political approach to nation-building. This, though, would have meant grappling with Vietnamese on their own terms and supporting their efforts to build their own new, noncommunist world. So often denigrated, noncommunist nationalism in South Vietnam is now better understood, but the moment that this matters is long gone. Reduced to its essence, as pointed out by the Nationalist Chinese advisory effort, this meant it was never enough simply to fight against something. Rather, one needed to know what one was fighting for.[14]

It may be assessed that a failure to appreciate this point was the greatest casualty of Vietnam. Robert Komer, as a key player, addressed the matter from an organizational angle in barbed commentary,[15] but it was other perceived lessons that informed subsequent American approaches in Afghanistan and Iraq. From the beginning, it was clear that the revised American approach to irregular challenge, embodied in the so-called 'Petraeus manual,'[16] was written based upon the mistaken premise that the military, particularly the Army, had misunderstood the nature of the Vietnam War and thus failed to engage in a population-centric approach. Ignoring the parameters of conflict, though, was not the issue. Misapplication lay in the area of implementing the armed shield behind which South Vietnam could engage in nation-building with U.S. assistance. The never-resolved conundrum posed by the communist side's main forces could not be resolved, and they could never be driven from the field to such extent as to allow the South Vietnamese to focus upon local security. By the time a proper balance between military operations and pacification was arrived at, American will was no longer there to sustain the effort.[17]

This was also the fate of American and allied efforts in Afghanistan and Iraq. Were systems diagrams of those misguided adventures to be constructed, they would appear as one with Vietnam. Only details would need to be altered as appropriate to the cases. Matt Dearing examines the misadventures of nation-building in northern Afghanistan, where a search for a foundation upon which to build the new-order has slowly sunk in the soft soil of warlordism and its attendant criminality. Jeanne Godfroy and Liam Collins delve into similar concerns with respect to Iraq. Both cases, their unique aspects notwithstanding, serve to bring home the point made earlier: Armed efforts in irregular warfare – counterinsurgency, in these cases – exist for the purpose of creating the conditions for politics to operate. Violence is a shaping mechanism, and what unfolds is first-past-the-post. The winner gets to dictate the politics that follow. As outsiders, the American role was to assist in creating a context for governance so that a handoff could occur to civil processes and local security forces. That much was understood in Afghanistan and Iraq. Washington's hubris lay in thinking today's practitioners understood the process (and its reduction to doctrine) better than practitioners in the past.

In reality, as the articles of Dearing and Godfroy/Collins bring home powerfully, it was the same inability as outsiders to conceptualize and implement viable approaches to state-building (aka nation-building) that proved a bridge too far. That the rebels in both cases, inspired by a mix of resistance to occupation and ideology wrapped in the idiom of political Islamism, were objectively 'on the wrong side of history' was quite irrelevant. Rebels invariably are – but only so long as they are not victorious. Leaders, to return to the point made earlier, are not followers, and for armed politicians to mobilize followers requires conditions which demand resolution. That particular solutions proffered, whether those of the Islamic State or the Khmer Rouge, are odious is a matter for counter, but that counter can only emerge from a cause that itself is worthy of support. Legitimacy is not a zero-sum decimal but the fluid basis for mobilization in support of one political option over another. Indeed, when the state is either unwilling or unable to mediate grievances of those for whom the political opportunity structure is closed, it ceases to have legitimacy among the masses.

Where we as outsiders fit in is painfully clear. It is stated by all authors in this volume and reiterated for the recent case of Niger (and Africa writ large) by Joe Guido. What approach is to be pursued if that which is being supported is at variance with our values? Governance exists to provide the three basics sought by any population – sustenance, security, and meaning. Its particulars stem from the political opportunity structure that it embodies. Though much has been written snidely condemning 'the liberal peace' that is the focus of international bodies and the United States and its allies, in particular, the argument that there are 'other options' is spurious. At least one would hope not to see the United States openly aligning itself in support of systems as odious as those espoused by authoritarian and outright dictatorial regimes. The present political orientation of Washington has ripped loose the sheet-anchor of devotion that ties the United States to the tenets of liberal democracy, but this serves only to thrust forward the point. What strategy can emerge, asks Guido, if not only the ends but the very end-state sought are unclear? All becomes but application of tactical finesse.

Values and ideologies are the very stuff of soft-power. The willingness of partners and local populations to throw in with us stems, at a most elemental level, from shared commitment. This may be as fundamental as sustenance and security, but more often than not motivation emerges from the quest for meaning, and the fact that the mechanisms of interest aggregation and articulation embodied in liberal democracy – which is the popular will enabled but also restrained by the rule of law – are those which ultimately are sought by populations.[18] Absent such partners, we as outsiders are unable to proceed, either tactically in operations or strategically in terms of crafting and implementing an approach that results in handoff and exit. Steve Miska and Sam Romano assess our failure to take this reality to heart by protecting the soft networks upon which all save the most direct kinetic action is based.

The pages above hardly make for uplifting reading. This may astonish but it does not surprise. The time is out of joint. As a nation we have become a population that has as little idea of what it wants as it does of how to get it. Small wonder, then, that in armed politics, the U.S. military has experienced what David Ucko, in the conclusion to this volume, calls 'systems failure.' Unable to harness means in ways appropriate to achieve ends, we have increasingly fallen back upon that which we do best, tactical action. Whether 'nights raids' – search and destroy for the 21st Century – or drone strikes – 'jungle bashing' in every way save the presence of better intelligence – the end is the same, 'long war' gone endless, because there is no political end-state towards which the action is directed. In this, we see strategic bankruptcy on full display.

It was neither our intention to produce such a conclusion nor to hold up U.S. inadequacy. Nevertheless, it must be pointed out that there have been alternatives. We began by observing that the Colombian case achieved its more satisfying trajectory with full participation of American players.[19] The same is true of cases such as Thailand (against the CPT), the Philippines (against the CPP/NPA/NDF), and Peru (against Shining Path).[20] El Salvador now appears less lustrous as an exemplar than it once did, but it cannot be ignored as a salutary economy of force effort that resulted in what for a time was a rather more laudable democratic polity than now extant.[21] What such cases share is the primacy of democratic politics as strategic focus in actuality as opposed to only verbiage. In none of the cases, though, did this come immediately or in an off-the-shelf form that could achieve quick results. Controversy, too, was a constant, but all saw emergence of an end-state that allowed the U.S. role to be drawn down in a satisfactory fashion. That would seem to be a fitting counterpoint to the thrust presented here.

Notes

1. Marks, "Regaining the Initiative".
2. Though not focused on this topic specifically, the larger issue, as presaged by its title, is treated extensively in the superb recent work by Nolan, *The Allure of Battle*.
3. Every political system is comprised of a structure that either speaks to and facilitates individual and group opportunity – or does not. For democratic systems, legitimacy is essential; for authoritarian systems, power is central. Intellectuals consume themselves endeavoring to theorize on and demonstrate the extent to which democracy exists through mystification and building an intangible structure of false consciousness. Gramsci remains a particular favorite of this genre, and he offers a great deal that is useful; but the vulgar Marxism that holds individuals are incapable of exercising agency due to systemic entrapment founders whenever adequate safeguards are in place to allow the exercise of free will (e.g., secret ballots, a free press, the rule of law). Benchmark original work on the political opportunity structure is Eisinger, "The Conditions of Protest Behavior," 11–28.
4. An astute assessment can be found in Canfield, "The Futility of Force," 62–79.

5. For superb discussion of the first, see Holt, *Into the Land of Bones*; for the second, Cheesman, *The Auxilia of the Roman*, also Meyer, *The Creation, Composition*; for the third, see the recent Cusick, *Wellington's Rifles*.
6. Mandatory reading for both the Revolutionary War and the tactical state of the irregular art at the time is the work by the German partisan participant, Ewald, *Diary of the American War*; see also Ewald's, *Treatise on Partisan Warfare*, which was originally published in 1785; for theoretical and operational context, see Heuser, ed., *Small Wars and Insurgencies*.
7. For an excellent recent treatment of the subject, see Hay, "An End to Empire".
8. In which Gandhi is brutalized for his effrontery in claiming equal rights legally (as a British citizen) and in terms of status (he was a lawyer) when resident in Durban, South Africa; see *Gandhi* (Columbia, 1982); available at Amazon.
9. Best single work on both individuals and the sources of their system is Finch, *A Progressive Occupation*.
10. *Summary of the 2018 National Defense Strategy of the United States*, 1. Available at https://dod.defense.gov/Portals/1/Documents/pubs/2018-National-Defense-Strategy-Summary.pdf (accessed 5 November 2018).
11. Hoffman, "Sharpening Our Military Edge".
12. Boot, *The Savage Wars of Peace*, xxiv.
13. Phillips, *Why Vietnam Matters*.
14. For Chinese observations see A. Marks, *Counterrevolution in China*.
15. Komer, *Bureaucracy Does its Thing*.
16. Army FM 3-24/MCWP 3-33.5, *Counterinsurgency*.
17. For the strategic conundrum, see Andrade, "Westmoreland was Right"; for proper balance, Andrade and Willbanks, "CORDS/Phoenix"; for nonmilitary approaches, Hunt, *Pacification*; for present state of knowledge on the nature of the conflict, O'Dowd, "What Kind of War is This?"
18. This would seem to be the oft-misunderstood point of Fukuyama, *The End of History*.
19. The most comprehensive treatment to date of what the U.S. actually provided to support the Colombian effort is Berrios, "Critical Ingredient"; for assessment of conflict outcomes at this point, see Ospina et al., "Colombia and the War-to-Peace Transition", as well as Ospina and Marks, eds., *¿FARC: Derrota Militar y Victoria Política*.
20. Originally treated in articles which appeared in *Small Wars and Insurgencies*, these cases were consolidated in Marks, *Maoist Insurgency Since Vietnam*. Incorporation of expanded treatment of the U.S. role for the first case may be found in Marks, "Thailand: Anatomy of a Counterinsurgency Victory".
21. See Ucko, "Counterinsurgency in El Salvador".

Disclosure statement

No potential conflict of interest was reported by the authors. The views expressed are those of the author and do not reflect the official policy or position of the National Defense University, the Department of Defense, or the US government.

Bibliography

Andrade, Dale. "Westmoreland was Right: Learning the Wrong Lessons from the Vietnam War." *Small Wars and Insurgencies* 19, no. 2 (September 2008), 145–181. Available at: https://www.tandfonline.com/doi/pdf/10.1080/09592310802061349 (accessed 19 October 2018).

Andrade, Dale and James H. Willbanks. "CORDS/Phoenix: Counterinsurgency Lessons from Vietnam for the Future." *Military Review*, 86, no. 2 (2006): 9–23. Available at: https://ia802806.us.archive.org/11/items/DTIC_ADA489376/DTIC_ADA489376.pdf (accessed 19 October 2018).

Army FM 3-24/MCWP 3-33.5. *Counterinsurgency*. Washington, DC: Headquarters, Department of the Army, December 2006. Available at: https://fas.org/irp/doddir/army/fm3-24.pdf (accessed 19 October 2018).

Berrios, Carlos G. "Critical Ingredient: US Aid to Counterinsurgency in Colombia." *Small Wars and Insurgencies* 28, no. 3 (June 2017), 546–575. Available at: https://www.tandfonline.com/doi/pdf/10.1080/09592318.2017.1307610 (accessed 19 October 2018).

Boot, Max. *The Savage Wars of Peace: Small Wars and the Rise of American Power*. NY: Basic Books, 2002.

Canfield, Daniel T. "The Futility of Force and the Preservation of Power: British Strategic Failure in America, 1780-83." *Parameters* 42, no. 3 (Autumn 2012), 62–79. Available at: https://ssi.armywarcollege.edu/pubs/Parameters/articles/2012autumn/Canfield.pdf (accessed 19 October 2018).

Cheesman, George Leonard. *The Auxilia of the Roman Imperial Army*. Oxford: Clarendon Press, 1914. Available at: https://archive.org/details/auxiliaofromanim00cheerich/page/n5 (accessed 19 October 2018.

Cusick, Ray. *Wellington's Rifles: The British Light Infantry and Rifle Regiments, 1758-1815*. NY: Carrel Books, 2015.

Eisinger, Peter K. "The Conditions of Protest Behavior in American Cities." *The American political science review* 67, no. 1 (March 1973), 11–28. Available at: http://www.jstor.org/stable/pdf/1958525.pdf?refreqid=excelsior:24750156a2de852b089b3daff48d82a6 (accessed 2 June 2017).

Ewald, Johann. *Diary of the American War: A Hessian Journal*. Translated by Joseph P. Tustin. New Haven, CT: Yale University Press, 1979.

Ewald, Johann. *Treatise on Partisan Warfare*. Translated by Robert A. Selig and David Curtis Skaggs. NY: Greenwood Press, 1991.

Finch, Michael P.M. *A Progressive Occupation? The Gallieni-Lyautey Method and Colonial Pacification in Tonkin and Madagascar, 1885-1900*. NY: Oxford UP, 2013.

Fukuyama, Francis. *The End of History and the Last Man*. NY: Free Press, 1992.

Gandhi (Columbia, 1982). Available at Amazon.

Hay, William Anthony. "An End to Empire? British Strategy in the American Revolution and in Making Peace with the United States." Ch. 12 In *Justifying Revolution: Law, Virtue, and Violence in the American War of Independence*, edited by Glenn A. Moots and Phillip Hamilton, 264–285. Norman, OK: University of Oklahoma Press, 2018.

Heuser, Beatrice, ed. *Small Wars and Insurgencies in Theory and Practice, 1500–1850*. London: Routledge, 2018.

Hoffman, Frank "Sharpening Our Military Edge: The NDS and the Full Continuum of Conflict." *Small Wars Journal*, 27 June 2018. Available at: http://smallwarsjournal.

com/jrnl/art/sharpening-our-military-edge-nds-and-full-continuum-conflict (accessed 5 November 2018).

Holt, Frank L. *Into the Land of Bones: Alexander the Great in Afghanistan*, 1st ed. w/new Preface. Berkeley, CA: University of California Press, 2012.

Hunt, Richard A. *Pacification: The American Struggle for Vietnam's Hearts and Minds*. Boulder, CO: Westview, 1995.

Komer, Robert. *Bureaucracy Does its Thing: Institutional Constraints on U.S.-GVN Performance in Vietnam*. Santa Monica, CA: RAND, August 1972.

Marks, Thomas A. *Maoist Insurgency Since Vietnam*. London: Frank Cass, 1996.

Marks, Thomas A. *Counterrevolution in China: Wang Sheng and the Kuomintang*. London: Frank Cass, 1997.

Marks, Thomas A. "Regaining the Initiative: Colombia versus the FARC Insurgency." Ch. 10 In *Counterinsurgency in Modern Warfare*, edited by Daniel Marston and Carter Malkasian, 209–232, pb/rev. ed. NY: Osprey, 2010.

Marks, Thomas A. "Thailand: Anatomy of a Counterinsurgency Victory." *Military Review* 87, no. 1 (Jan-Feb, 2007), 35–51. Available at: http://www.au.af.mil/au/awc/awcgate/milreview/marks.pdf (accessed 19 October 2018).

Meyer, Alexander *The Creation, Composition, Service and Settlement of Roman Auxiliary Units Raised on the Iberian Peninsula*, PhD dissertation, Duke University, 2012. Available at: https://dukespace.lib.duke.edu/dspace/bitstream/handle/10161/5566/Meyer_duke_0066D_11377.pdf?sequence=1 (accessed 19 October 2018).

Nolan, Cathal J. *The Allure of Battle: A History of How Wars Have Been Won and Lost*. NY: Oxford UP, 2017.

O'Dowd, Edward C. "'What Kind of War is This?'." *Journal of Strategic Studies* 36, no. 6–7 (June 2014), 1027–1049. Available at: https://www.tandfonline.com/doi/abs/10.1080/01402390.2014.891982 (accessed 19 October 2018).

Ospina, Carlos and Thomas A. Marks, eds., *¿FARC: Derrota Militar y Victoria Política?* Bogotá: Editorial Oveja Negra, 2017.

Ospina, Carlos, David Ucko, and Thomas A. Marks, "Colombia and the War-to-Peace Transition: Cautionary Lessons From Other Cases." *Military Review* 96, no 4 (July-August 2016), 2–14. Available at: http://usacac.army.mil/CAC2/MilitaryReview/Archives/English/MilitaryReview_20160831_art010.pdf (accessed 19 October 2018).

Phillips, Rufus *Why Vietnam Matters: An Eyewitness Account of Lessons Not Learned*. Annapolis, MD: Naval Institute Press, reprint 2017.

Summary of the 2018 National Defense Strategy of the United States, 1. Available at https://dod.defense.gov/Portals/1/Documents/pubs/2018-National-Defense-Strategy-Summary.pdf (accessed 5 November 2018).

Ucko, David. "Counterinsurgency in El Salvador: The Lessons and Limits of the Indirect Approach." *Small Wars and Insurgencies* 24, no. 4 (October 2013), 669–695. Available at: https://www.tandfonline.com/doi/full/10.1080/09592318.2013.857938 (accessed 19 October 2018).

1 The Mexican War

Frontier expansion and selective incursion

Craig A. Deare

ABSTRACT
Mexico's defeat in the war that (in the U.S.) takes the country's name resulted as much from the strategic context created by unrealized nation-building that followed independence as it did from American tactical supremacy. Three centuries of Spanish empire did not translate into national military excellence due to the decades of revolutionary upheaval that followed the sudden decapitation occasioned by Napoleon's ouster of the monarchy in Madrid. That the occupation which followed major combat provided salutary lessons learned in dealing with guerrillas rather than a Vietnam-like litany of quagmire eventuated from the conscious designs of military leadership steeped in the same Napoleonic dynamic that had produced our opponent. The United States wisely chose to leave issues of state-building and governance to the Mexicans themselves, while annexing the sparsely populated northern remnant of Spanish empire.

The case of the still-expanding United States of America in mid-nineteenth century and its conflict with Mexico represents a compelling story of the ends justifying the means. At this juncture at the outset of the twenty-first century, there is precious little thought given – in the U.S. at any rate – regarding how acquiring vast swaths of territory ostensibly owned and/or controlled by external powers actually came about, particularly where armed conflict is involved. The interaction between British, French, and Spanish concerns in the late 1700s/early 1800s in what are now the 48 contiguous states of the union was a continuation of their colonial designs over yet unconsolidated terrain. Although this article focuses on how the U.S. pursued its perceived national interest in both geostrategic as well as blunt military terms, some space must be dedicated at the outset to setting the larger stage.

Setting the stage

The broader strategic context of the early nineteenth century and the evolving experiment of American governance was a dynamic environment. France, Britain, and Spain (among other European powers) competed for control over much of the New World. Indeed, success in the American Revolution against King George was part of that great game as France bet on the colonialists to advance her interests more than out of any solidarity with the American upstarts. Spain's three century run at empire, beginning with the Habsburgs in the early 1500s, and continuing with the Bourbons from 1700 on, began to crumble in the early 1800s. Prior to the Spanish crown's expansion into Central and South America, Hernan Cortés – following his victory over Cuauhtémoc and the Aztecs – began to consolidate and expand the Spanish empire in the space that now embodies significant parts of North and Central America. These new domains were known as New Spain. Spanish territorial control in North America at the turn of the nineteenth century thus included much of Florida, the Gulf Coast, and the expanse of land west of the Mississippi basin.

Spain's territorial losses in what we now recognize as the continental U.S. over the course of several years resulted from both geopolitical struggles on the European mainland and internal, ongoing tensions throughout the Spanish empire in the Americas. The French Revolution of 1789 had little immediate impact, but Napoleon's aggression against the Spanish monarchy in the 1809–1810 timeframe, coupled with independence movements in Mexico and beyond, combined to spell the beginning of the end of Spain's control in the Americas. When King Carlos IV and King Ferdinand abdicated to Napoleon Bonaparte in 1808, Napoleon gave the crown of Spain to his brother Joseph. Across the Atlantic in New Spain, Viceroy José de Iturrigaray formed a provisional government, but it was simply a matter of time before Spain would lose control completely. The internal power struggles in Mexico were too advanced to contain. This independence movement is a story unto itself, but suffice to say that Mexico was embarking on a transition to self-government that was quite unlike that of its northern neighbor. From 1810 to 1821, a series of internecine power struggles ensued, and eventually on 27 September 1821, General Agustín Cosme Damián de Iturbide, supported by the Army of the Three Guarantees, marched into Mexico City, and the independent Empire of Mexico was born.

It shared the continent, in particular, with the young representative democracy that was the United States. The fledgling constitutional republic in the 1840s was a fascinating place, an evolving socio-political and economic experiment. Of particular moment, the relationship between the commanders-in-chief and the senior ranking general officers was quite unlike what today passes as effective civil-military relationships. Individual personalities played an even stronger role in the policymaking process than they do today, especially since the nation and its institutions had only 60 years of development. Washington, Jefferson, and Adams in the beginning, and then Jackson in his own way, had a profound influence in how the armed forces of the nation would develop.

Of concern to us here, in the 1840s, a situation obtained where the Democratic Party and the Whig Party were vying for political control. In this antebellum period, the concept and, perhaps even more importantly, the manner of the growth of the national experiment remained a matter of contention. Among myriad other issues, the question of westward expansion was on the ballot, so to speak, and the Democrat and Whig camps offered different propositions. James K. Polk, an exemplary acolyte in the Andrew Jackson expansionist camp, emerged as the Democratic Party's presidential candidate in 1844. No novice to the political scene, after several years in the Tennessee legislature, Polk had spent 14 years as a member of Congress, culminating as the Speaker of the House from 1835 to 1839. After a stint as the governor of Tennessee, he emerged as the consensus candidate for president on the ninth ballot, when no agreement could be reached among the early favorites. He was elected the eleventh president in 1845, simultaneously becoming the eleventh Commander in Chief of the armed forces.

Polk was elected in a setting where the Democratic Party was clamoring for westward expansion, specifically the 'recuperation of Oregon' and the 're-annexation of Texas.' This is not the place for a full treatment of the history of the Republic of Texas, but the matter sparked a coming together of expanding U.S. territorial ambitions under the emerging doctrine of Manifest Destiny with continuing political instability and weakness in the newly independent Mexico.[1] The result was 15 years that saw the 'transfer' of more than half of Mexico's territory to the United States. It is worth entertaining the question of whether the land of *Tejas y Coahuila* (as Texas was referred to in Mexico) was actually Mexico's territory or only territory claimed but not effectively controlled by Mexico. Or even more pointedly, perhaps the territory in question was best characterized as land previously *claimed* by Spain – again, the majority of the land was not effectively occupied and controlled by Spaniards – and then became territory without a true legal owner after the collapse of the Spanish government to Napoleon, an argument that it was never really Mexican territory to begin with.

In any event, back in the States, we encounter the reality of the evolving civil-military dynamic of the post-War of 1812. Only months after the British burning of the White House, General Andrew Jackson defended New Orleans against a larger, veteran force. Jackson's fame and representation was such that his subsequent presidential election was a mere formality. His populist personal style and political orientation resulted in the strengthening of the Democratic Party but also produced a strong opposition to those tactics, the evolving Whig party. Jackson's legacy would endure, however, as one of the lieutenants in his army was James K. Polk. He defeated Martin Van Buren from the Whig party in part on the strength of his support for western expansion.

President Polk's achievements as president are actually rather impressive. As historian Richard Bruce Winders argues:

> President James K. Polk was one of the most successful commanders-in-chief of the United States has ever produced. He led the nation in its first major war where the opponents were not Europeans or Native Americans. He formulated the strategy that sent five armies onto foreign soil. He oversaw the greatest military expansion that Americans of his day ever witnessed. His troops won victory after victory, occupying large sections of the enemy's territory...It is odd that, with all these accomplishments, Polk remains unknown to most Americans.[2]

The U.S. Army of 1845 was still in a process of becoming a stable institution. The enduring legacy of an all-powerful executive hung over the political psyche, and the notion of a standing army was anathema to the country's leaders and citizens. It does not surprise, therefore, that only a few years after Jackson's success in New Orleans, the Army was in lamentable shape. The U.S. Congress had authorized a strength of 8,615 officers and soldiers, though the true number was significantly less due to sickness and desertions, leaving the actual numbers closer to 5,000. Congressional guidance had established a force of 14 regiments and 10 staff departments, but the force was at less than 60 percent strength.

Beyond those stark realities, in the years prior to the War between the U.S. and Mexico, another complicating factor was the nature of civil-military relations. The armed forces of today's environment attempt to be as apolitical as possible; the model senior general and flag officers are not associated with any political party or explicit ideological bent. Their task is to translate strategic policy objectives into effectively organized, trained, and equipped operational combat units and supporting infrastructure. In 1845, the senior general officers of the day – major generals in that period – represented opportunities for the commander-in-chief to appoint, and for the Senate to confirm, important politico-military actors. Given the relatively reduced size of the force and number of commissioned officers, there were known personalities with political tendencies; choosing the men to lead this force represented an intensely personal decision for the country's leaders.

At this point in time, the two key protagonists were Winfield Scott and Zachary Taylor, both senior general officers and profoundly different – in terms of personality, professional background, operational approach, and political orientation. In that each of these two key actors has books written about them, only a very superficial treatment will fit in these spaces.[3] The larger point to keep in mind is that President Polk's larger geostrategic objectives were shaped, in significant part, by the individual backgrounds of two of the senior Army officers of the day.

The senior officer, by date of rank, was Major General Scott, 'Old Fuss and Feathers' – earlier known as 'Young Fuss and Feathers,' nicknames that stemmed from his recognized penchant for the finer things in life, ranging from food to manners of dress, pomp and circumstance, and the like. Appointed general-in-chief of the Army in 1841, his meteoric rise was an affront to the more traditionally grown general officers. There were numerous open rifts between Scott and his contemporaries. Volunteering in the Army in 1808, shortly thereafter accepting a commission as a captain of light artillery he was a lieutenant colonel a brief four years later, at the age of 26, primarily due to intellect and hard work. Congress appointed him brigadier general on 9 March 1814, at the age of 29. A serious scholar of European doctrine and tactics, Scott earned a reputation as one of the most effective trainers and leaders in the Army. His brigade fought the British successfully at battles in New York during the War of 1812, and he was seriously wounded at Niagara. As a 30 year old brevet major general, he was number four in terms of seniority behind General Andrew Jackson and two others. From 1817 and over the course of the next 30 years, Scott's military writings – influenced greatly by French and other European conventional tactics of the day – would have an important influence on the evolution of U.S. Army doctrine. As noted by Russell Weigley, 'In strategy he was at his best in a war of limited objectives which could be pursued by maneuver and occupation of territory rather than by ruthless destruction.'[4]

Following an entirely different career path was Zachary Taylor, referred to by his devoted troops as 'Old Rough and Ready.' Taylor entered the Army in 1808, commissioned as a lieutenant of infantry. Quite distinct from Scott's accelerated pace to general officer, Taylor rose gradually through the ranks, establishing himself an effective Indian fighter with a solid combat record, punctuated by an important victory on Christmas Day 1837 during the Seminole War. For that achievement, he was thereafter known as the Hero of Okeechobee. The commander of the U.S. 6th Infantry, he received a brevet promotion to brigadier general for his distinguished performance at Lake Okeechobee.

As President Polk envisioned his range of options against Mexico to achieve his strategic objectives, he initially placed Taylor in charge of the Army of Occupation. Polk distrusted Scott, a Whig whose undisguised presidential ambitions made him a serious threat to the Democratic Party. For this reason, the president removed him from any operational role in the impending war. Though also a Whig, Taylor was with solid justification viewed as a soldier's soldier, eschewing the trappings of senior officers and preferring a more Spartan setting, and thus as a more appealing alternative for Polk's purposes.

On the diplomatic front, Polk sent an envoy, John Slidell, to Mexico to negotiate a settlement on U.S. claims regarding Texas, as well to purchase California. The Mexican government did not receive Slidell as it had severed diplomatic relations with the U.S. In circumstances that remain contested to the present, an ongoing border dispute led to the deployment of Taylor and his forces from San Antonio to the Rio Grande, which the U.S. claimed as the boundary between the U.S. and Mexico. This positioning occurred within a context of Mexico continuing to reject an independent Texas and lack of agreement over the actual location of the border, the Rio Grande or the Rio Nueces. With Taylor occupying territory across the Rio Grande from Matamoros, the stage had been set for Polk to achieve his geostrategic goals.[5] It is from this perspective that we move into aspects relating to the war itself.

The road to war

Though various interpretations have been advanced, the picture tends to be less than flattering to the U.S. side. The case of Texas independence from Mexico and its eventual incorporation as a U.S. state; the provocations by Taylor's forces along the Rio Bravo; the lead up to and the U.S. invasion of Mexico at Veracruz and movement to Mexico City; and the treaties following the war, all are subjects worthy of more detailed research (see Figure 1) for major military movements and actions). Viewed in isolation, it is possible to become lost in the nuances of domestic politics in each country, as well as the broader bilateral relationship between the two young republics. If one applies a geostrategic perspective, it was but a matter of time for the U.S. desire of a secure continental-wide territory to move decisively to achieve that status. As historian T. Harry Williams accurately summarizes, 'The Mexican War has always occupied an ambiguous position in the national historical consciousness...it has been denounced as a wicked war of aggression against a weaker neighbor or justified as an inevitable phase in the expansion of a virile and superior people.'[6] What is of moment in this treatment is the residual issues that remained after what a later generation, speaking of another time and place, would call 'a splendid little war.' They might have noted that it was actually the second.

Texas was the proximate cause. Historically, despite its being part of the Spanish Empire since the early sixteenth century, and subsequently part of Mexican territory in the early nineteenth century, Texas was woefully underpopulated. In an effort to remedy this, the Mexican government granted Moses Austin, a U.S. pioneer, a concession to bring in settlers (with the caveat that all be members of the Catholic faith). Substantial colonization

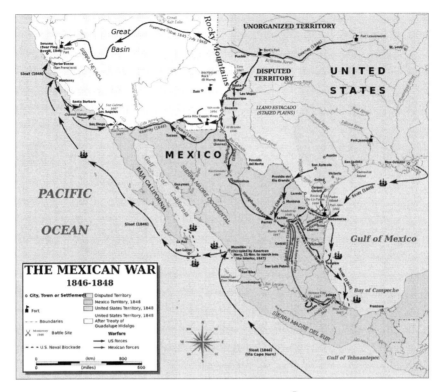

Figure 1. Major Movements during the U.S.–Mexico War.[7]

resulted. Observing the changing demographics of the area and perceiving U.S. designs on the territory, Mexico attempted to place restrictions of further immigration, as well as abolishing slavery in 1829 to dissuade U.S. slaveholders from moving there. This situation was exacerbated by a series of policy decisions (to include revoking the 1824 Constitution) taken by General Santa Anna, elected in 1833 to one of his 11 presidencies. The result was a Texas declaration of secession in November, 1835, followed by a formal declaration of independence in March 1836.

A majority of those pushing for independence were newly arrived settlers, powerfully influenced by conceptions of democratic control of local politics and redress of grievances. Initial willingness to compromise was increasingly at odds with the dictates of a centralized, authoritarian state. Conflict erupted when a Mexican force under Santa Anna's brother-in-law, General Martín Perfecto de Cós, entered Texas in 1835. Charged with pacification of a territory that had grown to 30,000 inhabitants (of whom only 4,000 were estimated to be ethnic Mexicans), Cós found himself outfought in urban battle at San Antonio and was forced to withdraw with the honors of war in December. There followed late in the year a powerful invasion by a force comprised mainly of veterans under Santa Anna himself. As San Antonio and Goliad were strategic points on the route to the areas of main 'Anglo' settlement, they were turned into strongpoints. This, however, occurred haphazardly and as much by individual accident as systemic design. Total defeat resulted in March 1836, with significant atrocity committed by the Mexicans at Goliad. As the only Texan forces remaining in the field retreated, Santa Anna split his forces into largely unsupported columns and proceeded with what he anticipated would be mopping up.

Rather than being intimidated by the loss at the Alamo, Texans rallied to the cause, surprising and defeating the column accompanied by Santa Anna at the Battle of San Jacinto in April 1836. Santa Anna was captured. Here we have yet another element of Mexican shame – in addition to Mexican anger at the U.S. – at actions taken by a Mexican leader more concerned with his own well-being versus the national interest. Santa Anna sent word (the Texans used a captured Mexican soldier as a courier) to the second-in-command, General Vicente Filisola (another Spanish general who had switched sides and joined Iturbide), that he was to remove all his forces from Texas in order to spare Santa Anna's life. He complied. Additionally, Santa Anna signed the treaties, the *Tratados* de *Velasco* – one public, one secret – that promised not to take up arms against Texas (the public version) and to recognize Texas' independence (the secret version). Texas, it seemed was free.

It was during this period that Santa Anna was sent to Washington D.C. (his first time aboard a train) to discuss his guarantee of the independence of Texas. While he was gone, the Mexican congress deposed Santa Anna, and because he had no authority to sign the treaties – he had been deposed – the Mexican government did not recognize Texas independence. To the contrary, Mexico would continue to attempt to reincorporate Texas as part of its territory, although Santa Anna – recognizing that doing so by force would be unlikely – would sign an armistice in 1843.

In the interim, however, the domestic political situation in Mexico at the time continued to be chaotic. The Mexican congress adopted *las Siete Leyes* (the Seven Laws) in lieu of the Constitution of 1824, the net effect of which was to limit civil rights, move away from federalism, and promote centralized power in the hands of the president. Among other disruptive events, the French landed forces at Veracruz in 1838 in response to Mexico's default on French loans and its rejection of French citizens' demands for compensation for property losses (the Pastry War). Santa Anna, after returning from the U.S. in 1837, was back in the game and led the successful ouster of the French forces (losing his left foot in the process). He then joined other Mexican forces in ousting President Bustamante by coup. He reassumed the presidency for a short while, turned it over to Nicolás Bravo, reclaimed power, was ousted and subsequently reinstated by competing Congressional pronouncements.

At this point we return to the events discussed above. Both countries made their claims regarding the actions that took place in 1845 and 1846, and merit additional study. Mexico's perspective on the matter, however, is that U.S. decisions demonstrated intent to 'take' Texas one way or the other. The argument has a number of elements, beginning with the claim that the U.S. violated the 1828 border treaty in which the U.S. recognized Mexican sovereignty over that territory. Mexicans also view this action as a violation of international law (such as it was in the mid-nineteenth century), and also established the precedent that the U.S. could annex other lands along the border at our whim. The Mexican Congress authorized the military mobilization necessary to preserve the territorial integrity of Mexican territory in accord with the established borders recognized by the U.S. from 1828 to 1836, yet never 'declared war' against the U.S.

In the U.S., the issue of whether to incorporate Texas and continue westward expansion was a divisive domestic political matter. In broad terms, the Democratic Party was favorable to the notion of Manifest Destiny, westward expansion, and the annexation of Texas, with the Whigs generally against the notion, in part because of the concern of adding another southern pro-slavery state to the union. With the presidential election of 1844 approaching, the Democrats chose James Polk over Martin Van Buren – Polk favored annexation, Van Buren opposed. Polk went on to win the presidential election, but before he was inaugurated, the U.S. Congress voted to admit Texas into the union as a state despite Mexico's warning that doing so would be a cause for war. Though not immediately the case, relations were severed by Mexico. The U.S. claimed additional territory beyond the traditional western boundary of the Nueces River to the Rio Bravo del Norte. Mexico rejected this claim as well.

Debate continues as to whether President Polk actually wanted to go to war with Mexico. This view holds that he simply wanted to acquire lands west of Texas to include present day New Mexico, Arizona, and California, as well as territory north of those states, and was prepared to purchase the territory. At the same point in time, Polk was attempting to reach an agreement with Britain regarding the Oregon territories (an area encompassing the present day states of Washington, Oregon, and Idaho). Concerned that Mexico would not simply sell those lands to the U.S., Polk may have believed that by intimating a possible war with Mexico that would be sufficient to lead to a negotiated solution.

Divided internally, some Mexican generals believed war with the U.S. was necessary. One of them, General Mariano Paredes Arillaga, overthrew the president, José Juaquín Herrera, with the intention of preparing the nation for war. Mexican popular opinion was split between those who favored military action versus a negotiated solution, but there was a strong consensus that Texas must not leave Mexico and most certainly not become a U.S. state. With Paredes in power in early 1846, forces were sent north to Matamoros. In April 1846, a U.S. Army unit on reconnaissance patrol about 30 miles from Taylor's forces found the large Mexican formation on the U.S. side of the Rio Grande and was routed. Taylor's forces subsequently engaged successfully with General Arista's formations in the Battles of Palo Alto and Resaca de la Palma, the first two major engagements of what would become the Mexican War. This was the spark that Polk needed, and on 11 May 1846, he appeared before Congress and declared that Mexico had 'shed American blood on America soil.' Despite the anti-expansionist stance of the Whigs, they joined the Democrats in declaring war on Mexico on 13 May 1846.

The domestic perspective

President Polk's choice of senior military leadership with regard to the unfolding war with Mexico, as noted earlier, involved a choice between two Whig generals, but on his mind was which would ultimately pose a greater political challenge. Polk, it has been noted, had opted for Taylor to serve as the General of the Occupation. Despite his hopes that the domestic political scene would produce alternatives, the initial reports from the southern border only served to strengthen 'Old Rough and Ready' and his standing as a possible electoral rival. Taylor's victories at Palo Alto and Resaca de las Palmas raised his profile as a future Whig presidential candidate. Nevertheless, Polk promoted Taylor to major general.

Time passed, though, and Taylor did not press the offensive in Monterrey, thus losing the possibility of an early victory. Polk found himself with the growing political strength of Taylor even as the geostrategic situation remained unresolved. Consequently, he opted for old 'Fuss and Feathers,' Winfield Scott. Despite his antipathy for Scott, Taylor had emerged as the more challenging political concern. In the fall of 1846, Scott was made the commander of the Army of Occupation.

While Polk may not have wanted a war and may have believed that, if war were to occur, it would be short, the reality proved quite different. The conflict lasted 16 months and cost both countries dearly in terms of blood and treasure. The military details of the war are quite interesting, filled with tactical innovation and brilliance, blunders and miscalculations, as well as gallantry and valor by both sides. The U.S. Army displays 10 streamers for the Mexican War. There were campaigns by Taylor's forces in Texas, New Mexico, and Northern Mexico; Kearney's troops in California and the Pacific Coast; and Scott's forces from Veracruz to Mexico City. The war was the first 'overseas deployment' of U.S. forces, and as such was a tremendous challenge for the young nation in a variety of ways. The success of the Continental Army had been based, in large part, on the effectiveness of militia citizen-soldiers as they supplemented General Washington's regular forces. A standing army was viewed with suspicion by much of the citizenry and its elected representatives. The establishment of the U.S. Military Academy at West Point in 1802, for instance, had not been universally supported – and Jackson had tried to eliminate it. As Weigley notes, 'The great structural question throughout most of the history of American military policy was that of the proper form of military organization in a democratic society, approached through a running debate over the proper weights to give to citizen soldiers and to military professionals in the armed forces of the United States.'[8] Primarily for these reasons, the congressionally authorized strength of the entire Army in 1845 was less than 10,000.

For his part, President Polk's concern that the majority of officers in the Army either belonged to the Whig party or were thought supportive of Whig philosophy affected his decision-making regarding how to prosecute the war. Examples abound, ranging from the appointment of volunteer generals (with the title General of Volunteers) to a preference for volunteer regiments to be the backbone of the Army for the duration of the war. During the course of the conflict, Polk appointed 13 generals of volunteers, and each was a loyal Democrat. As might be expected, regular Army units performed more effectively than the volunteer regiments, battalions, and companies. Leadership challenges resulted in large part from integration of volunteers with regular units.

The manner in which the federal government and the states each called for volunteers added additional confusion. Regular Army officers and soldiers held most volunteers in low esteem. In fact, a comparison of casualties is rather striking. Though both suffered from battlefield and disease/accident deaths, for volunteer regiments the latter category was disproportionately large, reflecting different approaches to unit discipline and procedures. The regular army unit with the highest number of battle deaths was the 8th U.S. Infantry, with 102; it also suffered 178 deaths by disease/accidents. On the volunteer side, the most extreme case was the 6th Illinois Regiment, which saw one death in battle but 296 through disease/accident.[9]

Approaches to battle itself strongly reflected individual command personalities. With the examples of both the American Revolution and the War of 1812 far in the past, the most effective American commanders – Scott, Taylor, Kearney, and Wool – all employed conventional tactics of the day, indeed, European tactics characteristic of the pre-Napoleonic era. Zachary Taylor was renowned for his direct approach, preferring a direct assault to an envelopment or turning movement. For his part, Winfield Scott was recognized for his detailed planning and preference for maneuver. His movement from Veracruz to Mexico City is acknowledged as a case study of avoiding well-established defensive positions through effective employment of his engineering assets. In all cases, however, the effects of conventional combat – bayonets, lances, bullets, and artillery shells – were experienced by soldiers of both countries, and the surgical limitations of the day were hard-pressed to save the seriously wounded. Fierce fighting was present throughout the theater, from Palo Alto and Resaca de las Palmas, to Buena Vista, Matamoros, Monterrey, Veracruz, Churubusco, Cerro Gordo, and Chapultepec.

After several months of combat in northern Mexico, President Polk – acknowledged as an actively participatory commander-in-chief – recognized that success in those operations would likely be insufficient to achieve his strategic objectives. According to Winders, Polk had proclaimed on 30 May 1846, that 'I declare my purpose to be to acquire for the United States, California, New Mexico, and perhaps some of the Northern Provinces of Mexico.'[10] Polk determined that to achieve those ends, it would be necessary to take the capitol of the country in Mexico City. After initial thoughts of an incursion in Tampico, it was later agreed that occupying Veracruz, and from there a movement to Mexico City, would be required. With Taylor occupied in the north, and Kearney in the west, the task would fall to Scott.

The amphibious assault and subsequent siege by Major General Winfield Scott against Veracruz in March 1847 was one of the first operations of its kind. In fact, Scott had to order the construction of boats with shallow draft for the purpose of being used as landing craft. Scott maneuvered his forces from Veracruz to Mexico City, largely avoiding Mexican defenses when possible. As but one of many examples of tactical innovation, the Battle of Contreras merits a brief recounting. Major General Scott, with four divisions under his control – David E. Twiggs, William J. Worth, John A. Quitman, and Guideon J. Pillow – was en route to Mexico City. As Scott approached the city of San Agustin to the east of Mexico City, General Santa Anna was in a defensive position with approximately 30,000 troops; in that Scott's four divisions totaled fewer than 10,000, he elected to avoid a direct assault. General Scott directed his engineer, Captain Robert E. Lee (USMA Class of 1829) to build a road across a lava field to bypass that position, a move which was completely unexpected and thus effective. During the next several days, as Scott maneuvered his forces around Santa Anna's defenses, Lee would make three successive night crossings across the Pedregal lava field, earning him a brevet promotion to lieutenant colonel by General Scott, characterizing it as 'the greatest feat of physical and moral courage performed by any individual' during the entire campaign.[11] Given Scott's maneuvers in and around Contreras, Santa Anna directed his units to fall back and prepare defenses at Churubusco, where direct engagement could no longer be avoided.

The Mexico City campaign would earn the Army battle streamers at Cerro Gordo, Contreras, Churubusco, Molino del Rey, and the culminating victory at Chapultepec Castle on 13 September 1847 which concluded the war. General Scott's dispatch to the Secretary of War on September 18th reported the following losses of his campaign:

> 19 August 2020. – Killed, 137, including 14 officers. Wounded, 877, including 62 officers. Missing (probably killed), 38 rank and file. Total, 1,052.
>
> September 8. – Killed, 116, including 9 officers. Wounded, 665, including 49 officers. Missing, 18 rank and file. Total, 789.
>
> 12 September 2013, 14. – Killed, 130, including 10 officers. Wounded, 703, including 68 officers. Missing, 29 rank and file. Total, 862.
>
> Grand total of losses, 2,703, including 383 officers.[12]

A brief review of this particular battle is necessary due to the national importance Mexico has given to what historians recognize as the facts evolving into the myth we have today. It is true that on that day in 1847, U.S. forces took the castle and the hill upon which it sits, defeating a smaller force. In one of the bloodiest battles of the war (and the single day in which he suffered his greatest losses), Scott and his forces won the battle of Molino del Rey on September 8th; that battle took place based on faulty reconnaissance and thus a mistaken assumption that a direct assault on a Mexican cannon founder at that location. After that costly victory, Scott halted, hoping that the Mexican government would agree to peace terms. But it was not to be, and Scott concluded that he would have to fly the Stars & Stripes from the *Palacio Nacional*.

The last fortress defended by the Mexican Army was located at Chapultepec Castle; it held tactical value as it was heavily fortified, sat on a 200 foot hill, and dominated much of central Mexico City. But it also held an intrinsic and emotional importance for Mexico in that it was built during the colonial period as a royal castle for the Viceroy (the only royal palace in the Americas), and in September 1847 served as the Mexican military academy. General Nicolás Bravo occupied the position with between 1,000 and 2,000 men, including the corps of cadets of the Mexican Army's military academy. The day prior, Scott initiated an artillery barrage on the fortress, continuing throughout the day. The morning of the 13th, two U.S. divisions attacked from the south and west, finally breaching the walls via ladders and engaging in close combat with the guardians. Despite valiant resistance, U.S. forces overwhelmed the Mexican defenders, eventually capturing the Mexican flag and replacing it with the U.S. standard. General Bravo ordered a retreat, and those able withdrew to the east; Bravo was captured before he could escape. Mexican losses were great, estimated at approximately 1,800 killed and wounded, with another 800 captured. Sources differ as they recount the story, but General Scott's message to the Secretary of War gives his conclusion:

> On the other hand, this small force has beaten on the same occasions in view of their capital, the whole Mexican army, of (at the beginning) thirty-odd thousand men – posted, always, in chosen positions, behind intrenchments, or more formidable defences of nature and art; killed or wounded, of that number, more than seven thousand officers and men; taken 3,730 prisoners, one-seventh officers, including thirteen generals, of whom three have been presidents of this republic; captured more than twenty colours and standards, seventy-five pieces of ordnance, besides fifty-seven wall-pieces, twenty-thousand small-arms, an immense quantity of shot, shells, powder, &c. &c.
>
> Of that enemy, once so formidable in numbers, appointments, artillery, &c., twenty-odd thousand have disbanded themselves in despair, leaving, as is known, not more than three fragments – the largest about 2,500 – now wandering in different directions, without magazines or a military chest, and living at free quarters upon their own people.[13]

The final major operational engagement concluded, it was a matter of time before the Government of Mexico would offer its surrender. And for his operational success, and thus the related strategic impact, Scott received a brevet promotion to lieutenant general, the first officer to be awarded that rank since George Washington during the Revolutionary War.

Here in Scott's summary we find the seeds of Mexican self-resentment and internally oriented shame. Because of Mexico's lack of unity, the collective nation did not defend itself as it could and/or should have. When the federal government requested men to augment its forces, many states answered in the negative, saying in essence, 'Not our problem.' It's quite one thing to lose a fight fair and square; it's quite another to have an invading force of lesser size and capability invade your territory and defeat you on your own turf. So beyond the legitimate anger and animosity against the enemy, the indignity and dishonor of not having pulled together as a nation is another factor that cannot be ignored.

Now negotiating from a very different position of strength, President Polk was able to move forward with what he indicated he sought at the outset of the war: 'We go to war with Mexico solely for the purpose of conquering an honorable and permanent peace…We shall bear the olive branch in one hand, the sword in the other.'[14] On 2 February 1848, the government of Mexico signed the Treaty of Guadalupe Hidalgo; Mexico surrendered 890,000 square miles of territory comprising the areas in present day states of California, Arizona, New Mexico, Nevada, Colorado, and parts of Utah and Wyoming. Mexico also accepted that Texas was now formally part of the U.S. The U.S. government agreed to pay $15 million for the territories. Mexico had lost more than half of its territory to a U.S. government intent on gaining access to and control of territory from sea to shining sea by any means necessary, including military force.

Adding some additional insult to injury, several years later, President Santa Anna (in power yet again, as silly as that may seem), in the midst of continuing turmoil in Mexico, sold the U.S. additional territory. Following the defeat in the *Intervención Estadounidense en México* (as the conflict is known in Mexico), the political divisions between Liberals and Conservatives continued to hamper progress and prolonged instability in the country. Santa Anna returned from exile and assumed power in April 1853, and in dire need of funding due to ongoing economic weakness, sold 29,640 square miles of now southern Arizona and New Mexico for $10 million in la *Venta de La Mesilla* (known in the U.S. as the Gadsden Purchase).

The long term implications of these major events have had tremendously significant implications for the fundamental nature of the bilateral relationship between the U.S. and Mexico; in ways large and small, they continue to influence virtually every interaction between the two countries. As historian Michael Scott Van Wagenen captures succinctly, 'the memory of the U.S.-Mexican War' has been 'indelibly etched in the minds of Mexicans and easily overlooked by Americans.'[15] Another American historian, Otis Singletary, writing as recently as the 1950s, offered this view:

> Still another reason for our apparent indifference to the Mexican War lies rooted in the guilt we as a nation have come to feel about it. The undeniable fact it was an offensive war so completely stripped it of any moral pretensions that no politician of that era ever succeeded in elevating it to the lofty level of "crusade." The additional fact that we paid Mexico fifteen million dollars after it was over – "conscious money," some called it [a reference to Grant] – seemed to confirm the ugliest charges of those who denounced the war as a cynical, calculated despoiling of the Mexican state, a greedy land-grab from a neighbor too weak to defend herself.[16]

Concluding thoughts

In the spirit of U.S. experience in Irregular Conflict, the U.S. engagement in the war with Mexico represents a departure from the Army's more typical form of warfare against the American Indians. Given a unique combination of factors which led to Winfield Scott's tenure as the chief writer of Army doctrine and tactics from the termination of hostilities with Great Britain until the Civil War. Scott's research and studies, based largely on eighteenth century European tactics, supplemented by Napoleon's experience, led him to write a series of Army manuals in the 1820s, 1830s, and 1840s.

The Mexican War, and the various campaigns waged from Texas in the east to California in the west, and from Matamoros in the north, the Veracruz and Mexico City in the south, represent a unique chapter in the story of U.S. warfare. Unlike the largely defensive orientation of the Revolutionary War, with the occasional and effective offensive action, the operational concept in the Mexican War had to be much more offensive in orientation. Scott's understanding of the need to avoid decisive engagements during the movement to Mexico City – both to avoid incurring significant losses as well as to limit inciting the Mexican population's wrath – demonstrated a keen understanding of the political aspect of the conflict. This level of sophistication regarding the national psyche in Mexico should represent a profound lesson for U.S. operational commanders as they engage in offensive operations in foreign lands.

Putting aside the morality factor regarding the justification of the U.S. actions vis-à-vis Mexico, one must acknowledge that President Polk had clearly defined policy and strategic objectives and was effective in ensuring his operational commanders understood the concept. Although Polk attempted to increase the number of Democratic general officers in the Army in the volunteer realm, he was sufficiently realistic to accept that he needed the competence of Scott to carry out the Mexico City campaign. The larger and more important point is the importance of envisioning the desired end state prior to embarking upon any military adventure; as blatantly obvious as this may seem, recent U.S. adventures in both Iraq and Afghanistan serve to remind us that this is not always the case. And without clearly identified political goals, all the operational and tactical brilliance in the world will only achieve limited military objectives.

Notes

1. One of the best treatments may be found in Fehrenbach, *Lone Star*, Pt. II, 'Blood and Soil: The Texans.'
2. Winders, *Polk's Army*, 4–5.
3. For example, Lewis, *Trailing Clouds of Glory*; and Johnson, *Winfield Scott*.
4. Weigley, *The American Way of War*, 56.
5. For an evenhanded treatment, see Merry, *A Country of Vast Designs*; for a decidedly more critical approach, Greenberg, *A Wicked War*
6. Williams, *The History of American Wars*, 144.
7. Map downloaded from Creative Commons. https://upload.wikimedia.org/wikipedia/commons/0/0b/Mexican%E2%80%93American_War_%28without_Scott%27s_Campaign%29-en.svg
8. Weigley, xx.
9. Ibid., 142–154.
10. Winders, 187.
11. Bauer, *The Mexican War*, 294.
12. Major-General Winfield Scott, at Mexico City, to William L. Marcy, Secretary of War, at Washington, D.C. Dispatch communicating Scott's report of the battles

for, and occupation of, Mexico City; available at: http://www.dmwv.org/mexwar/documents/mexcity.htm.
13. Ibid.
14. Mahin, *The Olive Branch and the Sword*, 2.
15. Michael and Scott, *The Enduring Legacies of the U.S.-Mexican War*, 2.
16. Singletary, *The Mexican War*, 5.

Disclosure statement

No potential conflict of interest was reported by the author.

Bibliography

Bauer, K. Jack. *The Mexican War, 1846–1848*. New York, NY: Macmillan, 1974.
Fehrenbach, T.R. *Lone Star: A History of Texas and the Texans*. Cambridge, MA: DaCapo Press, 2000.
Greenberg, Amy S. *A Wicked War: Polk, Clay, Lincoln, and the 1846 U.S. Invasion of Mexico*. New York, NY: Vintage, 2013.
Johnson, Timothy D. *Winfield Scott: The Quest for Military Glory*. Lawrence, KS: University of Kansas Press, 1998.
Lewis, Felice Flanery. *Trailing Clouds of Glory: Zachary Taylor's Mexican War Campaign and His Emerging Civil War Leaders*. 2nd ed. Tuscaloosa, AL: University of Alabama Press, 2010.
Mahin, Dean E. *The Olive Branch and the Sword: The United States and Mexico, 1845–1848*. New York, NY: McFarland, 1997.
Merry, Robert W. *A Country of Vast Designs: James K. Polk, the Mexican War and the Conquest of the American Continent*. New York, NY: Simon & Schuster, 2009.
Mexican War Map downloaded from Creative Commons https://upload.wikimedia.org/wikipedia/commons/0/0b/Mexican%E2%80%93American_War_%28without_Scott%27s_Campaign%29-en.svg
Scott, Major-General Winfield, at Mexico City, to William L. Marcy, Secretary of War, at Washington, D.C. Dispatch Communicating Scott's Report of the Battles For, and Occupation Of, Mexico City http://www.dmwv.org/mexwar/documents/mexcity.htm
Singletary, Otis A. *The Mexican War*. Chicago, IL: University of Chicago Press, 1960.
Wagenen, Michael, and Scott Van. *The Enduring Legacies of the U.S.-Mexican War*. Amherst, MA: University of Massachusetts Press, 2012.
Weigley, Russell F. *The American Way of War: A History of United States Military Strategy and Policy*. Bloomington, ID: Indiana University Press, 1973.
Williams, T. Harry. *The History of American Wars: From Colonial Times to World War I*. New York, NY: Knopf, 1985.
Winders, Richard Bruce. *Polk's Army: The American Military Experience in the Mexican War*. College Station, TX: Texas A&M University Press, 1997.

2 Birth of the Cold War
Irregular warfare first blood in Greece

Andrew Novo

ABSTRACT
While often held up as a model of successful American counterinsurgency, the Greek Civil War presents a unique case. Peculiar local conditions and geopolitics contributed to the defeat of communist forces in Greece. A firm British and later American commitment to combating communism stood in contrast to ambiguous support from the Soviet Union in an area they considered outside of their sphere of influence. Strong nationalist feeling among the Greek population buttressed support for the government and undermined the 'internationalist' concessions of communist forces. These characteristics make the extrapolation of broader lessons focused on victory through the application of overwhelming American resources and the financing of local forces problematic. If lessons are to be gleaned from this case, they should focus on the critical roles played by internal political dynamics and geopolitics in undermining the strength of the insurgent forces and how these provided a stable platform from which the counterinsurgents could operate.

Introduction: the Greek 'test tube'

American participation in the Greek Civil War represented several watersheds. It signalled that America's deep involvement in European politics would not come to an end with the surrender of Germany. Neutrality in the dirty business of 'power politics' on a global scale would also be problematic. The Second World War had fatally wounded the British Empire. British dominance in the Eastern Mediterranean – a feature of international affairs since the time of Napoleon – was ending. The collapse of British power was rapid, surprising many in Washington.[1] In March 1947, British policymakers explicitly requested that America take over its responsibilities for supporting the Greek government in order to prevent a communist takeover. A week after this request, an official in the British Foreign

Office was forced to admit that 'no time must be lost in plucking the torch of world leadership from our chilling hands.'[2]

America's commitment to Greece demonstrated a broader commitment to fighting the spread of communism and Soviet influence, which were seen as interchangeable at the time. Confronting the Soviet Union was a fundamental change in American policy. 'During and after the war, major United States policies were predicated ... [on] unity among the great powers.'[3] Soviet actions in the postwar world made such unity untenable. American policymakers had to accept new realities, sometimes against their preferences, and craft a strategy to oppose Soviet consolidation of Eastern Europe. Close political, economic, and military ties among the non-communist states were soon seen as the only hope for survival 'in the face of the centralized and ruthless direction of the Soviet world.'[4] Open conflict between communist and anti-communist forces in Greece was the first active manifestation of this previously latent violence between the Soviet Union and its erstwhile allies. In spite of this, violence between left and right grew out of the experiences of the national schism exacerbated by the German occupation. Understanding the Greek Civil war requires more context than can be provided by the Cold War alone.

In spite of the high stakes, the United States entered the Greek conflict reluctantly, with hesitation and with significant restraints. There was debate concerning both the scale and scope of aid. Whether or not the United States would commit ground forces remained a key bone of contention. Leaders in the Greek government were not entirely trusted within American circles. Their capacity to stabilize their country was called into question. Their divisive politics was criticized, and there were debates about whether they would be good custodians of the resources sent over by the United States. There were tensions between those who wished to avoid American involvement in Greek domestic politics and those who believed that only strong American influence on critical aspects of the Greek government could lead to victory.

In intervening in the Greek Civil War, America may have picked up a burden with reluctance, but it also did so with clear strategic imperatives. If Greece was 'lost' to communism, Soviet control of the Balkans would be uncontestable. Turkey would be isolated, its ability to cooperate with the West prevented. Losing Greece and Turkey would cut off Britain from its vital interests in Egypt, Jordan, Iraq, and Iran. The emerging state of Israel would likely become a communist client. As a strategic linchpin, Greece would have to be defended from a communist takeover. The nature of this defense required careful thinking in Washington.

American resources were finite. The army was carrying out a significant demobilization. Commitments were piling up. Large occupation forces were maintained in Japan, on the Korean peninsula, and in Germany. Berlin was already under Soviet pressure. Communist forces were making headway in China. There were concerns about France's position in Southeast Asia and

Britain's control of Middle Eastern oil. Pulled in so many directions, the United States felt the need to measure its commitment to Greece. Growing tensions with the Soviet Union made Americans cautious about committing troops to an open battle with guerrillas backed by Moscow, since Russia might retaliate anywhere in the world. Nor was it clear that American troops were the proper instrument to solve the problems confronting the Greek state.

As a clash between communist and anti-communist forces, the Greek Civil War became a paradigm in the minds of American policymakers. In this paradigm, a violent communist takeover was stopped with American resolve, technical assistance, and an enormous injection of financial resources. Elsewhere in the world, in Vietnam, for example, policymakers believed a similarly robust response could also turn back the red tide. But this analysis was too simplistic. Parallels with other cases soon break down. During the Greek Civil War, the local and geopolitical situations were peculiar and are therefore problematic as a basis for generalization. First, the Soviet Union, for practical reasons, had acknowledged that they would not be able to exert political control in Greece, much to the frustration of the Greek Communist Party. Second, there was a reserve of anti-communist sentiment in Greece. Greece had a history of partnership with Britain dating from the same time period. It had (and maintains) a deep sense of its unique cultural and historical foundations, including the Athenian experiment with democracy two-and-a-half millennia ago. There was a Greek military that could recruit sufficient forces and, with British and American assistance, equip and train those forces to fight against the communist insurgents.

Communism in Greece could not play on nationalist aspirations to end colonial control. To the contrary, Greek communists toed the line set by Moscow, kowtowing to Bulgarian and Albanian claims to Greek territory. During the first half of the twentieth century, Greece mistrusted Bulgaria greatly. Bulgarian nationalism was in direct competition with Greek nationalism for territory. Greek communists paid a price with the Greek public for cooperating with Bulgarian communists. Communist forces relied for recruitment on the shortcomings of the Greek economy. Economic stability and communist oppression of those who were deemed insufficiently ideological further undermined recruitment prospects. In some cases, this led to outright impressment.

Third, the Soviet Union's material limitations meant that no substantive Soviet support would be routed to the Greek communists.

Fourth, divisions within the communist world, in this case the widening split between Tito and Stalin, eventually removed significant external support for the communists within Greece. Stalin would have welcomed Greece if it had been given, but he was highly skeptical that it could be taken. As long as doubts remained, along with fear of American retaliation or escalation elsewhere, he had no plans to expose the Soviet Union by any direct participation in the Greek struggle.

In spite of these limitations, the defeat of the Greek communists was not a foregone conclusion. From the time of the Bolshevik Revolution, Greece developed strong support for radical leftist politics. Counter to Marx, this was not the result of a highly industrialized economy but of a traditional agrarian one, characterized by widespread poverty. Only one-fourth of its land was arable. Rugged mountains occupied a large proportion of mainland Greece and only a few of its 200 or so inhabited islands provided much in the way of food production. Droughts were frequent in many areas. Until after the Second World War, many low-lying arable areas in flood plains were plagued by malaria.[5] These limitations created widespread poverty. Coupled with centuries of foreign rule, they led to networks of local and personal patronage and widespread skepticism of central government. It was in this context that communism first took root, soon after the Bolshevik Revolution.

Communism in Greece

Communism in Greece sprang from the unification of small radical left-wing parties within the Socialist Workers Party of Greece, founded in November 1918. Two years later, this party affiliated itself with the Comintern (the Communist International). In 1924, it accepted Lenin's 'twenty-one points.' It also renamed itself the Communist Party of Greece (Κομμουνιστικό Κόμμα Ελλάδας), KKE. During its early years, the party made little progress on the Greek political scene, which at the time was still dominated by the 'national schism' between supporters of the politician Eleftherios Venizelos and the supporters of King Constantine I.

Born on the island of Crete, Venizelos' political acumen and foreign policy made him a dominant, if divisive, character in Greek history for the first three decades of the twentieth century. In particular, he was a champion of the Great Idea (Μεγάλη Ιδέα), the irredentist goal of reuniting the Greek-speaking territories of the eastern Mediterranean into something resembling a new Byzantine empire. Venizelos' goals led him to support a series of conflicts against the Ottoman Empire and Bulgaria. These paid dividends, practically doubling the territory of the Greek state. At the outbreak of the First World War, Venizelos and his supporters found themselves in direct conflict with their pro-German monarch, Constantine I.[6] Debate over Greece's entry into the war was the root of the 'national schism.' Yet this single issue only highlighted more fundamental disputes over the role of the king in the country's government and the authority of the prime minister as the elected head of government.

The tug of war between Venizelos with his liberal, Western-leaning attitudes, and the pro-German, authoritarian tendencies favored by the king and many of his officers led to a confusing political merry-go-round. These tensions came to a head during the First World War. In February 1915, Venizelos, prime minister since 1910, was forced to the resign by the king and a number of royalist officers. Elections in 1915 brought him back to power, only to have the king force his resignation again later that year. A pro-Venizelist coup in Thessaloniki in August 1916 was followed by recognition (by the end of the year) of the breakaway government by the Entente powers. In June 1917, Constantine fled, and Venizelos returned to govern the whole country. In July, Greece declared war on the Central Powers. Territorial additions and an ambitious attempt to expand Greek control into Asia Minor at the expense of the disintegrating Ottoman Empire followed.

In November 1920, Venizelos surprisingly lost the national elections and went into self-imposed exile. A month later, King Constantine was recalled by plebiscite. With the king back in power, Venizelist officers and civil servant were purged. Although the war in Asia Minor continued, the great powers, perhaps due to the absence of Venizelos's deft diplomatic touch, withdrew their support. In September 1922, Greek forces suffered a series of crushing defeats at the hands of the Turkish armed forces. The cosmopolitan city of Smyrna, on the coast of Asia Minor, was burned by Turkish forces. Tens of thousands were incinerated or drowned. Hundreds of thousands fled as refugees. The Great Idea was dead in practice, if not in aspiration. Venizelos returned to negotiate its obituary with the Treaty of Lausanne in July 1923 and briefly served as prime minister at the start of 1924. Between July 1928 and May 1932, he was again the head of the Greek government, this time plagued by the economic hardships of the Asia Minor catastrophe, the subsequent population exchanges, and the Great Depression.

In this environment of political upheaval, social disjuncture, and economic hardship, the KKE made some inroads in Greek political life. Nevertheless, it was hamstrung by continued direct control from Moscow. Soviet policy imperatives contradicted widely held Greek national aspirations. For example, the KKE was forced to accept Moscow's position that 'non-Greek minorities in Macedonia and Thrace were oppressed by the settlement there of Greek refugees.'[7] This ran directly against dearly held and widespread irredentist beliefs in Greece during this period.[8] As Stalin consolidated his leadership, Moscow's control became more pernicious. In 1931, 35 leading Greek communists were summoned to Moscow. On Stalin's orders, 33 were executed. Nikos Zachariades, only 29 years old, was chosen as the leader of the party.[9]

A combination of the Great Depression, the influx of over a million refugees from Asia Minor, and the incompetency of parliament critically undermined the republic during the early 1930s.[10] The monarchy was restored after a corrupt plebiscite in 1935. Parliamentary elections in January 1936 left neither the Liberal heirs of Venizelos nor the two conservative, pro-monarchist parties (the People's Party and the General Popular Radical Union) with the absolute majority needed to form a government. The king and a group of royalists unsuccessfully tried to broker a coalition agreement between the two blocks, but failed.[11]

In March, rumors of a secret arrangement between the communists and the Liberal party crackled through the country.[12] On 13 April, the political crisis deepened with the death of the Prime Minister, Konstantinos Demertzis. The king turned to General Ioannis Metaxas, a conservative politician with strong royalist credentials, to serve as the interim prime minister. Metaxas asked for and received a vote of confidence from parliament. But parliament followed this vote with another to alter the electoral system in favor of proportional representation. Such a system was incapable of producing a clear governing majority in the context of Greece's fractious politics.

Metaxas, authoritarian by nature and contemptuous of both traditional parties, moved to consolidate his power. A strike of tobacco workers around Thessaloniki was followed with general strikes in the city. Army units were brought in to quell the unrest. After the start of the Spanish Civil War on 22 July, more strikes and demonstrations broke out in and around Athens. A general strike was announced for 5 August. Metaxas acted on 4 August. The constitution was suspended and parliament dissolved. Several leading communists were arrested, strikes were forbidden, and stringent censorship of the press was imposed.

Communists, who had previously sought to work within the Greek political system, were now firmly pushed out of it. The Metaxas dictatorship, or the 4th of August Regime (Καθεστώς της 4ης Αυγούστου) as it is commonly called in Greece, was a hungry imitation of Italian and German fascism. Personally pro-German and vociferously anti-communist, Metaxas launched a robust persecution of communists and suspected communists. Thousands were arrested, tortured, and imprisoned. As in fascist Italy, some were exiled domestically to isolated islands.[13] The energetic Konstantinos Maniadakis, head of the internal security services, was largely responsible for carrying out these policies and drove the Communist Party underground.

To consolidate support among poorer Greeks, there were grand social reforms such as the imposition of a 5-day, 40-hour work week, the introduction of a minimum wage, unemployment insurance, and mandated maternity leave. Metaxas formed a youth organization, which took as its emblem the *labrys*, a double-headed axe of Minoan origins, echoing the Roman *fasces*. Its members wore all-black uniforms with white ties and military-style black, peaked berets. These children would parade through the streets singing, 'We have but one father and chief: The Leader.'[14]

Metaxas attempted social engineering on a grand scale through often ludicrous methods. His pictures were printed on light bulbs. His catchphrases were printed on bus tickets. Enormous public festivals and celebrations were organized, particularly on the anniversary of 4th of August.[15] In addition to 'the father,' 'the chief,' and 'the leader,' the dictator styled himself 'the first worker' and 'the first peasant.'[16] Just how effective such propaganda was when conveyed through photographs of the pudgy and diminutive Metaxas, ankle deep in earth behind a plow in his pinstriped suit and rounded spectacles, is hard to imagine.

Invasion, occupation, and resistance

In spite of their similar approaches to domestic policy, relations between Mussolini's Italy and Metaxas's Greece were fraught. Mussolini regarded Greece, along with Turkey and Egypt, as 'vital enemies of Italy and its expansion.' Greece was among the countries ready to join with Britain to complete Italy's political and economic encirclement.[17] The outbreak of war, and the scale of Hitler's unexpected success in France, exacerbated Mussolini's paranoia. At the end of October 1940, the Greek government received an ultimatum from Mussolini. It was refused. An Italian invasion rolled forward from bases in Albania, but was stopped and then turned back. Consequently, in April 1941, nearly 700,000 German soldiers, supported by their Bulgarian allies, outflanked the Greek army – still deadlocked with Italian forces in Albania – and occupied Greece. British and Greek troops fought side by side against the Axis but could not prevent rapid defeat and occupation. Britain evacuated the troops that it could and established a Greek government in exile in Cairo. Axis occupation naturally led to another round of anti-communist persecution. Zachariades was arrested and sent to Dachau. Other leading Communists were arrested, imprisoned, and deported.

In Greece, as in many countries, the most committed (and effective) resistance movements were spurred and supplied by the radical left. Axis occupiers played on local economic, ethnic, religious, and political divisions, using a combination of 'coercion and seduction to win over native collaborators.'[18] German policies widened and hardened existing divisions and provoked new depths of hostility. Societies fractured between resisters and collaborators. Fascist sympathizers were enlisted in Security Battalions in an attempt to maintain Axis control and stamp out resistance.[19]

Economically, the occupation had a devastating impact. The entire tobacco crop, purchased at 1939 prices, was sent to pay for the cost of occupation. Agricultural stocks – olive oil, olives, raisins, and figs – were requisitioned to feed German troops. Textiles such as silk and wool were appropriated to clothe them or sent off to Germany. To further cover the cost of occupation, '[b]illions of drachmas were printed ... causing hyperinflation.'[20] This hyperinflation destroyed the status of salaried workers and created a black market based largely on barter. Axis occupation and the Allied blockade combined to create a famine by the autumn of 1941. The average laborer, who consumed 3000 calories per day in 1940, saw his intake drop to 875 during the winter of 1941–1942.[21] Reaction to this hardship from the Allies underscored the centrality of Britain, and not the United States, in Greek affairs. As Secretary of State, Cordell Hull made clear to the American ambassador in London: 'The general question of the policy to be adopted with regard to the relief of Greece ... is primarily for the British Government to decide.'[22]

Occupation and starvation sparked resistance. In September 1941, a group of six socialist parties and organizations joined to form the Greek Liberation Front, EAM (Εθνικό Απελευθερωτικό Μέτωπο). The KKE Central Committee exerted a powerful influence over EAM, but accounts tinted by Cold War animus often exaggerate the realities and present EAM as '[c]ommunist conceived, delivered, and motivated.'[23] At least for this period, this is not an accurate representation. More measured scholarship undertaken after the end of the Cold War acknowledges the critical role played by the Communist Party in the National Liberation Front as the best organized and only truly national group; but it also paints the picture of EAM as a broad, anti-fascist coalition, rather than a tool of communist ideology.[24] At the same time, EAM was not the only organized source of resistance. Also in September 1941, 'a group of Venizelist officers inaugurated a republican resistance organization that they named EDES (the National Democratic Greek League) [Εθνικός Δημοκρατικός Ελληνικός Σύνδεσμος].'[25] On 10 April 1942, EAM announced that it would field a guerrilla army, the National Popular Liberation Army, ELAS (Ελληνικός Λαϊκός Απελευθερωτικός Στρατός).[26] A month later, ELAS's first unit was established under the command of the committed communist leader Aris Velouchiotis.[27]

EAM/ELAS size and organizational strength made them the most effective anti-fascist resistance in Greece. Soon after ELAS formation, and with the Soviet Union engaged in its own desperate struggle, the communist leaders accepted 'British patronage of the resistance and the prospect of British hegemony after liberation.'[28] This proved critical not only for the course of resistance to the Germans but the future of postwar Greece. Officers from the Special Operations Executive arrived in September 1942 to assist in anti-Axis operations. A year later, these 400 officers were joined by another 200 Americans from the Office of Strategic Services. Although these advisors were anti-communist, their primary focus was defeating Germany.[29] This reality led to compromises for both the Western allies and the guerrillas in spite of their left-wing pedigree.

Many right-wing Greek political leaders and officers feared a communist takeover more than German occupation. Ethnic minorities such as Vlachs, Chams (ethnic Albanians), and Slavs from Macedonia held their own nationalist objectives, hoping to gain territory from Greece after the war's end. These collaborators hoped 'to blunt EAM/ELAS's rise to power inside Greece.'[30] They joined the Security Battalions in large numbers. Between September 1943 and September 1944, nearly 10 times as many Greek members of the Security Battalions were killed in anti-guerrilla activities as were Germans.[31] They, not the *Wehrmacht*, SS, or order police, were the primary targets of the Greek resistance. It was an indication of German 'success in fomenting civil war.'[32] This extended to conflict between various anti-German resistance groups, which quickly bubbled to the surface. ELAS and EDES clashed in February 1943. By May, 'in one British officer's words a "state of undeclared war" [existed] between ELAS and EDES in Epirus and Thessaly, with each side constantly arresting the other's members.'[33] There was little that the British could do to alleviate these growing tensions.

Italy's withdrawal from the Axis in September 1943 further complicated matters. Some 15,000 Italians from the occupation force asked the Allied Military Mission to retain their arms and join allied units as co-combatants.[34] More, in largely unknown numbers, linked up with partisan formations, bringing their weapons with them. The Pinerolo Division, 7000 strong, was dispersed in small units among ELAS mountain formations in Thessaly. But this large influx of armed and well-trained non-communists was a cause for concern to EAM/ELAS leaders. To quiet these fears, the Allied Military Mission agreed to scatter the Italians more widely. ELAS took full advantage. Early in the morning of 15 October, the Italian detachments were surrounded and disarmed in contravention of the ceasefire agreement.[35] The Italians were taken prisoner, held in makeshift concentration camps, and pressed into forced labor. ELAS also seized the Pinerolo division's 20 mountain guns and most of its other heavy equipment. This new stock of quality arms was immediately used to build a new ELAS division.[36]

Italy's withdrawal from the Axis not only provided men and arms for the resistance but signaled that the defeat of Nazi Germany was rapidly approaching. This set off a race for control of the postwar order in Greece. ELAS, now better armed than ever, turned its attention to seizing control of the country before the Axis withdrawal. Its hope was to preempt any British attempt to reimpose the monarchy.[37] In October 1943, ELAS launched attacks on all other resistance forces. Its goal was to eliminate rival bases of power and establish itself, along with EAM, as the only foundation upon which to build a new, independent, Greek government. To achieve this, it would need to eliminate its former partners in the resistance who held nationalist and monarchist beliefs. It would need to crush their non-communist left-wing colleagues. And it would need to overthrow their patrons, the British Empire, all the while fending off the recrudescent elements of German occupation, including the Security Battalions and Fascist collaborators within the Greek population.

'The Greeks have acted stupidly' – Stalin

A German withdrawal from Greece appeared imminent during the summer of 1944. Intent on seizing power, ELAS appealed to the Soviet Union for help through the head of the Soviet military mission to Tito. The organization was swimming against the tide. Fully a year before, Moscow had identified Greece as in the British sphere of influence.[38] At the start of 1944, this attitude was reinforced in a memorandum by the former Soviet ambassador in London, Ivan Maiksii, who argued to Molotov that

> the USSR is interested in Greece much less than in other Balkan countries, whereas England, in contrast, is seriously interested in Greece. In relation to Greece, therefore, the USSR should observe great caution. If democratic Greece, following the example of other Balkan countries, would also like to conclude a pact of mutual assistance with the USSR, we would have no reason to discourage it. However, if the conclusion of a bilateral Greek-Soviet pact caused some complications with England, one could try to deal with the problem by way of the conclusion of a trilateral mutual assistance pact between England, Greece and the USSR (as in the case of Iran).[39]

ELAS's goal in this period was to secure diplomatic assistance and military support from the Soviet Union and its allies in order to counter British influence. When Germany troops did withdraw in September 1944, Greek communists were intent on seizing power. Soviet military officers, who made their way to ELAS headquarters as Soviet troops pushed through Bulgaria, advised caution. This was consistent with the Soviet relegation of Greece to the British sphere of influence. Soviet troops, although advancing through Eastern Europe and the Balkans, would not enter Greece. On the ground, these officers opposed plans to seize power and suggested that the KKE should instead join the new government of national unity.[40]

Still, there were mixed messages. By late September, nearly 300 Soviet military officers were reported across towns in northern Greece. ELAS hoped that Soviet military units would soon follow them and begin operations to harass the retreating Germans, as well as provide the foundations for communist control. These forces never materialized. Within a few weeks, the Soviet officers disappeared. Stalin and Churchill had met in Moscow, where on 9 October, they drafted a 'percentages agreement' dividing influence in the Balkans. Greece, it was proposed, would be an area of 90% British and only 10% Soviet influence. Though the agreement was neither official nor binding, and the percentages themselves were little more than Churchill's shorthand on the issue, they were an indication of Stalin's attitudes about the realistic reach of Soviet power.[41] It was Stalin's view that Britain would not accept having her connection to the Eastern Mediterranean jeopardized by a Soviet presence in Greece. It was a bridge too far. Stalin would not cross it at the risk of escalating tensions with the British and Americans. Stalin even pressured Bulgaria, now a client of the Soviet Union, to relinquish the Greek territory it had annexed in 1941 with Germany's blessing.[42]

KKE, on the other hand, did not accept its demotion on Moscow's priority list. As fighting between ELAS and its rivals began, it sent another request for assistance, this one to Georgi Dimitrov, a Bulgarian partisan who served as one of Stalin's Balkan experts. As in previous cases, there was disappointment. Greek Communists, in Dimitrov's words, would 'not be able to count on active intervention and assistance from here.'[43] Perhaps because they felt stronger than they actually were, or perhaps in an attempt to force the Kremlin's hand, ELAS again ignored the realities being imposed on it from Moscow. Even without Soviet support, it would attempt to seize power in Greece.

In spite of Moscow's hesitance, ELAS attempted to take decisive steps on the ground. In April 1944, its units attacked the Republican resistance group EKKA (Εθνική και Κοινωνική Απελευθέρωσις), National and Social Liberation. EKKA was a small organization led by a republican officer, Demetrios Psarros, active in central Greece. Its membership was primarily Venizelist politicians and army officers; it advocated radical democratic programs.[44] Pressed by both the Germans and ELAS (which disarmed it at gunpoint twice), it was largely dependent on British aid for survival.[45] On 17 April 1944, ELAS's notorious commander, Ares Velouchiotes, demanded EKKA disarm and surrender its fighting force of roughly 350 men. When Psarros refused, ELAS forces, numbering some 4500, carried out a ruthless massacre. Reports stated than many of the EKKA fighters were killed after surrendering and then only after brutal torture.[46] Fighting between ELAS and collaborators continued throughout the spring and summer of 1944.

EAM had formed a secret police, the Organization for the Protection of the People's Struggle or OPLA, in summer 1943. Like Stalin's NKVD or the Soviet Cheka, it now 'combed the towns and countryside looking for victims.'[47] These were anyone connected with the right or the Axis occupation and anyone suspected of such connections. Many collaborators took to the hills and attempted to join groups such as EDES or the right wing and staunchly royalist 'X' organization. Others joined the infamous Security Battalions. As the Germans withdrew, ferocious violence raged between ELAS and non-communist forces from the Security Battalions and other groups.

It was typical for ELAS forces to surround an area once the Germans withdrew and then attempt to overpower whatever garrison remained before the British could arrive. In the Peloponnese, ELAS attacked and defeated three such garrisons in short succession between 8 and 15 September. An 'orgy of revenge' followed in which hundreds of people were killed. 'Many of the victims were gendarmes. The worst massacre happened at Meligalas, a few miles north of Kalamata, where, according to a sober right-wing account, about 1800 people were killed.'[48] While collaborators suffered for their support of the Germans, victims were just as often completely innocent civilians subject to arbitrary beating, deportation, and murder reminiscent of 'Jacobin and Soviet terror.'[49]

At the end of October, more than 7000 anti-communist forces gathered in northern Greece. These were a collection of right-wing bands, recrudescent elements of the Thessaloniki Security Battalions, and even partners of EDES. They took up defense positions near Kilkis. On 3 November, ELAS launch an assault with 7000 of its own well-trained men. After a nine-hour battle, ELAS, at the cost of 356 casualties, inflicted 1500 dead and wounded on the enemy.[50] Another 2200 were taken prisoners. Many were summarily executed; others were taken to detention camps in Thessaloniki.[51]

Emboldened by these successes, ELAS pushed to seize control of the entire country by force. The Greek government in exile, in coordination with the British government, set the matter on a collision course when it announced on 1 December that all guerrilla forces should disarm by 10 December. EAM called for a demonstration on 2 December in Athens. Authorities granted permission and then revoked it. The march went ahead anyway. Enormous numbers of pro-ELAS demonstrators took to the streets. They clashed with police, who opened fire on the crowd. More than two dozen demonstrators were killed and hundreds wounded. Many others were arrested.

A general strike was called for the next day. ELAS units, armed and in uniform, began to move into the suburbs of Athens, where they clashed with government forces and the few British troops on the ground. The right-wing militia, 'X,' attacked ELAS positions on the hill opposite the Acropolis as ELAS fighters assaulted police stations.[52] Although British and ELAS troops tried to avoid shooting at each other during this phase of the conflict, such 'neutrality' did not last long. Lieutenant General Sir Ronald Scobie, the British commander in Greece, ordered all ELAS operations to cease. On the evening of 5 December, with the full support of the British government, he authorized British troops to take 'full offensive action' against ELAS forces.[53]

New National Guard battalions were recruited, and the British sent reinforcements from Italy in order to bring the uprising under control. The ELAS offensive stuttered and then failed. Guerrilla attacks against the Germans were one thing. Attempting to assault and hold ground against the British regular army, another. By the end of the month, there were some 90,000 British troops in Greece. By Christmas, Prime Minister Churchill was in Athens to preside over a peace conference in an attempt to bring the fighting to a close. Soviet support for ELAS had not materialized. Stalin held to his agreement with Churchill and did not press the ELAS cause. Like many shrewd practitioners of *real politik*, Stalin had positioned himself to benefit from either outcome. An unexpected ELAS victory would further communism in Greece. An expected ELAS defeat, brought about by the use of British forces, would provide him with an excuse for similarly heavy-handed measures in Eastern Europe on the side of communist forces.

On 15 January 1945, Scobie agreed to a ceasefire. ELAS withdrew from Thessaloniki, the city of Patras, and began demobilizing in the Peloponnese. The 'December Events' *Dekemvriana* (Δεκεμβριανά) resulted in more than 230 British killed in action and more than 2000 wounded. Greek security forces had suffered another 1000 killed. ELAS had lost perhaps twice as many killed and had taken 20,000 Greeks as hostages.[54]

After ELAS's defeat, Stalin was scathing. 'I advised not starting this fight in Greece,' he commented acidly to Dimitrov. 'The ELAS ... have taken on more than they can handle. They were evidently counting on the Red Army's coming down to the Aegean. We cannot do that. We cannot send our troops into Greece either. The Greeks have acted stupidly.'[55] ELAS's 'stupidity' was a dramatic setback for the Greek left, but conditions were about to get even worse.

The failure of peace

Beaten in the field, EAM agreed to talk. Three senior representatives met with the British at the small town of Varkiza, not far from Athens, to discuss a peace agreement. EAM's representatives were Georgios Siantos, who had commanded ELAS formations during the *Dekemvriana* and was acting as Secretary General of KKE, Demetrios Partsalides, and Ilias Tsirimokos. Tsirimokos represented the Socialist Union of People's Democracy, ELD (Ένωση Λαϊκής Δημοκρατίας). On 12 February, the two sides came to terms. ELAS would demobilize. Both sides would release prisoners and hostages. There would be a general election and a plebiscite on the status of the monarchy.[56]

This promised return to normal governance spurred action, and hope, among Greek communists. Germany's surrender and the end of the war in Europe – with communist forces dominant from Berlin to Moscow and throughout the Balkans – reinforced such feelings. Nikos Zachariades returned from Dachau in May 1945, intent on building the Communist Party into an organ that could compete in election politics with other political parties on an even playing field.[57] However, Socialists such as Tsirimkos were alienated by the December fighting, deepening divisions within the left.

Zachariades attempted to reinvigorate the party and reshape it into a more pure ideological tool. Desertions among the rank-and-file had been significant following the December defeat. Additional members who were considered insufficiently doctrinal were purged. Others were sent to Athens for ideological training. The number of peasants in the party was reduced.

Agricultural laborers were forced to join the United Agrarian Party.[58] Zachariades imposed a degree of strict personal control on the ideologically pure core of the remaining communists. Political debate and collective leadership, which had characterized EAM during the occupation, evaporated as Zachariades drew on Stalin's personalized control for his model.[59]

Zachariades was not able to impose his vision with complete success. A few commanders, such as Aris Velouchiotis, wished to continue the fight. They refused to adhere to the terms of Varkiza. Other ELAS formations handed over old or useless weapons. Good weapons were buried for future use. Velouchiotis was denounced by Zachariades and expelled from the party. Government forces located him with a force of less than 100 men. He committed suicide rather than allow himself to be captured. His body was decapitated, and the head was put on display.[60] Suspicions remain that the communists were the ones who supplied information on his whereabouts to the government.

The beheading and exhibition of Velouchiotis was not an isolated act of brutality. Other small, left-wing groups that refused to adhere to the terms of Varkza continued to carry out low level attacks. But the greatest violence came from the right. Flush with victory, the right indulged in oppression worthy of the days of fascism. Under the cover of British support and Soviet absence, its most radical elements, including former members of the Security Battalions, carried out a purge of leftist elements in a 'White Terror' that included arrests, torture, and summary executions.

Within a month of the signing of the agreement at Varkiza, Harold Macmillan, as Minister Resident for the Mediterranean, communicated to Alexander Kirk, the Political Adviser to the Supreme Allied Commander, Mediterranean Theater that the 'Greek situation was not going so well.'[61] Two days later, the American Ambassador in Greece, Lincoln MacVeagh, reported that Siantos, Partsalides, and Tsirimkos were making the rounds protesting violations of the Varkiza agreement.[62] MacVeagh knew that the EAM representatives were not fabricating their claims. The Greek government, he wrote to Washington, had 'used its armed forces and organized bands to institute a reign of terror.'[63]

British politicians had promised to support the new Greek government, but there were two obstacles. First, the British were not convinced that the Greek government could be trusted to adhere to the terms of the Varkiza agreement. They were dissatisfied with the actions of Greek leaders and continued to pressure them to broaden their government and stop the most egregious acts of retaliation against leftists, largely to no avail. Second, and more importantly, the British lacked the resources to support Athens in a timely manner and to the extent necessary. Already in March 1945, they were in discussions with the Americans to share the cost of rebuilding Greece. The elections promised by the Varkiza agreement would take place under joint American, British, and French supervision. Russian observers were invited, but Stalin refused. As he explained to the British prime minister, supervision of elections 'could not be regarded otherwise than as an insult to that people and a flagrant interference with its internal life.'[64] In both Washington and London, it was understood that Stalin was withholding Soviet observers in Greece to deny America or Britain the right to deploy their own observers for upcoming elections in Poland or elsewhere in Eastern Europe.

Although the Greek government, with British backing, had more or less established control over the entire country by spring 1945, it was failing to prevent widespread and brutal reprisals against communists and former members of ELAS. As the British made clear to their American partners, they 'were constantly obliged to step in to see to it that [the] Greek Government kept their side of the Varkiza Agreement.'[65] British forces attempted (often half-heartedly) to contain the worst of the violence. Historian David Close goes so far as to argue that excesses were 'made possible only by British backing.'[66]

Regardless of the accuracy of this analysis, maintaining order in Greece was becoming progressively more difficult. There were conditions of 'anarchic banditry' as ELAS demobilized, KKE attempted to assert control, and the elements from the right continued their reign of terror.[67] Drought made the 1945 grain harvest extremely poor. Greece imported massive amounts of food simply to prevent famine. Government revenues could hardly keep pace with required expenses, whether security or food. Resort to the expedient of printing money served only to add inflation to the toxic troubles already plaguing the country.[68] Successive governments were unable to improve conditions. Plagued by their own deteriorating financial situation and unwilling to 'hold the ring' any longer, the British began discussing their withdrawal with the Americans, preparing for a 1 July 1945 departure. The Americans, concerned about stability in the country and not yet willing to take over responsibility, were arguing that they should remain at least until the end of the year.[69]

Greek communists were the beneficiaries of this suffering and unrest. Social dislocation 'gave fresh relevance to the traditional communist criticisms of the Greek state as authoritarian and associated with an economic oligarchy which represented the interest of the imperialist powers.'[70] Fears within the left that the society was slipping from their control grew as the March 1946 election date approached. A delegation from KKE traveled to Moscow and pressed Stalin for more aggressive action in Greece. Again, they were told to avoid open insurgency and participate in elections. In spite of Moscow's instructions, they boycotted the March elections.[71] As a result, the staunchly anti-communist United Alignment of Nationalists won a resounding victory and established a right-wing government with 55% of the vote and 206 of 354 seats in parliament.

In March or April, Zachariades traveled to Moscow alone and met with Stalin. Soviet leaders were critical of the election boycott. Nevertheless, Stalin consented to Zachariades discussing the potential for an armed struggle in cooperation with Tito. At the same time, he made clear that the Greeks should 'avoid an untimely armed intervention by the British, and ... [search] for a compromise.'[72] The possibility of a compromise was pushed further away in September. A referendum to maintain the monarchy passed with 68.4% of the vote, in spite of the vehement objections of the left. Violence by left-wing bands increased.[73]

On 28 October 1946, a partisan command was founded with Markos Vaphiades at its head. In December, the guerrilla groups were renamed the Democratic Army of Greece (Δημοκρατικός Στρατός Ελλάδας), DSE. In many ways, DSE can be seen as the successor of ELAS, but 'communist control was much tighter and the ideological stakes were less ambiguous.'[74] The goal was to overthrow the Greek government by force, using guerrilla tactics at first, then creating a counter-state, and finally eliminating the government in Athens. Leaders and armed groups that had 'sought refuge across the border' during the White Terror now 'began entering Greece and forming large bands. Throughout the mainland, but primarily in the northern districts, these returning avengers unleashed an impressive hunt for right-wing sympathizers, mostly government appointees in the village councils, as well as gendarmes.'[75] Hundreds were killed and wounded; hundreds more were impressed into service for the revolution as DSE attempted to increase its size and 'to win and hold territory.'[76]

This latest wave of violence, uncertainty, and retribution worked for and against DSE. In 1946, recruits for the Democratic Army's cause were just as likely to be conscripts as volunteers. Many feared retribution from the right-wing if they returned to normal life 'or simply found no lawful means of livelihood at a time when under was widespread in the countryside.'[77] Nevertheless, recruits were in constantly short supply.[78]

In spite of DSE's weakness, Britain's broader position continued to deteriorate as the Varkiza agreement broke down. Under pressure across its empire, particularly in India and Palestine, practically bankrupt, and facing a host of domestic problems, Britain was eager to pass responsibility in Greece on to the United States. On 27 February 1947, the British Ambassador in Washington delivered an aide-memoire to the State Department. It announced that due to Britain's 'own situation,' support for the Greek government was no longer possible.[79] The British government hoped that the United States would assume the role of Greece's patron and continue the fight against the DSE. America had resisted assuming responsibility for Greece for years. Now, with the exigencies of the Cold War coming into focus, it chose to act decisively.

Enter the United States

It took the United States a little more than a week to formally acknowledge to the British that it was prepared to support the Greek government in its anti-communist efforts. The primary fear in Washington was that a communist victory in Greece would cause the spread of communism through Europe and the Middle East. Greece was the only non-communist country in the Balkans. It lay astride key routes in the Eastern Mediterranean to British imperial possessions, Middle East oil, and the Suez Canal. A communist Greece would put additional pressure on Turkey. In spite of the stakes, however, support for Greece was neither open-ended nor all-encompassing. Senior officials within both the State Department and the War Department crafted a strategy based on the deployment of a very small number of Americans to serve as technical advisors. These would be backed by the delivery of equipment to the Greek military and financial resources to the Greek government.

Support for Greece was a policy decision. But this policy decision was part of a broader strategy founded on the idea that the expansion of communism beyond the area currently under the military control of the Soviet Union would be detrimental to America's national security. The decision had been some time in coming and was a reflection of three key factors: (1) the transition from the more accommodating attitude of Roosevelt to the more confrontational attitude of Truman vis-à-vis the Soviet Union. (2) The belief that American power was needed to prop up the post-1945 settlement, because the traditional European powers were unable to do so. As argued by Dean Acheson, the acting Secretary of State, the issues in Greece were 'only part of a much larger problem growing out of the change in Great Britain's strength.'[80] And (3) the fear that communist control would spread like a pandemic were it not contained.

The shift had been some time in coming. Its implementation as policy required important changes in America's posture. In specific relation to Greece and Europe, implementation rested on three pillars: the Truman Doctrine, the Marshall Plan, and the formation of NATO.[81] The first two would have a major impact on the Greek Civil War. The last would solidify its result once the fighting had died down.

To counter the specters of sustained instability and a communist takeover, Truman was prepared to offer 'immediate aid' to Greece and Turkey. Just a week after Acheson's memo, Truman stood before a joint session of Congress and delivered a speech enunciating what would be called the 'Truman Doctrine.' Truman argued that Greece would not be able 'to survive as a free nation' without American support. Its 'very existence' was 'threatened by the terrorist activities of several thousand armed men, led by Communists.' The Greek government, with is meager resources, was unable to cope with the situation. Britain, Greece's erstwhile patron, was 'reducing or liquidating its commitments in several parts of the world, including Greece.' Since the United Nations was unable to act with sufficient alacrity, the United States for reasons of its own national security needed to act and provide support.[82]

Truman claimed that a successful communist takeover in Greece would undermine free institutions and democratic governments throughout Europe. It would isolate Turkey and all but ensure the spread of communism through the entire Middle East. He asked Congress for USD 400,000,000 over the following 15 months and the authorization to send American civilian and military personnel to Greece.

While Truman pitched to Congress his idea to save Greece from communism, Zachariades was back in Moscow attempting to convince Stalin to support the insurgency. He claimed that with Soviet support, DSE could rise to a strength of 50,000 and take control of Greece. It now seemed that Stalin was willing to listen. On 20 May, he met privately with Stalin,

> 'war materials and diplomatic backing were guaranteed by Moscow.' The KKE was encouraged to submit a 'wish list' of needed *matériel*. Shipments of weapons and supplies from Bulgaria and Yugoslavia to the Greek insurgents increased in volume, and the fighting in northern Greece intensified as the government troops were initially unable to do much more than defend large towns that came under attack.[83]

As Zachariades attempted to press his advantage, the Greek-American cooperation swung into motion. Truman's announcement was followed by a flurry of diplomatic correspondence between Washington and Athens aimed at formalizing the new bilateral ties. These focused on establishing the mechanisms through which American aid could be brought to Greece and directed toward building the Greek military into a force capable of conducting anti-guerrilla operations and supplying it with the necessary equipment.[84] The formal agreement was concluded on 20 June 1947 between Konstantinos Tsaldaris, then serving as deputy prime minister and foreign minister, and Ambassador MacVeagh.[85]

A month later, direct links were established between the U.S. Army Group Greece and the leaders of the Greek military. In late July, American personnel visited military bases and inventoried stocks of *matériel*. At a conference with senior officers, they discussed the Greek army's requirements.[86] By 2 August, the first American aid ship, carrying military supplies arrived in Piraeus. Over the course of the month, another 10 arrived.[87] Though significant American resources reached Greece, there were major issues that required work. A number of Greek leaders consistently requested American support in increasing the size of the army. Dwight Griswold, the assertive Chief of the American Mission for Aid to Greece, clashed with the more mild-mannered American ambassador, Lincoln MacVeagh. Deepening American contact within the Greek military and government also revealed serious deficiencies. Greek commanders were cautious. Approximately 15% of the men under arms were over the age of 60.[88]

Communist forces were unable to hold towns of any size, but large parts of country remained under their control. After seven months of anti-guerrilla operations, the situation was, as the CIA described it 'a deteriorating stalemate.'[89] The Greek army, operating in difficult, often mountainous terrain with poor roads (factors which favored the guerrillas) and without sufficient operational expertise, had 'failed' at both the tactical and strategic level.[90] The Greek government's American patrons were not pleased with the progress. On 3 November, Truman approved an expansion of the U.S. military role in Greece designed to correct these shortcomings and to break the deadlock.

A new entity, the Joint US Military Advisory and Planning Group (JUSMAPG), was created. Its mandate was to '[f]ormulate plans for the employment and coordination of the armed forces of Greece ... furnish advice concerning the military situation in regard to security and maintaining internal security in Greece ... [and] Furnish operational advice.'[91] The number of American advisors increased more than 10-fold, from 14 to 170.[92] As part of their new mission, they would provide guidance to the Greek government at every level. At the national level, the most senior members of JUSMAPG, particularly its new head, Lt. General James Van Fleet, in coordination with policymakers in Washington, would be in a position to restructure elements of the Greek army itself. Communist forces also made a political play to break the deadlock during this period. Before Christmas 1947, General Markos declared a 'Government of Free Greece,' hoping for recognition from communist members of the international community. It did not come.

A victory for democracy

In Washington, the deadlock raised the old question of whether American troops should be committed to the Greek Civil War. Loy Henderson, the State Department's Director of the Office of Near Eastern and African Affairs, argued that Greece was now 'the test tube which the peoples of the world are watching in order to ascertain whether the determination of the Western powers to resist aggression equals that of international Communism to acquire new territory and new bases for further aggression.'[93] In his view, unless the United States was willing to assert that its determination to prevent the conquest of Greece by the Soviet Union was 'stronger than that of the would-be aggressors to take Greece,' failure was inevitable.[94] Henderson's recommendation was the commitment of American regular troops to Greece on a sufficient scale to eradicate guerrilla activity. Nothing less than American boots on the ground was sufficient to demonstrate American resolve. This prescription, however, was not universally accepted. It stemmed from a fundamental divergence in diagnosis between Henderson (and his supporters within the NSC and military) and others, led by George Kennan, the chief of the State Department's Policy Planning Staff, and Dwight Griswold.

Henderson focused on the power of communist forces and their intervention in Greece. His fear was that a lack of American resolve would embolden foreign intervention and bolster domestic support for the communists. Kennan argued that the underlying cause for support of the communists was Greece's economic disintegration. The failure of the Greek economy and mistrust of the government were essential to support for the radical Left. These problems would not be solved by committing American forces to fight guerrillas. Griswold made this argument clearly to Marshall in a memorandum from January 1948: '[I]ntensification of the military campaign will impose excessive pressure on civilian economy with resultant certainty of runaway inflation.' A communist victory, in his view, would only be possible through invasion (which he thought unlikely) or because of an 'economic breakdown and general popular rejection of present political and social structure [sic]. The strongest allies of the Communists at the moment are increasing prices, inflation, and governmental inefficiency and malpractices of which the neglect of the refugees is a typical examples.'[95] The Central Intelligence Agency concurred with Griswold.[96]

In many ways, 1948 represented a high-watermark for the Democratic Army. The 'Markos Junta,' as the Americans called it, declared itself Greece's legitimate government at the close of 1947. By the start of 1948, American estimates placed guerrilla control at over a third of the rural population and half of the territory of the country.[97] Unexpectedly, however, the ground was crumbling beneath the communists' feet.

None of DSE's patrons in Moscow, Belgrade, Sofia, or Tirana could supply it with resources to compete with supplies streaming in from Washington. As David Close notes, 'For every mule load of foreign aid reaching themselves [DSE], a ship load reached their opponents. At least one soldier was executed for remarking on this contrast.'[98] Just as significantly, 1948 witnessed the escalation of the feud between Stalin and Tito. The split between Belgrade and Moscow placed the Greek communists in a difficult position:

> From an ideological point of view the Greek Communists leaned towards the Stalin line of thought (still the fountainhead of world Communism to the KKE) but practical politics and inherent nationalist feelings caused differences of opinion as to whether it was wisest to be open and frank at this critical juncture. Most of their eggs were in the basket held by Yugoslavia, and they would be difficult to retrieve, place elsewhere or replace. If they opted for Yugoslavia, they would be cut off from other Balkan aid; and, while Albania, Bulgaria and Rumania's share of assistance to the Democratic Army was not as great in volume or as immediately

vital as that of Yugoslavia, it was quite appreciable, and if deprived of it the Democratic Army would again also be heavily handicapped.[99]

Successive offensive actions by the Greek army pushed the guerrillas back with heavy casualties. They were still able to take refuge across the border. They had not been eradicated, but their strength was declining. DSE had reached a maximum effective strength of 26,000 in March 1948.[100] This was slightly more than half the number Zachariades had told Stalin he needed to seize control of the country. As casualties mounted, new recruits were almost always conscripts. As early as October 1947, the CIA reported that more than half of DSE's strength were 'forced recruits.'[101] By 1948, 'a quarter of the DSE were women, while four-fifths ... were aged under twenty-five, many being young teenagers.'[102]

Recruitment was a priority, because casualties were mounting. A determined defense on the Grammos mountain range in central Greece was dislodged by the army. Government forces lost 6740 men, while DSE lost 4500. Although dislodged, DSE formations managed to slip away. In 1948, DSE launched a new series of offensives designed to extend its control over the country. A new front was opened in the Peloponnese. Small towns such as Karditas, Noussa, and Karpenision were captured in December 1948 and January 1949. But these victories came at a cost in experienced fighters.[103]

This deteriorating position, both domestically and internationally, led to radical changes. Markos Vaphiades, who wished to continue the fight as a guerrilla campaign, was sidelined by Zachariades. During the Fifth Plenary Session of the Central Committee of the KKE held on 30–31 January 1949, Vaphiades was dismissed 'both as head of the Democratic Government and as commander of the Democratic Army ... [he] and his supporters were [then] expelled from the Central Committee of the KKE.'[104] To the south, in the Peloponnese, DSE guerrilla formations were smashed. In the north, Zachariades again tried to force the issue and achieve a military victory in the field. DSE's defensive mountain positions were again overrun.

After the loss of 2200, the survivors retreated across the border to Albania during August 29–30.[105] This time they would not return. Albania's dictator, Enver Hoxha, had announced that all Greeks found on Albanian soil 'would be disarmed and detained.'[106] Two months later, unable to continue the struggle in any meaningful way, the movement announced on Democratic Army Radio that 'its army had decided to "cease-fire" to "prevent the complete annihilation of Greece".'[107] The Civil War was over.

Aftermath

As the remnants of the Democratic Army withdrew across the border to Albania, the Greek nation was finally in a position to count the cost and rebuild after decades of conflict. During the first half the twentieth century, generations of Greeks had known nothing but war: the two Balkan Wars in 1912 and 1913, the First World War in 1917–1918, and the Greco-Turkish War of 1919–1922. These had been followed by the Greco-Italian War of 1940–1941, the German invasion and Axis occupation of 1941–1944, and the Civil War 1946–1949. Between 1922 and 1940, the country also struggled with the impact of the Asia Minor Catastrophe, the population exchange with Turkey, the Great Depression, and the Metaxas dictatorship. The Axis occupation and the Civil War left an even more staggering economic cost. There were 2000 destroyed villages and 400,000 destroyed buildings. Nearly a million Greeks were refugees or displaced persons.[108] More than 7% of Greek population had suffered a violent death between 1940 and 1949. Another 12.5% were permanently disabled by disease.[109] Food had to be imported to prevent famine. The country was essentially in a state of ruin.

With the end of the Civil War, Greece began a new phase of relative political stability and exceptional economic recovery. Marshall Plan aid combined with reparations and foreign grants to lay the foundations for a period of extraordinary economic growth. Between 1948 and 1951, the United States pumped USD 376 million into Greece, the equivalent of nearly USD 3.75 billion in today's terms. It had the desired effect. GDP growth in the period 1951–1961 averaged 6.2%. Per capita GDP rose 5.2% over the same period.[110] Certainly, there was a significant margin for growth since Greece's economy had been so devastated by the German occupation and Civil War, but new investment, the deployment of new technologies in agriculture and industry, and infrastructure projects all made an important contribution. In 1960, Greece received 115 million Marks from West Germany in war reparations, nearly USD 4 billion in today's terms.

Between 1960 and 1973, Greek economic growth was even more impressive. Some observers spoke of a 'Greek economic miracle,' which returned an average annual GDP growth rate of 7.7%. Exports of goods and services grew at the even faster pace of 12.6% annually. These figures made Greece the fastest growing economy in Europe during this period and the second fastest growing economy in the OECD, trailing only Japan.[111]

In contrast with the economic success, the political picture was ambiguous. The fundamental, long-standing political problems and social tensions which played out in the National Schism, the Civil War, and a seemingly unending cycle of democrats and dictators had not been resolved. American intervention had enabled the defeat of communism and prevented the emergence of a Soviet puppet state on the Mediterranean. Yet American involvement, precisely because it was deep and decisive, had in many ways made it more challenging for the Greeks to develop solutions to their domestic problems.[112] These problems would not go away. Learning nothing and forgetting nothing, the political system retained weaknesses and tensions present from its formation. Tensions between King and Cabinet, between the army and the government, between left and right were still not resolved.

When the young king, Constantine II, clashed in 1965 with the newly elected liberal Prime Minister, George Papandreou, the old divisions reopened dramatically. Five different prime ministers rode the merry-go-round between Papandreou's dismissal in July 1965 and the military coup of April 1967. This dictatorship, commonly called the Junta (Χούντα) or the Regime of the Colonels (καθεστώς των Συνταγματαρχών), lasted until it was brought down by popular unrest following the Turkish invasion of Cyprus in July 1974. Only then was Greece able to rid itself of monarchy and military dictatorship and begin the long, slow road to peaceful democratic governance. Still, divisions between the left and the right remained. The scars of the Civil War, the coup, and the Junta had not faded. In many ways, they continue to define divisions within Greek politics and Greek society today.

Conclusion: a model victory?

America's investment paid off. Greece was preserved from a communist takeover. In 1952, its position within the Western orbit was solidified when, along with Turkey, it joined the North Atlantic Treaty Organization (NATO). In 1981, it joined the European Community. The tensions, contradictions, and fissures of the Civil War were not eliminated but slowly began to recede. For the United States, the successful intervention in the Greek Civil War became a vindication of the policy of containment. The Truman Doctrine and the Marshall Plan had identified issues of core national interest, articulated a policy to sustain those interests, and then furnished the tools to implement that policy.

Victory in Greece did not presage a broader defeat of communism. To the contrary, the United States was soon on the back foot in a number of confrontations. On 1 October 1949, just before DSE announced its ceasefire in Greece, Mao Zedong declared the establishment of the People's Republic of China. In 1950, Communist North Korean troops crossed the 38th parallel. President Truman declared: 'Korea is the Greece of the Far East. If we are tough enough now, if we stand up to them like we did in Greece three years ago, they won't take over.'[113] In 1957, Eisenhower justified an expanded American role in Vietnam with a similar logic.[114] In his memoirs, Lyndon Johnson commented on the parallels between Greece and Vietnam.[115] It was the Greek experience – 'a successfully fought proxy war featuring a counterinsurgency campaign against communist guerrillas and marked by the use of napalm – [that] became a model for involvement in Vietnam.'[116]

But the parallels were dangerously imperfect for Greece to be applied broadly. Stalin acknowledged that the Soviet Union could not project power in Greece to match British and American resources. Soviet resources were limited. Their material commitment to Greece was very small. Neither was Stalin willing to risk a confrontation at that time, in that place, for that prize. Within Greece, there was a solid base of support for British and (later) American intervention. The United States claimed to be (and was) supporting the establishment of a political order founded on democratic principles (however flawed), including regular elections. This was in line with the wishes of a majority of Greek citizens. There was no question of American attenuation of Greek sovereignty in the long term. American intervention was a continuation of a wartime partnership first undertaken by the British. It was not neocolonialism.

President Truman built an effective political consensus to resist communism in Greece. The massive outlays of the Marshall Plan, American military aid to Greece, and the subsequent formation of NATO solidified a clear and substantive American commitment to Greece in particular and Europe more generally. Greece's geography and the insistence of American policymakers of its importance to security in the Eastern Mediterranean and the Middle East made this commitment possible. In spite of the seriousness of the situation, there was no commitment of conventional American military units. The number of Americans in-country peaked at 508 military personnel serving as advisors and trainers in March 1949.[117] Only four were killed in action.

American aid focused on supplying and organizing the Greek military to fight (and win) its own war. This was part of a clear recognition that American soldiers were not the right tool to end the insurgency. At the same time, the critical underlying factors that provided support to the communist forces were identified and reduced. Griswold and Kennan correctly diagnosed that poverty, corruption, and the failure of society were the greatest recruiting tools for the communists. Ameliorating these economic ills undermined communist efforts at recruitment and left them reliant on forced conscription. As a result, they were unable to regenerate their strength.

If this in a sense is a general diagnosis and prescription, the interplay of local and international factors was unique in Greece. No conflict is a purely local affair, nor is any conflict purely dictated by the exigencies of geopolitics. Each conflict represents its own unique blend of the two. In Greece, as articulated by David Close, polarization was a reflection of the struggle for power at both the domestic and international levels. Domestically, the fight was between the Greek Communist Party and anti-communist forces. Internationally, it was part of the contest between the West, led by the United States, and the forces of international communism, spearheaded by the Soviet Union.[118] On the domestic level, economic factors, geography, and ethnicity played their role. Communities chose sides because of these factors and sometimes simply as a means for survival.

As Griswold and Kennan argued, the problem in Greece was not primarily a military one. It did not have a military solution. The Greek armed forces could not eliminate communist guerrillas as long as the communists could recruit new members, fall back to positions outside of Greece, and receive supplies from abroad. At the same time, the Greek communists lacked the strength to seize control of the country through military means. As demonstrated during the *Dekemvriana* and again between 1947 and 1949, they were not even able to hold towns of any significant size. American troops would not have fundamentally altered this dynamic.

On the debit side, their presence could have undermined the legitimacy of the Greek state, provoked Soviet intervention (which remained indirect and half-hearted), and escalated the economic hardships confronting Greece. Instead, policymakers such as Griswold and Kennan accurately diagnosed the problem as hinging on recruitment, government legitimacy, and economics. Improving the economic situation in Greece, curbing the worst of the government's corruption, insisting on more inclusive governance, and taking advantage of the split between Tito and Stalin were the surest ways to strategic success.

America's deep commitment to Greece stood in stark contrast to the ambiguous and minimal support offered by the Soviet Union to the Greek communists. Greece's Balkan neighbors, communist countries such as Albania, Yugoslavia, and Bulgaria, provided limited support to the Greek Democratic Army. They were constrained by their own material limitations and the hesitancy of Stalin to provide the KKE greater support. Over time, the distancing of Yugoslavia from Moscow's orbit further isolated Greek communists in the international sphere, leaving them more vulnerable.

This isolation of the Democratic Army, combined with its dwindling forces, compelled its leadership, particularly Zachariades, to push for a military decision as the political situation deteriorated. The shift to 'positional warfare' was a reflection not of the Democratic Army's strength but of its weakness. Contrary to popular claims, the Greek communists did not fail because they attempted to hold territory. They were always successful in holding some rural and mountainous areas; they were never able to take and hold towns of any size. Their tactic of luring the Greek military to smash itself on strong defensive positions failed in both 1948 and 1949 at the cost of significant casualties. In 1949, they were unable to escape in sufficient numbers to fight another day.

DSE's forces were always outnumbered by the Greek army by four, five, or six to one, and never reach more than *half* the strength their leaders thought necessary to succeed through military means. This combination of factors, notably absent from the dynamics of South-east Asia, led to

American victory and communist defeat in Greece. These were not strategic or tactical practices that could be easily duplicated elsewhere.

Notes

1. Gaddis, *The Long Peace*, 55.
2. TNA (UK), FO 371/61053, Minute by F.B.A. Randall, 10 March 1947.
3. FRUS, *1947. General*, Memorandum by Bohlen, 30 August 1947, 763.
4. Ibid., 764.
5. Pepelasis and Thompson, "Agriculture in a Restrictive Environment," 147.
6. Among other factors contributing to his pro-German stance, Constantine was married to Kaiser Wilhelm II's sister.
7. Close, *The Origins of the Greek Civil War*, 19.
8. Stefanidis, *Stirring the Greek Nation*, 5.
9. Close, *The Origins of the Greek Civil War*, 20.
10. Gerolymatos, *Red Acropolis, Black Terror*, 25.
11. Kousoulas, *Modern Greece*, 165-6.
12. Cliadakis, "The Political and Diplomatic Background," 129.
13. Under Mussolini, this practice was known as *confino*.
14. Petrakis, *The Metaxas Myth*, 51.
15. Ibid.
16. Ibid., 52-59.
17. Gooch, *Mussolini and His Generals*, 451.
18. Close, *The Greek Civil War*, 1.
19. Convicts, including those with histories of violence and mental instability, were also recruited into these battalions.
20. Hondros, "Greece and the German Occupation," 45.
21. Hondros, "Greece and the German Occupation," 47.
22. FRUS, *1942, Europe*, Document 717, Secretary of State Cordell Hull to US Ambassador to the UK John Winant, 3 December 1941. Telegram 868.48/1172.
23. O'Ballance, *The Greek Civil War*, 50.
24. Smith, "'The First Round' – Civil War During the Occupation," 58-9.
25. Gerolymatos, *Red Acropolis, Black Terror*, 73.
26. O'Ballance, *The Greek Civil War*, 51.
27. See note 25.
28. Close, *The Origins of the Greek Civil War*, 76.
29. Ibid., 103.
30. Hondros, "Greece and the German Occupation," 49.
31. Ibid., 51-2.
32. Close, *The Origins of the Greek Civil War*, 90.
33. Ibid., 102.
34. Woodhouse, *Modern Greece*, 251.
35. Ibid.
36. O'Ballance, *The Greek Civil War*, 67.
37. See note 35.
38. Roberts, "Moscow's Cold War on the Periphery," 60.
39. Maiksii quoted in Roberts, 60.
40. Iatrides, "George F. Kennan and the Birth of Containment," 137.

41. According to many accounts, including Churchill's own, he drafted the percentage numbers, and Stalin ticked them to signal his agreement. Such penciled affirmations were typical of Stalin, who condemned hundreds of thousands to death with similar tick marks on execution orders for the NKVD during the Great Terror of 1937-8 and the shooting of Polish prisoners of war in 1940.
42. Iatrides and Rizopoulos, "The International Dimension of the Greek Civil War," 88.
43. Banac, *The Diary of Georgi Dimitrov*, 345.
44. Koliopoulos and Veremis, *Greece, The Modern Sequel*.
45. Close, *The Origins of the Greek Civil War*, 94.
46. Ibid., 113.
47. O'Ballance, *The Greek Civil War*, 92.
48. Baerentzen and Close, "The British Defeat of EAM, 1944-5," 79.
49. Kalyvas, "Red Terror."
50. See note 48.
51. Kalogrias and Dordanas, "Η αναγνώριση των μη εαμικών αντιστασιακών οργανώσεων (1945–1974) [The recognition of the non-EAM resistance group, 1945–1974]."
52. Baerentzen and Close, "The British Defeat of EAM, 1944-5," 86.
53. Ibid.
54. O'Ballance, *The Greek Civil War*, 108.
55. Banac, *The Diary of Georgi Dimitrov*, 352-3.
56. O'Ballance, *The Greek Civil War*, 112.
57. Close, *The Origins of the Greek Civil War*, 166.
58. Ibid.
59. Richter, *British Intervention in Greece*, 240.
60. Close, *The Origins of the Greek Civil War*, 167.
61. FRUS, *Diplomatic Papers, 1945, European Advisor Commission, Austria, Germany*, Telegram from Kirk to the Secretary of State, 8 March 1945, 116.
62. FRUS, *Diplomatic Papers, 1945, The Near East and Africa, Vol. VIII*, Telegram from MacVeagh to the Secretary of State, 10 March 1945, 116.
63. FRUS, *1945, Vol. VIII*, Telegram from MacVeagh to the Secretary of State, 10 March 1945, 117.
64. FRUS, *1945, Vol. VIII*, Aide Memoire from the British Embassy to the Department of State, 126.
65. FRUS, *1945, Vol. VIII*, Telegram from Alexander Kirk to the Secretary of State, 22 March 1945, 125.
66. Close, *The Origins of the Greek Civil War*, 162.
67. Close and Veremis, 97.
68. Close, *The Origins of the Greek Civil War*, 167-8.
69. FRUS, *1945, Vol. VIII*, Telegram from Alexander Kirk to the Secretary of State, 15 April 1945, 126.
70. Close, *The Origins of the Greek Civil War*, 170.
71. Iatrides, "George F. Kennan and the Birth of Containment," 138.
72. Ibid.
73. TNA, CREST-CIA, Central Intelligence Group, "The Greek Situation," 7 February 1947, 4.
74. Mazower, 7.
75. Koliopoulos and Veremis, *Greece, The Modern Sequel*, 89.

76. Ibid, 90.
77. See note 67.
78. Koliopoulos and Veremis, *Greece, The Modern Sequel*, 103.
79. TNA, RG 59 Box 7057, "Aide Memoire," 21 February 1947 from the British Ambassador.
80. FRUS, *1947 Vol. III*, The Acting Secretary of State (Acheson) to the Secretary of War (Patterson), 5 March 1947, 197. https://history.state.gov/historicaldocuments/frus1947v03/pg_197.
81. The North Atlantic Treaty Organization came into effect in 1949. Greece and Turkey joined as part of the first expansion in 1952.
82. President Harry S. Truman's Address Before a Joint Session of Congress, 12 March 1947, http://avalon.law.yale.edu/20th_century/trudoc.asp.
83. Close, *The Origins of the Greek Civil War*, 139.
84. Jeffrey, *Ambiguous Commitments and Uncertain Policies*, 286-8.
85. FRUS, 1947, *The Near East and Africa, Vol. V*, "Editorial Note," 204.
86. TNA, RG 49: Box 7057, American Mission to Greece, "Monthly Historical Report," August 1947, 9.
87. Ibid., 1-3.
88. Karlin, "Training and Equipping is Not Transforming," 50.
89. TNA, CREST-CIA, ORE 51, "The Current Situation in Greece," 20 October 1947, 4.
90. Ibid., 5.
91. TNA, RG 59: Box 7059, DoD "Directive Governing the Establishment and Operation of the Joint US Military Advisory and Planning Group in Greece, Forrestal to Marshall, 5 January 1948.
92. Karlin, "Training and Equipping is Not Transforming," 58.
93. FRUS, *1948, Vol. IV*, Memorandum by the Director of the Office of Near Eastern and African Affairs (Henderson) to the Secretary of State, 9 January 1948, 14.
94. Ibid., 9.
95. FRUS, *1948, Vol. IV*, Memorandum from Griswold to Marshall, 14 January 1948, 29.
96. TNA, CREST-CIA, "Consequences of Certain Courses of Action With Respect to Greece," 5 April 1948, 1.
97. Close, *The Origins of the Greek Civil War*, 209.
98. Ibid., 214.
99. O'Ballance, *The Greek Civil War*, 180.
100. Close and Veremis, 108.
101. TNA, CREST-CIA, ORE 51, "The Current Situation in Greece," 20 October 1947, 5.
102. Close, *The Origins of the Greek Civil War*, 120.
103. Close, *The Origins of the Greek Civil War*, 217.
104. O'Ballance, *The Greek Civil War*, 186.
105. Close, *The Origins of the Greek Civil War*, 219.
106. O'Ballance, *The Greek Civil War*, 200.
107. Ibid., 201.
108. Gerolymatos, *Red Acropolis, Black Terror*, 196.
109. Ibid., 197.
110. Geronimakis, "Post-War Economic Growth in Greece, 1950-61," 258.
111. Thomadakis, "The Greek Economy."
112. Iatrides and Rizopoulos, "The International Dimension of the Greek Civil War," 101.
113. Truman, *Harry S. Truman*, 461.

114. Gerolymatos, *Red Acropolis, Black Terror*, 231.
115. Ibid., 232.
116. Ibid.
117. Karlin, "Training and Equipping is Not Transforming," 92.
118. Close, *The Origins of the Greek Civil War*, 11.

Disclosure statement

No potential conflict of interest was reported by the author.

Bibliography

Primary Sources

Foreign Relations of the United States (FRUS). 1943. *The Near East and Africa*. Vol. IV.
Foreign Relations of the United States (FRUS). 1945. *The Near East and Africa*. Vol. VIII.
Foreign Relations of the United States (FRUS). 1946. *The Near East and Africa*. Vol. VII.
Foreign Relations of the United States (FRUS). 1947. *The Near East and Africa*. Vol. III.
The National Archives (TNA). CREST-CIA. https://www.cia.gov/library/readingroom/collection/crest-25-year-program-archive
The National Archives (TNA). RG 49 and RG 59

Secondary Sources

Allison, Graham, and Kalypso Nicolaides, eds. *The Greek Paradox: Promise Vs. Performance*. Cambridge: The MIT Press, 1997.
Baerentzen, Lars, and David H. Close. "The British Defeat of EAM, 1944-5." In *The Greek Civil War*, edited by David Close, 79. 1993.
Banac, Ivo, ed. *The Diary of Georgi Dimitrov* Translated by Jane Hedges, Timothy Sergay, and Irina Faion. Yale: Yale University Press, 2003.
Cliadakis, Harry. "The Political and Diplomatic Background to the Metaxas Dictatorship, 1935-36." *Journal of Contemporary History* 14, no. 1, Jan., (1979): 117–138. doi:10.1177/002200947901400106.
Close, David, ed. *The Greek Civil War, 1943-1950: Studies in Polarization*. London: Routledge, 1993.
Close, David. *The Origins of the Greek Civil War*. London: Longman, 1995.
FRUS. *1942, Europe: Diplomatic Papers*. Vol. II. Washington: The Government Printing Office, 1942.
FRUS. *Diplomatic Papers, 1945, European Advisor Commission, Austria, Germany*. Vol. VIII. Washington: Government Printing Office, 1945.
FRUS. *1947. General: The United Nations*. Vol. I. Washington: Government Printing Office, 1947.
Gaddis, John L. *The Long Peace: Inquiries into the History of the Cold War*. Oxford: Oxford University Press, 1987.
Gerolymatos, André. *Red Acropolis, Black Terror: The Greek Civil War and the Origins of Soviet-American Rivalry, 1943-1949*. New York: Basic Books, 2004.
Geronimakis, S. "Post-War Economic Growth in Greece, 1950-61." *Income and Wealth* 11, no. 1, Mar., (1965): 257–280. doi:10.1111/j.1475-4991.1965.tb00992.x.

Gialistras, S.A. *The Greek Nation once More Stems a Barbarian Onslaught*. Translated by G.A. Trypanis. Athens, 1950.

Gooch, John. *Mussolini and His Generals: The Armed Forces and Fascist Foreign Policy, 1922-1940*. Cambridge: Cambridge University Press, 2007.

Gounaris, Vasilis, ed. *Ήρωες των Ελλήνων: Οι καπετάνιοι, τα παλικάρια και η αναγνώριση των εθνικών αγώνων 19ος–20ός αιώνας [Heroes of Greece: The captains, the brave men, and the recognition of the national struggles, 19th–20th centuries]*. Athens: Hellenic Parliament, 2014.

Hondros, John L. "Greece and the German Occupation." In *The Greek Civil War*, edited by David Close, 45. 1993.

Iatrides, John O. "George F. Kennan and the Birth of Containment: The Greek Test Case." *World Policy Journal* 22, no. 3 (2005): 126–145. doi:10.1215/07402775-2005-4005. Fall.

Iatrides, John O., and Nicholas X. Rizopoulos. "The International Dimension of the Greek Civil War." *World Policy Journal* 17, no. 1 (Spring 2000): 87–103. doi:10.1215/07402775-2000-2009.

Jeffrey, Judith. *Ambiguous Commitments and Uncertain Policies: The Truman Doctrine in Greece, 1947-1952*. Lanham: Lexington Books, 2000.

Joes, Anthony James. *America and Guerrilla Warfare*. Kentucky: University Press of Kentucky, 2000.

Kalogrias, Vaios, and Stratos Dordanas. "Η αναγνώριση των μη εαμικών αντιστασιακών οργανώσεων (1945–1974) [The recognition of the non-EAM resistance group, 1945–1974]." In *Ήρωες των Ελλήνων: Οι καπετάνιοι, τα παλικάρια και η αναγνώριση των εθνικών αγώνων 19ος–20ός αιώνας [Heroes of Greece: The captains, the brave men, and the recognition of the national struggles, 19th–20th centuries]*, edited by Vasilis Gounaris, 174–176. Athens: Hellenic Parliament Foundation, 2014.

Kalyvas, Stathis N. "Red Terror: Leftist Violence during the Occupation." In *After the War Was Over: Reconstructing the Family, Nation, and State in Greece: 1943-1960*, edited by Mark Mazower, 149. Princeton, NJ: Princeton University Press, 2000.

Karlin, Mara E. "Training and Equipping Is Not Transforming: An Assessment of US Programs to Build Partner Militaries." Unpublished Doctoral Dissertation. Baltimore: Johns Hopkins University, 2012.

Koliopoulos, John S., and M. Veremis Thanos. *Greece the Modern Sequel: From 1831 to the Present*. New York: New York University Press, 2002.

Koliopoulos, John S., and Thanos M. Veremis. *Greece, the Modern Sequel: From 1831 to the Present*, 71. New York: New York University Press, 2002.

Kousoulas, D. George. *Modern Greece: Profile of a Nation*. New York: Charles Scribner's Sons, 1974.

Mazower, Mark, ed. *After the War Was Over: Reconstructing the Family, Nation, and State in Greece, 1943-1960*. Princeton: Princeton University, 2000.

O'Ballance, Edgar. *The Greek Civil War, 1944-1949*. New York: Praeger, 1996.

Pepelasis, A.A., and Kenneth Thompson. "Agriculture in a Restrictive Environment: The Case of Greece." *Economic Geography* 36, no. 2, Apr., (1960): 145–157. doi:10.2307/142149.

Petrakis, Marina. *The Metaxas Myth: Dictatorship and Propaganda in Greece*. London: IB Tauris, 2006.

Powers, Richard J. "From Greece to Vietnam, and Back?" *The Western Political Quarterly* 22, no. 4, Dec., (1969): 846–861. doi:10.2307/447039.

Richter, Heinz. *British Intervention in Greece: From Varkiza to Civil War*. Virginia: Hollowbrook Publishers, 1985.

Roberts, Geoffrey. "Moscow's Cold War on the Periphery: Soviet Policy in Greece, Iran, and Turkey, 1943-9." *Journal of Contemporary History* 46, no. 1, Jan., (2011): 58–81. doi:10.1177/0022009410383292.

Sakkas, John. *Britain and the Greek Civil War, 1944-1949: British Imperialism, Public Opinion and the Coming of the Cold War*. Hemsbach: Peleus, 2013.

Smith, Ole. "'The First Round'– Civil War during the Occupation." In *The Greek Civil War*, edited by David Close, 58–59. 1993.

Stefanidis, Ioannis. *Stirring the Greek Nation: Political Culture, Irredentism and Anti-Americanism in Post-War Greece, 1945-1967*. Hampshire: Ashgate, 2007.

Thomadakis, Stavros B. "The Greek Economy: Performance, Expectations, & Paradoxes." In *The Greek Paradox: Promise Vs. Performance*, edited by Graham Allison and Kalypso Nicolaides, 43. Cambridge: The MIT Press, 1997.

Thorpe, Andrew. "'In a Rather Emotional State?' the Labour Party and British Intervention in Greece, 1944-5." *The English Historical Review* 121, no. 493, Sep., (2006): 1075–1105. doi:10.1093/ehr/cel212.

Truman, Margaret. *Harry S. Truman*. New York: William Morrow, 1973.

Veremis, Thanos. *The Military in Greek Politics: From Independence to Democracy*. Montreal: Black Rose Books, 1997.

Woodhouse, C.M. *Modern Greece: A Short History*. London: Faber and Faber, 1986.

3 Organizing for the 'gray zone' fight
Early Cold War realities and the CIA's Directorate of Operations

David P. Oakley

ABSTRACT
Despite its portrayal as something new, the concept of the 'gray zone' is not novel. It was the Cold War battleground in which the USA and the Soviet Union waged rival unconventional campaigns, and it was there that the newly formed Central Intelligence Agency (CIA) was given responsibility for operating. This was not the organization's original purpose, but Cold War exigencies forced Washington to improvise and build an organization with unique capabilities. These early years shaped the CIA's operations directorate, creating two distinct cultures within the larger agency, one focused on intelligence collection and the other focused on covert action.

Introduction

In recent years, the concept of 'gray zone' operations has loomed large. 'Fighting and Winning in the Gray Zone,' 'Mastering the Gray Zone: Understanding a Changing Era of Conflict,' and 'Owning the Gray Zone,' are just a few of the titles discovered in a quick Google search.[1] A number of scholars and practitioners describe this zone between war and peace as novel and as posing a unique challenge to the USA. A few acknowledge similarities to earlier times, but most tend to exaggerate the uniqueness of the current environment.[2] Although the 'gray zone' may be a useful concept for military planners, who tend to focus on the dichotomy between war and peace, it is in fact not new for the broader national security profession or vastly different from challenges the country has previously faced. The identification of the contemporary operational environment as novel and a 'conceptual no man's land for strategists and military planners' ignores, or at least under-appreciates, previous experiences.[3] This ahistorical view is costly, because it neglects how the USA previously organized to wage unconventional campaigns in the gray zone.

During the Cold War, the USA and the Soviet Union faced the unfathomable possibility of a nuclear exchange; hence both sought to gain advantage through other ways. Both sought to 'shift international rules, norms, distribution of goods, and patterns of authority to their benefit,' by leveraging an unconventional 'gradualist campaign' against the other.[4] The Soviet Union infiltrated the US government, its business community, news agencies, and even Hollywood prior to World War II, not only to gain access to secrets but to influence the American population.[5] Despite Stalin's paranoia which led to the self-destruction of his intelligence networks in the USA,[6] the Soviet Union maintained significant capabilities and in 1947 reestablished the Communist Information Bureau (COMINFORM).[7] The COMINFORM was responsible for running front organizations that denounced Western governments and pushed for policies favorable to the Soviet Union. Through the running of 'academic conferences' and organizations with innocuous names such as the 'Women's International Democratic Federation,' the COMINFORM tried to convince people of Soviet benevolence and Western war-mongering.[8] In the Cold War gray zone, the Soviet Union exploited all its perceived strengths and attacked its adversaries' vulnerabilities. The Soviets, for instance, praised their 'cultural achievements,' while denigrating America for its race problems and the inconsistency of pushing for freedom abroad while maintaining segregation at home.[9]

Early in the Cold War, the US government wrestled with how to respond to Soviet moves around the world.[10] The post-war American national security structure had been influenced by the Pearl Harbor experience and built in response to a surprise yet conventional attack. It thus was not well-suited for the fluid Cold War context that posed challenges not yet fully appreciated. Since the USA had never waged this type of 'war,' the government sought nonconventional approaches.[11] The newly formed Central Intelligence Agency (CIA) was given responsibility for operating in the gray zone. This was not the original purpose for the organization, but Cold War exigencies forced the USA 'on the fly' to build an organization with unique capabilities. These early years shaped the CIA's operations directorate, creating two distinct agency cultures, one focused on intelligence collection and the other focused on covert action.

This article explores the early years of the CIA, with a particular focus on its organizational evolution in response to the Cold War gray zone. This article does not seek to be a comprehensive study of the CIA's early operations, but rather, looks to understand policy decisions that shaped why and how the CIA's operations directorate evolved during its early years. The early years of the CIA's operations directorate are important for four reasons. First, despite what some scholars and practitioners argue, it highlights that wrestling with how to operate in a gray zone is nothing new even if technology increases the tactical options currently available. Second, it highlights how the USA structurally responded to previous gray zone challenges and how this response shaped the organization and mission of the CIA's operations directorate. Third, it highlights the incremental measures the USA took in both policy and organization to wage an unconventional war against the Soviet Union. Finally, it provides the history of how two distinct cultures developed not simply within the agency but within the CIA's operations directorate itself. One of these cultures was devoted to spying, the other to warfighting in the irregular arena.[12] Such a development had not been envisaged at the agency's 1947 founding but evolved as America faced challenges in the gray zone between war and peace.

Numerous authors have documented the early history of the CIA, but there is little literature that focuses on how Cold War requirements created these two distinct cultures within the CIA's operations directorate. Amy Zegart, for instance, in *Flawed by Design: The Evolution of the CIA, JCS and NSC*, highlights the different agency cultures – those of Directorate of Intelligence (DI) and the Directorate of Operations (DO) – but does not go into detail about the division within DO itself.[13] Similarly, Douglas Stuart's *Creating the National Security State: A History of the Law that Transformed America* captures the CIA's shift from 'intelligence coordination' to covert action to show how one mission became more dominant, but he does not explore the rise of the different DO cultures.[14] Richard Immerman's *The Hidden Hand: A Brief History of the CIA* highlights how 'historical circumstances, organizational interests, and bureaucratic politics' influenced the CIA's evolution 'from an agency established to collect, analyze, and disseminate intelligence to an instrument for engaging in covert, frequently paramilitary operations.'[15] Although this paper agrees and benefits from Immerman's perspective on the importance of the Cold War in shaping the CIA, his discussion focuses on the broad purpose of the CIA, while this article examines the operations directorate. These authors and others provide a rich history of the CIA's early years, but there is a need, from the perspective of the American way of warfighting in irregular conflicts, to better understand why and how the DO's two cultures, which remain to this day, developed early in response to the gray zone between war and peace.

Building an espionage organization in an uncertain environment

In November 1944, William Donovan, the director of the Office of Strategic Services (OSS), sent President Franklin Roosevelt, his old Columbia Law School classmate, a memorandum that captured his vision for a postwar intelligence service.[16] Donovan believed the subordination of the OSS to the military, as had been the case during World War II, was a wartime reality that should not be carried forward. According to Donovan, post-war America required an intelligence service that reported directly to the president and not through executive departments. Roosevelt, who was largely annoyed by Donovan's persistence, sent the post-war intelligence recommendation to the State, Navy, and War Departments, most likely realizing the push-back it would receive.[17] Two months later, the JCS Strategic Survey Committee (JSSC) submitted its response to Donovan's recommendation.[18] Although the three flag officers on the committee agreed with Donovan's assertion that a central intelligence service was needed, they disagreed that its director should report directly to the president. Instead, the JSSC recommended the director report to a 'National Intelligence Authority' composed of the Secretaries of State, War, and Navy, as well as a representative from the Joint Chiefs of Staff (JCS).[19] This arrangement would not only guarantee the three departments maintained their internal intelligence capability but would also ensure they controlled any new national intelligence organization.

President Roosevelt and Donovan were never particularly close, but Donovan's relationship with President Truman was even more precarious.[20] Unlike his predecessor, Truman embraced transparent government and believed that a clandestine intelligence organization was a wartime necessity no longer required.[21] On 20 September 1945, five months after assuming the presidency, he issued Executive Order-9621, a terse statement eliminating the OSS and moving elements of the organization to the State and War departments.[22] Part of this move involved the transfer of OSS clandestine collection capability to a new separate War Department organization called the Strategic Services Unit (SSU). The SSU was led by Brigadier General (BG) John Magruder, an experienced intelligence officer who had served as Donovan's deputy during World War II. Despite President Truman not wanting a 'Gestapo'-like organization during peacetime, Secretary of War Robert Patterson and Deputy Secretary of War John McCloy were hesitant to release capability that might be needed in an uncertain future. By establishing the SSU, they ensured the retention of OSS clandestine collection capability while also keeping this capability independent from the Army.[23]

The five months between the disbandment of the OSS in September 1945 and the creation of a Central Intelligence Group (CIG) in January 1946 were a transitional period in American-Soviet relations. During the latter years of WWII, it was uncertain whether the USA and the Soviet Union would end the war as victorious partners or distrusting foes. Roosevelt enjoyed a friendly relationship with Stalin and believed the USA, Soviet Union, and Great Britain and China could serve as 'four policeman' imposing 'order on the rest of the world.'[24] Truman initially maintained this positive perspective on Soviet-American relations, but his confidence began to fray in late 1945 as the Soviet Union attempted to extend its influence into Turkey and Iran. The fraying unraveled in February 1946 when Stalin delivered a speech blaming capitalism for WWII and claiming Allied victory proved the supremacy of the communist system.[25]

Two weeks after Stalin's speech, from the US Embassy in Moscow, George Kennan sent his 'Long Telegram' analyzing Soviet strategy.[26] Therein, he asserted that Moscow's strategy was to 'advance the relative strength of USSR' in relation to Western 'capitalist powers.' As part of this strategy, the Soviets would use proxies to operate 'on an unofficial plane' to counter the Western powers economically, militarily, and culturally.[27] The resonance of his telegram showed that policy-makers were finally understanding the threat posed by the Soviets and the need for a response.[28] It was in this environment that Truman took the first-step towards building an independent intelligence organization.

On 22 January, Truman issued his directive establishing the National Intelligence Authority (NIA) and creating the Central Intelligence Group (CIG). Truman's directive maintained the influence of the State, War, and Navy Departments in the new structure by making them responsible for both coordinating intelligence through their positions on the NIA and filling CIG positions with officials from their departments. Through this action, Truman embraced the recommendations of the War and Navy Departments, while ignoring Donovan's recommendation for a separate intelligence organization that reported directly to the president. Truman initially envisioned the CIG's role as providing 'strategic and national policy intelligence' to the president and other elements of the executive branch.[29] CIG would serve more as a compiler and disseminator of intelligence, while the intelligence organizations within the State, War, and Navy Departments would serve as product producers. Despite National Intelligence Authority No.1 giving the CIG limited responsibility, the open-ended language in Truman's 1946 letter maintained the possibility of expanding the CIG's role when necessary to further national security[30] (a vagueness in language that would appear again in the 1947 National Security Act).

Less than a month after the formation of the CIG, Rear Admiral (RADM) Sidney Souers, a former Missouri businessman and newly appointed Director of Central Intelligence (DCI), issued Central Intelligence Group Directive No. 1, establishing an ad hoc committee to review the SSU and recommend the organizational elements and capabilities that should be retained.[31] The committee was chaired by Brigadier General (BG) Louis J. Fortier, a member of the CIG who had served as an intelligence officer and division commander during World War II before returning to intelligence after the war. The Fortier Committee recommended maintaining the SSU's clandestine capability but moving it from the War Department to the CIG.[32] This was in line with General Magruder's recommendation to retain an independent clandestine collection capability that could service national intelligence and not merely departmental intelligence requirements.[33]

Although the War Department was one of the three departments composing the NIA and therefore responsible for directing the CIG, the recommendation to move the SSU to the CIG was significant, because it would separate the SSU from any one department's control.

DCI transferred the SSU capabilities to the newly established Office of Special Operations (OSO) in October 1946.[34] SSU only existed for a year, but during this short period it protected and maintained the US clandestine collection capability that had originally been developed for WWII combat operations but would be essential in the Cold War gray zone.[35] OSO would serve as the organization responsible for 'all organized espionage and counter-espionage operations outside the United States.' The Assistant Director for Special Operations reported to the DCI but would service intelligence collection requests from executive departments.[36] Although the State, War and Navy Departments were members of the NIA and served as the DCI's 'supervisory body,' the establishment of the OSO under the DCI and not within a department ensured maneuver space for the new organization, even if it ultimately received its marching orders from the three departments.[37]

Similar to the SSU, the CIG proved a transitional organization replaced by an independent intelligence agency reporting directly to the National Security Council (NSC). The Central Intelligence Agency (CIA) created by the 1947 National Security Act more closely resembled Donovan's original recommendation.[38] The CIA's coordination responsibility and its authority to conduct 'all organized espionage and counter-espionage outside the United States' were functions executed previously by the CIG and the SSU, but the language granting the CIA authority to 'perform such other functions and duties related to intelligence as the NSC might direct' was significant.[39] Despite the paramilitary and covert action campaigns of the OSS during WWII, the SSU had 'abandoned all covert paramilitary and propaganda activities'; and while the OSO's founding memorandum said it could conduct 'semi-covert activities' to further its espionage mission, the OSO was not established for covert action.[40] The vague language in the 1947 National Security Act provided the legal justification for the CIA to assume a covert action role. As the unconventional conflict between the USA and the Soviet Union heated up, having this capability operating in the gray zone would become important.

Adapting in response to the gray zone threat

A year after the 'Long Telegram' and four months before the public became familiar with Kennan's concerns through his *Foreign Affairs* article, President Truman articulated his new doctrine before a joint session of Congress. The eponymous doctrine, articulated in response to Soviet moves in Greece and Turkey, established it was American policy to assist countries battling communist insurgencies.[41] Three months later, Secretary of State George

C. Marshall announced the economic recovery plan for Europe, the 'Marshall Plan' written by the State Department's Policy Planning Staff under the guidance of its director, George Kennan. Kennan believed the central threat facing Europe was not the Soviet Union or communism but the economic conditions that 'made the European society vulnerable to exploitation by totalitarianism.'[42] This meant the Marshall Plan was not merely about economic recovery but about using American economic resources and other elements of soft-power as weapons to battle for the 'hearts and minds' of Europe.[43] Economic altruism was good, but leveraging the resulting image of principled strength was key in a contest with the Soviets. The only issue was the USA did not have a 'peacetime' organization to conduct the covert psychological operations to contest this ground.[44]

Realizing this shortfall, the State-Army-Navy-Air Force Coordinating Committee (SANACC) – the latter member newly formed after splitting from the Army – established an ad hoc subcommittee in late 1947 'to determine whether at the present time the USA should utilize coordinated psychological measures in furtherance of the attainment of its national objectives; if so, what organization is required and what should be its terms of reference.'[45] The subcommittee concluded the USA had to take immediate 'coordinated measures' to counter Soviet propaganda efforts and to 'influence' foreign populations. It recommended this responsibility fall upon the Secretary of State, with coordination from the military services and the newly established CIA. The issue of covert psychological operations was deemed so important that the fledgling National Security Council (NSC) took up the issue during its second meeting in November 1947.

In December 1947, the NSC adopted the SANACC subcommittee's recommendation, while also expanding the CIA's role. The Agency would not only provide 'appropriate foreign intelligence' for psychological operations, but the Director of Central Intelligence (DCI) would be responsible for initiating and conducting 'covert psychological operations,' while ensuring coordination with Defense and State.[46] NSC-4 was not fully supported by DCI Roscoe Hillenkotter, the Department of Defense (DoD), or the State Department. Hillenkotter understood the potential blowback his organization could face running covert psychological operations, while DoD was concerned that the CIA's new responsibility would enter DoD's lane. The State Department's concern was slightly different. It did not want to get its hands dirty conducting covert psychological operations, but it believed such operations were part of foreign policy and wanted to plan and direct them.[47] Although Hillenkotter was not excited about CIA's new responsibility, he was even less enthusiastic about the State Department trying to direct CIA operations.[48]

Despite earlier concerns about the CIA's role in psychological operations, the council issued NSC 10/2 on 18 June 1948, expanding CIA's responsibility beyond just 'psychological operations' to all 'covert operations.'[49] To ensure proper coordination, the directive established the '10/2 Panel,' which included representatives from State, Defense, and the JCS. They were responsible for working with the CIA and reviewing covert action proposals.[50] To assume responsibility for this expanded mission, the NSC established the Office of Special Projects. Although this office would reside in the CIA, the Secretary of State would have responsibility for appointing its director and 'providing it policy guidance.'[51] This new set-up gave State the ability to influence CIA operations, while maintaining some distance from the perceived dirtiness of covert activity. Although not completely under the CIA's authority, the establishment of the Office of Special Projects placed foreign intelligence collection and covert operations under the same organization. While NSCID No. 5 clarified Agency authority for foreign intelligence collection and NSC-4 gave it responsibility for psychological operations, the establishment of a covert action office alongside an espionage intelligence office was the first step in establishing two distinct operational cultures within the CIA.[52]

George Kennan asked Allen Dulles to lead the Office of Special Projects, but Dulles, who expected a Republican victory in the 1948 Presidential Election, declined the position in hopes of becoming DCI. Kennan then selected Frank Wisner, a State Department official and former World War II Office of Strategic Services (OSS) officer to run the organization.[53] A brilliant mind, Wisner established what he referred to as 'the Mighty Wurlitzer,' a propaganda machine that used public and private organizations to provide operational cover, garner public support, and convince the third-world of communism's evil.[54] Although the Office of Special Projects soon changed to the Office of Policy Coordination (OPC), it retained the responsibility for conducting covert actions in the gray zone.[55]

In November 1948, the NSC published *NSC-20/4: U.S. Objectives with Respect to the USSR to Counter Soviet Threats to U.S. Security*. NSC-20/4 identified Soviet objectives, analyzed the Soviet threat, and provided 'U.S. objectives and aims' regarding the USSR. This document appears to be the first NSC guidance on countering Soviet actions following the establishment of OPC two months earlier, but its influence on policy is contestable.[56] Nonetheless, it originated with Kennan, the State Department official who pushed for OPC and the man who selected its first director. Kennan believed OPC operations 'might well enhance possibilities for achieving American objectives by means short of war' and wanted the opportunity to employ them.[57]

In April 1950, George Kennan's replacement as the head of the State Department's Policy Planning Staff released NSC-68, introducing 'containment' as America's new strategy for countering the Soviet Union. Despite NSC-68's aggressive military posture and expansive approach, Paul Nitze's document continued elements of Kennan's NSC-20/4.[58] Most notably, it included NSC-20/4's 'methods short of war' that focused on using American power and influence to demystify the Soviet Union and affect the attitudes of its population.[59] This element of NSC-68 required the continuation of covert psychological operations that Wisner and his OPC crew had been conducting.

As the CIA was evolving to handle both foreign espionage and covert action, the NSC was trying to determine if the Agency was structured, organized, and missioned properly to meet US intelligence needs in the gray zone. To this end, the NSC selected Allen W. Dulles, the former OSS station chief in Berlin and Kennan's preferred choice for the OPC directorship, to lead a committee reviewing the CIA.[60] As part of its review, the Dulles-Jackson-Correa Committee looked at both the CIA's foreign intelligence and covert action organization and mission. The committee's final report argued that covert action and foreign intelligence collection should be integrated into a single 'operations division' to ensure proper coordination.[61] NSC-50, though not issued immediately, ordered the phased implementation of the recommendations.

General Walter Bedell Smith, who took over for Roscoe Hillenkoetter in October 1950, hesitated to combine the OPC and OSO. Smith's reluctance stemmed from his disregard for OPC personnel, his preference for OSO operators, and a belief that he could ensure coordination without integration.[62] Despite Smith's concerns, the CIA established the Directorate of Plans in August 1952 and appointed Allen Dulles its first director.[63] The implementation of the Dulles-Jackson-Correa recommendation to combine foreign intelligence collection and covert action into one directorate thus embedded two distinct cultures within the CIA's operations directorate that still exist today. The foreign intelligence culture sought sources who clandestinely collected intelligence to inform policy-maker decisions. This group largely looked to report the world as it was. The covert action side was more 'offensive in nature' and 'looking to shape reality.'[64] Despite inherent friction in combining an organization that 'stole secrets' with one that shaped reality, the requirements of the Cold War gray zone determined the course of action.

As the CIA reorganized the operations directorate to integrate espionage and covert operations, the NSC was expanding the need for the latter against the Soviets. On 23 October 1951, NSC issued an update to NSC 10/2 that reaffirmed the CIA's lead role in covert operations, while also expanding and intensifying American covert operations against the Soviet Union. Through NSC 10/5, the council sought to 'place maximum strain' on the Soviet Union and its relationship with its 'satellites' and other communist countries, while strengthening the image of the USA and establishing the underground networks necessary to conduct 'covert and guerilla operations in strategic areas.'[65] This directive came five months after President Truman directed the Secretary of State, Secretary of Defense, and DCI to establish a Psychological Strategy Board (PSB) to coordinate America's psychological operations and to evaluate its effectiveness.[66]

Allen Dulles finally achieved his goal of becoming DCI with the election of General Dwight Eisenhower to the presidency in November 1952. In Eisenhower, Dulles found a leader who understood intelligence and the options covert operations offered in the Cold War gray zone.[67] On 10 July 1953, Congress directed a second Hoover Commission to investigate the structure and function of the executive branch.[68] Partially in response to the Hoover Commission's Clark Task Force that would soon investigate 'CIA operations,' the Eisenhower administration tapped World War II legend Jimmy Doolittle to lead a commission investigating the effectiveness of CIA covert actions.[69] The Doolittle Commission's report was a vigorous defense of CIA leadership of covert operations, as well as the use of covert action to counter the Soviets. Although the report was positive in its assessment of CIA management of covert operations – highlighting that covert action's 'placement in the overall organization of government is proper' and that the CIA was 'gradually improving its capabilities' – it did recommend a few areas requiring improvement. These included a reduction in cost and 'personnel,' together with improved 'coordination' with other agencies and departments. Most notable, though, the Doolittle Commission recommended expanding CIA covert operations in the gray zone as an element of American strategy, further solidifying the operations directorate's dual culture of foreign intelligence collection and covert action.[70]

Wurlitzer to rifles or moving from gray to black

In February 1961, less than a month after President John F. Kennedy's inauguration, McGeorge Bundy, Kennedy's National Security advisor, and Bundy's deputy, Walt Rostow, discussed the need to review the challenges posed by communist insurgencies.[71] The impetus behind the discussion was Kennedy's request that DoD 'examine means for placing more emphasis on the development of counter-guerrilla forces.'[72] Whereas Eisenhower looked to embrace covert action to counter Soviet moves, Kennedy was interested in expanding American counter-guerrilla operations against communist backed insurgents. Rostow and Bundy's meeting eventually resulted in the Counter-Guerrilla Warfare Task Force that was established to look at 'how could we organize our military and civil assets-including covert assets to make guerrilla operations unattractive or to deal with them if they start? What doctrine should we organize the government for the task?'[73] Selected to lead the task force was Richard Bissell, the CIA's Deputy Director for Plans, a highly regarded officer who oversaw both the successful development of the U2 spy plane in 1954–1955 and the disastrous Bay of Pigs invasion in 1961.[74]

The Bissell Committee published its report a month after Kennedy's Military Representative, General Maxwell Taylor, argued the USA had to 'decide how it will cope with Krushchev's "wars of liberation" which are really para-wars of guerrilla aggression.'[75] Similar to the Taylor report, the Bissell Committee concluded that Soviet 'subversive intervention' throughout the Third World was posing a 'critical problem' for the USA, a problem the USA was not organized to confront in substantive fashion. Reflecting criticism that was eerily similar to America's Iraq war four decades later, the task force argued the USA was not structured to wage a conflict that required a whole-of-government approach.[76] The outcome of the Bissell Committee was National Security Action Memorandum (NSAM) 124, which established the Special Group Counter-Insurgency to ensure 'the organization, training, equipment and doctrine of the US Armed Forces and other US agencies abroad and in the political economic, intelligence, military aid, and informational programs conducted abroad by State, Defense, AID, USIA, and CIA.'[77]

Although the CIA conducted counterinsurgency-type operations in Vietnam in the mid-1950s, it reduced its involvement from 1956 to 1961. Kennedy's election brought a turnabout that led to increased CIA involvement beginning in 1961, the same year the Bissell Committee and Taylor reports were published.[78] The CIA presence in Vietnam would result in the largest station in CIA history until the wars in Iraq and Afghanistan.[79] Although the CIA continued operating in the gray zone, the Vietnam War brought the conflict with the Soviets further into the black.

Conclusions

The recent gray zone emphasis results in catchy-titled articles and speaks to a permeable boundary between war and peace as something recent. This ignores a substantial history of engagement with irregular challenges. The CIA's Directorate of Operations came of age during the Cold War in the gray zone between war and peace. Thus it developed two distinct cultures, one culture focused on foreign intelligence collection, the other on covert action. The coexistence of covert action and clandestine foreign intelligence collection in the same organization has caused some friction since the CIA's early years. Both covert action and paramilitary operations are offensive in nature, looking to shape reality, while foreign intelligence collection looks to understand the world.

At times, CIA leaders have been concerned with covert action being employed too often as the president's favored foreign policy. Nonetheless, leaders have understood that covert action was a necessary tool and that housing it within the operations directorate provided the compartmentalization and deniability such action required.[80] This maintained a viable capacity for action as required. Although not always ideal, maintaining the two cultures was the best possible approach,[81] an approach that allowed the CIA to operate across the spectrum of war and peace.

Notes

1. Barno and Bensahel, "Fighting and Winning in the Gray Zone."; Mazarr. *Mastering the Gray Zone*.; and John Chambers, "Owning the Gray Zone."
2. For a view highlighting the long history of the challenge, see Brands, "Paradoxes of the Gray Zone."
3. Freier, *Outplayed*.
4. Mazarr, *Mastering the Gray Zone*, 10–33.
5. See Klehr, *Spies*.
6. See Weinstein and Vassiliev, *The Haunted Wood*..
7. See Healey, "The Cominform and World Communism, 339–49."
8. Wilford, *The Mighty Wurlitzer, 70*.; Stonor Saunder, *The Cultural Cold War*.
9. Wilford, *The Mighty Wurlitzer*, 100; Saunder, *The Cultural Cold War*, 18.
10. Stuart. *Creating the National Security Stat, 7*..
11. Mazarr, *Mastering the Gray Zone*, 43.
12. United States Department of Defense, *DoD Dictionary of Military*.DoD defines Unconventional Warfare-Activities as those conducted to enable a resistance movement or insurgency to coerce, disrupt, or overthrow a government or occupying power by operating through or with an underground, auxiliary, and guerrilla force in a denied area. DoD defines Irregular Warfare as a violent struggle among state and non-state actors for legitimacy and influence over the relevant populations.
13. Zegart. *Flawed by Design*, 185
14. Stuart. *Creating the National Security State*, 265.
15. Immerman, *The Hidden Hand*, 20-21.; and Wilford, *The Mighty Wurlitzer*.also provides a rich background on the rise of covert operations within the CIA. One of the best books on the history of CIA covert action is *Executive Secrets: Covert Action and the Presidency*, by William J. Daugherty, a scholar and former CIA officer who was also one of the Iranian hostages. He writes about this experience in his book, *In the Shadow of the Ayatollah: A CIA Hostage in Iran*.
16. Donovan to Roosevelt, 18 November 1944, in "The Donovan Plan for the Establishment." ; and Perisco, *Roosevelt's Secret War, 64*.
17. Alvarez and Mark, *Spying Through a Glass Darkly*, 12.
18. Rearden, *Council of War, 11*. The JSSC was created in November 1942 as "an elite advisory body dedicated to long-range planning,".
19. U.S. Joint Strategic Survey Committee, "Report by the Joint Strategic Survey Committee to the JCS on JCS 1181 and JIC 239/5." . The JSSC position was supported by the Lovett Committee, which was tasked by the Secretary of War in November 1945 to review the "foreign intelligence activities of the Nation and of the War Department." See https://history.state.gov/historicaldocuments/frus1945-50Intel/pg_71 (accessed 21 November 2017) for more information.

20. Perisco, *Roosevelt's Secret War*, 64.
21. Douglas Waller, *Wild Bill Donovan*, 321.; and Schroeder, *The Foundation of the CIA: Harry Truman*, 195–198.
22. Truman, "Executive Order No. 9621 "Termination of OSS and Disposition of Functions".
23. Alvarez and Mark, *Spying Through a Glass Darkly*, 16–17.
24. Gaddis, *Strategies of Containment*. 10.
25. Hamby, "Harry S. Truman: Foreign Affairs." ; and Stalin, "Meetings of Voters of the Stalin Electoral District."
26. Gaddis, *George F. Kennan*, 217–218.
27. Kennan, "George Kennan to George Marshall." . Part Four of Kennan's 'Long Telegram' described the Soviet Union's use of covert methods as part of their overall strategy. According to Kennan, the Soviets not only used fellow communists in other countries but non-governmental organizations to "undermine major western powers" and sow internal discord within Western societies, while "accepting no responsibility' for these groups.
28. Kennan, "George Kennan to George Marshall," 218.
29. National Intelligence Authority, *National Intelligence Authority Directive*. ; and Truman, *1946–1952: Years of Trial*., Kindle Location 1568–1572. In his memoirs, Truman stated, "The war taught us this lesson – that we had to collect intelligence in a manner that would make the information available where it was needed and when it was wanted, in an intelligent and understandable form. If it is not intelligent and understandable, it is useless. On becoming President, I found that the needed intelligence information was not coordinated at any one place. Reports came across my desk on the same subject at different times from the various departments, and these reports often conflicted".
30. National Intelligence Authority, *National Intelligence Authority Directive* .. The section in question reads, "perform such other functions and duties related to intelligence affecting the national security as the President and the National Intelligence Authority may from time to time direct."
31. Schroeder, *The Foundation of the CIA: Harry Truman, 195–198*.; and Central Intelligence Group, *Central Intelligence Group Directive No. 1*.
32. Darling, Berkowitz, and Goodman, *The Central Intelligence Agency*, 116; and "Fortier Committee to the Director of Central Intelligence (Souers)."
33. Alvarez and Mark, *Spying Through a Glass Darkly*, 24.
34. Ibid., 34.
35. Ibid., 24.
36. Executive Director to the Director of Central Intelligence (Souers), "Functions of the Office of Special Operations."
37. William M. Leary, *The Central Intelligence Agency, 21*.; There were other clandestine organizations operating in the immediate aftermath of WWII. For example, the Army's Special Services Branch "The Pond" was conducting clandestine collection activities and passing the information to elements within the State Department. See Alvarez and Marks' book *Spying Through a Glass Darkly*, 28.
38. U.S. Congress, *The National Security Act of 1947*.
39. Stuart, *Creating the National Security State*, 230; and National Security Council, *National Security Council Intelligence Directive No. 5*.

40. Alvarez and Mark, *Spying Through a Glass Darkly*, 30; and Executive Director to the Director of Central Intelligence (Souers), "Functions of the Office of Special Operations."
41. Truman, "Address Before a Joint Session of Congress."
42. Gaddis, *George F. Kennan: An American Life*, 265–267.
43. Darling et al., *The Central Intelligence Agency*, 245.
44. Pisani, *The CIA and the Marshal Plan*, 68. The author makes clear policymakers understood that the Marshall Plan had to be coordinated with efforts to counter Soviet psychological operations.
45. Ad Hoc Subcommittee of the State-Army-Navy-Air Force Coordinating Committee, *SANACC 304/11*.
46. Souers, *Executive Secretary (Souers) to the Members of the National Security Council*.; and Central Intelligence Agency, "Coordination and Policy Approval of Covert Operations."
47. Darling, et al., *The Central Intelligence Agency*, 245.
48. Gaddis, *George F. Kennan: An American Life*, 317.
49. Department of State Office of the Historian, *U.S. Covert Actions*. NSC 10/2 assigned CIA responsibility for "propaganda; economic warfare; preventive direct action, including sabotage, demolition and evacuation measures; subversion against hostile states, including assistance to underground resistance movements, guerrillas and refugee liberations groups, and support of indigenous anti-Communist elements in threatened countries of the free world. Such operations should not include armed conflict by recognized military forces, espionage, counter-espionage, and cover and deception for military operations."
50. Central Intelligence Agency,"Coordination and Policy Approval."
51. Gaddis, *George F. Kennan: An American Life*, 317; Wilford, *The Mighty Wurlitzer*, 27.
52. From National Archives and Records Administration, *RG 59, Records of the Department of State*.; and Department of State Briefing Memorandum, "Coordination of Foreign Measures (NSC 4) Psychological Operations (NSC 4-A)."
53. Wilford, *The Mighty Wurlitzer*, 27.
54. Ibid., 7.
55. Ibid., 27.
56. Elizabeth Edwards Spalding, *The First Cold Warrior*, 165–169. According to Spalding, NSC 20/1 also provided guidance, but focused on Russia and not the entire Soviet Union; and Gaddis, *George F. Kennan: An American Life*, 326–327.
57. Gaddis, *George F. Kennan: An American Life*, 318 and 326–327.
58. Thompson, *The Hawk and the Dove*, 107–113..
59. Executive Secretary of the National Security Council, *United States Objectives and Programs*.
60. Dulles and Correa Committee, *The Central Intelligence Agency*. The NSC asked the Committee to investigate: "a) The adequacy and effectiveness of the present organizational structure of the CIA; b) The value and efficiency of existing CIA activities; c) The relationship of these activities to those of other Departments and Agencies; d) The utilization and qualifications of CIA personnel."; and Kinzer, *The Brothers*.
61. The committee understood the need for covert action to be informed by foreign intelligence collection, but it is uncertain if they also appreciated the

friction that would arise with having these two missions within the same organization.
62. Darling, et al., *The Central Intelligence Agency*, 412; and Wilford, *The Mighty Wurlitzer*, 46.
63. Central Intelligence Agency's Center for the Study of Intelligence, *The Creation of the Intelligence Community*.
64. Oakley, *Subordinating Intelligence.*, 295.
65. Executive Secretary of the National Security Council, *A Report to the National Security Council*.
66. Harry S. Truman, *Directive Establishing the Psychological Strategy Board.*; and Central Intelligence Agency, "Coordination and Policy Approval." NSC-10/5 slightly changed the "10/2 Panel" by adding a representative from the PSB, thus becoming the "10/5" panel The Eisenhower administration in September 1953 renamed the PSB as the Operations Coordinating Board (OCB) and removed the OCB representative from the panel. NSC 5412 required the DCI to "consult with the OCB and with other government departments and agencies as appropriate to ensure that covert operations with consistent with U.S. polices." NSC-5412/1 directed that the DCI "consult with the Planning and Coordination Group (PCG) of the OCB and made the PCG the "normal channel for the policy approval of covert actions." Adjustments were made again in 1957 with NSC-5412/2, when it was made permissible for "sensitive" operations with no "military implication" to be approved "solely by the Secretary of State."
67. Wilford, *The Mighty Wurlitzer*, 153; and Prados, *Presidents' Secret Wars*, 108.
68. Houston, "Central Intelligence Agency."
69. Greenberg, "The Doolittle Commission of 1954.", 688; Doolittle Commission, *Report on the Covert Activities of the Central Intelligence Agency* (Washington, D. C., 26 July 1954); available at: https://www.cia.gov/library/readingroom/docs/CIA-RDP86B00269R000100040001-5.pdf (accessed 8 April 2018).
70. Greenberg, "The Doolittle Commission of 1954," 690; Doolittle Commission, *Report on the Covert Activities of the Central Intelligence Agency* (Washington, D. C., 26 July 1954); available at: https://www.cia.gov/library/readingroom/docs/CIA-RDP86B00269R000100040001-5.pdf (accessed 8 April 2018).
71. Central Intelligence Agency, *Background of Counter-Guerrilla*.
72. Kennedy, *National Security Action Memorandum No. 2*.
73. \ Bissell, *Reflections of a Cold Warrior*, 149.
74. Ibid, 92.
75. Taylor, *Report on General Taylor's Mission*.
76. Counter-Guerrilla Warfare Task Force, *Elements of US Strategy to Deal*.
77. Kennedy, *National Security Action Memorandum No. 124.*. Membership included the President's Military Representative, the Attorney General, the Deputy Undersecretary of State for Political Affairs, the Deputy Secretary of Defense, the Chairman of the Joint Chiefs of Staff, the DCI, the National Security Advisor, and the Administrator for the Agency for International Development.
78. Ahearn, *Vietnam Declassified*.
79. Douglas Jehl, "2 CIA Reports Offer Warnings on Iraq's Path."; and Miller, "CIA Expanding Presence in Afghanistan."
80. Helms, *A Look over My Shoulder*.
81. Oakley, *Subordinating Intelligence.* 295–296.

Disclosure statement

No potential conflict of interest was reported by the author. The views portrayed in the article are the author's own and do not reflect official policy or position of the DoD, CIA, or any other United States Government organization.

Bibliography

Ad Hoc Subcommittee of the State-Army-Navy-Air Force Coordinating Committee. *SANACC 304/11: Psychological Warfare*. Washington, DC. November 7, 1947. Accessed November 23, 2017. https://history.state.gov/historicaldocuments/frus1945-50Intel/d249.

Ahearn, Thomas L. *Vietnam Declassified: The CIA Counterinsurgency*. Lexington, KY: University Press of Kentucky, 2010.

Alvarez, David, and Eduard Mark. *Spying through a Glass Darkly: American Espionage against the Soviet Union, 1945–1946*. Lawrence, KS: University of Kansas Press, 2016.

Barno, David, and Nora Bensahel. "Fighting and Winning in the Gray Zone." *War on the Rocks*, May 19, 2015. Accessed November 21, 2017. https://warontherocks.com/2015/05/fightting-and-winning-in-the-gray-zone

Bissell, Richard M., Jr. *Reflections of a Cold Warrior: From Yalta to the Bay of Pigs*. New Haven, CT: Yale University Press, 1996.

Brands, Hal "Paradoxes of the Gray Zone." *Foreign Policy Research Institute*. February 5, 2016. Accessed April 8, 2018. https://www.fpri.org/article/2016/02/paradoxes-gray-zone/

Central Intelligence Agency. "Coordination and Policy Approval of Covert Operations." February 23, 1967. Accessed November 23, 2017. https://www.cia.gov/library/readingroom/docs/DOC_0000790232.pdf

Central Intelligence Agency. Background *of Counter-Guerrilla Warfare Task Force Report*. Accessed April 8, 2018. https://www.cia.gov/library/readingroom/docs/CIA-RDP83-000368R000500150037-0.pdf

Central Intelligence Agency's Center for the Study of Intelligence. *The Creation of the Intelligence Community Founding Documents*. Washington, DC: GPO. Accessed November 23, 2017. https://www.cia.gov/library/publications/intelligence-history/creation-of-ic-founding-documents/creation-of-the-intelligence-community.pdf

Central Intelligence Group. *Central Intelligence Group Directive No. 1: Survey of the Activities of the Strategic Services Unit*. February 19, 1946. Accessed November 22, 2017. https://history.state.gov/historicaldocuments/frus1945-50Intel/d104

Central Intelligence Group. "Memorandum from Executive Director to the Director of Central Intelligence (Souers)." *Functions of the Office of Special Operations*. October 25, 1946. Accessed November 22, 2017. https://www.cia.gov/library/readingroom/docs/CIA-RDP80R01731R001100010009-4.pdf

Chambers, John. "Owning the Gray Zone." *Army Times*, November 6, 2016. Accessed November 21, 2017. https://www.armytimes.com/opinion/2016/11/06/owning-the-gray-zone/

Counter-Guerrilla Warfare Task Force. *Elements of US Strategy to Deal with Wars of National Liberation*. December 8, 1961. Accessed April 8, 2018. https://www.cia.gov/library/readingroom/docs/CIA-RDP83-00036R001100160001-1.pdf

Darling, Arthur B., Bruce Berkowitz, and Allen E. Goodman. *The Central Intelligence Agency: An Instrument of Government to 1950*. State College, PA: Pennsylvania State University Press, 1990.

Department of State Briefing Memorandum, "Coordination of Foreign Measures (NSC 4) Psychological Operations (NSC 4-A)." December 17 1947, Accessed March 23 2018 https://history.state.gov/historicaldocuments/frus1945-50Intel/d256

Department of State Office of the Historian. *U.S. Covert Actions and Counter-Insurgency Programs*. Accessed November 23, 2017. https://history.state.gov/historicaldocuments/frus1964-68v16/actionstatement

Donavan, William J. "William Donovan to Franklin D. Roosevelt." *The Donovan Plan for the Establishment of a Central Intelligence Authority*. November 18, 1944. Accessed November 21, 2017. https://www.cia.gov/library/readingroom/docs/Donovan_plan_to_to_establish_central_intelligence_authority_18_Nov_1944.Pdf

Doolittle Commission, *Report on the Covert Activities of the Central Intelligence Agency*, Washington, DC, July 26 1954, Accessed April 8 2018 https://www.cia.gov/library/readingroom/docs/CIA-RDP86B00269R000100040001-5.pdf

Dulles, Jackson, and Correa Committee. *The Central Intelligence Agency and National Organization for Intelligence*. Washington, DC. January 1, 1949. Accessed November 23, 2017. http://sttpml.org/wp-content/uploads/2014/04/CIA-Dulles-Jackson-Correa-RDP86B00269R000500040001-1.pdf

Executive Secretary of the National Security Council. *United States Objectives and Programs for National Security*. Washington, DC. April 7, 1950. Accessed March 15, 2018. https://www.trumanlibrary.org/whistlestop/study_collections?coldwar?documents?pdf/10-1.pdf

Executive Secretary of the National Security Council. *A Report to the National Security Council on NSC 10/5*. Washington, DC. October 23, 1951. Accessed April 8, 2018. http://orchestratingpower.org/lib/National%20Strategies/NS%20subordinate%20strategies/Polwar%20Psywar/1951,10,23%20NSC%2010-5.pdf

Executive Director to the Director of Central Intelligence (Souers), "Functions of the Office of Special Operations." October 25 1946, Accessed November 22 2017 https://www.cia.gov/library/readingroom/docs/CIA-RDP80R01731R001100010009-4.pdf

Freier, Nathan P. *Outplayed: Regaining Strategic Initiatives in the Gray Zone*. Carlisle, PA: Strategic Studies Institute, U.S. Army War College, 2016. June.

"Fortier Committee to the Director of Central Intelligence (Souers)." 14 March 1946, Accessed November 22 2017 https://history.state.gov/historicaldocuments/frus1945-50Intel/d105

Gaddis, John Lewis *Strategies of Containment: A Critical Appraisal of American National Security Policy during the Cold War*. Oxford, U.K.: Oxford University Press, 2005.

Gaddis, John Lewis *George F. Kennan: An American Life*. New York, NY: Penguin Group, 2011.

Greenberg, H M. "The Doolittle Commission of 1954." *Intelligence and National Security* 20 (2005): 687–694. doi:10.1080/02684520500428160.

Hamby, Alonzo L. "Harry S. Truman: Foreign Affairs." Accessed April 8, 2018. https://millercenter.org/president/truman/foreign-affairs

Healey, Denis "The Cominform and World Communism." *International Affairs* 24, no. 3 (July 1948): 339–349. Accessed April 12, 2018. https://www.jstor.org/stable/3018651?seq=1#page_scan_tab_contents.

Helms, Richard *A Look over My Shoulder: A Life in the Central Intelligence Agency*. New York, NY: Random House Inc, 2003.

Houston, Lawrence "Central Intelligence Agency General Counsel (Houston) Memo to the Director of Central Intelligence (Dulles) on the "Hoover Commission"." 8 July 1954. Accessed April 8, 2018. https://www.cia.gov/library/readingroom/docs/CIA-RDP86B00269R000100130069-1.pdf

Immerman, Richard *The Hidden Hand: A Brief History of the CIA*. Malden, MA: John Wiley and Sons, 2014.

Jehl, Douglas "2 CIA Reports Offer Warnings on Iraq's Path." *New York Times*, December 7, 2004. Accessed April 8, 2018. http://www.nytimes.com/2004/12/07/front%20page/world/the-conflict-in-iraq-intelligence-2-cia-reports-offer.html

Joseph Stalin, "Meetings of Voters of the Stalin Electoral District." speech, Moscow, Soviet Union, 9 February1946, Accessed November 25 2017 http://digitalarchive.wilsoncenter.org/document/116179.pdf?v=a831b5c6a9ff133d9da25b37c013d691

Kennan, George. "George Kennan to George Marshall "Long Telegram"." *Harry S. Truman Administration File, Elsey Papers*, February 22, 1946. Accessed November 21, 2017. https://www.trumanlibrary.org/whistlestop/study_collections?coldwar?documents?pdf?6-6.pdf

Kennedy, John F. *National Security Action Memorandum No. 2: "Development of Counter Guerrilla Forces"*. February 3, 1961. Accessed November 29, 2017. https://fas.org/irp/offdocs/nsam-jfk/nsam2.jpg

Kinzer, Stephen. *The Brothers: John Foster Dulles, Allen Dulles and Their Secret World War*. New York, NY: Henry Holt and Company, 2013.

Klehr, Harvey *Spies: The Rise and Fall of the KGB in America*. New Haven, CT: Yale UP, 2010.

Leary, William. *The Central Intelligence Agency: History and Documents*. Tuscaloosa, AL: University of Alabama Press, 1984.

Mazarr, Michael J. *Mastering the Gray Zone: Understanding a Changing Era of Conflict*. Carlisle, PA: U.S. Army War College, December 2015. Accessed November 21, 2017. http://publications.armywarcollege.edu/pubs/2372.pdf

Miller, Greg "CIA Expanding Presence in Afghanistan." *Los Angeles Times*, September 20, 2009. Accessed April 8, 2018. http://articles.latimes.com/2009/sep/20/world/fg-afghan-intel20

National Archives and Records Administration, RG 59, Records of the Department of State, Records of the Executive Secretariat, NSC Files: Lot 66 D 95, NSCIDs (Top Secret). March 23, 2018. Accessed April 8, 2018. https://fas.org/irp/offdocs/nscid05.htm https://www.cia.gov/library/readingroom/docs/Index_of_NIA_Directives_Undated.PDF

National Intelligence Authority. *National Intelligence Authority Directive No. 1: "Policies and Procedures Governing the Central Intelligence Group"*. February 8 1946. Accessed November 22, 2017. https://www.cia.gov/library/readingroom/docs/Index_of_NIA_Directives_Undated.pdf

National Security Council. *National Security Council Intelligence Directive No. 5: "Espionage and Counterespionage Operations"*. December 12, 1947. Accessed November 22, 2017. https://fas.org/irp/offdocs/nscid05.htm

Oakley, Dave *Subordinating Intelligence: The DoD/CIA Post-Cold War Relationship*. Lexington, KY: University Press of Kentucky, Forthcoming.

Perisco, Joseph *Roosevelt's Secret War: FDR and World War II Espionage*. New York, NY: Random House Publishing Group, 2002.

Pisani, Sallie *The CIA and the Marshal Plan*. Lawrence, KS: The University of Kansas Press, 1991.

Prados, John *President's Secret Wars: CIA and Pentagon Covert Operations from World War II through the Persian Gulf*. Chicago, IL: Ivan R. Dee Publisher, 1996.

Rearden, Steven L. *Council of War: A History of the Joint Chiefs of Staff, 1942-1991*. Washington, D.C.: Joint History Office, 2012.

Schroeder, Richard E. *The Foundation of the CIA: Harry Truman, the Missouri Gang, and the Origins of the Cold War*. Columbia, MO: University of Missouri Press, 2017.

Souers, Sidney. *Executive Secretary (Souers) to the Members of the National Security Council, "Psychological Operations"*. December 9, 1947. Accessed November 23, 2017. https://history.state.gov/historicaldocuments/frus1945-50Intel/d253

Spalding, Elizabeth Edwards. *The First Cold Warrior: Harry Truman, Containment, and the Remaking of Liberal Internationalism*. Lexington, KY: University Press of Kentucky, 2006.

Stonor Saunder, Frances. *The Cultural Cold War: The CIA and the World of Arts and Letters*. New York, NY: New Press, 2013.

Stuart, Douglas *Creating the National Security State: A History of the Law that Transformed America*. Princeton, NJ: Princeton University Press, 2008.

Taylor, Maxwell D. *Report on General Taylor's Mission to South Vietnam*. November 3, 1961. Accessed April 8, 2018. https://www.cia.gov/library/readingroom/docs/CIA-RDP86B00269R000200030001-5.pdf

Thompson, Nicholas. *The Hawk and the Dove: Paul Nitze, George Kennan, and the History of the Cold War*. New York, NY: Henry Holt and Company, 2009.

Truman, Harry S. *Executive Order No. 9621: "Termination of OSS and Disposition of Functions"*. September 20, 1945. Accessed November 21, 2017. https://www.cia.gov/library/readingrooms/docs/CIA-RDP83-00036R000200110009-7.pdf

Truman, Harry S. *National Intelligence Authority Directive No. 1: "Organization of the Central Intelligence Group"*. February 8, 1946. Accessed November 22, 2017. https://www.cia.gov/library/readingroom/docs/Index_of_NIA_Directives_Undated.pdf

Truman, Harry S. *Address before a Joint Session of Congress*. Washington, D.C., March 12, 1947. Accessed November 22, 2017. http://avalon.law.yale.edu/20th_century/trudoc.asp

Truman, Harry S. *Directive Establishing the Psychological Strategy Board*. Washington, D.C., June 20, 1951. Accessed November 26, 2017. http://www.presidency.ucsb.edu/ws/?pid=13808

Truman, Harry S. *1946-1952: Years of Trial and Hope*. Boston, MA: New World City, 2014.

U.S. Congress *The National Security Act of 1947, Public Law 253, 80th Cong., 1st sess., S. 758*. Accessed April 8, 2018 https://global.oup.com/us/companion.websites/9780195385168/resources/chapter10/nsa/nsa.pdf

U.S. Joint Strategic Survey Committee. "Report by the Joint Strategic Survey Committee to the JCS on JCS 1181 and JIC 239/5." January 29, 1945. Accessed November 21, 2017. https://www.cia.gov/library/readingroom/docs/CIA-RDP90-00610R000100130007-6.pdf

United States Department of Defense, *DoD Dictionary of Military and Associated Terms*. March 2018, Accessed November 26 2017 http://www.dtic.mil/doctrine/new_pubs/dictionary.pdf

Waller, Douglas *Wild Bill Donovan: The Spymaster Who Created the OSS and Modern American Espionage*. New York, NY: Simon and Schuster, 2011.

Weinstein, Allen, and Alexander Vassiliev. *The Haunted Wood: Soviet Espionage in America-The Stalin Era*. New York, NY: Random House, 1999.

Wilford, Hugh *The Mighty Wurlitzer: How the CIA Played America*. Cambridge, MA: Harvard University Press, 2008.

Zegart, Amy *Flawed by Design: The Evolution of the CIA, JCS, and NSC*. Stanford, CA: Stanford University Press, 2009.

4 Counterinsurgency in Vietnam – schizophrenia until too late

Rufus Phillips

ABSTRACT

Insurgencies remain political projects, and thus the American experience in Vietnam remains relevant in any search for approaches. A population-first strategy – with tactics compatible with protecting people and winning their willing support – is essential, as much for success in local pacification as in retaining support in the homeland which has deployed its personnel abroad to assist another state. In the actual area of operations, decentralization of effort is required to get as close as possible to the population base being targeted by the insurgents. This remains essential for all mobilization in support of a polity, regardless of the extent to which insurgent challenge is grounded in grievances or simply based on coercive power.

The non-medical definition of schizophrenia speaks to an approach characterized by inconsistent or contradictory elements. This split-minded understanding of counterinsurgency prevailed in Vietnam, particularly on the American side, until the important elements of a more holistic approach were knit together in the aftermath of the enemy's 1968 Tet Offensive. Central to adaptation was the change, on the American side, to an integrated Civil Operations and Revolutionary Development Support (CORDS) organization (originally established in 1967); on the Vietnamese side, to an accelerated pacification plan and a more focused Revolutionary Development effort. Also key was the change in US Military Assistance Command, Vietnam (MACV) command from General Westmoreland to General Abrams. Strands of effective, previously developed concepts and programs, including a better understanding of the political and psychological side of war, were woven into a common design fostered by an integrated advisory organization that produced real results. What follows is an assessment of how we and the Vietnamese got there, in much of which the author was directly involved.

Background

Beginning in the summer of 1954, after the Geneva Accords had divided Vietnam at the 17th Parallel into North and South, there was a chance for South Vietnam to build an independent government and to develop a new military and political approach to pacification of the rural areas where the communist-dominated Viet Minh guerrilla movement remained strong. An inexperienced US Army Infantry second lieutenant, I arrived in Saigon on 8 August 1954, 3 days before the Ceasefire Agreement under the Geneva Accords went into effect. The South was in political turmoil. I was detailed to the CIA-supported Saigon Military Mission headed by the legendary Colonel (USAF, later Major General) Edward G. Lansdale.[1]

He had earlier developed a winning counterinsurgency strategy and set of tactics in the Philippines against the rural-based, communist-led *Hukbalahap* (Huk) movement.[2] In 1948, the Huks were on the verge of winning control of the Philippines. The Philippine government was corrupt and incompetent. Its army was poorly led, taking on the Huks with conventional military tactics and often alienating the civilian population. Lansdale became the advisor to an extraordinary Filipino leader, Ramon Magsaysay. As Secretary of Defense, Magsaysay changed the army's approach. Adopting an 'all-out friendship or all-out force' policy, Magsaysay persuaded the army to put the security and well-being of the population first while aggressively using small unit combat operations and psychological warfare to pursue and defeat the Huk guerillas. This was combined with a surrender program offering the Huks resettlement in peace on farms they could own with government help. During a crucial congressional election in 1951, which President Quirino was illegally trying to fix, Magsaysay had the army guard the polls to ensure voters would not be intimidated, either by the President's goons or the Huks. The President's party lost the first truly honest elections after independence, restoring Filipino faith in their democratic system. Magsaysay became so popular he later ran for President in 1953, winning in a landslide.[3]

Protecting the civilian population and ensuring their security and well-being were put ahead of killing Huks and force protection. Military civic action, in which each soldier was indoctrinated to believe he derived his authority from the people and was honor-bound to protect and help them, became the order and practice of the day. Popular support for the Huks was winnowed away, and the movement largely collapsed when its hard-core communist leader, Luis Taruc, turned himself in, saying he no longer had a cause worth fighting for.[4]

Lansdale took a similar approach to establishing security in the South Vietnamese countryside in 1954–1955. I was assigned to work with the Vietnamese army and became the lone advisor on two large pacification operations occupying large swaths of South Vietnamese territory previously controlled for 9 years by the communist-dominated Viet Minh.[5] Under the terms of the Geneva Accords, the communists evacuated their combatants north, while the French Army and subordinate Vietnamese army evacuated south along with hundreds of thousands of civilian refugees. There was an obvious need for the South Vietnamese to extend government into areas formerly under communist control. The only institution available for this purpose was the South Vietnamese army, but it had never been involved in civic action, only combat. It had never conducted independent operations under the French in less than battalion size, was demoralized after Geneva, and had a chief of staff who spent the fall of 1954 plotting a coup against the newly arrived Prime Minister, Ngo Dinh Diem. By the end of 1954, coup plotting was foiled so that the army could begin seriously considering its pacification mission and conversion to a territorial security force grounded in civic action. No one knew whether the Viet Minh would reinitiate active resistance with stay-behind cadre in the zones they were evacuating, so we had to help prepare the army for possible combat as well as for an active civic action effort to win the support of the population.

During the first occupation operation in Camau at the tip of the Delta south of Saigon, the troops were initially taught to respect the population mainly through lectures. Army truck drivers were instructed to stop running over people and their livestock when passing through villages. After one such lecture, I witnessed the same drivers get back into their trucks and go barreling off through villages, scattering people and chickens, right and left. Obviously, just lectures were not going to do the job. The first occupation was thus a learn-as-you-go affair. Communist resistance was passive not active, and the operation went off without serious adverse consequences but without creating a strongly positive relationship between the army and the population.

Consequently, in preparing for the next occupation in central Vietnam in April 1955, an area containing about 2 million people, the army with our help undertook much more intensive training in troop behavior and civic action. Preparations were made to render medical assistance and to provide rice and other help for a deprived population, as well as to repair knocked-out roads and bridges. Repeated indoctrination sessions went all the way down to the individual soldier, with skits illustrating good and bad behavior. The army as servant of the people and civic action – actively helping the population – was instilled as every soldier's duty down to the lowest private.

As a result, no untoward incidents between the troops and the population were recorded during the operation. Towards its end, people came out of their huts, voluntarily offering drinking water to the soldiers. (It was the dry season, and daily temperatures climbed over 100° F.) The popular response in turn generated real pride in the ranks. The population's initial fear and indifference turned into active support as the local people began identifying arms caches left behind by the Viet Minh (the existence of these caches clearly indicated they intended to return), as well as fingering active Viet Minh stay-behind cadre.

Counterproductive official policy

After Lansdale left in 1956, US policy insisted that the Vietnamese Army give up its territorial security role and be reorganized and trained as regular infantry divisions to oppose an overt North Vietnamese invasion over the 17th parallel.[6] This left a security vacuum in the rural areas which was to be filled by a new Civil Guard, but this was ill-trained and ill-equipped. The training mission was given to Michigan State University, which recruited retired US police chiefs as advisors.[7] A village-level self-defense corps (SDC) was organized but received little training and was armed only with obsolete French rifles and machetes along with an occasional pistol and shotgun. Hence, when the North Vietnamese reignited the insurgency in South Vietnam in 1958, the South Vietnamese army, the civil guard, and the SDC were not organized or prepared to ensure population security.

There had been an earlier Vietnamese central government effort in 1ate 1955 to train and send teams of civilians to work in the villages. A Civic Action Commission (also rendered as The Special Commissariat for Civic Action) was formed as a separate government body dependent on the presidency. Initially funded by the nascent South Vietnamese government from limited funds and with some CIA seed money, the effort was headed by an ex-Viet Minh, Kieu Cong Cung, He had once risen to the rank of brigadier in the Viet Minh forces before he refused to join the Communist Party and went underground to avoid a fatal purge. I became his advisor, and teams were trained and launched.

During 1956, anxious to get out of anything which smacked of nation-building, CIA headquarters reached an agreement with ICA (the economic aid agency) in Washington to turn over civic action to the Saigon aid mission (USOM).[8] The mission, ignoring the potential for insurgent revival – a mirror image of US policy towards the Vietnamese Army – decided to focus on Vietnamese industrial development as the route to future South Vietnamese economic independence (and a reduction in US aid).[9] The mission refused to support civic action with community development advisors and counterpart funds, promising only to provide some equipment for village development use. The first aid shipment of some 24,000 scissors would not arrive until the end of 1956.

Civic action thus became more of a propaganda program supporting the government's communist denunciation campaign. While imprisoning many and killing some cadre in the communist infrastructure, the effort also alienated non-communist ex-Viet Minh elements who could have been won over. On the positive side, there was a land reform program in the Delta, but it was underfunded (the USA refused to contribute, unlike a similar, highly successful program on Taiwan).[10] The result was a political vacuum, particularly in the Delta, enhancing the insurgent revival. Subsequently, the growth of the insurgency was blamed on the Diem government, but we also were much at fault. Taking Lansdale out too early and not heeding his vision were significant errors. It was reflective of the blindness inherent in turning over US assistance to the standard conventional bureaucratic approach of treating South Vietnam 'as if Saigon had suddenly become Stockholm'.[11]

Fast-forward to 1961, enter considerably more Americans and more American support under President Kennedy to help the South Vietnamese foil the rising Vietcong insurgency.[12] A new MACV, headed by General Paul Harkins, was set up, incorporating the existing Military Assistance Advisory Group (MAAG), which was reinforced. American officers assigned to MAAG were inserted as advisors to the Province Chiefs (mostly military officers).[13] MACV placed military advisors at the corps, division, and battalion levels of the regular Vietnamese Army (ARVN). Yet the last American war experience had been in Korea, a conventional conflict. Lansdale, by this time a brigadier general in the Pentagon (Chief of Special Operations/OSD), had tried to convince McNamara and the Joint Chiefs in 1961 that what was needed was a 'people first' approach to counterinsurgency, the new buzz word of the time. Few understood this. The military side of the counterinsurgency effort, with the exception of Special Forces working with the hill-dwelling Montagnards,[14] would become largely a conventional approach to killing insurgents as the main objective.

Secretary of Defense Robert McNamara had asked Lansdale for comments on an evaluation system he was creating to determine if our side was winning. It was all body-counts, weapons captured, and other quantitative measures. After looking it over, Lansdale said, 'Something's missing, the x factor'. McNamara was perplexed as Lansdale explained that the 'x factor' consisted of 'the feelings of the Vietnamese people'.[15] McNamara couldn't put a number on it, so it never penetrated his mind. Bean counting was substituted for practical indicators that meant something in an unconventional war. As a result, an intelligent American overall military approach to counterinsurgency never got off the ground. Lessons about winning population support were ignored.[16]

New directions

I had become re-involved in the conflict in 1962, when I was asked by USAID in Washington to take a month's leave of absence from the family engineering business to go back to South Vietnam. I was to survey how our economic aid office, USOM/Saigon, could constructively become involved in counterinsurgency. Bert Fraleigh, a genius in rural development whom I had gotten to know in Laos, joined me from the USAID Mission in Taiwan. While I explored, with direct visits to the provinces, what the Vietnamese were already doing to counter the insurgency, Bert looked into the potential within USOM and the Vietnamese government for rural development.[17]

The Vietnamese had adopted the Strategic Hamlet Program, which was at its heart a village self-defense, self-government, and self-development program, as their main response to the Vietcong insurgency.[18] Curiously, I found that though the Vietnamese had prepared a detailed description of the program, few on the US side knew about it. This was remedied by a quick translation at my request. The program was promising but with a choked pipeline in Vietnamese government funding, poor planning in a number of provinces (with too much uncompensated population relocation), and lacking in economic and social development and robust security support. Except for one experimental province in central Vietnam, there was little tie-in between combat operations by regular Vietnamese Army (ARVN) units and the strategic hamlets. While senior American MACV advisors at the corps and division level were advising ARVN units of battalion size or larger to conduct sweeps (the predecessor to 'search and destroy' operations), many provinces had inadequate security forces to keep larger Vietcong guerrilla units away from the hamlets.

Bert and I prepared a *Report on Counterinsurgency in Vietnam*,[19] which not only analyzed the insurgency and the Vietnamese government response but recommended restructuring and decentralizing USOM/Saigon, with a new and largely independent Office of Rural Affairs to support counterinsurgency in the rural areas. At the time, USOM, with a total American staff of 110, had only three stationed outside Saigon. Based on trips to five provinces and talks with Vietnamese officials from the local level to President Diem, the report analyzed the insurgency and the government's response as well as US support to date. It then examined the availability of the USA and Vietnamese resources which could be brought to bear. Finally, it recommended a new organization within USOM/Saigon specifically designed to address the insurgency in the rural areas where it was based. An initial list of specific activities for support was prepared along with an itemized budget for the use of a US$10 million local currency fund already set aside for counterinsurgency support.[20] President Diem was persuaded to allow a joint Vietnamese-American committee at the provincial level to administer actual expenditures. The program was approved by the acting Director of USOM/Saigon. I suddenly found myself boxed in by the program I had developed with little grounds for refusing a Vietnamese and American request that I come back to run it.

The result was that when I came home and was asked by the White House to leave my job and return, I could not refuse joining the fight. By September 1962, I was back in Saigon in charge of Rural Affairs, putting funds and representatives into the provinces in active collaboration with the Vietnamese. Rural security improved as our support took hold in those provinces where the province chief had a real concern for the security and well-being of the population. Inadequate security support at the provincial level, however, continued to plague the effort. Exceptions were those provinces with outstanding Vietnamese province chiefs or those where the Vietcong was weak or where a regular ARVN unit (usually a regiment) had been specifically assigned as back-up.

ARVN divisions were generally kept intact and had areas of responsibility covering several provinces. Continuing to be deployed in large unit sweeps, based on intelligence often 24 hours old, units made little contact in most operations. An exception was the infamous battle of Ap Bac on 2 January 1963, where regular ARVN troops were ambushed by a well dug-in, heavily armed Vietcong force and suffered heavy casualties (including three American advisors killed).[21] While American military provincial advisors were clearly tied in with the strategic hamlet program, MACV headquarters and the corps and division advisory levels were not; and with few exceptions were more interested in traditional combat operations. There was an over-reliance on air support and indiscriminate artillery interdiction, too often striking civilians but hitting few Vietcong. There was little understanding at higher military circles that the war could be fought more effectively by protecting and winning over the population. This was accompanied by little civilian or military appreciation at the top of the conflict's political and psychological aspects.[22]

The disconnect between regular army units and the civilian population was also in large measure responsible for troop misbehavior, which alienated villagers. The 'people first' doctrine instilled in the army back in 1955 and 1956 had been lost. There was talk of civic action, but few American military advisors to ARVN units understood it or thought it important. Things were different with the American provincial level military advisors. They could see first hand the connection between good troop behavior and civic action in fostering positive reactions from the population. They could see especially how this helped gain intelligence about the Vietcong as well as fostering participation in local self-defense. Unfortunately, these advisors were mandatorily rotated after a year, often with no overlap, and with the incoming individual normally having little prior orientation or training. There were exceptions, but by the time most understood the local situation and had established personal relationships, their 1-year tour was nearly over.[23]

Role of armed capacity

In many provinces, the lack of effective backup military support for the hamlets made permanent security difficult if not impossible. When properly armed and at least minimally trained, the hamlet militia could resist small-scale VC incursions. The village-level SDC was the next line of defense, but it was often poorly trained and under-armed, at a time when more and more VC were armed with AK-47s smuggled in from Cambodia or sent down the Ho Chi Minh Trail. Again, it was at the provincial level that most MAAG advisors understood the importance of the SDC. At higher levels, its needs received little attention. At the next highest level in the provinces, the Civil Guard was mainly deployed in static duty, guarding bridges and provincial and district headquarters.

General Harkins, the head of MACV, issued an order in February 1963 that explained the importance of 'clear and hold' operations and support for the Strategic Hamlet Program, declaring it 'absolutely essential' that Vietnamese army resources be applied to this effort. However, the emphasis at division and corps levels remained on large-unit sweeps. A MAAG 'lessons learned' report of June 1962 had condemned sweep operations as 'indicative of poor intelligence', recommending that they 'should be avoided'.[24] This was ignored, as was another recommendation that participating troops and commanders needed to be 'civic action minded'. Troop abuses continued. It was hard to figure out why the top level of MACV remained so impervious to its own first hand, field-based recommendations, but this was the reality.

To question military tactics openly would have brought Rural Affairs into direct conflict with General Harkins about a subject civilians were thought not qualified to speak on. A further complication was Ambassador Nolting's endorsement in April 1955 of increased air interdiction. He claimed that it had few unfavorable side effects. Reality was quite the opposite. Rural Affairs was never asked for comment, nor were the MAAG provincial advisors, although together we were well aware of the adverse side effects.

Lt. Col. Charles Bohannon (USA ret), whom I brought over from the Philippines to help start the Vietnamese government's surrender program (*Chieu Hoi*), had been deeply involved in the anti-Huk campaign as Lansdale's deputy. He had been a decorated scout platoon commander with a division in the Pacific theater during World War II – wounded in action in the Philippines – and had most recently spent half a year bringing the Lansdale approach to Colombia as part of a special CIA assessment mission. He had even written a book about how the Huk campaign was won.[25] We thought Bohannon's reputation and expertise might influence changes in the MACV's approach. We began giving MACV verbal reports about harmful Vietnamese army actions and suggested a training focus on civic action, but little happened. Later, written memos were sent, again without much reaction. What we had been able to do with two much less disciplined and untrained Vietnamese army divisions back in 1956 was explained but without effect. Civic action indoctrination was again urged, but the idea received no priority within MACV.[26]

In its first systematic attempt to change military tactics, Rural Affairs focused in 1963 on the largely indiscriminate use of firepower by US aircraft when fired upon, even from friendly villages, as well as on the bombing and shelling of suspected VC locations where civilians were present. I sent a memo to Ambassador Nolting with a copy to MACV emphasizing that winning the support of the people was the main way to defeat the insurgency. What that meant 'was [that] ... so long as actions taken in the war contribute to winning the people, they contribute to winning the war. When they do not contribute to winning the people, they contribute to losing the war'.[27] Mistaken, but all too prevalent in practice, was the view that 'those who do not support the government, or are not in government-controlled areas, must suffer for this (after all, war is hell) ... After suffering enough they will either blame the VC or will come over to government controlled areas to escape the bombs ... their lot when the VC are around'.[28]

I argued there were two reasons why the USA should neither countenance nor support such actions. 'No one should be punished for actions beyond his control or forced on him by fear of his life ... [and] when punishment is possibly unjust, as well as excessive, it is certain to create hatred for those that inflict it'. We should 'absolutely prohibit any attacks by U.S. aircraft or pilots on ... targets where the absence of women and children cannot be positively determined. So called Free Fire Zones, which could be shelled or bombed indiscriminately, should be eliminated'. The memo concluded, 'This war is not an isolated phenomenon. The actions that we take, or support, here in Vietnam, must be viewed in that context, and as they may be made to appear long after our major involvement here has ended'.[29]

The difference in outlook and understanding of the reality of the insurgency and the effectiveness of our counterinsurgency efforts, particularly in the critical area of the Delta, came to a head at a September 1963 meeting at the White House. As a prelude, there had been a political uprising of the Buddhists resulting in a government raid on the Pagodas in early July.[30] This had in turn convinced newly arrived Ambassador Lodge that the only solution to increasing Vietnamese political unrest and a diminishing war effort was a military coup against President Diem and his brother Nhu. An early effort to organize a coup by the generals had failed and President Kennedy was trying to figure out what to do next, either continue Lodge's effort to give covert support to a coup, or soldier on with both Diem and Nhu in power.[31]

Metrics for success

To find out whether we were winning the war, President Kennedy sent two emissaries to Saigon, one from the State Department, Joseph Mendenhall, and one from the Pentagon, Major General Victor Krulak, to report back on the 'true' state of affairs. Their reports were so at variance that President Kennedy asked, 'The two of you did visit the same country?'[32] Temporarily in Washington at the time, I was called into the same meeting and asked to report directly to the President shortly after Mendenhall and Krulak. I told him everything I knew about the current situation and recommended he send my old boss, General Lansdale, the only American Diem really trusted, to see if Diem could be persuaded to send his brother Nhu out of the country so relations could be patched up with the army and the Buddhists. Kennedy thanked me about recommending Lansdale (the President's response is inaudible on the recording but absolutely clear in my memory).

He then asked what I thought of the military situation. I responded that I had just been in Long An Province south of Saigon, where 60% of the more recently constructed strategic hamlets had been overrun by the Vietcong. We were not winning the war in the Delta. Later in the meeting, I would get into a direct argument with General Krulak, who stressed that we were winning the war military. I replied, 'When someone says that this is a military war ... I don't believe you can say this about this war. This is essentially a political war, because it's a war for men's minds'.[33]

This caused a sensation, because General Krulak had just claimed we *were* winning the war handily, *particularly in the Delta*. This was what General Harkins thought. He only listened to favorable reports. The Vietnamese Secretary of Defense, however, had confirmed my conclusions as had the ARVN officer in charge of the strategic hamlet program at the national level. General Harkins attempted to have me replaced, but when Secretary McNamara and General Taylor paid a visit about a month later, my conclusions were confirmed. This was symptomatic of the degree to which the wrong tactics and a willingness at the top to listen only to good news had skewed official military views.

Much of what has been written about the Strategic Hamlet Program classified it as an outright failure.[34] Unfortunately, Americans with direct on the ground experience with the program – such as the author, my Rural Affairs deputy (Bert Fraleigh), or Rural Affairs provincial representatives – were not interviewed. The truth was more complex. The program came under attack by the Vietcong in the summer of 1963, particularly in the Delta. Progress had not only been halted in most of the Delta, with the exception of the two provinces of Vinh Binh and Kien Hoa, but also where the program had been overextended with insufficient security. In these areas, hamlets were being overrun. This was particularly true in Long An

Province. However, the program remained largely stable in I, II, and III Corps (with the exception of Binh Duong Province, north of Saigon) until the coup against Diem, the Buddhist problem notwithstanding. The notion (advanced by Neil Sheehan, for example) that it had alienated a significant number of peasants, who were then converted into Vietcong, was simply not correct. The program had deficiencies and weaknesses, but they could have been corrected, and some correction was underway when the Vietnamese Strategic Hamlet Central Committee issued an order in Sept 1963 to stop building new hamlets and concentrate on consolidating those existing. Even Nhu came to understand that it was over-extended, with too many hamlets in combat zones where they lacked adequate security.

What really killed the program was the *aftermath* of the coup and what took place under the military junta. They gave the effort only lip service, changed existing province chiefs and many district chiefs, regardless of merit, disbanded many of the militia protecting the hamlets, and allowed ARVN to become consumed by internal rivalries. Then, USOM under Killen dissolved the provincial tri-partite committees impeding effective funding and nullifying the American constructive advisory role. The same basic approach was subsequently re-named and reinvigorated with the advent of Revolutionary Development and CORDS, and in that second try it became successful.

There were other important developments in counterinsurgency strategy, tactics, and programs during 1962–1963, which would add to a viable approach later. One such program with a strategic political cast was *Chieu Hoi*, a Vietnamese government surrender program that was estimated to take 200,000 Vietcong off the battlefield by 1972.[35] Rural Affairs, with a hand in its initial development, provided budgetary and advisory support. Also highly significant were two programs developed by a particularly imaginative and able chief in Kien Hoa Province in the Delta, Lt. Col. Tran Ngoc Chau. One was the creation of census-grievance teams which interviewed hamlet residents to identify grievances and obtain intelligence about Vietcong supporters. Grievances against government officials and forces were then addressed by Chau.

The other program was the formation of counter-terror teams. Based on intelligence gathered by the Census-Grievance process, these small teams conducted raids against Vietcong cadre. An attempt was first made to persuade families identified as Vietcong supporters to get their sons and daughters to return without retribution. If this did not succeed pursuit by the CT teams followed.[36] USOM could not support this kind of operation, so I introduced Chau to a CIA friend who began providing funds and spreading the idea to other provinces. This would become the Phoenix program, with excesses in some provinces with poor leadership and indifferent American advice, but a vital instrument of counterinsurgency after Tet.[37]

There were experimental armed propaganda teams organized by Frank Scotton, supported initially by the field operations part of the Saigon US Information Service (USIS).[38] The concepts and experience from this operation, similar CIA-supported political action teams, and early provincial civic action teams supporting strategic hamlet development were folded into the creation of Vietnamese Revolutionary Development teams operating in the provinces. A special training center was set up to school these teams which were recruited from the provinces.

Over the next 5 years, little came of my memo about controlling the use of largely indiscriminate bombing and shelling. The 'we had to destroy it to save it' approach would intensify during the later American direct intervention phase of the war under Gen. William Westmoreland. This turned too much of South Vietnam, as Lansdale phrased it, into 'a lush tropical bombing range', alienating not only many Vietnamese but the American public as well. We were going to win the war ourselves by decimating the Vietcong and the North Vietnamese, who presumably were going to give up so we could then turn the country back to the South Vietnamese. All the lessons about revolutionary warfare were forgotten, if they had never been learned. As General Maxwell Taylor would later reflect just before he died, we failed to understand our enemy, the North Vietnamese, our South Vietnamese allies, and ourselves.

The damaging effect of such highly destructive tactics came to a head in Saigon during a second Vietcong offensive, called 'Mini-Tet', in the spring of 1968, after the major Tet Offensive in January.[39] General Lansdale had been back in Saigon since 1965 as a State Department civilian in our Embassy, trying to implement pacification and political development. I had been coming out periodically to help him. In May, as part of mini-Tet, a small Vietcong unit invaded a heavily populated, poor but pro-government area, District Eight, on the south side of the Saigon River and began lobbing mortar shells into Saigon. Under Westmoreland's orders, American forces replied with intensive shelling and bombing. Through Lansdale's intercession the bombardment was stopped but not before destroying over 5000 dwellings, killing 200 civilians, wounding 200, and creating 40,000 refugees. Incredibly, some of the Vietcong were still there until arms were given to the local population who drove them out. I visited District Eight in June to see what had happened, and the devastation was horrific. Strangely, the American officer directing artillery against District Eight had been previously responsible, as an advisor to the Indonesian Army, in persuading them to conduct civic action. Now, he opposed having his Saigon barrage stopped.[40]

As he was taking over command from Westmoreland, General Abrams had seen the immense destruction wrought by American firepower while flying over the city. He decreed that no further bombing would be conducted in the greater Saigon area without his personal permission. This started the change in military operations, giving priority in most instances to population security and protection with compatible combat tactics. (General Ewell's operations in the Delta in 1968 and 1969 were an exception.[41])

Search for an approach

By now well known, improper metrics and the search for 'what worked' had ultimately led in late 1967 to the unification of the American military and pacification facets of the war into a single unity, Civil Operations and Revolutionary Development Support (CORDS) program, under military command.[42] This combined approach to pacification, though, did not really begin to take hold until after Abrams' assumption of command and the failure of the Tet and min-Tet offensives in 1968. On the one hand, it merged military and civilian action, and between those with a real appreciation derived from on-the-ground exposure there was substantial agreement. On the other hand, missing was the development of a common understanding at the American top in Vietnam of what was needed politically – and then focusing on persuading the Vietnamese to pursue that understanding.

This occurred with Vietnamese government Revolutionary Development and with CORDS in support on the American side.[43] Moreover, on-the-ground American advice and support became much more relevant and useful due to specialized training for both civilian and military advisors at the Vietnam Training Center in Washington. The CORDS advisory force greatly improved in effectiveness, with good leadership from the top, exemplified by William Colby with steadfast support from General Abrams, and many more Vietnamese-speaking personnel serving multi-year assignments.

Also notable in positive effect in the countryside were some political actions taken by the Vietnamese national government. A complete land reform was implemented with considerable positive effect on villager attitudes, particularly in the Delta. Allowing rural men subject to a national draft to serve in local defense forces boosted those forces. Later, village elections were initiated. By the end of 1971, most of the South Vietnamese countryside was secure, but this came too late as American public support died after 1968. South Vietnam eventually succumbed in 1975 to an all-out conventional North Vietnamese invasion.[44]

In assessing the relative success of the earlier Rural Affairs program, followed by CORDS support for Vietnamese Revolutionary Development, what stands out and should be considered basic elements for effective counterinsurgency almost anywhere are the factors below. This list is not all-inclusive as experience since Vietnam has shown that certain innovations can achieve signal impact, such as using centrally organized special operations to eliminate key insurgent leadership.

Before proceeding, several other contextual factors must be outlined. Most fundamentally, of course, the host national government in its actions has to show that it offers a more compelling political cause than the insurgents. Insurgencies, no matter the involvement of factors such as religion or identity (e.g. ethnic or tribal), are essentially political not military projects, though one should never downplay the role of raw power in any contest involving violence. Also, it was clear from the Vietnam experience and now in Afghanistan that insurgent sanctuary in an adjacent country must be eliminated or radically reduced. The elements listed below also assume that taking action has been preceded by a thorough analysis of a particular insurgent threat's organization, operations, and political and psychological basis for its support. A realistic assessment is needed to host government political, governance, and security capabilities and capacity for improvement (not to speak of our own capabilities). Finally, critical to enduring success, there needs to be a commonly shared political strategy with the host government to effect the changes necessary to gain and sustain widespread and willing population support (in short, government based on democratic principles).

With this said, the essential counterinsurgency factors, as derived from the Vietnam case, are:

- A population-first strategy and tactics compatible with protecting people and winning their sustainable support.
- A decentralization of the effort to get it as close as possible to the population base which the insurgency is exploiting.
- A bottom-up approach to providing security, with the development of local militia and a tiered security system which ties in local security with successive levels of reinforcement.[45]
- A local intelligence effort, done by locals under regional (e.g. provincial) control, to interview villagers on an individual basis about the insurgents, combined with information about grievances to improve local government responsiveness.
- A local level effort (e.g. provincial) to mount successful counter-terror teams to pursue insurgents who do not return to their families or join the surrender program.
- A surrender program which offers a chance for insurgents to come in, be placed in rehabilitation and skills training centers, and be absorbed back into society.
- Organization of indigenous security, development, and information teams at the local level (e.g. provincial) to assist villages in self-defense and development, and to provide public information (indigenous but

similar to the best model of American provincial development teams in Afghanistan). US Special Forces, based on the Afghan local police example, have proved particularly effective in this area.
- A sustainable economic, social, and political development program targeted at the local population (e.g. village) based on self-help principles to the maximum extent possible, with villagers taking ownership of the improvements. (The idea is not always to try to effect instant change but to provide evidence which creates hope for a better future for the inhabitants' children.) Funds should be decentralized through the intermediate to the local level (e.g. provinces to the villages), where elected councils make project decisions (similar in concept to the Afghan Solidarity Program). A similar approach needs to be implemented in poorer urban neighborhoods to cement popular support and help provide intelligence about hostile infiltrators.
- A focus at the host country national level, in the form of a coordinating inter-governmental commission, to provide overall guidance and logistical and financial support for the effort.
- Organization of the indigenous regular and special armed forces in a territorial manner, which provides for coordination with provincial governments and enables a rapid response to insurgent forces massing for attack.
- Fusing (if at all possible) the American advisory effort into a combined military and civilian organization, decentralized to the regional level (e.g. provinces), with as few intervening levels of command as possible, under either the American military in-country command (if there is one) or the American ambassador (with a special high level supporting staff). The size of the organization should be kept to a minimum. The head of this counterinsurgency organization must have direct access to all levels of the host government and its armed forces to be truly effective. Military and civilian personnel assigned to this effort should receive special training to include languages. To achieve adequate local understanding, mutual trust and consistency in relationships, advisors should be assigned in a way that allows for either longer than usual or repeated tours with special leave arrangements as necessary.
- Measured and controlled use of kinetic support, especially airpower, to ensure that it is discriminant enough not to constitute a recruiting tool for the insurgency. As noted previously, it is a general rule that actions taken in the counterinsurgent war which contribute to winning the people contribute to winning the war. When they do not contribute to winning the people, they contribute to losing the war.
- Patience and persistence. These are necessary at the very top of the US government to commit to the long-haul as results which have a chance of lasting are never achieved easily or quickly in this context. We must

understand that only the host country's government can defeat insurgencies. We can provide effective help, if we know what we are doing, but we cannot do it ourselves. Host country minds have to be changed by deeds rather than words.
- Full and frank education of the American public about what this kind of war is about, why it takes time and persistence, why some casualties are inevitable if our help is to be effective, and what victory looks like. For the host country, this is the cessation of armed struggle and the return of the insurgents to the political process. Easy to say; the Devil is always in the details.

Notes

1. For most recent biography, see Boot, *The Road Not Taken*.
2. For overview of the insurgency, though not the counter to it, see Kerkvliet, *The Huk Rebellion*; also, Pomeroy, "Source Materials on Philippine Revolutionary Movements," 74–81; and Kerkvliet, "Additional Source Materials on Philippine," 83–90; for roots of conflict, Mitchell, *The Huk Rebellion in the Philippines*.
3. For details, see Starner, *Magsaysay and the Philippine Peasantry*.
4. Some elements remained unreconciled and, encouraged by dysfunctional government, re-emerged later but at a relatively low level; for ideological tensions within the movement, see Carlson, "Born Again of the People," 417–458.
5. The Viet Minh in Vietnam and Indochina – like the Huks in the Philippines – were a communist insurgency that included numerous non-communists motivated by a wide variety of concerns. The precise 'communist' content of Vietmind nationalism has been the a subject of debate but, the ideology in fact, dominated all insurgent objective formulation and decisionmaking. See, for example, Tuong, *Vietnam's Communist Revolution*.
6. For details, see Spector, *Advice and Support*.
7. Group archives may be accessed at: http://vietnamproject.archives.msu.edu/browse_term.php?term=Michigan%20State%20University.%20Vietnam%20Advisory%20Group&cat=Subjects
8. For complete history of the effort, see Hunt, *Pacification*.
9. For details, see Dacy, *Foreign Aid, War, and Economic Development*.
10. For details, see Wurfel, "Agrarian Reform in the Republic of Vietnam," 81–92; also, Prosterman, "Land Reform in South Vietnam," 26–44.
11. Boot, 298.
12. On this topic, the classic remains Pike, *Viet Cong*.
13. See Cosmos, *MACV*.
14. See Kelly, *Vietnam Studies*.
15. Phillips, *Why Vietnam Matters*, xiii; see endnote 1 for original source.
16. For a measured discussion, see Daddis, *No Sure Victory*; for excellent comparative framework, see Connable, *Embracing the Fog of War*.
17. For problems encountered, perhaps illustrative of much that occurred in South Vietnam, see *Debrief of a Former Senior AID Official (Saigon, Vietnam), 1957–1967, No. 12681A*.

18. For a summary description, see "The Strategic Hamlet Program, 1961–1963," 128–159.
19. Phillips, "A Report on Counterinsurgency."
20. Ibid. Activities proposed by the report included: funds for emergency relief for Vietnamese and Montagnard refugees from VC areas; funds to pay villagers in-kind (rice) for relocation and hamlet development; pay for elected hamlet chiefs and councils; training for civic action teams to work in hamlets; training of elected hamlet chiefs and of hamlet militia; a self-help program for building hamlet improvements after elections for hamlet chiefs and committees; construction materials on self-help basis for hamlet schools; a series of agriculture and livestock development programs; and a miscellaneous fund to fill in the unanticipated gaps. Support for a surrender program, *Chieu Hoi*, was later added in 1963.
21. Two of the best known journalists from this period were present at the battle. See Sheehan, *The Battle of Ap Bac*, which is the relevant portion of his much longer, award-winning *A Bright Shining Lie*; and Halberstam, *The Making of a Quagmire*, For recent treatment, see Toczek, *The Battle of Ap Bac, Vietnam*.
22. To explain just why this gap in comprehension existed has occupied more than a few observers; see esp. Halberstam, *The Best and the Brightest*. Ironically, Halberstam's *The Making of a Quagmire*, now recognized for its keen insights, was but a moderate success at its 1965 publication.
23. Useful for its comparative framework, Ramsey, 24–81.
24. Phillips, *Why Vietnam Matters*, 152 (original document is in the Phillips collection at the Texas Tech Vietnam Center and Archive).
25. Bohannan and Valeriano, *Counterguerrilla Operations* (republished 2006). For Bohannan work in Colombia, see Rempe, *The Past as Prologue?*
26. It is useful to compare these observations with those of the Taiwan advisory mission that was present at the same time and filing similar reports. See Marks, *Counterrevolution in China*, 196–210.
27. Memorandum to Ambassador Nolting from Phillips, "Bombs, Rockets, Shells, Popular Support and the U.S. Interest" (original document in Phillips collection, Texas Tech Vietnam Center and Archive), 6 August 1963; see also Phillips, *Why Vietnam Matters*, 338 (n. 23).
28. Ibid.
29. Ibid.
30. See esp. Miller, "Religious Revival and the Politics of Nation Building," 1903–1962; also Hung, "The Buddhist Crisis in the Summer of 1963 in South Vietnam," 21–37.
31. Numerous excellent sources are now available on this topic; see esp. Miller, *Misalliance*.
32. See Burleigh, *Small Wars, Faraway Places*, 473.
33. JFK Library, "Vietnam – Mendenhall and Krulak Reports." For the best known treatment of the province, see Race, *War Comes to Long An*; an updated, expanded edition was published by the same press in 2010.
34. For example, Catton, *Diem's Final Failure*.
35. For details, Koch, *The Chieu Hoi Program, 1963–1971*.
36. Chau, *Vietnam Labyrinth*, 179–184.
37. Of the several works available, see Andrade, *Ashes to Ashes*.
38. For a general account of how various approaches to armed Revolutionary Development teams emerged, see Scotton, *Uphill Battle*.

39. Details at Willbanks, *The Tet Offensive*.
40. Phillips, *Memorandum to the Vice President*.
41. For specific singling out of the counterproductive practices involved, see Long, *Doctrine of Eternal Recurrence*, 18.
42. The name was later changed to Civil Operations and Rural Development Support program. For overview, Andrade and Willbanks, "CORDS/Phoenix, 9–23; also, Honn et al., "A Legacy of Vietnam," 41–50.
43. See, for example, Ferguson and Owens, *Revolutionary Development in South Vietnam*.
44. For the Vietnamese perspective, see Hosmer, Kellen, and Jenkins, *The Fall of South Vietnam*.
45. Security is essential for all political action; for specifics of local defense, see Marks, "At the Frontlines of the GWOT," 42–50.

Disclosure statement

No potential conflict of interest was reported by the author.

Bibliography

Andrade, Dale. *Ashes to Ashes: The Phoenix Program and the Vietnam War*. Lanham, MD: Lexington Books, 1990.
Andrade, Dale, and James H. Willbanks. "CORDS/Phoenix: Counterinsurgency Lessons from Vietnam for the Future," *Military Review* (March-April 2006), 9–23. https://www.hsdl.org/?abstract&did=483580
Bohannan, Charles T. R., and Napoleon D. Valeriano. *Counterguerrilla Operations: The Philippine Experience*. New York, NY: Praeger, 1962. republished 2006.
Boot, Max. *The Road Not Taken: Edward Lansdale and the American Tragedy in Vietnam*. New York and London: Liveright Publishing Corporation, 2018.
Burleigh, Michael. *Small Wars, Faraway Places: Global Insurrection and the Making of the Modern World, 1945–1965*. New York, NY: Penguin, 2014.
Carlson, Keith Thor. "Born Again of the People: Luis Taruc and Peasant Ideology in Philippine Revolutionary Politics." *Historie Sociale/Social History* 41, no. 82 (November 2008): 417–458. https://hssh.journals.yorku.ca/index.php/hssh/article/download/38707/35115 doi:10.1353/his.0.0049.
Catton, Philip E. *Diem's Final Failure*. Lawrence, KS: University Press of Kansas, 2002.
Chau, Tran Ngoc. *Vietnam Labyrinth: Allies, Enemies and Why the U.S. Lost the War*. Lubbock, TX: Texas Tech University Press, 2012.
Connable, Ben. *Embracing the Fog of War: Assessment and Metrics in Counterinsurgency*. Santa Monica, CA: RAND, 2012. https://www.rand.org/content/dam/rand/pubs/monographs/2012/RAND_MG1086.pdf
Cosmos, Graham A. *MACV: The Joint Command in the Years of Escalation, 1962–1967*. Washington, DC: Center of Military History, 2006. https://history.army.mil/html/books/091/91-6/index.html
Dacy, Douglas C. *Foreign Aid, War, and Economic Development: South Vietnam, 1955–1975*. New York, NY: Cambridge University Press, 1986.
Daddis, Gregory A. *No Sure Victory: Measuring U.S. Army Effectiveness and Progress in the Vietnam War*. New York, NY: Oxford University Press, 2011.

Debrief of a Former Senior AID Official (Saigon, Vietnam), 1957–1967, No. 12681A. Michigan State University Vietnam Group Archive. http://vietnamproject.archives.msu.edu/fullrecord.php?kid=6-20-1ADA

Ferguson, Ben R., and Edgar Owens. *Revolutionary Development in South Vietnam: The Next Step*. Trip Report, Saigon: 2 January 1967. pdf.usaid.gov/pdf_docs/Pnadw017.pdf

Halberstam, David. *The Making of a Quagmire: America and Vietnam during the Kennedy Era*. rev ed. New York, NY: Rowman & Littlefield Publishers, 2007.

Honn, Mandy, Farrah Meisel, Jacleen Mowery, Jennifer Smolin, and Minhye Ha. "A Legacy of Vietnam: Lessons from CORDS." *InterAgency Journal* 2, no. 2 (Summer 2011): 41–50. thesimonscenter.org/wp-content/uploads/2011/08/IAJ-2-2-pg41-50.pdf

Hosmer, Stephen T., Konrad Kellen, and Brian M. Jenkins. *The Fall of South Vietnam: Statements by Vietnamese Military and Civilian Leaders*. Santa Monica, CA: RAND. December 1978. https://www.rand.org/content/dam/rand/pubs/reports/2005/R2208.pdf

Hưng, Nguyễn Quang. "The Buddhist Crisis in the Summer of 1963 in South Vietnam Seen from a Cultural-Religious Aspect." *Religious Studies Review* 3, no. 1–2 (2009): 21–37. www.vjol.info/index.php/RSREV/article/viewFile/4575/4356

Hunt, Richard A. *Pacification: The American Struggle for Vietnam's Hearts and Minds*. Boulder, CO: Westview Press, 1995.

Kelly, Francis J. *Vietnam Studies: U.S. Army Special Forces, 1961–1971*. Washington, DC: Department of the Army, 1973. https://history.army.mil/html/books/090/90-23-1/index.html

Kerkvliet, Ben. "Additional Source Materials on Philippine Radical Movements." *Bulletin of Concerned Asian Scholars* 3, no. 3–4 Summer-Fall, (1971): 83–90.

Kerkvliet, Ben. *The Huk Rebellion: A Study of Peasant Revolt in the Philippines*. Berkeley, CA: University of California Press, 1982.

Koch, J. A. *The Chieu Hoi Program in South Vietnam, 1963–1971*. Santa Monica, CA: RAND. January 1973. https://www.rand.org/content/dam/rand/pubs/reports/2006/R1172.pdf

Long, Austin. *Doctrine of Eternal Recurrence: The U.S. Military and Counterinsurgency Doctrine, 1960–1970 and 2003–2006*. Santa Monica, CA: RAND, 2008. https://www.rand.org/pubs/occasional_papers/OP200.html

Marks, Thomas A. *Counterrevolution in China: Wang Sheng and the Kuomintang*. London: Frank Cass, 1998.

Marks, Thomas A. "At the Frontlines of the GWOT: Colombia Success Builds upon Local Foundation." *Journal of Counterterrorism & Homeland Security International* 10, no. 2 (2004): 42–50.

Miller, Edward. *Misalliance: Ngo Dinh Diem, the United States, and the Fate of South Vietnam*. Cambridge, MA: Harvard University Press, 2013.

Miller, Edward. "Religious Revival and the Politics of Nation Building: Reinterpreting the 1963 'Buddhist Crisis' in South Vietnam." *Modern Asian Studies* 49, no. 6 (November 2015): 1903–1962. https://search.proquest.com/docview/1720973518/fulltextPDF/A4451D0B1D924679PQ/8?accountid=12686 doi:10.1017/S0026749X12000935.

Mitchell, Edward J. *The Huk Rebellion in the Philippines: An Econometric Study*. Santa Monica, CA: RAND. January 1969. https://www.rand.org/content/dam/rand/pubs/research_memoranda/.../RM5757.pdf

Phillips, Rufus. "A Report on Counterinsurgency in Vietnam." Phillips collection, Box 1, Folder 28. https://vva.vietnam.ttu.edu/advanced_search?utf8=%E2%9C%93&advanced=true&v0=&t0=text&f0=keyword&op1=AND&v1=&t1=text&f1=key

word&op2=AND&v2=&t2=text&f2=item_number&op3=AND&v3=&t3=text&f3=title&op4=AND&v4=2397&t4=text&f4=coll_num&op5=AND&v5=01&t5=text&f5=box&op6=AND&v6=28&t6=text&f6=folder

Phillips, Rufus. *Memorandum to the Vice President*, Report from Saigon, June, 1968, Hoover Institution, Lansdale Collection, Box 59, folder Phillips. doi:10.1055/s-0028-1105114.

Phillips, Rufus. *Why Vietnam Matters: An Eyewitness Account of Lessons Not Learned*. Annapolis: Naval Institute Press, 2008.

Pike, Douglas. *Viet Cong: The Organization and Techniques of the National Liberation Front of South Vietnam*. Cambridge, MA: The MIT Press, 1966.

Pomeroy, William. "Source Materials on Philippine Revolutionary Movements." *Bulletin of Concerned Asian Scholars* 3, no. 3–4 (Summer-Fall 1971): 74–81.

Prosterman, Roy L. "Land Reform in South Vietnam: A Proposal for Turning the Tables on the Viet Cong." *Cornell Law Review* 53, no. 1 (1967): 26–44. https://www.google.com/search?q=land%20reform%20south%20vietnam&cad=h

Race, Jeffrey. *War Comes to Long An*. Berkeley, CA: University of California Press, 1972. (updated, expanded ed. 2010).

Ramsey, Robert D. III. *Advising Indigenous Forces: American Advisors in Korea, Vietnam, and El Salvador*. Ft. Leavenworth, KS: Combat Studies Institute Press, 2006.

Rempe, Dennis M. *The past as Prologue? A History of U.S. Counterinsurgency Policy in Colombia, 1958–66*. Carlisle, PA: Strategic Studies Institute, Army War College. March 2002. https://archive.org/details/The-Past-as-Prologue-A-History-of-US-Counterinsurgency-Policy-in-Colombia-1958-66-2002

Scotton, Frank. *Uphill Battle: Reflections on Viet Nam Counterinsurgency*. Lubbock, TX: Texas Tech University Press, 2014.

Sheehan, Neil. *A Bright Shining Lie: John Paul Vann and America in Vietnam*. NY: Vintage, 2009.

Sheehan, Neil. *The Battle of Ap Bac*. NY: Vintage, 2014.

Spector, Ronald H. *Advice and Support: The Early Years, 1941–1960*. Washington, DC: Center of Military History, 1985. https://history.army.mil/html/books/091/91-1/index.html

Starner, Francis L. *Magsaysay and the Philippine Peasantry: The Agrarian Impact on Philippine Politics, 1953–1956*. Berkeley, CA: University of California Press, 1961.

Toczek, David M. *The Battle of Ap Bac, Vietnam: They Did Everything but Learn from It*. Annapolis, MD: Naval Institute Press, 2007.

Tuong, Vu. *Vietnam's Communist Revolution: The Power and Limits of Ideology*. New York, NY: Cambridge University Press, 2016.

US Department of Defense. "The Strategic Hamlet Program, 1961–1963." In The Pentagon Papers. Gravel. Vol. 2. Boston: Beacon Press, 1971. 128–159. (Ch.2); available at. https://www.mtholyoke.edu/acad/intrel/pentagon2/pent4.htm

Vietnam – Mendenhall and Krulak Reports. JFK Library, Tape 109/A44; JFK Library and Museum. https://www.jfklibrary.org/Asset-Viewer/Archives/JFKPOF-MTG-109-004.aspx

Willbanks, James. *The Tet Offensive: A Concise History*. New York, NY: Columbia University Press, 2008.

Wurfel, David. "Agrarian Reform in the Republic of Vietnam." *Far Eastern Survey* 26, no. 6 (June 1957): 81–92. https://www.jstor.org/stable/3024364?seq=1#page_scan_tab_contents doi:10.2307/3024364.

5 Turning gangsters into allies
The American way of war in Northern Afghanistan

Matthew P. Dearing

ABSTRACT

The American way of war in Afghanistan presents a conundrum for proponents of 21st-century state-building projects. How can liberal peace proponents engage in efficient state building without sacrificing their ideals? The US learned that state-building allocates a degree of command and control to powerbrokers operating in the shadows to launder aid money, traffic illicit narcotics, and engage in extrajudicial punishments. These clients failed to represent the liberal values foreign patrons endorsed, because the latter not only offered resources without conditions but also rewarded bad behavior. This issue is examined by looking at the case of post-2001 northern Afghanistan, where powerful warlords should have held greater control over their paramilitary forces, limited predatory behavior, and built stronger relationships with the community. Instead, warlords-turned-statesmen expanded their material and social influence in the north, while holding onto the informal instruments of racketeering and patronage that overwhelmed Western ideals and shaped the predatory state present in Afghanistan today. Moreover, paramilitaries were influenced by material, social, and normative incentives that rewarded violent and predatory behavior and further eroded already weak community control mechanisms at the subdistrict level.

The picture of United States Special Forces and Afghan paramilitaries riding together on horseback at the dawn of the 2001 invasion of Afghanistan brought hope to many Afghans wearied by decades of internecine war. The US mission to eliminate Al Qaeda and overthrow the Taliban regime would become a nation-building effort less than one week after the initial US invasion.[1] But as the American way of war in Northern Afghanistan evolved, the United States was faced with a conundrum: how to rebuild a state without sacrificing ideals? The United States had no intention of implementing a Marshall Plan or sending a half-million American troops to secure ungoverned spaces. Instead, it would subcontract security to regional warlords and their paramilitary groups—hoping to transition a collapsed state into a stable and viable regional partner. Despite pledges to unite and secure a divided nation, paramilitaries and their warlord patrons preyed on the civilian population, engaged in systematic resource capture, and embraced an anti-Pashtun agenda in the north, ultimately prolonging a much needed political settlement and further eroding trust in community institutions.

This case study of American reliance upon gangsters in northern Afghanistan describes a patron-client relationship that was strongly leveraged by a market of protection[2] that gave paramilitaries free reign to mobilize with limited restrictions on the target, function, and character of their protection racket. Paramilitaries worked for patrons at the individual and organizational levels, often with cross-functional purposes, expanding the influence of warlord protectorates, while undermining Western state formation objectives. Moreover, patrons offered an open checkbook to their clients, failed to follow through on conditions or in many instances, set up conditionality, and rewarded bad behavior. The north is a hard case as the expectation is that strong warlords should have greater control over their armed actors and a better relationship with the community writ large. This was not the case. Paramilitaries were influenced by material, social, and normative incentives that rewarded violent and predatory behavior and further eroded already weak community control mechanisms at the subdistrict level. Patron relations with local communities were hostile, undermining civil society and reinforcing militia behavior that freely engaged in predation against the civilian population.

The incentive structure in the north was a lucrative market of protection where patrons relied upon social relations from the era of state collapse to engage in criminal activities such as extortion rackets, murder, and a deepening of patronage control over the north. Social norms between patrons and clients were extractive and exemplified a celebration of retribution and violence over enemies; they rewarded successful clients through resource provisions, security relationships, and formalization in the security sector. The patronage system further eroded the effects communities had over violence wielders. While warlord-turned-statesmen such as Atta Mohammad Noor and Abdur Rashid Dostum represented the pinnacle of paramilitary achievement through state capture, they did so without full control over the use of force, yet were still determined to expand their material and social influence in the north. In some cases they exhibited strong elements of coalition building, equitable distribution of material and social incentives, and public displays of prudence and cooperation—all of which helped encapsulate militias into the Afghanistan state-formation project.

However, they also held onto the informal instruments of racketeering and patronage that overwhelmed Western ideals and shaped the future of the predatory state. While eliminating illicit opium cultivation on the one hand, they provided support and patronage to a more profitable shadow market for opiate processing and trafficking. While reigning in violent militias that served under their command during the intramujahedin war and the overthrow of the Taliban regime, they remobilized illegal armed groups when the central government failed to provide security against the Taliban's incursions in the north. And while they had deep penetration in nearly all facets of their provinces, they could not manage all paramilitary groups; in part due to the difficulty of controlling armed groups, but also the profitability of using these groups to control the market of protection. Instead of relying upon local communities to manage and control paramilitaries, patrons largely ignored them and depended upon civil war social networks to expand their control.

In this case study on northern Afghanistan, I use a partial process-tracing method to outline the relationship between patrons and clients in post-2001 Afghanistan. I rely on primary source documents including government and international organization reports, public speeches and social media, and interviews with US, Afghan, and NATO officials and scholars in the period 2008–2016. While this case focuses on the north and in particular two key patrons (Abdur Rashid Dostum and Atta Mohammad Noor), it is far from representative of all provinces and districts in the north. Dostum and Noor were warlords with strong roots in the two most powerful parties in the north, Jombesh-i Milli and Jamiat-i Islami, and would later develop into two of the most powerful figures in the country—Dostum as First Vice President of Afghanistan under Ashraf Ghani's administration, and Noor as Provincial Governor of Balkh for over a decade.[3]

Focusing on these individuals is an important starting point for a broad understanding of American warfare in northern Afghanistan. I start the study with a brief discussion of the literature on patron-client relations, or clientelism. I then look at the emerging market of protection after the collapse of the Taliban regime, the failed process of militia disarmament, and the protection racket industry. These provide a foundation for understanding the difficulty American patrons faced as they harnessed militia movements. Finally, I analyze how a collective norm of retribution enabled state predation and erosion of community cohesion.

Clientelism refers to a relationship between systems, institutions, or individuals predicated on resource provisions and expected outcomes. A resource provider (patron) provides negotiated material or social provisions to a recipient (client) in exchange for actions, loyalty, or some other agreed upon settlement.[4] The exchange may be established directly via dyadic relationships or through a system of brokers and networks.[5] Recent research has focused on the role of decentralization or devolution of authority at the state level to substate actors, with a consequent rise of armed clientelism or 'the private appropriation of public goods through violence or the threat of violence', with Colombia serving as a prominent case of both insurgent and right-wing paramilitaries reducing the state's monopoly of force through armed clientelism.[6] In state formation, patrons often devolve the use of force to clients, a process that may undermine long-term goals of state formation and prioritize short-term imperial victories.[7] Ultimately, third-party states, such as the United States, seek to maximize their influence through the liberal peace by subcontracting to clients performing security functions states traditionally controlled. Ladwig's study of patron-client relations in counterinsurgency is an important recent addition, arguing that poorly or unconditioned aid from patrons fails to ensure better client behavior; but when aid is appropriately conditioned, clients are more apt to abide by US requirements.[8] Ludwig's contribution serves as a central hypothesis for this study.

State formation and the emerging market of protection

The history of the US invasion of Afghanistan is well documented.[9] At the outset of the invasion, the Bush administration relied upon a 'light footprint' model to gain decisive victory and refocus on a broader campaign in the Global War on Terror (GWOT). In an effort led by 15,000 Northern Alliance fighters, small, mobile US special operations teams, and a crippling aerial campaign, US forces quickly subdued the Taliban.[10] The US mission from the outset was clear—decapitate Al Qaeda leadership and its supporters. Longer and more complex issues such as postconflict security and the establishment of a new central government were of less concern to the Bush Administration.[11] On 9 November 2001, the Taliban retreated from Mazar-e Sharif as the Northern Alliance, backed by US Special Forces and CIA paramilitary officers, captured the city and effectively took control of the northern territories of Afghanistan.

The light footprint of the US invasion required the use of proxy forces to serve as the main ground element. Prior to the invasion, the United Front, also known as the Northern Alliance, controlled only the Panjshir Valley, the Shomali Plains, and small pockets of resistance throughout the country. While weakened from years of civil war, the army was able to muster about 20,000 men for combat.[12] As patrons, the US offered cash, resources, and power, which Dostum and Noor would distribute to their networks, allowing them to mobilize forces and reestablish their roles as the most powerful figures in northern Afghanistan.[13] On 21 October 2001, Dostum overtook the village of Bishqab on the banks of the Dar-ye Suf south of Mazar, continuing up the river valley. Atta took Ac'capruk on the Balkh River, meeting Dostum's troops in Mazari Sharif on 10 November. Three days later, Kabul fell, and 2 weeks later, the Taliban's forces in Kunduz surrendered.[14]

In the nascent stages of the Taliban's collapse, the retaking of major cities such as Mazari Sharif, exemplified in part a continuation of the civil war and transference of power from one mujahedin party to another. The confusion of power distribution meant that while warlords were able to mobilize fighters, they hardly had significant control over their actions, particularly outside the role of direct military engagements. Moreover, US forces had limited oversight over Dostum and Noor's men, and were focused primarily on counterterrorism operations. Factionalization reminiscent of the intramujahedin war resurfaced in the north, as Jamiat and Jombesh forces collided, and the leading warlords emerged as new statesmen. At the local level, regaining Taliban-held territory for their US patrons brought opportunities for militias to loot, pillage, and engage in the emerging market of protection.

The Taliban were not the only targets of Jombesh militias and other Northern Alliance forces. In November 2001, Jombesh forces focused on locating Al Qaeda members or affiliates and disarming local villages that surrounded Jombesh military bases. For the most part, these searches also gave Jombesh the opportunity to engage in anti-Taliban retribution by terrorizing Pashtuns, and ransacking whole villages. Documented by Human Rights Watch, 40-armed Uzbeks plundered a Pashtun village, Nauwarid Janghura on 15 November.[15] In some cases, Jombesh would disarm villagers peacefully, assess the wealth of the area, and depart, only later to return with the intention of comprehensive looting. In nearly all the cases of predation investigated by Human Rights Watch, criminals went unpunished. In the weeks and months following the US invasion, competing militias controlled villages and district centers, and civilians were subject to predation. Militia commanders had limited control over their forces and failed to prevent wide-scale banditry, rape, and murder in the north.[16] One Jombesh commander told village elders appealing for reprieve, 'Now is not the time for complaining', while another responded, 'You did the same thing to us before, now we will do the same to you'.[17]

The deliberate disarmament of Pashtuns offered opportunity for minority groups to seek vengeance for transgressions that appeared all too recent. In fact, the demise of the Taliban did not mean an end to hostility, just a new phase, presenting new obstacles to intracommunal reconciliation. In December 2002, around 300 Hazara militiamen arrived at the village of Bargah-e Afghani, a Pashtun enclave in Chimtal district of Balkh province. The village was disarmed two days prior by Manzullah Khan, a Jombesh commander who ensured the village would remain secure by leaving a dozen of his own soldiers to guard it. However, his men were unable to stop the hundreds of Hazara bandits seeking retribution, spoils, and the execution of 37 residents.[18]

In the post-Taliban era and the aftermath of the Bonn Process, interparty disputes grew more intense, particularly among groups neglected by the new government.[19] Disenfranchised Taliban, left out of the new government, were instead given the opportunity to play spoiler by engaging in antistate violence.[20] The historical tension between Jombesh and Jamiat was ripe with interparty competition, and it was not uncommon for each to make alliance with common enemies to upset the other.[21] The alliance among northern militias was fragile as infighting ensued early on for control over portions of Kunduz and Balkh. Noor also sought to capture territory west in Uzbek-dominated areas of Jowzjan and Faryab, while Dostum sought to monopolize power east of his strongholds. The new Minister of Defense, Marshall Fahim, a powerful Jamiat party leader encouraged Atta to weaken Dostum through buying off of key local commanders, engaging in divide and rule tactics.[22] By controlling key ministries in Kabul, Jamiat could leverage resources to areas historically controlled by Dostum in an effort to marginalize his influence.[23] In the Bonn process, the new Afghan state was established with the Interim Administration through allocation based on factional division. Each political faction was awarded power in order to 'ethnically balance' the administration, and each faction was awarded jobs based not on merit but patronage. Instead of interagency cooperation among departments in the new state, the situation bred competition as each network sought state funds and power.[24]

The emerging market of protection first centered on the strategic city of Mazari Sharif. In January 2002, up to 5,000 Jamiat and Jombesh forces prepared to battle over resources, influence, and territory in the city. Smaller clashes between faction commanders first erupted around neighboring Sari Pul, Balkh, and Kunduz provinces, killing up to 40.[25] By February, the United Nations Assistance Mission Afghanistan (UNAMA) initiated a security commission between Noor, Dostum, and the Hazara leader, Mohaqqeq, in order to establish a 600-man multiethnic police force and encourage demobilization of armed groups in the city.[26] However, by spring, the number of militia increased to nearly 10,000, and the police force was penetrated with Noor and Jamiat loyalists. Complaints waged by citizens of the police engaging in predation went largely unchecked as the UNAMA commission had weak control over the Jamiat security forces in place.[27] Within a few months, the warlords were able to come to some basic agreements on customs collection and sharing within the province and the start of a disarmament process for their militias.[28]

In 2003, armed conflict erupted between Dostum and Atta's militias leading to at least 70 deaths in the north. One October battle near Mazari Sharif involved the use of heavy weapons such as tanks and mortar fire. At the same time, at least 80 irregular militia units under Jamiat control were operating illegal checkpoints throughout the city. While international observers implored Dostum and Atta to keep their lower-level commanders from engaging in mayhem in the city and countryside, a UN advisor noted that removing either of the two warlords could make the situation 'unbalanced'.[29] Of the two generals, it appears Atta held a more commanding presence over Balkh province.[30] Yet mutual relations between the two commanders and between their subordinate militias still remained tense, and an objective, third-party security presence was required to rebuild trust and enforce the writ of Kabul. The process of demobilizing, disarming, and reintegrating militias into society actually became an entry point in the market of protection, facilitated by patronage networks but also the growing need for armed security.

Meet the new boss, same as the old boss

The rise of a new Afghan state raised expectations and opportunities among paramilitaries, namely for jobs, land, and a better future. At the same time, international patrons pressured the Afghan state and northern warlords to demobilize militia forces through the Disarmament, Demobilization, and Reintegration (DDR) program. Jamiat, which had already captured the Ministry of Defense and Interior, began appointing their own militia commanders as officers in the new army and police.[31] While this served as a way to rein in some paramilitary groups, state patrons continued to use paramilitaries to further their control over the north and empower these forces over competitors. As the insurgency expanded in the north, organizational patrons abandoned DDR for the expediency of local security forces, while individual patrons utilized paramilitary clients to engage in shadow economies and expand their political, territorial, and social control in the new Afghan state.

The first phase of demobilization of paramilitary groups in the post-Bonn Afghanistan involved the Japanese-led Afghan New Beginnings Program (ANBP), announced in February 2003.[32] From the start, the program was flawed. First, while the ANBP sought to collect weapons from anti-Taliban militias and offer new jobs, it gave no security assurances, leaving a void in a third-party security provider. Absent a 'credible guarantor' of security for those disarming, the program was bound to stumble.[33] The very groups the program intended to capture—militias in the north—only turned in some arms, hoarding, and redistributing others throughout their communities.[34] Second, while the program started in October 2003, Atta and Dostum did not intend to disarm their militias and only submitted their men to the program in the spring of 2005, primarily because they never thought the program targeted their militias. The DDR program was run by the Ministry of Defense (MoD), a Jamiat-controlled institution, so many of the Jamiat forces escaped the program altogether, particularly given the threat of civil war among factions in the north.[35] Third, the ANBP was unable to collect a sufficient amount of heavy weapons. According to the program just 56% of weapons previously registered were collected, and only 36% of those turned over were serviceable.[36] Fourth, the counseling process of demobilized militiamen was largely an arbitrary act, as Giustozzi notes. Coordination among different agencies, technical studies on local livelihoods, and adequate training opportunities were lacking. In addition, DDR failed to prevent the old patronage system from recapturing inductees.[37] Many local commanders in the north who should have been put through DDR were wrapped up in patronage relationships to Jamiat, Jombesh, or American Forces engaged in counterterror operations outside the scope of DDR review.

When the first phase of the UN demobilization program was finished in mid-2005, many of the important powerbrokers maintained their networks and links with illegally armed groups and criminal networks.[38] The second phase, scheduled to begin in 2006, was to disarm those groups that did not participate in phase one, but there was a growing need by US and Afghan patrons to use militias for village-level security while the Afghan Army developed and Taliban insurgency appeared to be spreading.[39] In 2007, fears of insecurity and neglect emerged in the northern provinces as Afghan and NATO security forces focused more on the Pashtun east and south. Still, patrons had plenty of informal militia to engage with. In 2005, there were 1,870 informal militias identified with a total membership of 136,835. By 2007, the programs dismantled at least 274 groups, reintegrated about 62,000 militia members, and recovered more than 84,000 weapons; by 2010, less than half (759 groups) were disbanded.[40]

Patrons used informal incentives to maintain client loyalty. Jamiat militias that turned in weapons during DDR were promised Noor's care in the years to come, ensuring, in part, continued loyalty of decommissioned militias and his ability to recall these reserve forces as needed. Land parceling was another incentive Noor used to temper his former militiamen, gifting 1,500 parcels of land, 450 m^2 each, to members of his militia. He also seized and allotted government land to former commanders, who reaped huge profits selling at inflated prices.[41] Noor and his associates manipulated the property market by locating state offices on and around allotted land, then reselling the land to private or state ventures at a substantial profit. Militia commanders were often inserted into shareholder relationships between business and security professionals, where the decommissioned militia then served as a private-security enterprise, enforcing contracts, bribes, and securing new property rights.[42]

Atta also awarded commanders high-level appointments in the provincial government, positions in his private companies, or business associations, ensuring loyalty in his administration and protecting his clients still tied to criminal activities.[43] This system served to further the interests of Noor, both state and private networks. In addition, it sent a signal that the market of protection extended to other profitable industries such as business, investment, and government enterprise. If one controlled the market of protection in the north, the opportunity to corner other markets increased exponentially.

As violence and Taliban threats increased in the north, the market of protection expanded as other provincial and district strongmen sought to advance their positions and gain leverage over the central government by mobilizing their pre-2001 militia networks. The German Provincial Reconstruction Team was the primary international force in Kunduz after 2004, and it was not until 2009 that American forces significantly reinforced troop levels in the province in response to a growing insurgency in the north.[44] By the fighting season of 2009, with insurgent attacks at their peak, Kunduz provincial governor Mohammad Omar requested additional security forces from Kabul. Ignored at first, the governor mobilized local mujahedin commanders, primarily Turkmen, Tajiks, and Uzbeks who had fought the Taliban in 2001. The Uzbek Ibrahimi family drew upon its resources in Imam Sahib district, while Nabi Gachi organized his Turkmen networks in Qal-e Zal district. Even some Pashtuns organized, such as Mohammad Omar's Itihadi faction in Khanabad.[45] However, as Goodhand and Hakimi note, the rise of paramilitary groups 'had little to do with protecting communities and was primarily about protecting the new power structures at the provincial level'.[46]

The initial growth of militias seemed to inspire financial support from Kabul as a way to control and garner sway. This, though, had the effect of raising interest and anticipation of state financial support and inspired previously disarmed groups to reunify and enter the market of protection. At first apprehensive, the Ministry of Interior and National Directorate of Security (NDS) agreed to supply up to 1,500 militiamen in Kunduz. NDS chief, General Mohammad Daud, worked with his brother-in-law, Mir Alam, a powerful Jamiat commander, to recruit and command the auxiliary security response in Kunduz.[47] Mir Alam was commander of the 54th Division in the 6th Corps of the Northern Alliance and was one of the largest contributors of weapons during the northern disarmament process, providing over 900 of the 2,600 weapons turned in.[48] General Daud reportedly accepted any recruits Alam brought him, most of whom were products of the anti-Soviet jihad and the anti-Taliban resistance.

These prestate formation alliances allowed militias and patrons to rely upon personal networks and avoid the constraints of community control or formal security institutions such as the police and army. While the National Directorate of Security provided weapons and funds, it did not include sufficient oversight, command, or control, essentially giving the militias unfettered access to the market of protection.[49] The absence of a formal agreement between patrons and clients led to confusion when resource expectations went unmet. Commanders expected patrons to supply the informal armed groups with at least weapons and 60% of a regular police salary. One group of 50 men in Tarbuz Guzar claimed to be serving for over 14 months with no pay: '(…) the government encouraged us to arm ourselves. District government officials promised to help us, but so far nothing has come from them'.[50]

These informal agreements frequently broke down when pressured by financial or political instability. By September 2010, the new Kunduz police chief, Abdul Rahman Sayedkhaili, distributed cash to militias, and the Interior Minister, Besmillah Khan, reportedly supplied Sayedkhaili with USD 100,000 to distribute to local militia commanders and pay insurgents who had reintegrated.[51] Ahead of the parliamentary elections in 2010, the US deployed special operations troops to target Taliban infiltration into Kunduz. This, when coupled with Sayedkhaili's cash payouts to militias, resulted in Taliban being nearly expelled from the province in January 2011; but they struck back hard with a suicide attack that killed the district police chief and ended the Ministry of Interior's cash payout program. This is an important turn of events replicated in Ghazni province one year later: A powerful government patron supporting militia clients with resources is targeted by insurgents, undermining the program and showcasing the fragility of patronage-based security programs.[52]

By early 2011, militias in Khanabad district alone had reached upward of 4,000 according to the district police chief, Nizamuddin Nashir.[53] Contesting territory, the groups fought amongst each other, some with high-powered weapons such as mortars and rocket launchers, and more than 100 were killed.[54] At the beginning of August 2011, a directive was issued for militia in Khanabad to surrender their weapons or face a military showdown. Ten days later, only 13 'heavy weapons, such as rockets and missiles' were turned in, not even a fraction of the arms held by the armed groups. Many refused to disarm out of fear of becoming victim to their rivals, demanding employment in the police. It increasingly became difficult to control the variety of militia. One NDS official commented that some were playing both sides, working with Taliban and with the government.[55]

With or without funds from Kabul, some of the militia ran side businesses to fund their existence, and allegedly had support from the highest levels in Balkh. In the first 7 months of 2010, there were 60 recorded kidnappings in Balkh, up from 42 in 2009. Two such kidnappings involved prominent businessmen, Haji Gul Ahmad Zargar and Oil Ismail Jamshidi; the former rescued by police, the latter freed after his family paid a USD 400,000 ransom. According to Human Rights Watch interviews and internal documents, Noor had several (three are named) commanders on payroll who operated criminal gangs and 'secret bodyguard' units involved in kidnappings, ransom extortions, and murders.[56]

The resources Noor provided to his militia in Balkh were enough for commanders to mobilize forces but not enough to prevent militia from profiting off the new market of protection. Human Rights Watch documented 'serious human rights abuses' by Noor's militias, which by one report numbered 452 men in violation. In order to control his forces, Noor allegedly paid the Balkh district chief of police USD 30,000 monthly.[57] As the scale of militia predations increased, Noor used security institutions such as Afghan Local Police and Afghan National Police as transfer programs to reintegrate militia. This served two purposes: institutionalizing militia, and reshaping the provincial security institutions with Noor's own clients rather than appointments from Kabul. One official told Human Rights Watch that in Balkh, '80% of the Afghan Local Police (ALP) are Noor's people'.[58] Even with this close oversight, Noor had limited control over his commanders skimming from the resources flowing from the provincial center or taxing locals.[59]

A final note on incentives highlights the role of trafficking in expanding the militia system. Just as much as the narcotics trafficking industry is dependent upon licit economies to operate, it is also dependent upon the market of protection to facilitate transport and trade from field to border. The transition to formal politics forced new statesmen like Noor to take their criminal relationships underground. Their ties to illicit industries such as narcotics trafficking required degrees of separation from the public realm. A new criminal underworld emerged, led by 'businessmen' with strong connections to the political 'upperworld'. Illegal militia in Kunduz who failed to transfer to formal paramilitary programs used trafficking as a way to finance their operations, in addition to kidnapping for ransom and taxing citizens for protective services.[60] Whereas warlords previously dealt with multiple drug traffickers, the formalization of warlord politics led to the elimination of competition and consolidation of the trafficking market. The opium economy, while operating in the shadows, is not without a sophisticated coalition. The networks within the system rely upon trust, praxis, and hierarchical relationships. Social bonds link elements of the supply chain by ethnicity, tribal affiliation, or marriage. These nongovernmental systems of influence serve to facilitate what Goodhand describes as combat, shadow, and coping drug economies in Afghanistan. The warlord patrons are 'embedded' within these socioeconomic systems which are dependent upon 'reciprocal interpersonal networks'.[61]

Control failures

The Afghan Local Police in Kunduz had one of the worst reputations among local police forces in all of Afghanistan. In 2014, UNAMA found that more than half of all the recorded civilian casualties caused by ALP (16 killed and

47 injured) occurred in the northeastern provinces.[62] Northern patrons employed two important methods to control their paramilitary clients. At the organizational level, US and Afghan forces built security institutions to capture and steer the power of paramilitary groups toward enhancing stability across the provinces. At the individual level, patrons applied methods of coercive coalition building through paramilitary clients to extend their influence over people and territory, and gain greater control over violence. The degree to which patrons at the individual and organizational levels could harmonize their interests, determined the effect control measures had over paramilitary clients.

Given the growing insurgent threat in the north and the prominence of illegal armed groups after 2008, officials made it a policy to abandon DDR and 'regularize' existing militias by bringing them into the security sector, encouraging patron networks to wholesale transfer units into mandated *tashkiels* without regard for vetting and training requirements. One way the US attempted to bring disparate militias together was under the Critical Infrastructure Protection (CIP) force. Militia in the program were assigned 'critical infrastructure' to guard, such as roads, bridges, or government facilities. This, as was the case with other irregular forces, served as a stop-gap measure until more official programs, such as Afghan Local Police, were approved and implemented. In 2010, Regional Command North organized 1,200–1,700 militiamen in four northern provinces (Balkh, Kunduz, Jowzjan, and Faryab) into the program so that the US would have some element of control over them.[63] Still, forces were untrained, self-armed, without standard uniforms (many just wearing a yellow armband), and typically loyal to one of the powerful warlords in the north.[64]

The Critical Infrastructure Protection force was short-lived for four main reasons. (1) While the militias received resources from organizational patrons, the amount and type were deemed inadequate by the militias. (2) The militias were primarily comprised of Uzbek and Tajik ethnicities and overwhelmingly focused their activities upon extortion and predation of Pashtun minorities, whom they viewed as Taliban sympathizers. (3) Forces were mobilized by militia commanders outside the realm of the bureaucracy, and the former demanded personal loyalty and often brought in outsiders from other villages. (4) US and NATO reportedly failed to notify the Afghan President of the CIP, essentially running the program independently of the Afghan bureaucracy and failing to garner longer-term organizational support.[65] Leaving community elders outside the selection and monitoring process, together with insufficient flow of institutional resources, allowed paramilitaries to operate outside their institutional framework and focus on the market of protection.

Militias run amok

Misbehavior by paramilitaries in the CIP was one example of how the funding process between patrons and clients alone was not enough to ensure loyalty. Though CIP forces received funds and supplies from their NATO benefactors, the force commanders claimed such support was insufficient. When NATO failed to meet expected resource allocations, the paramilitaries felt neglected and fell back on their alliances with original patrons such as Mir Alam, Dostum, and Noor. When the CIP program dissolved, some of the paramilitaries were accepted into the Afghan Local Police program, but the supply of illegal armed groups far-surpassed the demand limits put in place by the Ministry of Interior, leaving many more militias in place.

In Kunduz, CIP were located in Qala-e Zal (225 men), Chahrdara (150 men), and Aliabad (150 men) districts. In Qala-e Zal, the forces fell under command of Nabi Gechi, who assigned individuals as commanders of local villages.[66] Gechi's Turkmen forces collected protection tax from the population, as well as food, wheat, chicken, and other bulk products his militia could consume or resell. Under the CIP program, his men collected a regular salary; but when the program ended, his men continued to freelance as hired guns and more broadly as roving bandits. In Qala-e Zal district, Gechi held a monopoly on protection, challenged only by Taliban and supported by US and Afghan governments.[67]

Despite state support, Gechi had numerous critics, particularly among Pashtuns claiming grievances. Provincial councilman Amruddin Wali complained that Gechi used his position to unfairly tax the population, and many others complained of abuses. Gechi outlasted the critics to become Afghan Local Police commander, with a hundred of his men included.[68] These men were notorious for violating their duty to remain defensive and frequently employed search missions in Pashtun-dominated villages such as Bajaorai. There, they engaged in plunder campaigns, a tactic that sowed fear in addition to enriching the forces.[69]

Militia outside of ALP oversight went unpaid and routinely extorted locals for cash, food, fuel, or other supplies. Commander's Emergency Response Funds (CERP), a US discretionary spending program for battlefield commanders, were used to pay CIP monthly salaries of USD 150 per officer and USD 200 per commander.[70] Even with these funds, a Swedish report argued in 2011 that the CIP 'will likely commit more violations against basic human rights than the regular police due to lack of education and oversight'. The report concluded there was 'no mechanism for disciplinary actions against CIP within the Afghan sphere'—essentially militias run amok. Such an environment could only drive the population to 'join or support the insurgency'.[71]

To be fair, Gechi and other militia commanders were placed in a tough position. State or international resourcing was often interrupted by a variety of factors. This could place commanders in a precarious position. One official noted how Gechi was forced to use his own funds to pay his militia when state resourcing failed to arrive. Like any good businessmen, commanders planned raids and engaged in taxation in order to have a reserve fund in anticipation of future revenue losses. In addition, state funds simply did not meet revenue demands. ALP and other militia in Kunduz all suggest low pay and supplies were used as justifications for collecting taxes from locals.[72]

Not all militia engaged in the same operating tempo. Much depended upon the commitment and oversight of the commander. Some were quite active with defensive patrols, conversing with the public, and collecting intelligence. Others lounged around observation posts and waited on the random spot check by US, NATO, or Afghan forces to conduct joint patrols. As a direct counterinsurgency force, CIP and ALP both faced high levels of combat stress and operations, more than militias focused purely on entrepreneurial engagements. In terms of opportunity cost, the CIP or ALP was often a risky endeavor in the market of protection. In the summer of 2014, Chahardara district in Kunduz came under intense Taliban pressure.[73] The road from Qaria Yatim village to Kunduz city, which was only about a 1-km stretch, nevertheless saw as much as 75% of improvised explosive device (IED) incidents in the spring of 2014. At the Qarai Yatim ALP outpost, the ALP force saw some of the most intense combat of any of the ALP in Charhardara district, and the group argued it could not continue to sustain the fighting without additional government resources, such as food and equipment.[74] One resident who supported ALP complained regarding insufficient government support:

> The government always asks us to cooperate with, and we cooperate. We assigned our sons to the ALP to finally have peace here but the government has left the ALP alone. If the government does not support the ALP post in Mamakhel, the Taleban will arrest all ALP and we will not cooperate anymore, because if the government cannot defend their own police, how can they defend their own people?[75]

This quotation highlights that support for ALP meant more than just resource provision. It entailed oversight, armed back-up, and medical evacuation. The results of patron abandonment only fueled perceptions of neglect and insecurity. In the same month, an ALP commander posted in Yar Mohammad village in the same district decided to defect with nine of his men to the Taliban after being outnumbered and outgunned.[76] In the Gor Tepa area of northern Kunduz city, the ALP saw similar resource constraints.[77] Cecchinel argued that the neglect of ALP by state administrators led to a competition between the Taliban and ALP over collection of *ushr*, or religious tax, on the population to fund their exclusive protection rackets. Over time, even villages cut off from the central government became used to paying a local tax for protection, either to the Taliban or the local militia commander. Inadvertently, state building via taxation took place on its own.[78]

Patronage, politicking, and community erosion

The second factor behind limited institutional control was the extent to which patronage from Kabul and the regional levels injected itself into local governance. Warlords at the regional level sought to maximize their control over issues at the periphery and used paramilitary clients to enforce or maintain their rule of law. While in one sense this was part of the state formation process—extending the writ of the state—it was overwhelmingly a personality-based state that warlords pushed upon the citizenry through armed coercion. Supported by US and NATO forces, warlord rule undermined the very tenets of US 'village stability operations' that encouraged local democratic governance.[79] Reliance on warlords formalized and legitimized patronage networks by handing local authority to the Jamiat-controlled Ministry of Interior and National Directorate of Security. In Chahrdara, Afghan Local Police were established under the influence of Mir Alam and other militia commanders (some affiliated with Jombesh) without consultation or approval from local community leaders.[80]

While in some instances, local police were established with community support, in general, the ALP in Balkh and Kunduz were not 'local' and did not have buy-in from all communities. As US and international Special Forces units worked alongside many of these militia commanders after the US invasion of Afghanistan, they relied upon the commanders to provide written lists of names for formal selection into CIP or ALP. For example, one senior Afghan government official in Kunduz province explained: 'I was at the head of Kunduz provincial ALP selection council. Our list on the selection and recruitment of ALP was not taken into account and none of the current ALP members is in that list. The Americans themselves recruited those people, while they are only responsible for equipping and training them'.[81]

Fearing inaction by state authorities or retribution, local governments were either incapable of stopping paramilitary formations or unwilling to get involved.[82] Paramilitaries were products of larger political positioning beyond the subdistrict level, which limited local sovereignty over both the political decisions from Kabul and the militias implementing those decisions in their districts. This is an important contrast to cases such as *arbakai* (tribal militia) in southeast Afghanistan, where the periphery generally held more authority than the center on local matters and used it to rein in abuses by armed groups or negotiate settlements. Unresolved disputes between militias created power vacuums that advanced Taliban goals. For example, Mir Alam was the direct client to the Jamiat-controlled Ministry of Interior and

National Directorate of Security. He effectively controlled five districts in Kunduz, but he was not answerable to local community councils.[83]

NDS also organized militias that worked directly with Kunduz Governor Mohammad Omar. Human Rights Watch noted that Alam and Omar's militias often fought amongst themselves, creating insecurity in the province that did not previously exist.[84] Tensions between Alam and the provincial government escalated in 2014 when the new governor, Ghulam Sakhi Baghlani, reportedly sent three trucks of ammunition to the Taliban in hopes of aiding insurgents at the expense of Alam's growing power in the province. Alam's militia confiscated the truck enroute to Hazrat Sultan. Narratives spread of a government alliance with the Taliban as Taliban infiltration and influence in the province continued to expand after 2008.[85]

There was also a lack of community engagement at the district government level in Kunduz. Human Rights Watch found in 2014 that government security forces in Khanabad district had 'limited capacity to challenge the authority' of paramilitary groups. They found the situation in Khanabad 'of serious concern', with as many as 1,200 armed militiamen affiliated with several different groups competing for control of territory. The monopoly of violence was not in the government's hands and was challenged on many occasions in 2014. One government teacher who publicly opposed militia taxation of citizens was killed in August. In October, militia shot and killed another education department employee who refused to give higher marks to a student of one paramilitary commander. And in November, paramilitaries abducted 25 civilians in Kunduz city and severely beat five of them with their weapons. Yet just 2 months prior, in September, the NDS had continued to arm paramilitaries against Taliban incursions in Kunduz city, displaying pernicious support for militia behavior while neglecting the role that behavior had in aggravating civilian and local government grievances.[86]

Increasingly it seemed the NDS relied upon informal militias (which appeared to number about 2,000 active members and 3,000 reserve) to engage in defensive and counterinsurgency operations against the Taliban and to further the center's control over the periphery. The provincial council chief, Abdul Qadir Hussainkhel, believed the election was fueling militia mobilization in the province but argued Taliban had controlled parts of Dasht-i-Archi, Imam Sahib, and Chahrdara districts. In 2014, Alam set his sights on securing the presidential election results for the Jamiat-endorsed candidate, Abdullah Abdullah. As voting entered the second round in a close race with Ashraf Ghani, Mir Alam told one journalist 'he was in "emergency mode", ready to mobilize his network of commanders and militias if he should be called upon by Abdullah to "reject the results of the elections"'.[87] In August, Alam deployed as many as 3,000 paramilitaries in plain clothes at informal checkpoints throughout Khanabad and surrounding districts, in part to protect against the threat of Taliban attacks.

Part of the preelection maneuvering included a calculated effort by Marshall Fahim to remove the threat of Hezbi Islami influence spilling over from neighboring Baghlan province. This could be seen through the removal of Kunduz police chief Khalil Andarabi in October 2013; replaced by a Fahim confidant and local powerbroker, Ghulam Mustafa Mohseni, closely affiliated with Mir Alam. According to Cecchinel, the power move began when Andarabi launched a major anti-Taliban operation in Dasht-e Archi in September 2013. ANA and ANP were set to take the front lines in the clearing operation, while ALP and paramilitary groups, including Nabi Gechi, Mohammad Omar, and Mir Alam's fighters, were to serve as rear defense and holders of terrain. The offensive raid, made up of over 1,500 men, turned into a 'looting rampage' as militias pillaged homes and stole vehicles, personal possessions, money, and even livestock. When told to 'do whatever they wanted to demolish the Taliban', the forces did just that. Even elements of ALP were mixed with paramilitary bands ripping jewelry and money from residents' hands. The event served as impetus for Fahim to order Andarabi's removal from the Kunduz security apparatus and to centralize further Jamiat control over Kunduz. Meanwhile, Jamiat-affiliated militias continued to operate with impunity.[88]

Power imbalances were also seen in Chahrdara district in Kunduz, where the power structure benefited minority communities while selectively targeting the majority Pashtun population. Of 12 district government positions in 2012, at least 10 were held by Jamiat affiliated members, most of whom where non-Pashtuns. Only the district governor was affiliated with a Jamiat competitor, Hezbi Islami. Combined with unfair treatment by security forces and state neglect, the Pashtun residents sought protection through Taliban. This had a reinforcing effect. The more residents relied on Taliban for social and security services, the less reliant they were on state institutions. The government, in turn, separated itself from the population by engaging in anti-Taliban operations, which inevitably targeted the Pashtun demographic.[89] The annual 1230 Report to the US Congress in 2010 argued that 'Afghan perceptions of injustice and the abuse of power fuel the insurgency in many areas more than the Afghan Government's inability to provide services do'.[90]

The influence of community elders in the north was eroded by pressure from competing mujahedin commanders and insurgents, political posturing, and manipulation from the center to the periphery, adding to legacy impact of the anti-Soviet jihad, the civil war, and the international occupation. Community leaders were forced to cede local control to paramilitary groups and warlords vying for territorial and political power in the new government. Security institutions such as the ALP, which were manifestations of outside patrons and lacked institutional control, together with insufficient community membership and buy-in, further eroded social capital and made predatory behavior a more prevalent characteristic of paramilitary groups.

Cecchinel argues that in Chahrdara district, 'there is very little social cohesion (...) traditional and accepted ways of solving conflict barely exist'.[91]

In other instances, there seemed to be unclear messages from individual patrons such as Noor regarding the extent to which they supported paramilitaries, whether through resource distribution or public statements. In September 2009, Governor Noor accused the MoI of 'destabilizing the north' by arming 'Khadists' instead of 'reformed and professional officials'.[92] Noting the trust placed in him by Balkh residents and international forces as governor, he expressed his 'serious opposition to the establishment of *arbakai* in Afghanistan in general and in Balkh in particular'. However, Noor would shift views 1 year later when faced with a lack of security forces to engage Taliban threats.[93]

The CIP and ALP programs failed to offer short-term suitable control mechanisms on two accounts: First, program intent and patron intent were not aligned. CIP, controlled by ISAF, was outside the oversight and legal sanction of Kabul. ALP was controlled by a patronage system, managed by special forces, and disproportionally comprised of Jamiat or Jombesh-aligned guardians. Tribal elders and village councils were left out of the selection and monitoring phase, contrary to the institutional mandate outlined by Village Stability Operations.[94] Second, while patrons sought quick solutions to establishing local security and used large portions of their revenues to strengthen their networks, the flow of resources and support was inconsistent at the institutional level. This forced units to fall back on their patronage networks and the thriving market for protection.

Collective retribution

The final section addresses the shared norm of retribution and its influence on the patron-client bond in the north. While warlords made successful transitions to statesmen, they still embellished the warlord persona and maintained relations with predatory militias. Moreover, patron-client relations celebrated retribution and violence over perceived enemies and awarded those clients most successful in the market of protection through resource provisions, security relationships, and formalization in the security sector. The Dashti Leili massacre in late-November 2001 exemplified one of the first miscalculations of US strategy in Afghanistan, over-reliance and trust in proxy warfare and the inability of the patron to have accountability over the client. These issues were continually revisited in Afghanistan as state-building proceeded. Considered the greatest mass atrocity documented during Operation Enduring Freedom, the Dashti Leili massacre involved the mass execution of up to 2,000 Taliban prisoners by suffocation, thirst, or gunshot in the desert of Sheberghan in Sar-e-Pol province. Prisoners were transferred west from Kunduz to Sheberghan in locked shipping containers, a method of torture and execution frequently used by mujahedin parties during the 1990s civil war.[95] The Dashti Leili massacre demonstrated not only the limited control patrons have over armed clients in the emergence of state formation, but also the unique relationship between partner patrons and paramilitary clients that appears to have given tacit sanction for retribution.

Events preceding the Dashti Leili massacre likely led to rash and misguided decisions by Abdur Rashid Dostum and his militia commanders, who were left in charge of prisoner transfers. On 24 November 2001, an uprising of around 1,000 prisoners took place at Qala Jangi, a prison severely overcrowded and improperly run by Dostum's troops. Later analysis found Jombesh failed to properly inspect all prisoners transferred into the prison for weapons.[96] American and British soldiers secured the prison after two days of fighting and with aerial weapons support. As the smoke rose from Qala Jangi, prisoner transfers continued. Around 25 November, a large Taliban surrender took place in Yerganak, about 5 miles west of Kunduz. Both Dostum and Noor were present to monitor the surrender and prisoner transfer. Trucks reportedly shipped prisoners west to Qala Zeini, a prison on the road between Mazari Sharif and Sheberghan. There, prisoners were moved into freight containers (standard 40 ft × 8 ft × 8 ft) for the journey to Sheberghan, a prison with a capacity to house only 600 inmates. In Kunduz and in Qala Zeini, prisoners were locked in containers without food, water, or breathing holes. Within hours, many were crying out for water. One trucker tried to pry open holes and provide water, but Dostum's soldiers spotted and beat him. Those who survived what would be called the 'death convoy' spoke of prisoners chewing the flesh off others just to obtain fluids.[97]

Descriptions of the subsequent Dashti Leili massacre varied. One Afghan soldier who fled to Pakistan later wrote an editorial on the incident, saying, 'It was the most revolting and most powerful stench you could ever imagine: a mixture of feces, urine, blood, vomit, and rotting flesh'. State Department believed the number of deaths to be at 1,000, while another office estimated at least 1,500 and as high as 2,000. Another document reports that Northern Alliance commanders and Kabul elites were concerned with the negative perceptions Dashti Leili brought on them and encouraged balanced investigations that also looked into Taliban atrocities.[98]

Some reports contend Dostum was not present with the prisoner transport columns and that he told his men, 'In the interest of national reconciliation, we'll let these guys go home and we'll see if we can all live together'.[99] However, the abuse was carried out under his command, and the narratives evolved in a way that bolstered his image as a notorious warlord, only temporarily impeding his upward political trajectory. Years later, an FBI official overheard Guantanamo Bay detainees describe how the bodies were 'stacked like cordwood' in the shipping containers, and prisoners licked the perspiration off each other in an effort to quench their thirst.

The US invested heavily in Dostum as a paid associate of the CIA, and it appeared state interests would ensure that irregularities such as Dashti Leili were set aside. For example, then Deputy Secretary of Defense Paul Wolfowitz said regarding Dostum's culpability in the massacre, 'We're not going to be going after him for that'.[100] According to officials close to Dostum, he concedes that some were killed (at most 160) in the prisoner transport. Some also suggest the mass grave is a result of the Malik-led massacre of civilians in 1997–1998.[101]

Irrespective of the numbers, a massacre occurred. There are three interrelated themes to consider regarding how paramilitaries were able to engage in this massacre. These themes point to important factors contributing to the difficulty patrons have managing paramilitary clients. First, patron oversight of Dostum's militia was limited to counterterrorism activities, namely securing areas (the Mazar-i Sharif airfield in particular) and prisoners, and locating high-level Al Qaeda or Taliban representatives. US forces had little interest or capability to ensure human security for prisoners.[102] This exemplifies a tactical dilemma for international forces engaged in counterterrorism and counterinsurgency operations: Who is responsible for securing the population?[103]

Second, it is apparent from a 2002 Public Broadcasting Service interview with members of ODA team 585 that they were in complete awe of Dostum, his forces, and the unique situation they found themselves in. After the first meeting, a Chief Warrant Officer likens Dostum to 'Santa Claus' and calls the initial introduction to the Northern Alliance 'like the sand people from "Star Wars."' The team's captain calls Dostum 'phenomenal', while a staff sergeant reflects on the extraordinary experience of riding a horse in Afghanistan. Dostum proves his charismatic leadership from the start, outlining Taliban locations, when and how to approach, and impressing the team with his strategic focus. The team thus found Dostum to be more than an ally. They called him a 'friend'.

Reading through the interview transcript, it becomes clear that Dostum did an impressive job cultivating friendship with the ODA team.[104] One could certainly chalk this up as cultural misfire, but it illustrates a deeper and more fundamental problem: a prevailing Western perspective that the Northern Alliance's battle was just. Eliminating Taliban was somehow equivalent to 'liberation' of civilians, irrespective of the reality that for many innocent civilians, caught in the middle of what was still a civil war, it led to further contestation. For them, it was a continuation of the tyranny of war.[105]

It may also represent our own need for retribution after the 11th September terrorist attacks in the United States.[106] The Taliban gave support and refuge to Osama bin Laden and Al Qaeda, which made them just as much a target of US retribution.[107] That is not to say US forces condoned, supported, or had knowledge of the Dashti Leili incident. Most analysis suggests the US and forces on the ground only learned of the incident later. But the US patrons did share with Dostum and the Northern Alliance a common hatred and need for blood retribution. When international forces empowered the Northern Alliance with weapons, currency, and friendship, they gave these militias freedom to engage in predation and brutality against mutual patron-client enemies.

The second point gives way to the third—an issue the West proved it was keen to look away from—the right of retaliation. The internment of Taliban prisoners represented a symbolic gesture to enemies of the Northern Alliance that carried over to the creation of the new state: defeat, maltreatment, and exile. Viewed through the lens of near and far history, death by shipping container served a strategic purpose. First, it was punishment for the Qala Jangi uprising and a solution for the overcrowding problem. Second, in sending a signal to enemies and allies, Dostum exercised the right of his position as warlord of the north and the just retaliation for the recent blemish to his honor occasioned by the prison riot. Like Abdur Rahman Khan, the 19th-century Iron Emir, Dostum executed the right of the sovereign when a crime was committed in his presence; as it might be considered, a crime against the king.[108] Of course, Dostum could never publicly acknowledge his participation in such a crime committed in the presence of Western forces and under the auspices of Western liberation, but such a proclamation is of little importance when Pashtuns believed the event was meant as retaliation.[109]

When questioned about prisoner abuse, the ODA team denied witnessing any extreme behavior and defended Dostum's treatment of the prisoners. The team also chastised UN aid workers for their overly critical analyses of prisoner conditions at Qala Jangi, noting that Dostum's soldiers were in the same deplorable conditions as the prisoners. The team further noted that it fully explained 'basic human rights' to Dostum and the Northern Alliance commanders, and the consequences of failing to follow these standards. At the conclusion of the interview, the captain notes with a deep sense of nostalgia, 'We're all now part of that inner circle of the military commanders there'.[110]

More than money or jobs, joining a militia during the new state formation era was a masculine embrace of trouncing one's enemies and reclaiming agency, which seemed abandoned after years of civil war and Pashtun ascendancy. The northern non-Taliban groups had finally captured the state and had a visible target for their grievances. Public displays of violence and masculinity were celebrated, which gave figures such as Dostum and Atta public notoriety. Passing through Mazari Sharif, one cannot miss the numerous billboards of Governor Atta, pictured alongside other heroic figures such as Massoud, who sacrificed for the country.[111] These shrines are meant not only to empower Atta but also to build a collective national identity, rallying behind the strong and powerful who offer defense against those who challenge the (just) status quo.

While warlords-turned-statesmen had a sophisticated rebranding campaign in place to show their protective character, it did more to empower their political image and less to change paramilitary behavior. Dostum realized a coordinated public relations campaign was important if he had any hope of regaining the spotlight in Afghanistan's political future. The post-Bonn process in December 2001 left Jamiat a majority controller over Afghanistan's civil and security institutions, and Jombesh with a limited stake in the Afghan government. Jombesh and Dostum needed a change of image that displayed peace, cooperation, and reform, rather than conflict. Under advice of Western leaders, Dostum changed his military fatigues for a civilian suit and Afghan traditional garb. He also issued apologies for his role in the civil war and committed to changing the representation of the Jombesh party from military and male-dominated to a mixture of educated and intellectual, as well as female, leaders. The Second Jombesh Congress announced in 2002 that 6% of delegates and 4% of central committee members were women. In 2004, Aina television, a media network in the north, spread his image as 'the "traditionally styled" leader of the Uzbeks'.[112]

Noor also commanded respect not only through extensive provisions to his people but by shaping public opinion about Balkh and himself. Noor encouraged businessmen to invest in the renovation of the Shrine of Hazrat Ali, for which USD 500,000 was raised. Atta invested in the aesthetic of the city center, erected monuments and billboards commemorating the unique quality of Mazari Sharif. These were symbols of the greatness of the north as well as 'his own stature as a political figure'.[113] In terms of his past in the jihad, he said, 'I have no regrets (…) it was the best way of education about how to be organized and so it teaches one how to govern'.[114]

Mukhopadhyay notes that locals found Noor's commitment to the province dignified, with one commenting, 'These actions are making him a hero'.[115] In addition to building monuments, Noor sculpted his image in public appearances, television, and social media. Balkh Television, staffed with Jamiat-affiliated journalists, presented cordial reports on Noor. One journalist created a documentary featuring the heroism of Noor, *Eagle on Alborz Mountain Ridge*.[116]

Nabi Gechi, leader of the Turkmen militia discussed earlier, was known to brag to visitors that he fired over 120 explosives from a Russian grenade launcher into a suspected Taliban residence. He showed a *Vice* journalist video of the postdetonation aftermath, complete with bodies 'peppered with shrapnel'. His crew later stacked the bodies like 'cords of wood' and presented it as a gift to the Afghan National Police. In front of television cameras, the police chief hailed Gechi as a hero.[117] Characterizations of

Gechi, Dostum, or Atta as brave warriors focused more on their acts of violence than gestures of peace.[118]

There were opportunities to rein in the decades of violence that have characterized state collapse and state formation, such as the DDR-DIAG programs. Giustozzi argues there was a bureaucratic 'façade of respectability' that overshadowed the weakly implemented DDR-DIAG. The façade was intended to project an image of a successful Kabul regime and to encourage support for the international coalition, to state that what occurred in Afghanistan after 2001 was 'more noble than a mere strategic move'.[119] Since DDR was both controlled by Jamiat-affiliated warlords in Kabul seeking to capture the state, and ignored by US forces engaging in counter-insurgency and counterterror operations, the compromise with local powerbrokers—partnered with militias with limited control mechanisms to achieve short-term tactical goals—seemed a logical conclusion to why DDR-DIAG failed. The programs had to appear successful both in terms of winning hearts and minds among Afghans, the international community, and the American domestic electorate concerned with rising casualty rates. Yet partnering with militias in the north did not win hearts and minds. The evidence suggests it did more to undermine the state-formation process and expand a criminal-patronage network in the north.

US Department of Defense press releases (directed at Western media) of ALP success were generally one-sided and failed to appreciate viewpoints beyond government officials. For example, the Combined Joint Special Operations Task Force Afghanistan released a story in August 2013 on how ALP 'Guardians' in Charhdara district 'attribute their desire to serve their villages to a sense of loyalty and the desire to see their country develop into a safe place for all Afghans'. The story also quotes Kunduz Provincial Spokesman Enaytullah Khaliq regarding residents' faith in the Guardians, 'The ALP are successful because they are of the people. The people know and have confidence in them'.[120]

Months before the story, however, a number of abusive incidents involving ALP suggested the community had a different opinion regarding the Guardians. In February 2013, around 25 community elders lodged complaints with the district prosecutor's office regarding abuses by ALP Commanders Najib Ghafar Wahab and Sayed Murad. This was the second public complaint of residents to officials. The first had concerned a November 2012 incident where one of the commanders allegedly broke the arm and smashed the head of a young boy for staring at the commander. Another ALP commander allegedly forced local children to find and defuse an IED planted on the road by insurgents.[121] In addition, the Afghanistan Independent Human Rights Commission found that ALP were one of the least admired institutions among Kunduz inhabitants. One former government official called them 'forces without order, in other words—criminals'.[122]

Command and control: unwilling or unable?

When militias worked, there were typically formal lines of control, conditionality, and interorganizational praxis in place such as Ministry of Interior oversight and community buy-in. But for the most part, militia structures and processes were based on patronage networks that were open-ended. Giustozzi argues that Dostum's method of coalition-building was less through violence and coercion, and more through manipulation. He employed his ability to construct strong, elastic networks beyond immediate regional commanders, to mid- and low-level 'vavassors', as he called them. This was exemplified by his ability to build trust with local commanders in Faryab province and to find those with the greatest influence to implement his decisions. These happened to be those with the most extensive networks. When required, Dostum would use direct appointment of relatives or intermarriage to maintain control and build alliances with rival networks.[123]

The international community invested endless time and resources in these patronage systems and ensured their continuance at expense of formal institution building. Many counterinsurgency advisors have commented that the former are easier to manage, the latter are harder to implement. But this process further eroded community control mechanisms for the next generation in northern Afghanistan.

The end of the Taliban in the north and the rise of the state-formation era brought a period of violent reckoning against Pashtuns, a thriving market of protection, and weak national institutions that failed to capture paramilitaries into the disarmament process or employment in the national security forces. In part, the securitization of the Pashtun identity after 9/11 led to their abandonment by the state and to their being targeted by paramilitaries. Coupled with structural adjustments in the insurgency, the Taliban spread to the north and found refuge with aggrieved Pashtun communities. Politicking between Kabul and its periphery compelled warlords-turned-statesmen to remobilize their militia in response to Taliban advances. Moreover, the state-builders themselves (the US and NATO) endorsed the arming of paramilitary forces as a near-term counterinsurgency solution even while failing fully to support, control, or condition the forces. Even institutionalized militia such as the ALP failed to receive significant support in the face of the insurgent threat. While the rise of predatory paramilitaries was a result of a shared collective value of retribution, weak community controls, weak institutional controls, and a strong incentive structure centered on a thriving market of protection, patrons' under-reliance on community support had the most impact.

The passage of warlords to statesmen is indicative of the complexity of state-formation after civil war. Their influence over the market of protection allowed them to expand their personal power and wealth in northern Afghanistan, so that while they instituted protection through violence, they also plundered public resources for their personal benefit. Moreover, the international community's failure to assume responsibility at the outset of the invasion, as a third-party security provider, led to a fragmentation of social order in the north. Large-scale human rights violations occurred at the hands of militia fighters, often through orders by militia commanders, other times by a blind eye being turned to wide-scale banditry and retribution. The international community failed to guarantee human security or rebuild trust at critical moments in the state-formation process, instead contributing to the deconstruction of Pashtun identity as enemies in Afghanistan. It is no wonder Pashtuns sought to reempower their identity by filling offices of the bureaucracy.

The US commitment to paramilitary clients was a short-term instrument in state-formation with long-term implications. The 2014 Senate CIA Torture Report gives a public display of how easily even democratic states can abandon ideals of liberty, justice, and human rights to engage in systematic torture of foreign combatants. This behavior in the shadows at a minimum gave legitimacy to our trusted agents and clients to conduct their own projects that often ignored basic human rights and undermined the legitimacy of the new state.

Patron failure to control paramilitary clients may be more a function of will than capability. In most instances where patrons choose to oversee and control paramilitary groups, they do so with positive results. However, the utility of less control is an appealing option that creates space for paramilitary clients to conduct covert or illegal operations against difficult-to-reach enemies. When there is no limit to your enemies in the world, the desire to operate in the shadows is relentless, offering a reliable career for gangsters exploiting the market of protection.

Notes

1. The earliest sign of President Bush's embrace of a nation-building plan was during a 12 October 2001 news conference when he stated, 'It would be a useful function for the United Nations to take over the nation-building. I would call it the stabilization of a future government after our military mission is complete'.
2. The market of protection is a term I borrow from Lane, 'Economic Consequences of Organized Violence', and introduced in Dearing, 'A double edged sword'. It represents the industry in the use of force. In periods of state formation, consumers of protection (citizens) seek an efficient price/service ratio in the market, while producers of the service seek to monopolize and maximize profit. Legitimate governments are in the business of providing efficient (cost-effective) markets of protection, while challengers, such as bandits, mafia, and private security contractors, seek to provide less efficient markets that maximize profits.
3. Otherwise referred to as Jombesh and Jamiat; other popular parties include Hezbi Wahdat, Hezbi Islami, and Harakati Islami parties. See Giustozzi, *The Resilient Oligopoly*, 12–15.

4. See Piattoni, *Clientelism, Interests, and Democratic Representation*; and Robinson and Verdier, 'The Political Economy of Clientelism'.
5. See Mainwaring, *Rethinking Party Systems*; Weingrod, 'Patrons, Patronage and Political Parties'; and Kitschelt & Wilkinson, *Patrons, Clients, and Policies*.
6. Eaton, 'The Downside of Decentralization', 535.
7. Ahram, *Proxy Warriors*.
8. Ladwig, 'The Forgotten Front'.
9. See Berntsen and Pezzullo, *Jawbreaker*; Connors et al, *A Different Kind of War*; Grenier, *88 Days to Kandahar*; Stanton, *Horse Soldiers*; Schroen, *First In*; Gopal, *No Good Men Among the Living*; and O'Hanlon, 'A Flawed Masterpiece'.
10. By mid-October 2001, three ODA teams were on the ground; in mid-November, there were 10; and by December, there were 17. By the end of January 2002, over 18,000 bombs, including 10,000 precision munitions, had been dropped. See O'Hanlon, 'A Flawed Masterpiece'.
11. This is evident through the reading of internal administration correspondence and meeting notes held at the National Security Archives. For example, in November 2001, US foreign policy objectives began a sudden shift toward Iraq, where initial planning for the 'decapitation' of the Iraqi government was discussed between US Secretary of State Donald Rumsfeld and CENTCOM Commander General Tommy Franks. This planning came at the direction of the President, according to Woodward (2004) who asked Rumsfeld on 21 November, 'What kind of war plan do you have for Iraq?' There were already questions regarding how military forces should be utilized 'coming out of Afghanistan'. See Rumsfeld, *Talking Points Memo*.
12. Like Dostum, Noor's Seventh Corps had just a few hundred loyal men prior to the US invasion. In late 2001, they mobilized a few thousand men, and by the spring of 2002, Noor had between 4,000 and 5,000 men under his command. He also controlled up to 30 tanks, 25 armored personnel carriers, and 30 artillery pieces. Atta Mohammad Noor joined the mujahedin as a teenager and fought under a northern militia commander named Zabihullah. Under the Rabbani government in the 1990s, Noor commanded the 7th Corps of the Afghan Military Forces—a unit loyal to Jamiat Islami. See Connors et al., *A Different Kind of War*; Mukhopadhyay, *Warlords, Strongman Governors*, 80; and Schiewek, 'Keeping the Peace', 172.
13. In late 2001, the US supplied 767 tons of supplies and USD 70 million to Uzbek, Tajik, and Hazara forces—enough to raise a 50,000-man militia. Subsidies paying for Afghan Militia Forces were based in part on numbers of actual troops each faction held. From November 2001 to January 2002, each faction's militia numbers (on paper at least) expanded exponentially. Ismail Khan went from 2,000 to 25,000, and Dostum went from 1,200 to over 20,000, claiming he could bring in as many as 40,000. UNAMA and MoD both did surveys of the number of militiamen in Afghanistan; the first derived a figure of 94,000; the second produced one of 250,000. Giustozzi notes the latter figure is likely due to Ministry of Defense inflation in order to garner greater international resources. See Giustozzi, 'Bureaucratic Façade and Political Realities of Disarmament and Demobilization in Afghanistan', 182; Giustozzi, *Empires of Mud*, 89; and Schiewek, 'Keeping the Peace', 216.
14. Biddle, 'Afghanistan and the Future of War'.
15. Human Rights Watch, *Paying for the Taliban's Crimes*.

16. Gall, 'A Nation Challenged'; Afghanistan Independent Human Rights Commission, *From Arbaki to Local Police*, 34.
17. Human Rights Watch, *Paying for the Taliban's Crimes*, 27, 29.
18. *Ibid*.
19. In December 2001, the Bonn Conference established a Transitional Administration and appointed Hamid Karzai as interim chair. In June 2002, his position was confirmed at an emergency Loya Jirga.
20. Goodhand, 'Corrupting or Consolidating the Peace?'.
21. For example, while Jombesh and Jamiat were allied in the early days of the civil war (1992–1993), Jombesh broke the alliance in 1994 and joined with Hezbi Islami. In 1995, Jombesh joined with the Taliban, only to break the alliance and re-ally with Jamiat in 1996. However, the alliance broke again in 1997, when Jombesh allied again with the Taliban. Jamiat, for the most part stayed away from the Taliban, except for some reports that Atta's men supplied intelligence to the Taliban in order to have some of Dostum's men killed. See Christia, *Alliance Formation in Civil Wars*; and Giustozzi, *Empires of Mud*, 123.
22. In fact, Dostum was able to do the same to Jamiat military formations, reaching out to the Army Corps VII and VI in Balkh and Kunduz, converting two of the four divisions in Army Corps VII to Jombesh units. See Giustozzi, *Empires of Mud*, 150–51, 175; and Schiewek, 'Keeping the Peace', 192.
23. Mukhopadhyay, *Warlords, Strongman Governors*, 85–86.
24. Maley, *The Afghanistan Wars*, 236.
25. I am grateful for an anonymous reviewer's comment that clashes at this time were in Samangan, Faryab, Jowzjan, Balkh, and Sari Pul, but not Kunduz. There are conflicting accounts and I defer to Schiewek's study, which cites the last three provinces.
26. The force was comprised of 240 men from Jamiat, 180 from Jombesh, and 180 from Shia groups (Hezbi Wahdat and Harakat). See Schiewek, 'Keeping the Peace,' 192, 222.
27. Schiewek, 'Keeping the Peace', 172, 175; and Mukhopadhyay, *Warlords, Strongman Governors*, 546.
28. Schiewek, 'Keeping the Peace', 176.
29. Gall, 'For an Ancient Afghan Town'; and Constable, 'Afghan MilitiaLeaders Sign Truce'.
30. For example, when Yengi Qala village was ransacked by Hazara bandits, a Tajik villager placed a call to Atta, and within hours a truckload of weapons were delivered to the village. Later, a Jamiat commander was summoned to ensure the village remained free of Hazara banditry. See Human Rights Watch, *Paying for the Taliban's Crimes*.
31. Giustozzi, 'Bureaucratic façade', 184.
32. The ANBP was meant to disarm, demobilize, and reintegrate the Afghan Militia Forces into society. Combatants were registered and assigned a case-worker to interview and counsel the militiaman with work or training options. See: Giustozzi, 'Bureaucratic façade', 171–2. A second phased program implemented in 2006 called the Disbandment of Illegal Armed Groups (DIAG), focused on disarming and disbanding illegal armed militias that continued to exist past the ANBP phase. The initial phase of DIAG called for voluntary compliance; the second phase intended for negotiated compliance; and the final phase involved enforcement. See: Shaw, 'Drug Trafficking', 196.

33. Mukhopadhyay, *Warlords, Strongman Governors*, 540.
34. Semple, 'Citing Taliban threat'.
35. Giustozzi (2008) notes the DDR process was a bureaucratic façade and lacked political will by the very figures expected to endorse it—Jamiat and Jombesh party leaders contesting for territory in the north and new seats in the government.
36. Maley notes that the greatest achievement of the program was the decommissioning of heavy weapons such as tanks and artillery, not small arms. See Maley, *The Afghanistan Wars*, 252; and Giustozzi, 'Bureaucratic façade', 173.
37. Giustozzi, 'Bureaucratic façade', 174.
38. While 255 Provincial Council candidates were targeted for their association with these groups and pressured to renounce their ties before the September 2005 election, many kept informal alliances intact, while at least half of the 249-seat lower house of Parliament was made up of Islamists or former militia members. See Shaw, 'Drug Trafficking', 197; and Gall, 'Islamists and Mujahedeen Secure Victory'.
39. Suhrke, 'Reconstruction as modernization', 1301.
40. Shaw, 'Drug Trafficking', 196; United Nations Development Programme, 'Disbandment of Illegal Armed Groups'; and Semple, 'Citing Taliban threat'.
41. Mukhopadhyay, *Warlords, Strongman Governors*, 551–2.
42. Torjesen, 'Transition from war to peace', 57–8.
43. One former commander positioned as the head of the Criminal Investigations Directorate is alleged to have accepted and extorted bribes, stole confiscated cash from police raids, and engaged in criminal kidnapping and ransoms. See Giustozzi, *The Resilient Oligopoly*, 47; and Mukhopadhyay, *Warlords, Strongman Governors*, 553.
44. The German PRT worked largely within the formal Afghan institutions, only working through informal powerbrokers as necessary to mitigate conflicts. The US relied upon and empowered informal powerbrokers to more effectively fight counterinsurgency, but this was at the expense of longer-term stability and formal institution building. See Munch, *Local Afghan Power Structures*, 1–2, 17–21.
45. Giustozzi and Reuter, *The Insurgents of the Afghan North*, 25–27; Goodhand and Hakimi, *Counterinsurgency, Local Militias*, 33; and Reuter, 'Power plays in Afghanistan'.
46. Goodhand and Hakimi, *Counterinsurgency, Local Militias*, 36.
47. In late 2008, the provincial NDS chief of Kunduz, who was a junior commander to Alam in the 6th Corps, sought the latter's support for militia recruits. In July 2009, Vice President Fahim's convoy came under attack in Kunduz province. Soon thereafter, militia recruitment increased. See Heward, 'Legal, Illegal: Militia'.
48. Alam was also appointed police chief of Baghlan province after disarming in 2005, though he later remobilized his militia forces. See Heward, 'Legal, Illegal: Militia'; and Reid and Ally, *Just Don't Call it a Militia*, 30.
49. Reid and Ally, *Just don't call it a militia*, 27–28.
50. Tahir, 'Afghan village fight to keep Taliban at bay'.
51. Cash payments were reportedly distributed to insurgents, militiamen, and those working with regional strongmen, Kabul elites, or intelligence departments such as NDS through the CIA's secretive payout program. In one instance, funds were reportedly used to pay an Al Qaeda ransom fee to release

an Afghan diplomat. See Goodhand and Hakimi, *Counterinsurgency, Local Militias*, 33; Reuter, 'Power plays in Afghanistan', Rosenberg, 'Afghan leader confirms cash deliveries by CIA'; Rosenberg, 'Karzai says he was assured CIA would continue delivering bags of cash'; and Rosenberg, 'CIA cash ended up in coffers of Al Qaeda'.
52. Dearing, 'A Double-edged Sword'.
53. Pajhwok news claimed over 1,500 'tribal militiamen' were under loose control of the Ministry of Interior, while another 1,200 anticipated recruitment in the Afghan Local Police program.
54. Even Afghan Local Police were frustrated with illegal militias. One ALP Commander, Gul Afghan, planned to recruit his own side force to protect communities against the illegal militia causing problems for the ALP. See Reid and Ally, *Just Don't Call it a Militia*, 32, 40; and Reuter, 'Power Plays in Afghanistan'.
55. The inability to control clients was also evident when one of Mir Alam's subordinates, Commander Qadirak, engaged in a botched anti-Taliban operation in September 2012. Regarded by locals as *ghair-e qanuni*, or illegal, Qadirak was hoping to receive support from NDS or US Special Forces. Qadriak's men attacked Loy Kanam village, a Pashtun area they thought served as a Taliban refuge, and which Qadriak believed was involved in the killing of a relative. With 20–30 men, his militia attacked the village at night, pulling civilians from their beds and beating them in the streets. Twelve villagers were killed and eight wounded. The National Directorate of Security and the Ministry of Interior remained partial to these groups due to their degree of separation from the state, but officials such as the Provincial Governor called them 'irresponsible armed militias'. Mir Alam even publicly disavowed Qadirak and his men, claiming, 'These are not my men anymore'. Meanwhile, the Taliban used the issue to emphasize the predatory nature of the pro-government militia: 'These criminal groups were created and trained by the occupying American forces in an attempt to lower the number of American casualties and to improve security'. They also noted that Qadirak and his men were still at large and working for the government. While the state appeared to ignore Qadirak's behavior, his persistent predation on the population backfired when he began controlling access to public resources such as water. Khanabad district governor told journalists that after Qadirak cut off villagers' access to water supplies, they organized a plan to invite Taliban into their village. In August 2014, Taliban assassinated Qadirak, killing an additional 20 civilians in the clash. See Rubin, 'Afghan Rape Case Turns'; Heward, 'For a Handful of Bolani'; Matta, 'Afghan Forces Fail'; Ghanizada, '20 Civilians Killed'; and Reid and Ally, *Just Don't Call it a Militia*, 32.
56. Babak, 'Afghan Businessmen Prove Popular Targets'; and Human Rights Watch, *Today we Shall all Die*.
57. Human Rights Watch, *Today we shall all die*; and Abi-Habib, 'Ethnic militias fuel tensions'.
58. I also confirmed this rough percentage in multiple interviews with Afghan government officials.
59. In mid-2012, residents in Tandurak village established a local defense force with the support of Governor Noor to prevent Taliban infiltration into the village. Initially, weapons were provided by Noor's office (according to residents), and expectations were that the government would provide the

necessary resources for the militia. Over time, however, residents were coerced by militiamen to fund and support their armed presence, with many of the former equating the militia with Taliban. This process of coerced taxation was sometimes a passive form of predation that was evident in many local defense forces in Afghanistan. Residents believed aid was distributed from Noor to subclients, and then distributed to other clients such as militia commanders, local powerbrokers, and village elders. Residents noted that each level of distribution included skimming that was felt acceptable as long as residents 'get everything they need'. For the near term, residents were willing to side with the militia and Noor as they appeared to be the dominant power alliance and of most benefit to the village. See AIHRC, *From Arbaki to Local Police*, 34.
60. For similarities to the Colombia case, see Marks, 'FARC, 1982–2002', *passim*.
61. Shaw, 'Drug Trafficking', 198, 203; Heward, 'For a Handful of Bolani'; Goodhand, 'Frontiers and Wars'; and Schetter, Galssner, and Karokhail, 'Beyond Warlordism', 139.
62. One ALP commander in Dasht-e-Archi district harassed a resident to give him 2,500 Afghanis or two sheep on a monthly basis. When the man refused, the commander forced the man and his father to go down in a well. Water and dirt were poured over the men while ALP guarded the well. The men were imprisoned in the well all day and all night, and only released after village elders agreed to pay the ALP the ransom. The ALP Monitoring Unit within the Ministry of Interior failed to establish a significant presence at the provincial level in Kunduz, forcing it to rely upon provincial police chiefs to carry out its work. The political appointment of police chiefs and the patronage network of militias had come to incentivize the MoI to disregard complaints of ALP abuse. Pressure eventually built to rein in ALP abuses. In December 2014, four ALP members in Kunduz were convicted and sentenced for crimes against the population. In addition, an ALP commander charged with forced labor, intimidation, assault, and extortion was arrested in July 2014 and sentenced to 4-year prison. It is believed one of these cases involved an incident in Aliabad district, south of Kunduz city, where a rogue ALP officer attacked a family in Lala Maidan village, killing nine of its members. See UNAMA, *Afghanistan Annual Report*, 79–82; and Cecchinel, 'Taleban Closing in on the City'.
63. While Regional Command North recruited 1,200–1,700 men into the CIP, a German report noted there were approximately 3,000 militia in their area. See Deutscher Bundestag, *Antwort der Bundesregierung*.
64. In addition, the Afghan government responded to the proliferation of paramilitary groups in Kunduz by introducing two disarmament campaigns that failed to bring in substantial weapons. The first campaign in 2011 brought in only 51 disarmed individuals; while the second in August 2012, targeting Khanabad district, only achieved 12 weapons. See UNAMA, *Afghanistan Annual Report*, 82; Hewad, 'Legal, Illegal: Militia'; and Goodhand and Hakimi, *Counterinsurgency, Local Militias*, 34.
65. In 2011, reporters asked Karzai about the program during a visit to Germany. He expressed concern and dismay at their behavior. Shortly afterward, he announced the force would be disbanded. See Rosenberg and Rubin, 'Afghanistan to Disband'.
66. Nabi Gechi is a notorious Turkmen warlord based in Qala-e Zal district, a 95% Turkmen district. He seems to have significant buy-in from the local

community and the central government, but his brutality against insurgents and suspected insurgents is well known by residents. He also funded his operations predominately through taxation for his protective services, despite commanding over 300 militiamen in the CIP program. See Goodhand and Akimi, *Counterinsurgency, Local Militias*, 34; Sites, 'Swimming With Warlords'.
67. In October 2012, US commended Gechi for his leadership. See Raghavan, 'Afghanistan's Defining Fight'.
68. A Ministry of Interior report cites a limit of 100 ALP for Qala-e Zal district, but other reports cite between 200 and 240 armed men.
69. Cecchinel, 'The End of a Police Chief'.
70. Rosenberg and Rubin, 'Afghanistan to Disband'.
71. As referenced in Reuter, 'Power Plays in Afghanistan'.
72. Interview with Afghan intelligence official. Also see Cecchinel, 'Taleban Closing in on the City'; Hamdard, 'Gunmen Extort Locals' Livestock'; Afghanistan Independent Human Rights Commission, *From Arbaki to Local Police*.
73. Chahrdara is one of seven districts in Kunduz, comprised of around 70,200 residents. The district center is located about 10 kms southwest of Kunduz city. Approximately 60% of inhabitants are Pashtun, 17% Uzbek, 7% Turkmen, and 4% Arab. See Cecchinel, 'Back to Bad'.
74. Cecchinel, 'Taleban Closing in on the City'.
75. *Ibid*.
76. Cecchinel (Ibid) reported that due to Taliban offensives a number of ALP abandoned their posts in Dasht-e Archi district during the same period.
77. The head of the ALP at one checkpoint bellowed: 'The Kunduz governor and police chief do not care about our nation and the local police fighting for them, they are sitting in their offices under the AC, watching Indian and Turkish dramas all day'. See *ibid*.
78. By July 2016, Dasht-e Archi and Chahrdara districts were only under nominal government control. See Cecchinel, 'Far From Back to Normal'.
79. For more on village stability operations, see Moyar, *Village Stability Operations*. Also see Jones and Munoz, *Afghanistan's Local War*, 26. The authors share particularly interesting views on the stark difference between militia engaged with the community and those engaged against it: 'These forces are significantly different from warlord militias. Warlords are charismatic leaders with autonomous control of security forces who are able to monopolize violence within a given territory. Their militias are beholden to individuals, not to a community, making them fundamentally different from community policing forces. Warlords view themselves as above the tribe and, unlike traditional forces, do not answer to the jirgas or shuras'.
80. Cecchinel, 'Back to Bad'.
81. AIHRC, *From Arbaki to Local Police*, 23–24.
82. For example, tribal elders in Kobayi village, Kunduz complained to local officials regarding Mir Alam's militia activity and received no response. They later placed their complaint with the Ministry of Interior. See Heward, 'For a Handful of Bolani.'
83. See Cecchinel, 'Taleban Closing in on the City'; and Munch, *Local Afghan Power Structures*, 25, 29–30.
84. Human Rights Watch, *Just Don't Call it a Militia*, 39.
85. Cecchinel, 'Taleban Closing in on the City'; Bleur and Ali, 'Kunduz Deteriorates Futher'.

86. UNAMA, Afghanistan Annual Report 2014, 85–86.
87. Cecchinel, 'Taleban closing in on the City'.
88. In September 2010 and April 2011, complaints were voiced regarding Atta's militia in the Pashtun dominant districts of Charbolak and Chemtal in Balkh province. The 452 militiamen outnumbered the 280 policemen in the two districts. Residents claimed the militia prevented Pashtuns from voting in the 2010 parliamentary elections. Atta's commander noted he served under Atta's behest but that he was not ethnically biased. Less than 2 weeks before the election, 67 out of 84 polling stations located in Chemtal, Charbolak, and Sholgara districts were identified as facing 'high threat' of armed attack. See Cecchinel, 'The End of a Police Chief'; Abi-Habib, 'Ethnic Militias Fuel Tensions'; Shamshad TV, 'Analyst Says Pashtuns'; Weesa, 'Report Says Afghan'; and Arzu, 'Local Officials Express'.
89. Additional pressure on Pashtuns arrived in late 2009 to late 2010, when US Special Operations Forces engaged in kill/capture missions throughout the district. See Cecchinel, 'Back to Bad'.
90. Department of Defense, *Report on Progress*, 62.
91. See note 80 above.
92. Atta was interviewed by a political party newspaper and addressed accusations of attempts by MoI minister Mohammad Anif Atmar to undermine his influence and create instability in Balkh province. Atta noted that 25 militiamen previously affiliated with Hezbi Islami were supplied weapons by MoI and reportedly threw 'acid' on 'innocent schoolgirls' and murdered civilians and police. See Mojahed Weekly, 'Afghan Governor Accuses'; Payam-e Mojahed, 'Taliban Spreading Influence'; and Arzu TV, 'Afghan TV Shows Police'.
93. Atta's requests for increased police and other security forces in Balkh were rejected by President Karzai, compelling the governor to arm and supply militias around Mazari Sharif. The militia reportedly received no pay from the government and engaged in pillaging the population. See Abi-Habib, 'Ethnic Militias Fuel Tensions'; and Tolo TV, 'Afghan Governor Opposes'.
94. For example, Mir Alam and Mohammad Omar provided all of the ALP commanders to the first ALP units in central Kunduz. The process of community engagement in ALP was more a façade with US Special Forces providing selected, vetted, and trained guardians to the council for a ceremonial signing. See Goodhand and Hakimi, *Counterinsurgency, Local Militias*, 35–36.
95. For example, Malik Pahlawan, a Jombesh member, used shipping containers to execute enemies in 1997. In August 1998, Taliban also used shipping containers to asphyxiate possibly hundreds of Hazara, Uzbek and Tajik civilians during their capture of the northern city of Mazari Sharif. See Human Rights Watch, *The Massacre in Mazar-i Sharif*.
96. The US would receive its first casualty to the Afghan war at Qala Jangi, CIA operative, Johnny Michael Spann. This was also the prison where the US captured the infamous 'American Taliban' John Walker Lindh.
97. Barry, 'The Death Convoy of Afghanistan'.
98. The US Army's Combat Studies Institute official history of the Afghan war completely ignores the Dashti Leili event. A declassified report proposes there were likely hundreds of mass graves from the Civil War. Physicians for Human Rights, an organization advocating investigation of war crimes at Dashti Leili, alleged in a Freedom of Information Act (FOIA) request that US forces might have witnessed atrocities around Shiberghan Prison. The FOIA investigation by

Department of Defense found these allegations unfounded. In 2008, a UN official confirmed the mass graves were 'disturbed' by backhoes or bulldozers, and Afghan officials believed Dostum's militia might have destroyed evidence at the site. See Filkins, 'Afghan Militias Battle Taliban'; Lasseter, 'UN: Afghan Graves Disturbed'; United States, FOIA doc# 2027283053; 200802926; Secretary of Defense, FOIA doc#200802926.
99. CNN, 'House of War'.
100. See Williams, *The Last Warlord*, 267–271; Filkins, 'Afghan Militias Battle Taliban'; and Partlow, 'Dostum: a Former Warlord'.
101. Interviews with Afghan and US officials May 2017.
102. This is not to minimize the role humanitarian projects played. Once Mazari Sharif was secured, soldiers from the 96th Civil Affairs Battalion, 5th SFG, and 10th Mountain Division, as well as civilian specialists, organized a number of projects. By January 2002, a new hospital already treated around 8,000 patients. See Connors et al., *A Different Kind of War*, 91.
103. The two previously mentioned declassified reports describe one of the ODA teams embedded with the Northern Alliance as providing the 'best humanitarian treatment possible for the prisoners'. The team also advised Dostum in prison security, medical aid, and humanitarian assistance, while surveying the overall humanitarian situation. The second report confirmed the existence of mass graves and recommended that the best procedure for managing the 'Mass Grave Objectives' was to preserve the gravesite for future investigation. Logistics of doing so seemed impractical. For more, see Physicians for Human Rights, *Timeline of the Investigation*.
104. We see this characterization of the heroic and friendly Dostum in Western narratives such as the Brian Glyn Williams (2013) historical biography, *The Last Warlord*. He and Robert Young Pelton, a well-known adventure writer who was embedded with Dostum and ODA team 585 during the US invasion, brush off the accusations of a massacre as more myth than reality. See Williams, *The Last Warlord*, 267–270.
105. Human Rights Watch, *Paying for the Taliban's Crimes*; and Human Rights Watch, *Killing you is a Very Easy Thing for Us*.
106. The Federal Bureau of Investigation reported a 1,600% increase in anti-Muslim hate crime incidents in 2001 in the United States. See Federal Bureau of Investigation, *Confronting Discrimination in the Post-9/11 Era*.
107. For example, US President Bush made no distinction between our enemies and 'those who harbor them'. See Bush, *Address to the Nation*.
108. For more on the discussion of the Afghan sovereign's right to redress see Edwards, *Heroes of the Age*, 119–123.
109. It should be noted Dostum has denied all claims to knowledge of the incident and challenges the numbers contained in official reporting. He has created a public webpage directly addressing the Dasht-e-Leili incident. See Dostum's public website.
110. PBS, 'Interview: US Special Forces'.
111. Raghavan, 'Afghanistan's Defining Fight'.
112. Dostum commands the honor of leading the northern Uzbek population. In order to secure the Uzbek vote (roughly 10% of the electorate) in a close presidential election, Ashraf Ghani selected Dostum as his first running mate in 2014. Not just for his lamentable history, but for seemingly unhinged public outbursts, Dostum increasingly saw his status marginalized within the

administration on day-to-day functions. At a 2015 gathering, Dostum was seen in tears, shouting, 'No one returns my calls! The people made me a general, but no one even asks for my help.' At another event, Dostum claimed he would build a 20,000–man elite fighting force to clear the south of Taliban. And in Jowjzan province, he claimed that he persuaded 200 Taliban to reintegrate, when the figure was closer to 30 or 40, who actually were his own militiamen. Dostum appears to be searching for purpose and glory beyond his current position, which makes his status as second-in-line precarious. See Giustozzi, *Empires of Mud*, 188–190; Mashal, 'Afghan Vice President Raises Concern'; and Zee News, 'Dostum's Reintegration Campaign'. In recent years, he has groomed his son, Batur Dostum, to serve as heir apparent of the Jombesh party.
113. Mukhopadhyay, *Warlords, Strongman Governors*, 133; Raghavan, 'Afghanistan's defining fight'.
114. Peake, 'From warlords to peacelords?' 188.
115. Mukhopadhyay, *Warlords, Strongman Governors*, 135.
116. *Ibid.*, 152.
117. Sites, 'Swimming With Warlords'.
118. Brazen expressions of violence are common in this region of Afghanistan, where the most popular game is *buzkashi*, a Central Asian sport where a headless goat carcass is fought over by horsemen. In another case, a vigilante group calling itself Margh ('Death') vowed to martyr themselves to save Afghanistan from the threat of Islamic State militants. Dressed in *ninja*-like outfits adorned with colors of the Afghan flag, they appeared less threatening than Taliban or pro-government paramilitary groups. Revealed as more like a gathering of aging mujahedin commanders nostalgic for the anti-Soviet Jihad, they bear no more firepower than most Afghans, some with Kalashnikov rifles, others with farming tools. Their power was linked more to a growing narrative of self-defense against foreign invasion. Convinced by experience that their government could not protect them, they vowed to fight the Islamic State as they had fought the Soviets and the Taliban. See: Raghavan, 'Afghanistan's Defining Fight'.
119. Giustozzi, 'Bureaucratic façade and political realities', 189.
120. Combined Joint Special Operations Task Force—Afghanistan, 'Afghan Local Police'.
121. See note 80 above.
122. Interview with Afghan government official.
123. Giustozzi, *Empires of Mud*, 125–130.

Disclosure statement

No potential conflict of interest was reported by the author.

Bibliography

Abi-Habib, Maria. "Ethnic Militias Fuel Tensions in Northern Afghanistan." *The Wall Street Journal*, April 21 (2011): 14.
Afghanistan Independent Human Rights Commission (AIHRC). *From Arbaki to Local Police: Today's Challenges and Tomorrow's Concerns*. Kabul: AIHRC, 2012.

Ahram, Ariel. *Proxy Warriors: The Rise and Fall of State-Sponsored Militias.* Stanford: Stanford University Press, 2011.

Arzu TV. "Afghan TV Shows 'Police' Distributing Arms to Militias in North." *Mazar-e Sharif (Dari)*, September 26 2009.

Arzu TV. "Local Officials Express Concerns over Security on Election Day in Afghan North." Mazar-e Sharif (Dari), 1500 GMT, September 5 2010.

Babak, Qayum. "Qayum Babak: Afghan Businessmen Prove Popular Targets for Kidnappers." *St. Paul Pioneer Press*, December 6 2010.

Barry, John. "The Death Convoy of Afghanistan." *Newsweek*, August 25 2002. doi:10.1044/1059-0889(2002/er01)

Berntsen, Gary, and Ralph Pezzullo. *Jawbreaker: The Attack on Bin Laden and al-Qaeda: A Personal Account by the CIA's Key Field Commander.* New York: Three Rivers Press, 2006.

Biddle, Stephen. "Afghanistan and the Future of War." *Foreign Affairs* 82, no. 2 (2003): 31–46. doi:10.2307/20033502.

Bleuer, Christian, and Ali. Obaid "Kunduz Deteriorates Further: The Case of Khanabad." *Afghanistan Analysts Network*, October 28 2014.

Bush, George W. *President Bush Address to the Nation.* Congress. September 20 2001.

Cecchinel, Lola. "Back to Bad: Chahrdara between Taleban and ALP—A District Case Study." *Afghanistan Analysts Network*, September 6 2013.

Cecchinel, Lola. "Taleban Closing in on the City: The Next Round of the Tug-Of-War over Kunduz," *Afghanistan Analysts Network*, September 2 2014.

Cecchinel, Lola. "The End of a Police Chief: Factional Rivalries and Pre-Election Power Struggles in Kunduz," *Afghanistan Analysts Network*, January 31 2014.

Cecchinel, Lola. "Far from Back to Normal: The Kunduz Crisis Lingers On." *Afghanistan Analysts Network*, August 17 2016.

Christia, Fotina. *Alliance Formation in Civil Wars.* New York: Cambridge University Press, 2012.

CNN. "CNN Presents: 'House of War. The Uprising in Mazar e Sharif'," August 3 2002. doi:10.1044/1059-0889(2002/er01)

Combined Joint Special Operation Task Force—Afghanistan. 2013. "Afghan Local Police Prove Essential to the Stability of Kunduz Province," Sgt. James Walker, Press Release. August 7 2013. Kunduz.

Connors, Peter W., Donald P. Wright, James R. Bird, Steven E. Clay, Dennis F. Van Wey, Lynne Chandler Garcia, and Scott C. Farquhar. *A Different Kind of War: The United States Army in Operation Enduring Freedom, October 2001—September 2005.* Fort Leavenworth, KS: Combat Studies Institute Press, 2009.

Constable, Pamela. "Afghan Militia Leaders Sign Truce; 50 Slain in Fighting; Rivalry Still Threatens Plan for Disarmament." *The Washington Post*, A21. October 10 2003.

Dearing, Matthew P. "A Double-Edged Sword: The People's Uprising in Ghazni, Afghanistan." *Small Wars and Insurgencies* 28, no. 3 (2017): 576–608. doi:10.1080/09592318.2017.1307611.

Department of Defense. *Report on Progress toward Security and Stability in Afghanistan.* Washington, DC: U.S. Department of Defense, 2010.

Deutscher Bundestag [German Army]. "Antwort der Bundesregierung [Answer of the Federal Government]." November 29 2011.

Dostum, Gen, and Abdur Rashid. 2010. Public Website. http://generaldostum.com/

Eaton, Kent. "The Downside of Decentralization: Armed Clientelism in Colombia." *Security Studies* 15, no. 4 (2006): 533–562. doi:10.1080/09636410601188463.

Edwards, David. *Heroes of the Age: Moral Fault Lines on the Afghan Frontier*. Berkeley: University of California Press, 1996.
Federal Bureau of Investigation. Confronting Discrimination in the Post-9/11 Era: Challenges and Opportunities Ten Years Later. A Report on the Civil Rights Division's Post-9/11 Civil Rights Summit Hosted by George Washington University Law School October 19, 2011.
Filkins, Dexter. "Afghan Militias Battle Taliban with Aid of U.S." *The New York Times*, November 21 2009.
Gall, Carlotta. "For an Ancient Afghan Town, No End to War, with Rival Generals Now Clashing." *The New York Times*, November 5 2003.
Gall, Carlotta. "Islamists and Mujahedeen Secure Victory in Afghan Vote." *The New York Times*, October 23 2005.
Ghanizada. "20 Civilians Killed following Clashes in Kunduz Province," *Khaama*, August 11 2014.
Giustozzi, Antonio. "Bureaucratic Façade and Political Realities of Disarmament and Demobilization in Afghanistan." *Conflict, Security and Development* 8, no. 2 (2008): 169–192. doi:10.1080/14678800802095369.
Giustozzi, Antonio. *Empires of Mud: War and Warlords of Afghanistan*. New York: Columbia University Press, 2009.
Giustozzi, Antonio. *The Resilient Oligopoly: A Political-Economy of Northern Afghanistan 2001 and Onwards*. Kabul: Afghanistan Research and Evaluation Unit, 2012.
Giustozzi, Antonio, and Christoph Reuter. *The Northern Front*. AAN Briefing Paper. Kabul: Afghanistan Analysts Network, 2010.
Giustozzi, Antonio, and Christoph Reuter. *The Insurgents of the Afghan North*. AAN Thematic Report, Kabul: Afghanistan Analysts Network, 2011.
Goodhand, Jonathan. "Frontiers and Wars: The Opium Economy in Afghanistan." *Journal of Agrarian Change* 5, no. 2 (2005): 191–216. doi:10.1111/joac.2005.5.issue-2.
Goodhand, Jonathan. "Corrupting or Consolidating the Peace? the Drugs Economy and Post-Conflict Peacebuilding in Afghanistan." *International Peacekeeping* 15, no. 3 (2008): 405–423. doi:10.1080/13533310802058984.
Goodhand, Jonathan, and Aziz Hakimi. *Counterinsurgency, Local Militias, and Statebuilding in Afghanistan*. Washington, DC: United States Institute of Peace, 2014.
Gopal, Anand. *No Good Men among the Living: America, the Taliban, and the War through Afghan Eyes*. New York: Picador, 2015.
Grenier, Robert. *88 Days to Kandahar: A CIA Diary*. New York: Simon and Schuster, 2016.
Hamdard, Hidayatullah. "Gunmen Extort Locals' Livestock in Kunduz." *Pajhwok*, July 3 2014.
Heward, Gran. "Legal, Illegal: Militia Recruitment and (Failed) Disarmament in Kunduz." *Afghanistan Analysts Network*, November 10 2012.
Heward, Gran. "For a Handful of Bolani: Kunduz's New Problem with Illegal Militias." *Afghanistan Analysts Network*, October 8 2012.
Human Rights Watch. *The Massacre in Mazar-I Sharif* no. 7. Vol. 10. New York: Human Rights Watch, 1998.
Human Rights Watch. *Massacres of Hazaras in Afghanistan* no. 1. Vol. 13. New York: Human Rights Watch, 2001.
Human Rights Watch. *Paying for the Taliban's Crimes: Abuses Against Ethnic Pashtuns in Northern Afghanistan*. 14, no. 2, New York: Human Rights Watch, 2002.
Human Rights Watch. *"Killing You Is a Very Easy Thing for Us": Human Rights Abuses in Southeast Afghanistan* no. 5. Vol. 15. New York: Human Rights Watch, 2003.
Human Rights Watch. *"Just Don't Call It a Militia": Impunity, Militias, and the "Afghan Local Police"*. New York: Human Rights Watch, 2011.

Human Rights Watch. *"Today We Shall All Die" Afghanistan's Strongmen and the Legacy of Impunity*. New York: Human Rights Watch, 2015.

Jones, Seth G., and Arturo Munoz. *Afghanistan's Local War: Building Local Defense Forces*. Washington, D.C.: RAND, 2010.

Keefer, Philip. "Clientelism, Credibility, and the Policy Choices of Young Democracies." *American Journal of Political Science* 51, no. 4 (2007): 804–821. doi:10.1111/ajps.2007.51.issue-4.

Kitschelt, Herbert, and Steven I. Wilkinson. *Patrons, Clients and Policies: Patterns of Democratic Accountability and Political Competition*. Cambridge: Cambridge University Press, 2007.

Ladwig, Walter C. *The Forgotten Front: Patron-Client Relationships in Counterinsurgency*. Cambridge: Cambridge University Press, 2017.

Lane, Frederic C. "Economic Consequences of Organized Violence." *The Journal of Economic History* 18, no. 4 (1958): 401–417. doi:10.1017/S0022050700107612.

Lasseter, Tom. "UN: Afghan Graves Disturbed; Physicians Demand Probe." *McClatchy DC*, December 12 2008.

Mainwaring, Scott P. *Rethinking Party Systems in the Third Wave of Democratization: The Case of Brazil*. Stanford: Stanford University Press, 1999.

Maley, William. *The Afghanistan Wars*. 2nd ed. New York: Palgrave Macmillan, 2009.

Marks, Thomas A. "FARC, 1982-2002: Criminal Foundation for Insurgent Defeat." *Small Wars and Insurgencies* 28, no. 3, (June2017): 488–523. doi:10.1080/09592318.2017.1307612.

Mashal, Mujib. "Afghan Vice President Raises Concerns by Turning to Militias in Afghan Fight." *The New York Times*, August 18 2015.

Matta, Bethany. "Afghan Forces Fail to Halt Taliban Resurgence." *Al Jazeera*, August 29 2014.

Mojahed Weekly. Interview. "Afghan Governor Accuses Government of Distributing Weapons to Taliban," Kabul (Dari). September 27 2009.

Moyar, Mark. *Village Stability Operations and the Afghan Local Police*. MacDill Air Force Base: Joint Special Operations University Press, 2014.

Mukhopadhyay, Dipali. "Disguised Warlordism and Combatanthood in Balkh: The Persistence of Informal Power in the Formal Afghan State." *Conflict, Security and Development* 9, no. 4 (2009): 535–564. doi:10.1080/14678800903345812.

Mukhopadhyay, Dipali. *Warlords, Strongman Governors, and the State in Afghanistan*. Cambridge: Cambridge University Press, 2014.

Munch, Philipp. *Local Afghan Power Structures and the International Military Intervention*. AAN Thematic Report. Kabul: Afghanistan Analysts Network, 2013.

O'Hanlon, Michael E. "A Flawed Masterpiece." *Foreign Affairs* 81, no. 3 (2002): 47–63. doi:10.2307/20033162.

Pajhwok. "4,000 Gunmen to be Disarmed in Kunduz," August 1 2011.

Partlow, Joshua. "Dostum, a Former Warlord Who Was once America's Man in Afghanistan, May Be Back." *The Washington Post*, April 23 2014.

Payam-e Mojahed. "Taliban Spreading Influence in Konduz and Baghlan," (Dari and Pashto). September 9 2009.

PBS. "Interview: U.S. Special Forces ODA 595," *Frontline*. August 2 2002. doi:10.1044/1059-0889(2002/er01)

Peake, Gordon. "From Warlords to Peacelords?" *Journal of International Affairs* 56, no. 2 (2003): 181–191.

Physicians for Human Rights. Timeline of the Investigation. http://physiciansforhumanrights.org/issues/mass-atrocities/afghanistan-war-crime/timeline-of-the-investigation.html

Piattoni, S. *Clientelism, Interests, and Democratic Representation: The European Experience in Historical and Comparative Perspective*. Cambridge: Cambridge University Press, 2001.

Raghavan, Sudarsan. "Afghanistan's Defining Fight: Technocrats Vs. Strongmen." *The Washington Post*, April 12 2015.

Reid, Rachel, and Sahr Muhammed Ally. *"Just Don't Call It a Militia": Impunity, Militias, and the "Afghan Local Police"*. New York: Human Rights Watch, 2011.

Reuter, Christoph. "Power Plays in Afghanistan: Laying the Groundwork for Civil War." *Spiegel*, December 5 2011.

Robinson, J, and T. Verdier. "The Political Economy of Clientelism." *Scandinavian Journal of Economics* 115, no. 2 (2013): 260–291. doi:10.1111/sjoe.12010.

Rosenberg, Matthew. "A Group Taking Politics and Military Strategy to the Same Extremes." *The New York Times*, May 21 2013

Rosenberg, Matthew. "Afghan Leader Confirms Cash Deliveries by C.I.A." *The New York Times*, April 29 2013.

Rosenberg, Matthew. "Karzai Says He Was Assured C.I.A. Would Continue Delivering Bags of Cash," *The New York Times*, May 4 2013.

Rosenberg, Matthew. "C.I.A. Cash Ended up in Coffers of Al Qaeda." *The New York Times*, March 14 2015.

Rosenberg, Matthew, and Alissa J. Rubin. "Afghanistan to Disband Irregular Police Force Set up under NATO." *The New York Times*, December 27 2011.

Rubin, Alissa J. "Afghan Rape Case Turns Focus on Local Police." *The New York Times*, June 27 2012.

Rumsfeld, Donald. Talking Points Memo. National Security Archive. "The Iraq War—Part I: The U.S. Prepares for Conflict, 2001" Washington, DC: The George Washington University. September 22 2001.

Schetter, Conrad, Rainer Galssner, and Masood Karokhail. "Beyond Warlordism: The Local Security Architecture in Afghanistan." *International Politics and Security* 2 (2007): 136–152.

Schiewek, Eckart. "Keeping the Peace without Peacekeepers." In *Building State and Security in Afghanistan*, edited by Wolfgang Danspeckgruber with Robert P. Finn, 189–232. Boulder, CO: Lynne Rienner, 2007.

Schroen, Gary. *First In: An Insider's Account of How the CIA Spearheaded the War on Terror in Afghanistan*. New York: Presidio Press, 2007.

Secretary of Defense. 2008. Letter Deputy Secretary of Defense to Mr. Leonard S. Rubenstein. Case # 200802926 dated 4 August. Accessed via Afghanistan Documentation Project.

Semple, Kirk. "Citing Taliban Threat, Afghan ex-Militia Leaders Hoard Illegal Arms." *The New York Times*, October 27 2007.

Shamshad, TV. "Analyst Says Pashtuns Prevented from Voting in Afghan North," Kabul (Pashto), 1430 GMT, 20 September 2010.

Shaw, Mark. "Drug Trafficking and the Development of Organized Crime in Post-Taliban Afghanistan." In *Afghanistan's Drug Industry: Structure, Functioning, Dynamics, and Implications for Counter-Narcotics Policy*, edited by Doris Buddenberg and William A. Byrd, 189–214. Kabul: United Nations Office on Drugs and Crime, 2005.

Sites, Kevin. "Swimming with Warlords." *Vice*, July 5 2013.

Stanton, Doug. *Horse Soldiers*. New York: Scribner, 2009.

Suhrke, Astri. "Reconstruction as Modernization: The 'Post-Conflict' Project in Afghanistan." *Third World Quarterly* 28, no. 7 (2007): 1291–1308. doi:10.1080/01436590701547053.

Tahir, Muhammad. "Afghan Village Fights to Keep Taliban at Bay." *Radio Free Europe/Radio Liberty*, September 10 2010.

Tolo TV. "Afghan Governor Opposes Establishment of Tribal Force in North." Kabul (Dari) 1330 GMT, September 20 2009.

Torjesen, Stina. "Transition from War to Peace: Stratification, Inequality and Post-War Economic Reconstruction." In *Political Economy of Statebuilding: Power after Peace*, edited by Mats Berdal and Dominik Zaum, 48–62. London: Routledge, 2013.

United Nations Assistance Mission Afghanistan (UNAMA). *Afghanistan Annual Report on Protection of Civilians in Armed Conflict: 2013*. Kabul: UNAMA, 2014.

United Nations Development Programme, *Disbandment of Illegal Armed Groups Annual Project Report 2010*. Project ID 00043604. Kabul, Afghanistan, 2011.

United States Government. Dasht-e-Leili Afghanistan Massacre FOIA (2002-2008), Doc #: 2027283053 Released November 24, 2008. Accessed via Afghanistan Documentation Project.

United States Government. Dasht-e-Leili Afghanistan Massacre FOIA (2002-2008), Case # 200802926, Released 24 November 2008. Accessed via Afghanistan Documentation Project.

Weesa. "Report Says Afghan Governor Runs Tribal Militia to Maintain Security," Kabul (Pashto). April 23 2011.

Weingrod, A. "Patrons, Patronage and Political Parties." *Comparative Studies in Society and History* 10 (1968): 377–400. doi:10.1017/S0010417500005004.

Willams, Brian Glyn. *The Last Warlord*. Chicago: Chicago Review Press, 2013.

Woodward, Bob. *Plan of Attack*. New York: Simon and Schuster, 2004.

Zee News. "Dostum's Reintegration Campaign in the North Continues." *Zee News*, December 31 2014.

6 Iraq, 2003–2011: succeeding to fail

Jeanne Godfroy and Liam Collins

ABSTRACT
This study examines the US experience during the Iraq war, from the planning phase that began in 2001 to the withdrawal of US forces in 2011. It reveals a dearth of planning and intelligence leading up to the invasion; reluctance by conventional coalition military forces to conduct reconstruction, political and security capacity-building; and, later, full spectrum counterinsurgency operations. These forces took on some missions traditionally reserved for special operations forces, and they increasingly assumed diplomatic roles as they interfaced with the Iraqi leadership and local kingpins. Although these efforts yielded some impressive organizational learning and limited operational successes, they were hampered by lack of adequate preparation, a poor understanding of the human terrain, shortsighted strategies, and ultimately a dearth of political will to stay the course. The outcome was far from the model Middle East democracy envisioned by the invasion's architects, and the American experience in Iraq instead became a cautionary tale for military intervention.

The American-led Coalition invasion of Iraq in 2003 was an impressive – if imperfect – display of military might. Had the conflict ended there, the entire endeavor might have been heralded as an unprecedented military and strategic success. However, this undertaking did not end with the removal of Saddam Hussein's authoritarian regime. The next several years proved to be a harrowing, costly learning experience for the American leadership, military, and populace. The power vacuum generated by the elimination of a repressive government and American lack of preparedness for governing an entire country created near perfect conditions for long-standing rivalries and hostile armed groups to wreak havoc on the Coalition military and the Iraqi state.

In the months and years following the conclusion of major combat operations, conventional Coalition military forces reluctantly began reconstruction and political and security capacity-building, even as they engaged in counterinsurgency operations. They took on some missions traditionally reserved for special operations forces, including Foreign Internal Defense. Military leaders also increasingly assumed diplomatic roles as they interfaced with the Iraqi leadership and local kingpins. Although these efforts yielded some impressive organizational learning and limited operational successes, US endeavors were hampered by lack of adequate preparation, a poor understanding of the human terrain, shortsighted strategies, and, ultimately, a dearth of political will to stay the course. The outcome was far from the model Middle East democracy envisioned by the invasion's architects, and the American experience in Iraq instead became a cautionary tale for military intervention.

This article begins by reviewing the decision to invade Iraq, followed by a discussion of some of the key planning and intelligence failures leading up to the invasion. It continues with a description of how the Coalition's inability to understand Iraq's human terrain contributed to further blunders and describes what was actually happening in Iraq. The article continues with review of American efforts to formulate and implement a strategy to achieve stability and democracy in Iraq. The authors then highlight some of the more notable tactical and operational achievements of the US military during the conflict and conclude with their assessments of the most important lessons from the American intervention in Iraq.[1]

The decision to invade and liberate Iraq

The terrorist attacks of 11 September 2001 shook the American leadership to its core. A once distant adversary named al-Qaeda – whose assaults on United States citizens and interests had occurred far from American shores – had brazenly struck symbols of American financial and military might and taken over 3,000 lives in the process. Not since the Japanese assault on Pearl Harbor had the US been so threatened or the American public so galvanized to action. The difficulty was that Usama Bin Ladin's al-Qaeda was sponsored by a multitude of state and non-state actors all over the world. Thus, striking back to eliminate the threat would be neither a simple nor a direct affair. Any such effort would require a multi-pronged approach across many different geographic areas, including the elimination of terrorist cells on US soil.

When President George W. Bush was first presented with options to respond to the 9/11 attacks, most of the recommendations he received involved striking at al-Qaeda in Afghanistan and securing US territory from further attack. Secretary of Defense Donald Rumsfeld and his deputy, Paul Wolfowitz, wanted to move beyond direct attacks against al-Qaeda in Afghanistan. Wolfowitz in particular was adamant that, in order to solve the larger problem of terrorism, the US needed to avoid getting bogged down in Afghanistan in order to address other suspected state sponsors of terrorism, including Saddam Hussein and his Weapons of Mass Destruction (WMD) program. The way forward, argued Wolfowitz and Rumsfeld, was to aid opposition groups in Iraq with military action. Secretary of State Colin Powell, among others, was privately concerned that going into Iraq would shift focus from the war on terrorism and thought the Defense Department officials were overestimating the capabilities of the military to conduct two major operations at once within the US Central Command (CENTCOM).[2]

Ultimately, however, the DoD leadership, Vice President Dick Cheney, and, to an extent, the National Security Council (NSC) leadership, persuaded President Bush to look into military operations to remove Saddam Hussein and his Ba'ath Party regime from power.

Planning for Iraq

As Powell predicted, military leaders at the CENTCOM headquarters were incredulous when, shortly after Thanksgiving of 2001, Rumsfeld requested that they develop plans for invading Iraq. At the time, CENTCOM Commander General Tommy Ray Franks was focused on defeating al-Qaeda and the Taliban in Afghanistan, and on detaining or killing its leadership. CENTCOM did maintain some contingency plans to conduct military operations inside Iraq, but those were mostly defensive in nature, drawn against a scenario in which Iraq was the provocateur against Kuwait or others. Most Iraq analysts believed that the principal threat posed by Iraq was its WMD program, not terrorism, and they had directed considerable energy towards identifying the locations of Saddam's 900 or so suspected WMD sites. However, there were no military or other contingency plans specifically targeting those facilities.[3]

Furthermore, the links between Saddam and acts of terrorism against US territories were tenuous at best. Saddam had indeed provided financial and training support to Islamic terrorist organizations in the 1990s but had shied away from supporting al-Qaeda. There was one al-Qaeda affiliate in Iraq's northeastern province of Sulaymaniyah, Ansar al-Islam, comprised of Kurdish Islamists. An al-Qaeda operative named Abu Mus'*ab* al Zarqawi was working with them to perpetrate attacks against the Iraqi regime and the more secular Kurdish parties, but that region was geographically partitioned from Saddam's influence by the Northern No-Fly Zone.[4]

Therefore, it had not occurred to anyone within the US military leadership to create plans to forcibly remove Saddam Hussein's Ba'ath Party regime.

Planning failures

The plans that CENTCOM and its subordinate commands developed for the invasion and its aftermath were constrained by a combination of assumptions driven by historical analogies and wishful thinking, micromanagement from the Office of the Secretary of Defense (OSD), and military biases that favored large maneuver operations over stability and peacekeeping activities. The Pentagon's senior leaders were eager to showcase their strongly held belief that a small troop footprint combined with strategic air power could achieve the strategic objectives of removing the Ba'ath Party regime from power and replacing it with a free and democratic Iraq. That perspective had seemingly been validated by military operations in Afghanistan in October 2001 in which a small group of special operations forces assisted by the Northern Alliance and strategic air support successfully ousted the Taliban and dispersed al-Qaeda strongholds.[5] Rumsfeld himself determined that the strategic objectives of the Iraq campaign could be achieved with a small force of less than 30,000 personnel, and his insistence on reducing the size of the invasion force drove three major planning rounds involving successively smaller force footprints between January and October of 2002. After military leaders refused to depart from their established methods of deploying the force – the Time Phased Force Deployment List (TPFDL) – Rumsfeld, who deemed the process too slow, forced deployments for the invasion in small groups using Requests For Forces (RFFs) held for his signature authority.[6] The outcome of the Afghanistan success and Rumsfeld's micromanagement was a total ground force at least a full division smaller than what military leaders and planners believed was the minimum necessary for success.[7]

The planning for how to manage post-Saddam Iraq was driven by unrealistic expectations for what would happen after Saddam was removed from power. One such assumption was the conviction that the liberation of Iraq would proceed much like the Allied liberation of France in 1945. Like the non-Vichy French, Iraqis who had suffered under the Ba'ath party were expected to welcome a Coalition invasion with gratitude, and Iraqi leaders in exile could be repatriated to create and lead a new government built on democratic principles with the support of a professional civil services and non-Ba'athist security organizations such as the Iraqi Army that would remain intact after the regime's fall.[8]

CENTCOM and its subordinate commands likewise made some inaccurate estimates based upon their memories of the Gulf War. In particular, they believed that the non-sectarian, nationalist Iraqi Army would not put up much of a fight and that most units would surrender or capitulate during the invasion. That same army could then be recalled to help stabilize Iraq until a replacement Iraqi government took control of them. Military planners expected that the bulk of their assistance would then transition to humanitarian efforts to support Prisoners of War, displaced persons, and refugees from the fighting and to some limited reconstruction in neighborhoods and locals that had been neglected and repressed under Saddam Hussein.[9] These assumptions would ultimately be invalidated during the execution of the invasion, but commanders would not modify the plan based on the new reality they faced until months later.

In addition to being driven by poor assumptions, planning was uncoordinated and was largely ignored by the Defense Department and the military. Not until the summer of 2002 did the NSC establish an executive steering group to plan for post-Saddam Iraq, and this council was not well synchronized with the State Department's Future of Iraq project, which was responsible for identifying Iraqi expatriates who would build the successor government. OSD and the Joint Staff had their own post-invasion planning efforts ongoing as well, neither of which was coordinated with the NSC, the State Department, or ongoing military planning. One of those was the Office of Humanitarian Reconstruction and Assistance run by Jay Garner, a retired general officer, whose focus was on humanitarian assistance and reconstruction, less so on political governance structures or the running of a state.[10]

Interestingly, the most robust post-invasion planning took place inside Lieutenant General David McKiernan's Coalition Forces Land Component Command (CFLCC), which was responsible for the ground forces component of the invasion. A small portion of the CFLCC staff developed detailed lines of operation for governance, reconstruction, and humanitarian assistance using all four Army Civil Affairs Commands, regionally dispersed throughout the country, in a plan called ECLIPSE II after the allied plan to occupy Denmark after WWII.[11] However, apart from ECLIPSE II, military leaders such as General Franks were overwhelmingly focused upon the major maneuver operations for the invasion and the size of the forces they would have at their disposal. Most incorrectly believed that the State Department or other non-military agencies had plans and resources prepared for what came next.[12]

Intelligence failures

Invasion and post-regime plans were also hampered by significant intelligence deficiencies. Crucially, there was a shortage of reliable sources on the inner workings of the Iraqi regime and society. Intelligence analysis on Iraq during the periods between the end of the Gulf War in 1991 and the March 2003 invasion focused on Iraq's WMD program, the positioning of large Iraqi military formations and major weapons systems, and Iraqi air defense systems. There was almost no detailed examination of Iraqi society. What was available was often supplied by Iraqi expatriates, who, apart from having agendas that did not necessarily align with US policy interests – or Iraqi national interests, for that matter – tended to be disconnected from the Iraqi people who had remained behind and suffered under Saddam's rule. For their part, military intelligence analysts had institutional biases from the Cold War that favored information on enemy military hierarchy and conventional forces. They were far less concerned about the internal workings of Iraqi society or Iraq's numerous paramilitary organizations, including the Fedayeen.[13] The other major intelligence limitation was a seeming disregard for how Iraq's neighbors – namely Syria and Iran – would behave in the aftermath of the invasion. Some US strategic and military leaders assumed both regimes would be glad for Saddam's departure – or at the very least, ambivalent – and would not interfere in Iraq after the regime fell.[14]

The combined oversights of the strategic and military intelligence community ultimately led to some major adjustments to maneuver operations during the invasion itself, and they would leave the ground forces floundering in the aftermath of the regime's destruction.

Outcomes of the invasion

On 20 March 2003, Coalition naval, air, and ground forces followed special operations activity in northern and western Iraq with a ground invasion that originated in Kuwait. Although they faced an unexpectedly tenacious defense by paramilitary forces such as the Fedayeen in and around Iraq's urban areas, which they had intended to bypass, US and Coalition military forces succeeded in defeating the Iraqi military and forcing regime change in just under three weeks. US Army Colonel David Perkins' 2nd Brigade, 3rd Infantry Division, together with elements of the First Marine Expeditionary Force (I MEF), entered Baghdad for the first time on 5 April, and the city fell four days later. The Coalition adapted quickly to the unanticipated ferocity of the paramilitary attacks and the failure of their planned aviation deep attacks against Iraq's *Republican Guard* mechanized formations, but their rapid maneuver and overwhelming firepower would not provide them the with the same advantages after the regime's fall.[15]

As the US Army V Corps commanded by Lieutenant General William 'Scotty' Wallace and I MEF entered Baghdad, Wallace called the CFLCC operations chief Major General James Thurman for instructions, asking, 'Okay Bubba, we're here. Now What?'[16] The absence of an answer in any detail to this seemingly simple question revealed just how unprepared the Coalition military and US leadership were for the new situation that arose as the Iraqi state collapsed. This unexpected state of affairs – which began with looting and the complete dissolution of order – would necessitate a combination of offensive operations, intense policing, reconstruction, and building economic and governance capacity in nearly every major state function – a considerable commission for a comparatively small number of troops who lacked capacity for missions of that magnitude.

Although President Bush declared victory on 1 May 2003, the war was far from over.[17] Much of the country – including sizable portions of western and northern Iraq – remained unsecured and, with no authority to keep them in check, Iraqis alternately celebrated in the streets, looted abandoned buildings and government offices, and desecrated the private residences of Saddam and regime leaders. Coalition leaders were also either unaware of or ignored the reprisal attacks that ensued against Sunnis and Ba'athists, some of which had been years in the making. The White House and Defense Department also made some considerable changes in the leadership in Iraq at this critical time. Garner and the Office of Humanitarian Reconstruction and Assistance were replaced by Ambassador L. Paul Bremer and the Coalition Provincial Authority (CPA). Secretary Rumsfeld, who was unimpressed with the performance of McKiernan or Wallace during the invasion, removed CFLCC to Kuwait and replaced Wallace with very junior Lieutenant General Ricardo Sanchez. V Corps was then hastily re-designated as the Command Joint Task Force (CJTF-7) for Iraq. At CENTCOM, General Franks retired and was replaced by his deputy, General John P. Abizaid.[18] Although Abizaid had a wealth of knowledge and expertise on the Middle East, Iraq now found itself governed by civilian and military personnel who were relative amateurs when it came to the circumstances they confronted.

Failure to understand the human terrain

Inaccurate assumptions about how the Iraqi people and state would respond to the invasion and erroneous intelligence assessments about the Iraqi security forces were emblematic of a larger problem – the American military's fundamental lack of information or understanding about Iraq's complex human terrain. Disregard for Iraq's intricate social landscape generated tremendous gaps in what the US intelligence and community knew about Iraqi politics, society, and government, gaps that translated to significant shortcomings in future intelligence activities, detention operations, and the policies and strategies Coalition leaders would develop for the country.

What was really happening in Iraq – the foundations of resistance, insurgency, and civil war

The manner in which Saddam Hussein ran his security forces in the 1990s and into the 2000s would have a distinct imprint on the participants and methods used against the Coalition military by Iraqis who wished to resist its rule. Saddam's major anxiety after the Gulf War was not – as US planners believed – a US military invasion. He was far more concerned about being assassinated by his own people or forced from power in a coup as his predecessors had been. Most of his anxiety about external threats centered on Israel and Iran, and Saddam translated these concerns into a proliferation of internal security and competing specialized paramilitary and intelligence entities, including the Fedayeen. He also supported terrorist organizations that opposed the governments of Iran and Israel.

In the early 2000s, Saddam and his security and intelligence directorates became keenly interested in using assassinations, suicide bombings, and Improvised Explosive Devices (IEDs) against Iraqi opposition groups and Iranian targets. To that end, the Iraqi Intelligence Service (IIS) established the 'Ghafiki Project' to develop those capabilities. The IIS's M16 directorate trained some of its special mission units in explosives to build car bombs and other IEDs, while the M8 'Directorate of Liberation Movements' hosted Palestinian, Lebanese, Syrian, and North African fighters in paramilitary training camps. Through these camps, the IIS worked extensively to perfect IED construction and the more technical aspects of conducting terrorist attacks.[19]

All three of Iraq's primary ethno-religious groups – the Sunni Arabs, the Shi'a Arabs, and the Kurds – had their own agendas for post-regime Iraq and, in most cases, the militias with which to carry them out. At the time Baghdad fell, much of the mostly Sunni areas of Iraq, including Anbar, Salah a Din, Ninawah, and parts of At Tamim provinces, were untouched by the Coalition presence. Having never encountered or fought directly against the Coalition military, many Sunni tribal leaders believed they had not lost the war or, if they had, attributed the loss to Saddam's blundering. As the Coalition gradually injected more forces into Sunni territory and accepted the surrender of the remaining Iraqi units in Anbar, many of the local tribal leaders waited for the Coalition to approach them.

Far from being the Ba'athists US analysts thought them to be because they were Sunni, these tribal sheikhs viewed themselves as the natural allies of the Coalition as they shared a common enemy – Iran. They also expected that the US would enact a patronage system of government similar to the one they had enjoyed under Saddam. In exchange for a Coalition decision to put the Iraqi government in capable Sunni hands, these tribes intended to keep the Iranian-backed Shi'a out of Iraq and split oil revenues evenly with the US and its Coalition partners.[20]

Saddam's rapid fall from power created a temporary void that various Shi'a organizations attempted to fill. The first was that of the *marja'aiyah*, the senior Shi'a clerics and religious community in the holy cities of Karbala and Najaf. Although the leader of this community – Grand Ayatollah Ali al Sistani – remained more of a quietist force, his voice would eventually be drowned out by those of militants. Some segments of Iraqi Shi'a society had long-standing plans for how to achieve their interests after Saddam was removed from power. Captured documents revealed that the Iranian regime intended to use the Badr Corps – a militant wing of an Iraqi Shi'a party known as the Supreme Council for Islamic Revolution in Iraq (SCIRI) – to subvert American efforts to occupy Iraq by military and social means. This militia was also armed with lists of the names of senior Iraqi military personnel, Ba'athists, Iraqi pilots, and other Iraqi regime collaborators whom they planned to systematically execute. The Badr Corps began carrying out those assassinations during the invasion and continued to conduct them well into the fall and winter of 2003. SCIRI further intended for the Badr Corps to surreptitiously take over Iraqi institutions after the regime collapsed, and they successfully seized towns and government offices in southern Iraq in the power vacuum that ensued.[21]

Another party eager to fill the power vacuum was that of Muqtada al-Sadr. Sadr had remained in Iraq during Saddam's rule, and he and his martyred father's family and followers had survived Saddam's crackdown against the Shi'a. After the US invasion, he began arming his followers and branded them the *Jaysh al Mahdi* or Mahdi Army. The Sadrists gradually rose to power by assassinating their Shi'a competitors in SCIRI and other organizations.[22] Sadr's organization would eventually fracture into several armed groups of varying levels of militancy and links to Iran. The most extreme of these 'Special Groups,' as they were called, was the *Ahl Asaib al Haqq* or 'Leagues of the Righteous' organization headed by Qais al-Qazali and supported by Lebanese Hezbollah and Iran. This group would unleash some of the most lethal attacks on Coalition forces and would provide robust support to institutionally-led ethnic cleansing of Iraq's Sunni neighborhoods.[23]

The Kurds, too, participated in reprisal attacks, but they were also ambitious to extend their territory well beyond the 'Green Line' established by the Northern No-Fly Zone. The two major Kurdish political parties – the Kurdistan Democratic Party (KDP) and Patriotic Union of Kurdistan (PUK) – had well-trained militias that had supported US special operations forces during the invasion but that also served parochial Kurdish interests. As the Kurdish militias moved south during the invasion, they began to expand Kurdish territory in the oil-rich city of Kirkuk and Iraq's most populous northern city of Mosul. Kirkuk in particular was strongly tied to Kurdish identity, and most Kurds could not envision a future Kurdistan that did not have Kirkuk as its capital.[24] Overtime, the Kurdish parties and militias wove themselves into Iraqi national politics and the political and security institutions of Mosul and Kirkuk and continued to press for autonomy in Iraq. They also sent their people south to displace Arabs in those territories in de-facto seizures overtime.[25]

Poor policies and the wrong kind of intelligence in post-regime Iraq

The Coalition was not attuned to these social dynamics. Consequently, Coalition efforts and failures to restore order after the invasion understandably exacerbated – rather than mitigated – many of the simmering tensions and fault-lines in Iraqi society. The World War II analogies driving post-invasion planning persisted in the policies enacted by US leaders in Iraq in the months following the invasion. The American leadership intended to de-Ba'athify the country using the de-Nazification of post WWII Germany as a model. Accordingly, Bremer issued CPA Orders 1 and 2, preventing former senior Ba'athists (many of whom were senior leaders within the Sunni community) from ever holding government positions and dissolving all Iraqi security and military institutions, including the Iraqi Army. The latter was a highly respected symbol of Iraqi national pride, and its dissolution angered many Iraqis.[26]

That second order also made it impossible for the Coalition military to recall any Iraqi Army units to assist with security. Bremer then set up an Iraqi Governing Council consisting of expatriate Iraqi Shi'a and Kurds and a few token Sunnis who had no connection to the local population. One of the first acts of the Iraqi Governing Council was to call for all senior Ba'athists – many of whom were in professions that required them to join the Ba'ath Party – to be fired immediately, furthering discontent amongst the Sunnis and putting the onus of security squarely on the shoulders of the small invasion force.[27] This act, combined with the Coalition's failure to contact the Sunni tribes and the CPA's installation of a Shi'a dominated government, quickly disabused Sunni sheikhs and other leaders of the notion that the new regime was prepared to work in their favor and sent them into the open arms of former Ba'athist resistance.

Coalition blindness to these factors and others persisted for additional reasons. Policymakers and leaders of the institutional military back in Washington believed that the war was over, and they often dismissed or overruled what their leaders in Iraq were reporting. When, in the summer of 2003, Abizaid characterized enemy activity in Iraq as a 'classical guerilla-type campaign,' and used the term 'insurgency' to describe the hostilities against the Coalition, those politically unfeasible terms earned him the ire of Rumsfeld. Abizaid subsequently became more circumspect in his language, instead focusing on the actual behaviors rather than labeling the activity as insurgency or guerilla warfare.[28]

Another hurdle to creating an accurate picture of the situation in Iraq was the tendency of strategic intelligence organizations to create intelligence reporting that was irrelevant tactically while ignoring bottom-up reporting from tactical units who were encountering sectarian violence and local leaders with information on a regular basis. This failure was a holdover from the Cold War-era intelligence models that had proved unhelpful in understanding the enemy activity during the invasion. Analysts simply were not primed to recognize insurgent groups seeking to subvert the Coalition-backed Iraqi government or a growing civil war between Iraq's three primary ethno-religious groups. Instead, these analysts continued to explain the enemy in terms of large land forces and other paradigms that were poor fits for the intricate networks of political militias, former military organizations, and tribal and religious groups that overlaid all of the hostile activity in Iraq.[29]

US forces were also used to detecting enemy activities and intentions by monitoring large camps and military equipment or tracking al-Qaeda-level communications used by relatively small numbers of foreign fighters in Iraq. They were not accustomed to gathering and synthesizing a large quantity of Human Intelligence (HUMINT) – or any information at all for that matter – on tribal and other informal networks that came to prominence after Saddam's removal.[30] Those networks were constantly changing as US and Coalition forces' contact with local, provincial, and national leaders alternately empowered or marginalized traditional leaders and, in some cases, widened the growing divides in Iraqi society.[31] It would take years of on-the-job training and the development of additional personnel and systems focused on HUMINT, network-based, and cultural analysis before Coalition military forces would gain much traction in understanding the true source and nature of the resistance and reprisals ongoing in Iraq.[32]

Detention operations

Another large gap in the planning for the invasion and the reconstruction of Iraq was unpreparedness for the volume and type of personnel that would be held in US and Coalition military custody. The lack of planning, intelligence, and understanding of the Iraqi social and political landscape led many Coalition units to detain Iraqis in large numbers either in error or for minor offenses as they lashed back at attacks whose origins they simply could not understand. This treatment angered local leaders, who complained to Abizaid and others about the unlawful detention of their people.[33] There was also no clear guidance concerning how to handle civilian detainees, as well as a dearth of information and trained personnel for managing the growing population of 'unlawful enemy combatants' in Coalition custody. The lack of appropriate guidelines combined with angry and frustrated Coalition units created conditions for some interrogators and detention facility guards to use physical contact, demeaning behavior, and other forms of torture in detention facilities (in both Iraq and Afghanistan).[34] These deficiencies would eventually lead to scandal.

Between 25 October and 26 November 2003, soldiers from a recently-arrived reserve Military Police Company physically and psychologically tortured some detainees at the Abu Ghraib prison outside of Baghdad, and another detainee at the same facility died in the custody of a non-DoD organization.[35] The news of the abuses that took place at Abu Ghraib coincided with Marine operations in Fallujah in April 2004, spurring many Iraqis who were undecided about how to treat Coalition forces into sympathy or outright support for various insurgent organizations and armed groups. Iraqis released from Coalition custody for minor offenses later in the war, as well as those who eventually turned against the Iraqi insurgent groups, would later tell the Coalition that the reasons they began fighting the Coalition emerged from the abuses at Abu Ghraib.[36]

Abizaid, who recognized the devastating impact the Coalition's detention woes would have on Coalition efforts to stabilize the country and gain popular support, spurred the creation of Task Force 134 to manage the crowded and chaotic Coalition detention facilities across the country, conditions that led to deadly prison riots in the larger facilities. Like many other new organizations, however, the Task Force was never sufficiently manned or equipped for the immense task of detention operations, and detention and release problems remained a sore point for the Iraqis and rule of law in Iraq more generally. Task Force 134 also had no control over Coalition forces' continued indiscriminate targeting and detention of suspected insurgents, whose transgressions ranged from being in the wrong place at the wrong time to minor criminal offensives to major terrorist operations.[37]

Controlled prisoner releases designed to assuage various Iraqi communities sometimes backfired as terrorists and insurgents learned how to manipulate the Coalition detention system. Recidivism rates were high, and Coalition units became increasingly frustrated by having to repeatedly detain the same personnel, some of whom were linked to attacks on their soldiers.[38] Overtime, coalition detention facilities became temporary holding facilities for Iraq's most dangerous operatives, allowing leaders of organizations such as al-Qaeda in Iraq and the Iran-backed Special Groups to recruit, train, consolidate, and reorganize safely behind prison walls.[39]

Myopic strategizing

At the outset of the Iraq war, the US intended to create an Iraq that was free of links to terrorism and WMD and to replace Saddam Hussein's authoritarian Ba'ath regime with a more representative and democratic government that could be a partner for the US in the war on terrorism.[40] The principal means of achieving that end-state, however, was a military invasion with a more limited mission to destroy the Ba'ath regime power base, eliminate Iraq's WMD ability, and ensure Iraq retained its territorial integrity.[41] In the months following the toppling of Saddam Hussein, the Coalition military killed or captured most of the senior Ba'ath Party leaders, including Saddam himself in December 2003. Although some senior Ba'athists such as Izzat Ibrahim al-Duri and Muhammad Yunis al-Ahmed escaped to Syria and were able to fuel a Ba'athist-led resistance to the Coalition presence, there was very little chance they would succeed in restoring Saddam or the Ba'ath party to power.[42] WMD, too, were no longer a concern. After months of extensive searches and investigations, neither the DIA-led Iraq Survey Group nor military units on the ground could find any evidence that Saddam had a working WMD program after 1999.[43]

The remaining strategic objective – a stable, democratic Iraq – would prove far more difficult to achieve. Over the course of the next 8 years, the US would find that they had far less control than it imagined over Iraq's political processes, and it would instead spend the bulk of their resources attempting to control an increasingly volatile and complex security situation.

Initial attempts at a strategy in 2003

The absence of a solid post-war plan for Iraq led to hasty attempts by CPA and CENTCOM in the summer of 2003 to cobble together a strategy. At the end of July, Bremer's CPA produced a 57-page 'Strategic Plan and Vision for Iraq' that laid out what the Coalition needed to accomplish in terms of security, essential services, economic growth, and governance. This document, however, was a list of key tasks rather than a strategy, and it was not coordinated with any Iraqis of standing or the Coalition military it occasionally mentioned.[44] Separately, Abizaid crafted his own strategic framework for Iraq based on what he termed as the 'Five Is': the Internationalization of the Iraq effort across Coalition and UN partner contributions; Improvement of Intelligence about Iraq and the theater; Improvement in Iraq's physical Infrastructure; creation of comprehensive Information strategy; and Iraqization.

This last 'I' would become Abizaid's focus. He believed it was imperative that the Coalition put an Iraqi face on all security and political activities to build capacity quickly and, more importantly, make the Coalition presence more palatable to Iraqi citizens and regional players. As Iraqis gradually assumed more responsibility for governance and security, the Coalition military would withdraw. Under Abizaid's proposal, the US would be able to reduce its presence in Iraq from 155,000 troops in the fall of 2003 to fewer than 30,000 by the end of 2004 and continue to decrease in size until only a small deterrence force remained.[45]

Both Bremer's and Abizaid's plans for Iraq were based on overly optimistic assessments of the state of affairs and the ability of the Coalition leadership to mold Iraq's political and security institutions using American or Western models. They also necessitated considerably more resources than Washington was willing to provide. Iraqis were dissatisfied with the Iraqi Governing Council, which pitted expatriates with parochial interests against Iraqi leaders who had suffered under Saddam's rule, and was not truly representative of the Iraqi population. Ambassador Ryan Crocker, a senior US diplomat sent to assist Bremer with establishing an Iraqi-led government, found that the Iraqis had their own notions of how to govern and were not as malleable to US advice as anticipated. The members of the Interim Iraqi Government decided among themselves that each of the nine executive council members would lead the country for a month, beginning with Ibrahim al Ja'afari of the Shi'a Dawa party, and they would not be dissuaded from that disjointed method of governance.[46] The initial Iraqi government thus lacked both legitimacy and efficacy, which advanced Iraqi grievances and emboldened recruitment for insurgent and terrorist organizations.

A speedy US exit under Abizaid's proposal would necessitate capable Iraqi security institutions, institutions CPA had effectively dismantled with CPA Orders 1 and 2. To make matters worse, initial Coalition efforts to develop capable Iraqi security forces were disjointed, shortsighted, and under-resourced. CPA split the security force mission between two different organizations: the Coalition Police Assistance Training Team or CPATT under former New York police commissioner Bernard 'Bernie' Kerik, and the Coalition Military Assistance Training Team (CMATT) led by the former commander of the US Army Infantry School, Major General Paul Eaton. Kerik found the existing Iraqi police to be corrupt, absent, or otherwise incapable of performing any reasonable policing functions.[47] Meanwhile, Eaton, supported by a small team of military personnel and some contractors, was tasked with creating a new Iraqi Army consisting of 12,000 light infantry soldiers and officers. This New Iraqi Army (NIA) had no support functions, no mobility capability, and a mission of protecting Iraq from invasion from its neighbors.[48] And, unbeknownst to CPA, CJTF-7 divisions began recruiting and developing their own local security forces to assist them with providing security and stability. CJTF-7 eventually decided to create some standardization amongst these locally-grown security units and branded them the Iraqi Civil Defense Corps (ICDC).[49]

Despite growing unrest in Iraq and a steady increase in attacks against Coalition military forces, civilian and military leaders in Washington failed to acknowledge the urgency of the situation in Iraq. They either believed – or wished to believe – the war was effectively over in May 2003. By the end of 2003, sources of military personnel were scarce as US Army Reserve tours came to a close and the time constraints associated with Reserve and National Guard tour lengths began to take their toll on the total force. The Defense Department was eager for military units to redeploy so that they could be available for other contingency operations in the war on terror or to deal with North Korea, and Rumsfeld continued to demand a reduction in troop numbers to under 100,000 by the end of 2004.[50] Demands like these for reductions in resources, while consistent with strategic proposals to put the Iraqis forward and draw down the US commitment, were disconnected from the real needs of Iraqi political and security institutions.

Forcing the Iraqis to take charge, 2004–2006

The spring of 2004 proved to be tumultuous for the Coalition effort in Iraq on a number of fronts. Despite optimistic assessments to the contrary, Saddam's capture on 14 December 2003 had no impact on the deteriorating security situation, which exploded in April 2004 and continued its downward spiral for nearly 3 years. On 31 March 2004, four private security contractors with the Blackwater security firm were ambushed, killed, and dragged through the streets of Fallujah by insurgents. A few days later, CJTF-7 shut down the Sadrist *Al Hawza* newspaper because of its violent rhetoric and arrested one of Sadr's senior lieutenants.[51] This last action unintentionally ignited a two-front war for CJTF-7, with the Sunni insurgents and terrorist organizations in Anbar and the Sadrist *Jaysh al Mahdi* in eastern Baghdad and southern Iraq.

CJTF-7 ordered a Marine assault on Fallujah and sent the recently arrived 1st Cavalry Division to quell Sadr's militias in Sadr City. The Marines achieved some limited successes before Sunnis on the Iraqi Governing Council forced a Coalition withdrawal. Fallujah would remain a symbol of Sunni insurgent success and it became a safe haven from which future insurgent and terrorist operations were launched.[52] Sadrist violence expanded into Karbala and Najaf until Sadr, whose forces were being decimated at the hands of the Coalition military, issued a ceasefire and ordered his militia to stand down. The first battle of Fallujah and operations to quell the Sadrist uprising resulted in a total of 137 Coalition deaths, hundreds of wounded, and an unknown number of insurgent and militia casualties. The Sadrist uprising also created a lasting impression about the dangers associated with inciting the Shi'a to violence and opening up additional fronts in the Iraq conflict.[53]

As the violence simmered, the Coalition transferred the reins of government back to Iraqi leaders in accordance with UN Security Council Resolution (UNSCR) 1546, which mandated that Iraqi sovereignty be returned no later than 30 June 2004. The new Prime Minister, Ayad Allawi, would head the Interim Iraqi Government (IIG) until the Iraqis held free and fair elections sometime before the end of January of 2005.[54] New US civilian leadership and military units also arrived and replaced the only troops and commanders with any Iraq experience. CPA dissolved and was replaced by the US mission in Iraq led by Ambassador John Negroponte, Bremer returned to the US. CJTF-7, too, was replaced by the Multi-National Forces-Iraq (MNF-I), a four-star command led by General George Casey, Jr. with two subordinate three-star commands: The Multi-National Corps – Iraq (MNC-I) led by Lieutenant General Thomas Metz, and the Multi-National Security Transition Command – Iraq (MNSTC-I), led by Lieutenant General David Petraeus.[55]

The strategy that Casey and Abizaid attempted to construct for Iraq maintained an end-state of a secure, free, and democratic Iraq. They intended to achieve this by expanding the international effort in Iraq to support reconstruction, creating conditions conducive to democratic elections, and enabling the Iraqi security forces to stabilize the country. Casey's plan also included criteria that would justify the removal of US forces as the Iraqis met specific benchmarks in terms of governance and security among other factors. Iraqi municipalities that met those criteria would first be transitioned to local control, followed by Provincial Iraqi Control (PIC). Once the majority of Iraq's provinces successfully PIC'd, the Coalition would then return full control of all state functions to the Iraqi government. As these transitions to Iraqi control took place, Coalition forces would withdraw first from the cities, then the provinces, and would ultimately move to a position of strategic overwatch with a small regional footprint.[56]

In the meantime, MNC-I would lead 'full spectrum counterinsurgency' operations to restore stability and create space for the Iraqi security forces and budding local, provincial, and national councils and other governance structures to develop. The purpose of these operations was to drive a wedge between the insurgents and the Iraqi people by eliminating safe havens and ensuring the legitimacy and viability of Allawi's Interim Iraqi Government. MNC-I eventually succeeded in removing Sadr's militia from Najaf, and then turned to the Sunni strongholds of Samarra and Fallujah, eliminating safehavens in those areas by the beginning of 2005.[57] However, as plans to remove forces from Iraq's population centers progressed and MNC-I units became confined to larger Forward Operating Bases (FOBs), MNC-I gradually lost visibility on what was happening with the population and was limited in its ability to conduct the full range of counterinsurgency operations.

Although MNC-I's operations were essential to the success of the strategy, Abizaid and Casey viewed the main effort as the development of capable Iraqi security forces who could provide adequate security for the Iraqi elections and eventually assume full responsibility for securing Iraq. This was a colossal task given the state of the Iraqi security forces in 2004. The Iraqi units that actually showed up to fight had failed miserably in Fallujah, Sadr City, and Iraq's southern cities during the violence April, and the effort to continue to develop them had been haphazard and disjointed. Based on the recommendations of a report written by Major General Karl Eikenberry in early 2004, Abizaid established MNSTC-I to unify the disparate security force efforts and propel the Iraq security forces towards a future more suitable for the situations they would face. When Petraeus took command of MNSTC-I, he assumed responsibility for CPATT, CMATT, and the remaining operational ICDC forces, which were later re-branded as the Iraq National Guard (ING).

Petraeus's initial assessment of the security forces led him to three conclusions about how to proceed: Iraq needed far more forces of multiple specialties; the Ministries of Defense and Interior needed the capacity to build, support, and sustain those forces; and the military forces needed to change their mission from external security to one of assisting the Coalition in stabilizing Iraq's internal security. Allawi agreed to all three recommendations, but other Coalition leaders and US policymakers took considerably longer to be convinced as expanding the Iraqi Security Forces (ISF) effort would require a substantial increase in the number of military trainers, equipment, and money.[58] Training host-nation security forces had traditionally been the purview of US special operations forces as part of their Foreign Internal Defense doctrine, and no unit in the special operations community forces had never built an entire state military from the ground up. Petraeus's proposal would require the institutional Army and other military branches to prepare large numbers of personnel for that very specialized mission. In the short-term, MNSTC-I enabled the Ministry of Defense and Interior to recruit forces directly into the ISF to augment the numbers, but it scrambled to obtain sufficient Coalition military trainers to support the expanded ISF mission.[59]

The outcome of the combined efforts of MNC-I and MNSTC-I was that the Iraqis voted in national elections on 30 January 2005. Only 58% of eligible Iraqis voted, and Iraq's Sunnis largely boycotted the election proceedings. The Sunnis were thus left out of the political process as the Shi'a and Kurdish parties took control of the government. These circumstances further embittered the Sunni population, causing recruitment and retention problems for the ISF while simultaneously creating recruitment opportunities for Sunni terrorist and insurgent groups.[60] Zarqawi's al-Qaeda in Iraq organization took advantage of the election outcome to ignite a full-blown civil war. He attacked Shi'a population centers and officials with massive suicide bombings to draw the Shi'a into a sectarian conflict with the Sunnis, a conflict he believed he could win.[61]

Efforts to internationalize reconstruction in Iraq also waned in response to determined attacks from al-Qaeda. After international support for the war declined following a massive car bombing that killed 19 UN workers in 2003, Zarqawi realized he could continue to reduce international backing by targeting the less secure Coalition partner country compounds, including the Spanish and Italian contingents. Countries that had supported the post-war operations refused to maintain military commitments after their forces became targets for insurgent and terrorist organizations.[62] Although MNSTC-I successfully increased the size of the ISF from 100,000 in late fall of 2005 to over 210,000 by the end of 2005, the capability and loyalties of those units remained extremely questionable.[63] Despite these disturbing details, Abizaid and Casey pressed ahead with transitioning Iraqi locales and provinces back to Iraqi control and withdrawing Coalition forces out of the cities and onto Forward Operating Bases (FOBs). In 2006, Casey reduced the number of Forward Operating Bases from 112 down to 50, and the total force was reduced from 160,000 to 135,000.[64]

On 22 February 2006, al-Qaeda in Iraq bombed the Golden Dome Mosque in Samarra, an important Shi'a holy site. This act enflamed the Shi'a and brought the sectarian conflict into outright civil war. The Iraqi Army proved ineffective in its response, and the Iraqi police and other interior ministry forces began to reveal their ties with Shi'a militias and proprietary interests in the violence that ensued. Casey, however, saw the bombing and its aftermath as a temporary setback in light of a positive development on the governance front: Iraqis had elected a new parliament on 15 December 2005, and the Sunnis turned out in far higher numbers than they had in January. The new Prime Minister, Nuri al Maliki, was from the Shi'a Dawa party, thought to be a more forward-thinking political organization, just as Maliki himself was believed to be Dawa's comparatively weak compromise candidate.[65] As a result, Casey and Abizaid were reluctant to request additional forces, believing that a larger Coalition presence would only make the situation worse. Instead, Casey launched two combined Iraqi-American operations, Operations TOGETHER FORWARD I and II, between July and October of 2006 in an attempt to regain control of Baghdad.[66]

Helping the Iraqis to take charge, 2007–2009

While MNF-I worked to stabilize Baghdad during TOGETHER FORWARD I and II, a congressional panel led by James Baker and Lee Hamilton was making its own assessment of the situation in Iraq, and their conclusions were markedly different from those of Casey and Abizaid. The Iraq Study Group, as it was called, stated bluntly that US policy in Iraq was not working, and noted that increasing costs in American lives and money had thus far yielded violence that was only increasing in 'scope, complexity, and lethality.'[67] In addition to the Sunni insurgency and the sectarian conflict, the report identified Kurd-Arab competition in northern Iraq and the unhelpful contributions of Iran and Syria as sources of continued instability. The authors further noted that the US military was becoming overstretched with repeated deployments and that international patience with the Iraq war was waning. Among other things, the report recommended that the US tie any continued support to Iraq to the achievement of milestones on national reconciliation, security, and governance. Calling for a 'responsible transition,' the authors advocated embedding more US military personnel in the Iraqi security forces and increasing the size of the US contingent by 10,000–20,000 troops.[68]

A separate study conducted by the Joint Chiefs of Staff identified six major trends in Iraq, including an incapable Iraqi government, weak or nonexistent rule of law, and weak security forces as contributing factors to the chaos in the country. The Pentagon also backed proposals to build more capacity in the Iraqi security forces before drawing down US forces to a support role.[69]

These reports combined with his own intuition about the situation in Iraq convinced President Bush that the US needed a drastic shift in strategy from one of drawing down the US presence to one in which the US bolstered the Iraqis with more forces. Bush signaled his intent by changing some of the key defense and military officials who would be responsible for executing the new strategy. He replaced Rumsfeld with Robert Gates as Secretary of Defense, sent Ryan Crocker to be the new US Ambassador in Iraq, and replaced General Casey with General Petraeus as the commander of MNF-I. On 10 January 2007, Bush announced his new strategy, which was known as the 'Surge.' Instead of Abizaid and Casey's strategy of 'as the Iraqis stand up, we stand down,' the Surge was a more traditional counterinsurgency strategy of 'clear, hold, build': clearing areas of insurgents and armed groups; holding the territory with capable security forces; and then building new, legitimate governance and rule of law structures. The Surge forces would include five additional Brigade Combat Teams (BCTs) along with many additional teams of advisors to embed within the Iraqi security forces. The surge brigades began arriving in March 2007, bringing the total number of Coalition troops back up to 120,000.[70]

Crocker, Petraeus, and the MNC-I Commander, General Raymond Odierno, set about using those additional forces to 'buy the time and space for the government of Iraq to move forward with national reconciliation and delivery of public services.'[71] They were determined to move their forces out of Forward Operating Bases and into the population, fighting side-by-side with Iraqi forces where possible. The joint effort was intended to show the population that Coalition and Iraqi forces were capable of protecting them and, by default that the Iraqi government itself was qualified to rule Iraq.[72] Petraeus and Odierno sent forces to the most violent areas along the faultlines of warring factions. The first two Surge brigades were sent to Baghdad to protect Sunni neighborhoods from Shi'a militias, and highly specialized forces were sent to root out al-Qaeda in Iraq's vehicle borne IED network. The Baghdad operation – known by the Iraqi name of *Fardh al Qanoon* or 'Enforcing the Law' – was also intended to show that Iraqi security forces could secure and hold Iraq's capital city.[73] Odierno sent the three other Surge brigades into Baghdad's belts, the towns surrounding Baghdad that insurgents were using as safe havens.[74]

Maliki had created the Baghdad Operations Command to unify the Iraqi security forces under a single command in support of Coalition military operations. The difficulty was that many of the national military and police forces had become sectarian, and few capable non-sectarian Iraqi forces outside of the special operations community remained. Shi'a militias dominated the national police forces and were engaged in sectarian cleansing as well as targeting Coalition forces. Kurdish forces had no desire to leave their territories in northern Iraq to support operations in Baghdad. Many of the Sunni-dominated security forces in western and northern Iraq had abandoned their posts to join various threat groups.[75]

Fortunately for the Coalition, there were some unexpected forces at work that aided the counterinsurgency strategy. In mid-2005, Sunni tribal leaders in western and central Iraq had become progressively more frustrated with arrangements they had made with al-Qaeda to resist the occupation forces.[76] Zarqawi had subverted traditional tribal authorities, and the sheikhs had seen no gains for themselves or their constituents, particularly in the restive cities of Fallujah and Ramadi. Sheikhs from three large tribes in the area decided to join forces with the American units against al-Qaeda in a movement known as the Anbar Awakening, the Sunni Awakening, or the 'Sons of Iraq.'[77] In the summer of 2007, Odierno and Petraeus sent an additional two battalions of Marines to Anbar to capitalize on some reconciliation-related gains made by the Coalition units that brokered the Anbar Awakening. This movement gained traction outside of the belts and expanded into Anbar, Baghdad, and Tikrit.[78]

A UK general officer, Graeme Lambe, took the Awakening further by brokering engagements between the Sunni tribes and the Iraqi government at more senior levels. These engagements were intended to bring the Sunnis and other disaffected groups into political accommodation with the Iraqi government such that they would no longer have a reason to fight.[79] Eventually MNF-I and the US Embassy would work to get the Iraqi government to incorporate members of these tribal militias into the Iraqi security forces instead of maintaining them on US payrolls.[80] Some Iraqi Shi'a militias also appeared tired of fighting. In August of 2007, Sadrist militias and Iraqi police backed by the Badr Corps militia clashed in the holy Shi'a city of Karbala. The result was the death and injury of hundreds of civilians during a religious ceremony. Sadr subsequently declared a 'freeze' on militia activity, a ceasefire prohibiting the *Jaysh al Mahdi* from attacking Sunni neighborhoods, Iraqi security forces and, to an extent, Coalition forces as well. Although the 'freeze' did not prohibit the Iranian-backed Special Groups from continuing to attack and harass the Coalition and its Iraqi partners, it did significantly reduce sectarian violence and allowed Coalition forces more space to continue the Surge.[81]

In March of 2008, Sadrists attacked Maliki's national security advisor, and Maliki responded by launching his security forces into Sadrist strongholds in Basrah and Baghdad, effectively ending the 'freeze.' Caught off-guard, Petraeus and Odierno hastily decided to send Coalition troops to reinforce the Iraqi-led 'Charge of the Knights' operation. The joint effort decimated the Sadrist militias, many of them backed by Iran, in those areas. The battle also proved to be a huge political victory for Maliki, who had been facing a vote of no-confidence.[82]

Under the tutelage of Crocker, Petraeus, Odierno, and other Coalition leaders, the Iraqis also made important strides in governance and national reconciliation. Between January and October 2008, the Iraqi parliament rolled back a number of harsh de-Ba'athification measures it had implemented between 2005 and 2007, which had further alienated the Sunnis. The Iraqi government also delegated more authorities to the provincial governments, authorized amnesty for some insurgent activities, and, importantly, passed the 2008 budget. After much debate over the hotly contested city of Kirkuk, the parliament successfully passed an election law to allow provincial elections to take place.[83] In January 2009, Iraq held provincial council elections that removed many sectarian leaders from power. A secular Iraqi political conglomerate led by Ayad Allawi won the majority of votes for the national elections.

To outsiders, Iraq appeared to be 'rejecting militancy and embracing nationalism' as well as developing a new democratic culture. These political developments coincided with a sharp drop in violence from almost a thousand violent attacks per week in mid-2007 to fewer than 200 per week in 2009. Additionally, Coalition fatalities were down by 85%, and civilian casualties had dropped a staggering 90%, allowing some semblance of normalcy to return to most areas of Iraq.[84] General Odierno, who succeeded Petraeus as the commander of MNF-I in September 2008, had one memorable briefing in October in which there was not a single major attack or violent incident reported.[85] The Surge of Coalition forces moving in and amongst the population combined with the effects of the Sunni Awakening, the Sadrist 'Freeze,' and the passing of legislation conducive to democracy and national reconciliation had finally started turning Iraq in the direction the authors of the invasion had originally envisioned.[86]

Leaving authoritarian Iraqis in charge, 2009–2011

The Surge had indeed improved security and overall perceptions of Iraqi government legitimacy, but the ability of Iraqis to maintain and improve upon these conditions was uncertain. Continued stability and national reconciliation were dependent on Maliki's support for the Sunni Awakening militias, and his ability to manage diverse Shi'a factions and interests, curtail Kurdish ambitions in northern Iraq, and cope with continued interference and threats to intervene from Iran and Turkey, respectively. Unfortunately, Maliki's confidence in his abilities to address those challenges had only increased with the successful defeat of the Sadrists during the Charge of the Knights operation, even as his capability to govern became more questionable. Maliki's tolerance for the Coalition presence was simultaneously wearing thin, and Congress, the American people, and the incoming administration were likewise eager to find an honorable means of reducing or eliminating the US military commitment to Iraq.[87] Although Bush favored staying the course, Congress was not convinced of the Surge's success, and the Obama administration had given notice that withdrawal was imminent.[88]

In order to clarify the US long-term role in the country in a manner politically feasible to the Iraqi leadership, the US had negotiated in 2008 a Strategic Framework Agreement outlining political, economic, and other non-security goals for Iraq, as well as a Status of Forces Agreement (SOFA) to clarify the role US security forces would play and their legal status in the country. Both agreements were designed to make a continued US force presence in Iraq politically feasible for the Iraqi government and simultaneously develop more quantitative ways to ensure the eventual drawdown of US forces in Iraq. The agreements jointly advocated continued capacity-building in the Iraqi government and security forces but set a hard timetable for the withdrawal of all American forces from Iraqi cities by the end of June 2009 and the removal of all American troops from the country by the end of 2011.[89]

As the Coalition prepared to pull its forces back and out of Iraq, the political and security situation began to deteriorate. As the timeline for SOFA implementation approached, the Coalition realized that Maliki's government was unlikely to honor its commitment to maintain the Sunni tribal militias in the Iraqi Army or on the Iraqi payroll more generally.[90] Intra-Shi'a political battles were also in play, and the Kurd-Arab tensions in Northern Iraq continued to create flashpoints with the potential for disaster in and around Ninawah and Kirkuk provinces. Although Odierno and his forces managed to prevent all-out war from breaking out in northern Iraq, he and other Coalition leaders saw that they had less and less influence over Maliki, who was increasingly favoring Dawa party interest and becoming more authoritarian in the process.[91]

Neither the security situation nor Iraqi political developments were going as planned.

Nevertheless, the US remained committed to withdrawal, even as al-Qaeda in Iraq and Shi'a militias reinvigorated their operations. Al-Qaeda launched high-profile, vehicle-borne IED attacks targeting Iraqi civilians, the remaining US outposts, and Iraqi government facilities and personnel.[92] Although his party had lost the election, Maliki was not willing to relinquish the reins of government, and he refused to accept that he and his party had lost. Over the course of the next several months, the new US Ambassador, Christopher Hill, with support from the Obama administration, decided to back Maliki's claim, unwittingly allowing what some US and Coalition officials in the country termed a 'paranoid despot' to consolidate his power and that of the Iran-backed Shi'a militias his government was tied to. Maliki's authoritarian and sectarian policies and actions would ultimately lead his country back into civil war after the 2011 departure of US forces.[93]

Military adaptations and innovations

As the US civilian and military leadership muddled its way through transforming Iraq into a democracy, the US military made a number of significant innovations that greatly contributed to the success of the Surge and the reduction of violence. The Army and Marine Corps incorporated counterinsurgency back into their doctrines; the Coalition military developed impressive, comprehensive methods to counter the IED attacks that were wreaking havoc on the ground forces; and Coalition forces made crucial adjustments to the targeting process and improvements to their exploitation capability.

Updates to counterinsurgency doctrine

The 'Surge' strategy that Crocker, Petraeus, and Odierno employed from 2007 to 2008 was the culmination of some institutional soul-searching and doctrinal adjustments that the US Army and Marine Corps made after being frustrated in their efforts to strike back at attackers who had far less technology and firepower at their disposal than the Western militaries they targeted. During the early years of the Iraq war, the more forward-thinking members of the U.S. military realized that they had purged almost all of the lessons they had learned fighting insurgents in the Vietnam War. Although some military units, such as Major General Petraeus's 101st Airborne Division in Ninawah in 2003, Major General Peter Chiarelli's 1st Cavalry Division in Baghdad in 2004, and, later, Colonel H.R. McMaster's 3rd Armored Cavalry Regiment in Tal Afar in 2006, successfully experimented with counterinsurgency tactics and operations, these units' activities were the exception. Most of the Coalition forces largely operated in an ineffective manner.[94]

In 2006, Lieutenant General David Petraeus, who was then commanding the Combined Arms Center at Fort Leavenworth, Kansas, decided that the institutional military could benefit from a reintroduction of counterinsurgency doctrine for use in its operations in Iraq and Afghanistan. He expedited the development of the doctrine and published the new Army and Marine Corps counterinsurgency field manual on 15 December 2006. Petraeus then quickly incorporated the doctrine into the Army's combat training centers by updating the mock villages and contracting additional civilian role players to provide more realistic training environments. He ensured that the new doctrine was incorporated into the Army's professional military education programs in order to prepare the next generation of Army leaders for the types of operations they were most likely to encounter in the future.[95] These much-needed updates to Army and ground force operations proved instrumental to the effectiveness of not only the Surge strategy, but to the broader set of operations the US military would conduct in Iraq through the end of the war.

Countering IEDs

IEDs used in roadside bombings, vehicle bombings, suicide bombings, and the extremely lethal Iranian-built Explosive Formed Projectiles (EFPs) had a devastating impact on Coalition forces as they fought to counter insurgents, curb sectarian violence, and restore basic services in Iraq. Appalled by the scale of the IED problem, General Abizaid proposed that DoD initiate a 'Manhattan Project-like effort' to confront what he believed to be the 'number-one killer of American troops' in Iraq in 2003–2004.[96] The Army subsequently created an IED task force that eventually became the Joint IED Defeat Organization (JIEDDO).[97] Meanwhile, British, American, and Australian ordnance specialists were merged into a Combined Explosives Exploitation Cell (CEXC). This special operations organization gathered fingerprints and other forensic evidence to link devices to different IED cells, assisting units on the ground with targeting and eliminating IED networks.[98]

Improvements in protection for the ground forces were every bit as critical to countering IEDs as improved intelligence and forensic analysis. Initially, ground forces attempted to protect themselves using a combination of sandbags and metal welded to the sides of their vehicles, but these methods added little fortification and often increased casualties due to the spalling from the additional metal. Some units later added steel-plated cages to the vehicles to protect exposed gunners, and the military developed strap-on armor kits for the vehicles and rushed them to Iraq to protect unarmored vehicle fleets. The Army and Marine Corps also increased up-armored HUMMWV production and, overtime, replaced the unarmored vehicles entirely.[99]

Even up-armored HUMMWVs were extremely vulnerable from the blast effects of IEDs, and the US military investigated a variety of technical means to mitigate IEDs' destruction. Initial experiments with dogs and bees failed, and the military turned to electronic jammers to interfere with the signals sent to remotely detonated IEDs. The jammers worked well against radio-controlled IEDs, but failed against other deployment mechanisms. The military then fielded the Rhino – a heat source placed on a telescoping pole attached to the front of a vehicle – to deceive IEDs into deploying prematurely.[100] Although these new technologies were effective for a time, armed groups in Iraq frustrated them by quickly developing defeat mechanisms. In 2006, the US military began exploring the utility of V-shaped hull vehicles developed by the Rhodesians and South Africans in the 1970s. These vehicles, which had been used by some European nations for years, had been largely ignored by the US military leaders.[101] As IED attacks intensified, the US military tested several designs and eventually fielded a Mine Resistant Ambush Protected (MRAP) vehicle fleet. The MRAP had a higher ground clearance, a V-shaped hull, and angled sides, all of which offered significantly more protection than the up-armored HUMMWV. The deployment of MRAPs to Iraq saved hundreds of lives and contributed to the success of the Surge operations on the ground.[102]

Improving exploitation capability

A critical element of dismantling insurgent and terrorist organizations and armed militias was removing their key personnel from the battlefield and exploiting the intelligence gleaned from such operations. After 9/11, the US found itself pursuing a transnational terrorist organization, an actor it lacked the doctrine, capability, and often the authority to defeat. US and Coalition special operations forces excelled at killing or capturing high-value targets when provided the right intelligence, but they had little ability to follow-up quickly on their successes due to their limited capacity to exploit captured individuals, documents, and media.[103] As a result, al-Qaeda in Iraq was able to expand its operations at an alarming rate, conducting more than 50 suicide attacks that killed more than 275 people in a single month by 2005.[104]

While commanding the Joint Special Operations Command (JSOC) in 2006, Major General Stanley McChrystal realized that he needed to build his own network in order to defeat the complex networks his forces faced in Iraq and Afghanistan.[105] He flattened his command and built two Joint Inter-Agency Task Forces (JIATFs), which served as formal intelligence fusion centers full of interagency partners. McChrystal then expanded his informal network by inserting more than 75 liaison officers at other military units and government agencies and conducting daily video teleconferences attended by thousands of people in up to 72 different locations.[106] At the same time, he built a robust interrogation capability with a brand new tactical screening facility in Iraq and manned it with dozens of teams comprised of professional interrogators, intelligence analysts, and linguists. These teams were augmented with a document exploitation capability and an Intelligence, Surveillance, and Reconnaissance (ISR) fleet with enhanced signal intelligence features capable of finding and tracking multiple targets simultaneously.[107]

Simultaneously, McChrystal set about designing better targeting procedures to use these enhanced resources to their maximum potential. The result was the F3EAD process, and it proved to be particularly well suited for 'engaging high-value individuals' on Coalition targeting lists. McChrystal's teams would first *Find* enemy targets amidst 'civilian chatter' and then *Fix* their precise location using precision ISR assets. The teams would send the appropriate assets to *Finish* (e.g. kill or capture) the fleeting target.[108] During the next phase, *Exploitation*, the teams would collect and *Analyze* information from captured personnel, records, and electronic media to gain a better understanding of the enemy network; and that improved understanding would be *Disseminated* and used to *Find* new targets, beginning the cycle anew.[109]

F3EAD and McChrystal's special operations network decimated al-Qaeda in Iraq, among other organizations. The organization increased the number of operations against high-value targets from only 10 a month in 2004 to over 300 per month in 2006.[110] In June 2006, the task force located and killed Zarqawi, causing the terrorist organization to temporarily fracture.[111] By 2010, McChrystal's task force and its Iraqi counterparts had killed or captured most of al-Qaeda in Iraq's top leadership, dealing the organization a critical blow from which it would have to wait to recover until after the departure of US forces.[112]

Lessons learned: winning is not the same as ruling

The US and Coalition impressive adaptations in doctrine, operations, and tactics were unable to mitigate the impacts of flawed planning, fundamental misconceptions concerning Iraq's human terrain, and the inability of policymakers and military leaders to employ the resources and willpower to execute their lofty strategic goals. The invasion plan military leaders constructed for Iraq was shaped by unrealistic expectations, institutional biases, and other constraints that led to successful combat operations but resulted in years of floundering in the power vacuum that emerged with the decapitation of the state. Analogies to post-WWII Germany and Afghanistan proved to be unhelpful when applied to Iraq, and the US military's stubborn focus on maneuver operations detracted from its preparedness for the lawlessness, corruption, and hostilities it encountered after Saddam's fall. Additionally, Coalition leaders and members of the intelligence community – who seemed unable or unwilling to reach back to lessons from Vietnam – persisted in using inappropriate paradigms to understand and explain the hostile activities they observed.

The consequent U.S. failure to have an appreciation for Iraq's complex social and political history blinded the Coalition effort to how they were failing to meet Iraqi expectations for restoration of order and establishment of a more democratic government. The Coalition likewise ignored or overlooked reprisal attacks that engendered a vicious circle of violence and civil war, a quagmire the Coalition unwittingly exacerbated by blunders in detention operations. Strategies crafted in that context were myopically focused on defeating armed groups, creating capable, non-sectarian Iraqi security forces, and creating the conditions for elections. The rising unpopularity of the war in the US simultaneously eroded policymakers' original goal of establishing a democratic partner in the war on terror. Although the 'Surge' strategy of 2007 was successful in stemming the tide of violence and improving the legitimacy of the Iraqi government, the US government was unwilling to commit further resources to build on those gains, reneging on its commitment to the Iraqi people in the process. In the end, the US settled for the thinnest veneer of democracy, which proved to be a mask for yet another authoritarian government in Iraq.

The Iraq war also revealed some important limitations of the US in the areas of nation-building and creating security forces from the ground up. Contrary to military expectations, the State Department had neither the resources nor the mandate for nation-building and, while Foreign Service Officers assisted with those efforts in Iraq, their primary focus was negotiating agreements at higher levels of government. No other government agency existed to fulfil the intense demands of constructing state institutions at the local level, and military leaders were left to fill that gap as best they could on top of a lengthy list of other equally demanding responsibilities.

Just as telling was the revelation that the US military did not have the institutional capability or resources to develop host-nation security forces on a large scale, a mission that had traditionally been reserved for small numbers of special operations forces conducting Foreign Internal Defense missions. Despite those institutional limitations, recruiting, training, and enabling capable Iraqi security forces became a cornerstone of every strategy and military campaign US leaders in Iraq constructed between 2003 and 2009. Building capable Iraqi leaders, institutions, and security forces would have been a tall order in most circumstances, but achieving those outcomes while combating an insurgency and a civil war was a nearly impossible task.

By 2009, US political leaders and the American people had lost their appetite for a costly and unpopular war that had yielded few tangible gains in US national security. When US forces left Iraq in 2011, the US had expended nearly USD 1 trillion and had 4,484 personnel killed in action, with over 32,000 wounded. The Iraqi people suffered over 100,000 casualties in the same time frame.[113] The authoritarian government in Iraq under Maliki would eventually become more entrenched and beholden to Iranian interests, which seeded resentment in the Sunni population, laying the foundation for the Islamic State in Iraq (ISIS). Far from aiding US national security interests, Iraq became a haven for the same terrorist activities the invasion was designed to eradicate.

Notes

1. This article has been heavily influenced by the thoughts, writings, and sources of the Chief of Staff of the Army's Operation IRAQI FREEDOM Study Group, (hereafter referred to as the OIF SG), of which LTC Jeanne Godfroy had the privilege of being an active part of from 2013–2015. As such, it is critical that the authors reference the unpublished (at this time) manuscript produced by that effort, *The U.S. Army in the Iraq War, Volumes I and II*, and its other authors, COL Joel Rayburn, COL James Powell, COL Frank Sobchak, and COL Matthew Morton. This article reflects their thoughts, writings, and conclusions, and some of the primary sources cited here are actually taken from the manuscript as it stood in December 2016. Those sources include primary source interviews and documents, now declassified, that will be released once the manuscripts are published.
2. Woodward and Balz, "10 Days in September," http://www.washingtonpost.com/wp-dyn/politics/news/postseries/tendaysinseptember/.
3. Primary and secondary sources used by the OIF SG, Volume I, Chapters 2–3.
4. Woods, *Saddam and Terrorism*, 13–25; other primary source documents held by the OIF SG, Volume I, Chapters 2–3, 7.
5. Primary source interviews held by the OIF SG, Volume I, Chapter 2; for additional influences on these planning assumptions, see Gordon and Trainor, *Cobra II*, 37–42.
6. Primary source interviews held by the OIF SG, Volume I, Chapter 3; Gordon and Trainor, *Cobra II*, 110–117.
7. Primary source documents and interviews held by the OIF SG, Volume I, Chapters 2–3. Fontenot, Degen and Tohn, *On Point*, 73–74.
8. Primary source interviews held by the OIF SG, Volume 1, Chapter 2; Gordon and Trainor, *Cobra II*, 162–3.

9. Primary source interviews and documents held by the OIF SG, Volume I, Chapter 3; Fontenot, Degen and Tohn, *On Point*, 69.
10. Benshael, "Mission Not Accomplished," 68–77, 79–81; Primary source interviews and sources held by the OIF SG, Volume I, Chapter 3.
11. Gordon and Trainor, *Cobra II*, 165–6.
12. Primary source interviews held by the OIF SG, Volume I, Chapter 3.
13. Godfroy, "The Other Side of the 'COIN'," 1–4. This paper was produced with the support and resources of the OIF SG.
14. Ibid., 1.
15. Briscoe et al., *All Roads Lead to Baghdad* 448–69, 482–7, 497; and Fontenot, Degen, and Tohn, *On Point*, 161, 312–20, 332, 336, 343–5; primary source interviews and secondary sources from the OIF SG, Volume I, Chapter 4.
16. Primary source interview held by the OIF SG, Volume I, Chapter 4.
17. Cline, "The Other Symbol of George W. Bush's Legacy," https://www.usnews.com/news/blogs/press-past/2013/05/01/the-other-symbol-of-george-w-bushs-legacy. It is worthwhile to note – as this article does – that President Bush did not actually declare victory or sanction the 'Mission Accomplished' sign that was displayed. He declared the end to major combat operations in Iraq, a defacto declaration of victory.
18. Godfroy, "The Other Side of the COIN," 4.
19. Woods, *Saddam and Terrorism*, 4, 8, 13–25.
20. Godfroy, "The Other Side of the COIN," 12; Secondary source document used by the OIF SG, Volume I, Chapter 7. This particular secondary source contained analysis from numerous interviews with and intelligence on the Sunni tribes maintained by units in Anbar through 2007.
21. Godfroy, "The Other Side of the COIN," 13–14; Ware, "Inside Iran's Secret War for Iraq," 26–31; and Felter and Fishman, *Iranian Strategy in Iraq*, https://ctc.usma.edu/v2/wp-content/uploads/2010/06/Iranian-Strategy-in-Iraq.pdf.
22. Godfroy, "The Other Side of the COIN," 11–14.
23. International Crisis Group, "Iraq's Civil War, the Sadrists and the Surge," https://www.crisisgroup.org/middle-east-north-africa/gulf-and-arabian-peninsula/iraq/iraq-s-civil-war-sadrists-and-surge, accessed 15 September 2013; and Felter and Fishman, *Iranian Strategy in Iraq*.
24. Rayburn, *Iraq After America*, 178–9.
25. Primary source interviews and documents held by the OIF SG, Volume I.
26. Godfroy, "The Other Side of the COIN," 4–11; Primary source interviews and documents held by the OIF SG, Volume I, Chapters 7, 9.
27. Ibid.
28. Primary source material provided to the OIF SG from personnel at U.S. Central Command.
29. Primary source interviews held by the OIF SG, Volume I.
30. Ibid.
31. Hull, "Civil Warriors," http://dataspace.princeton.edu/jspui/handle/88435/dsp01z603qx56m.
32. Godfroy, "The Other Side of the COIN," 5–6; Materials held by the OIF SG, Volume I, Chapter 7.
33. Wright and Reese, *On Point II*, 208.
34. Report, James Schlesinger to Secretary of Defense Donald Rumsfeld, Independent Panel to Review DoD Detention Operations, 24 August 2004, 11–12, http://www.antiwar.com/rep2/abughraibrpt.pdf; Transcript, "Brian Whitman, W. Hayes Parks,

and Ambassador Richard Prosper," http://www.defense.gov/Transcript/Transcript.aspx?TranscriptID=2281; Bybee, "Standards of Conduct,", 2340-2340A; and Sanchez, *Wiser in Battle*, 151–4; primary source materials held by the OIF SG, Volume I.

35. Sanchez, *Wiser in Battle*, 151–4; Coalition Provisional Authority Ministry of Justice, *Prisons and Detention Centers in Iraq*; and Philip Gourevitch and Errol Morris, *Standard Operating Procedure*, 174–5. "Court Martial in Iraq," *60 min II*, 24.
36. McChrystal, *My Share of the Task*,172; and Ricks, *Fiasco*, 290.
37. Group Primary source interviews and sources held by the OIF SG for *The U.S. Army in Operation Iraqi Freedom*, Volume I; Bernard et al., *The Battle Behind the Wire*, 52–3.
38. Bernard et al., *The Battle Behind the Wire*, 57; Primary source materials held by the OIF SG for Volume I.
39. Interview, William Knarr, Lieutenant Colonel David Graves, and Mary Hawkins, Institute for Defense Analyses with Mullah Nadhim al Jabouri, 12 and 14 February 2011; Chulov, "ISIS: The Inside Story."
40. President George Bush, 26 February 2003, in the "National Strategy for Victory in Iraq," http://graphics8.nytimes.com/packages/pdf/international/20051130military-text.pdf, accessed 31 August 2017.
41. General Franks, *American Soldier*, 268, 329; primary source documents and interviews held by the OIF SG, Volume I, Chapter 2.
42. Primary sources and primary source interviews held by the OIF SG, Volume I, Chapters 7, 9.
43. Declassified documents held by the Institute for Defense Analysis and the OIF SG; Iraq Survey Group, Final Report and Key Findings, online, accessed 10 September 2017, https://www.globalsecurity.org/wmd/library/report/2004/isg-final-report/ .
44. Coalition Provisional Authority (CPA) Strategic Plan, 1 August 2003, Department of Defense FOIA library at http://www.dod.mil/pubs/foia/Reading_Room/CPA_ORHA/; Bremer, *My Year In Iraq*, 114–16.
45. Primary source documents held by the OIF SG, Volume I, Chapter 5.
46. Discussion, COL Joel Rayburn with a senior United States diplomat, April 2015, Washington DC; International Crisis Group, "Governing Iraq," 5; Allawi, *The Occupation of Iraq*, 191.
47. Primary source interviews and sources held by the OIF SG, Volume I, Chapters 6, 8.
48. Executive Summaries and meeting notes from the Commander of Multi-Security Transition-Command-Iraq, June-July 2004.
49. Ibid.
50. Garamone, "Predictability, Stability at Heart of Rotation Policy," http://archive.defense.gov/news/newsarticle.aspx?id=27835; U.S. Department of Defense Update on Force Rotation Plan, 26 November 2003, accessed 21 October 2015, http://www.defense-aerospace.com/article-view/release/29439/us-sends-extra-troops-tp-iraq-(nov.-27).html; and Primary source materials from the OIF SG, Volume I; Papers of General Casey, "Papers.".
51. Gordon and Trainor, *The Endgame*, 69–73.
52. Ibid.
53. Jaffe and Cloud, *The Fourth Star*, 128; and Gordon and Trainor, *The Endgame*, 67–73; Primary source interviews and sources held by the OIF SG, Volume I.

54. United Nations, "United Nations Security Council Resolution 1546," http://unscr/com/en/resolutions/doc/1546, accessed 8 August 2017; and Chadrasekaran, "U.S. Hands Authority to Iraq Two Days Early," http://www.washingtonpost.com/wp-dyn/content/article/2007/06/22/AR2007062200847.html.
55. Wright and Reese, *On Point II*, 157–177.
56. Primary source documents from MNF-I held by OIF SG, Volume I, Chapter 15.
57. Wright and Reese, *On Point II*, 177–180, 344–358.
58. MNSTC-I Executive Summaries and meeting notes for LTG David Petraeus, June-July 2004; Trip reports for LTG David Petraeus, August-October 2004.
59. MNSTC-I Executive Summaries and meeting notes for LTG David Petraeus, August 2004- January 2005.
60. MNSTC-I trip reports and meetings with Iraqi officials, January – March 2005.
61. Gordon and Trainor, *The Endgame*, 149–50.
62. Bailey, Iron, and Strachan, eds., *British Generals in Blair's Wars*, 80; Fisher, "Italy to Withdraw Its Troops from Iraq," http://www.nytimes.com/2006/01/20/world/europe/italy-to-withdraw-its-troops-from-iraq-by-end-of-the-year.html?mcubz=0; Full Text: British Broadcasting Company, "Al Qaeda Madrid Claim,"http://news.bbc.co.uk/2/hi/europe/3509556.stm; and United Kingdom, "Testimony of Sir Richard Sannatt to UK Government's Inquiry," http://www.iraqinquiry.org.uk/media/55290/20100728am-dannatt.pdf.
63. Gordon and Trainor, *The Endgame*, 144–146; MNSTC-I Executive summaries and trip reports, October 2004- May 2005.
64. Jaffe and Cloud, *The Fourth Star*, 200–210; and Gordon and Trainor, *The Endgame*, 138, 180–190.
65. Gordon and Trainor, *The Endgame*, 183–200; Cloud and Jaffe, *The Fourth Star*, 221; and Rayburn, *Iraq After America*, 23, 25–6.
66. Malkasian, "Counterinsurgency in Iraq," 301–302.
67. Baker and Hamilton, *The Iraq Study Group Report*, 3.
68. Ibid., 7–10, 38, 59, 61, 71.
69. Gordon and Trainor, *The Endgame*, 285–6, 302–8.
70. Kagan, "Enforcing the Law," http://www.understandingwar.org/iraq-project/publications/reports, 1–5, 7–8.
71. Sky, *The Unraveling*, location 2830.
72. Collins, "Military Innovation in War," 170, http://dataspace.princeton.edu/jspui/handle/88435/dsp01br86b3727; and Mansoor, "Army," 75–86.
73. Kagan, "Enforcing the Law," 1–5, 7–8.
74. Cloud and Jaffe, *The Fourth Star*, 255–58; and Gordon and Trainor, *The Endgame*, 348–66.
75. MNSTC-I notes; Gordon and Trainor, *The Endgame*, 335–41.
76. International Crisis Group, "Iraq After the Surge I," 11–13. https://www.crisisgroup.org/middle-east-north-africa/gulf-and-arabian-peninsula/iraq/iraq-after-surge-i-new-sunni-landscape.
77. Gordon and Trainor, *The Endgame*, 248–53.
78. Ibid., 406.
79. CPT Hull, "Iraq," 2–3.
80. Sky, *The Unraveling*, locations 3141–3147, 3199–3211, 3365–3385, 3471–3493.
81. International Crisis Group, "Iraq's Civil War, The Sadrists, and the Surge," 3–4, https://www.crisisgroup.org/middle-east-north-africa/gulf-and-arabian-peninsula/iraq/iraq-s-civil-war-sadrists-and-surge.
82. Rayburn, *Iraq After America*, 30–36.

83. Partlow and Abramowitz, "Iraq Passes Bill on Ba'athists,' http://www.washingtonpost.com/wp-dyn/content/article/2008/01/12/AR2008011201122.html; Rubin, "Ending Impasse, Iraq Parliament Backs Measures," http://www.nytimes.com/2008/02/14/world/middleeast/14iraq.html?mcubz=0; and Goode, "Iraq Passes Election Law, Setting Aside Kirkuk Status," http://www.nytimes.com/2008/09/25/world/middleeast/25iraq.html?mcubz=0.
84. Rayburn, *Iraq After America*, 44; and Biddle, Friedman and Shapiro, "Testing the Surge," 18–22.
85. Author was present for that meeting.
86. Biddle, Friedman, and Shapiro, "Testing the Surge," 18–22.
87. Sky, *The Unraveling*, kindle edition, locations 4466–4472, 5722–5748, 5864–5870.
88. Obama, "Responsibly Ending the War in Iraq," https://obamawhitehouse.archives.gov/blog/2009/02/27/responsibly-ending-war-iraq.
89. Gordon and Trainor, *The Endgame*, 529.
90. Hull, "Civil Warriors," 99.
91. Sky, *The Unraveling*, kindle edition, locations 5068–5094, 5126–5132, 5246–5303; Sullivan, "Maliki's Authoritarian Regime," 6–7, 28–37, http://www.understandingwar.org/sites/default/files/Malikis-Authoritarian-Regime-Web.pdf; and Rayburn, *Iraq After America*, 42–58. 60–64.
92. Adams, "2009 Command Report," 27–28. Dagher, "2 Blasts Expose Security Flaws in Heart of Iraq," ; Myers and Santora, "Election Date Set in Iraq as Bombs Kill Scores," ; and Williams, "Bombings in Iraq, Deadliest Since 2007."
93. Rayburn, *Iraq After America,* 4–6.
94. Collins, "Military Innovation in War," 140–151.
95. Ibid.,154–176.
96. Barry, "Iraq's Real WMD."
97. Smith, "Improvised Explosive Devices in Iraq, 2003–2009," 14.
98. U.S. Congress, House, Committee on Armed Services, Subcommittee on Oversight and Investigations, *The Joint Improvised Explosive Device Defeat Organization*, 23; and Phillips, "The Birth of the Combined Explosives Exploitation Cell."
99. Collins, "Military Innovation in War," 262–264.
100. Atkinson, "Left of Boom"; Zorpette, "Countering IEDs," http://spectrum.ieee.org/aerospace/military/countering-ieds; and Higginbotham, "U.S. Military Learns to Fight Deadliest Weapons," http://www.wired.com/magazine/2010/07/ff_roadside_bombs/all/.
101. McGriff, *Mine Resistant Ambush Protected Vehicles*, 15–16; and Guardia, *US Army and Marine Corps MRAPS*, 40.
102. Vanden Brook, "Armored Vehicles Cut IED Deaths"; and Carter and Gilmore, "Running the Numbers on MRAPs."
103. Collins, "Military Innovation in War," 65.
104. McChrystal, *My Share of the Task*, 186.
105. McChrystal, "It Takes a Network."
106. Priest and Arkin, *Top Secret America*, 253–255; and Colonel Liam Collins, interviews with former JIATF directors and deputy directors.
107. Collins, "Military Innovation in War," 345–347.
108. Flynn, Juergens, and Cantrell, "Employing SOF ISR Best Practices," 57.
109. Faint and Harris, "F3EAD."
110. COL Liam Collins, interview with Michael Flynn; McChrystal, *My Share of the Task*, 145.

111. McChrystal, *My Share of the Task*, 224–234.
112. Collins, "Military Innovation in War," 406–407.
113. Datablog, "War in Iraq," https://www.theguardian.com/news/datablog/2011/dec/15/war-iraq-costs-us-lives, accessed 15 July 2017; and Belasco, "The Cost of Iraq," http://www.au.af.mil/au/awc/awcgate/crs/rl1331110.pdf.

Disclosure statement

No potential conflict of interest was reported by the authors.

Bibliography

Adams, Bianka J. "2009 Command Report: Multi-National Division Baghdad, 1st U.S. Cavalry Division." 19 (2010): 27–28.
Allawi, Ayad. *The Occupation of Iraq: Winning the War, Losing the Peace*. New Haven: Yale University Press, 2008.
Atkinson, Rick. 2007. "Left of Boom Parts 2 and 3." *The Washington Post*, October 1–2.
Bailey, Jonathan, Richard Iron, and Hew Strachan. *British Generals in Blair's Wars*. Surrey, UK: Ashgate Publishing, 2013.
Baker, James A., III, and Lee H. Hamilton. *The Iraq Study Group Report*. New York: Vintage Books, 2006.
Barry, John. 2006. "Iraq's Real WMD." *Newsweek*, March 26.
Belasco, Amy. 2010. "The Cost of Iraq, Afghanistan, and Other Global War on Terror Operations since 9/11." Congressional Research Service, September 2. http://www.au.af.mil/au/awc/awcgate/crs/rl1331110.pdf.
Benshael, Nora. "Mission Not Accomplished." In *War in Iraq: Planning and Execution*, edited by Thomas G. Mankhen and Thomas A. Kearney, 130–133. New York: Routledge, 2008.
Bernard, Cheryl, Edward O'Connell, Cathryn Quantic Thurston, Andres Villamizar and Elvira N Loredo. *The Battle behind the Wire: U.S. Prisoner and Detainee Operations from World War II to Iraq*. Santa Monica, CA: Rand Corporation, 2011.
Biddle, Stephen, Jeffrey A. Friedman and Jacob N. Shapiro. "Testing the Surge: Why did Violence decline in Iraq in 2007?" *International Security* 37, no. 1 (2012): 18–22.
Bremer, Paul L. *My Year in Iraq: The Struggle to Build a Future of Hope*. New York: Simon and Schuster, 2006.
Briscoe, Charles, Kenneth Finlayson, and Robert W. Jones. *All Roads Lead to Baghdad: Army Special Operations Forces in Iraq*. Fort Bragg, NC: U.S. Special Operations Command History Office, 2007.
British Broadcasting Company. "Al Qaeda Madrid Claim." Accessed March 14, 2004. http://news.bbc.co.uk/2/hi/europe/3509556.stm
Bybee, J.S. 2002. "Standards of Conduct for Interrogation under 18 U.S.C., 2340-2340A." *Memorandum by Asst Attorney General for Alberto R. Gonzalez, Council to the President*, August 1.
Carter, Ashton B., and J. Michael Gilmore. 2012. "Running the Numbers on MRAPs: Reliable Data Proves the Vehicles are Worth the Money." *Foreign Affairs*, October 9.
Casey, George W. 2003. "Papers." No. 44-45. National Defense University. September–October.

Chadrasekaran, Rajiv. 2004. "U.S. Hands Authority to Iraq Two Days Early." *The Washington Post*, June 29. http://www.washingtonpost.com/wp-dyn/content/article/2007/06/22/AR2007062200847.html

Chulov, Martin. 2014. "ISIS: The Inside Story." *The Guardian*, December 11.

Cline, Seth. 2013. "The Other Symbol of George W. Bush's Legacy." *US News and World Report*, May 1. https://www.usnews.com/news/blogs/press-past/2013/05/01/the-other-symbol-of-george-w-bushs-legacy

Coalition Provisional Authority. 2003. "Strategic Plan." Department of Defense FOIA library, August 1. http://www.dod.mil/pubs/foia/Reading_Room/CPA_ORHA/

Coalition Provisional Authority Ministry of Justice. *Prisons and Detention Centers in Iraq: An Assessment and Recommendations for Prisons in a Free Society*. Baghdad, 2003.

Collins, Liam. *Interview with Michael Flynn*. New Haven, CT: Yale University, 2013

Collins, Liam. "Military Innovation in War: The Criticality of the Senior Military Leader." Doctoral Dissertation, Princeton University, 2015. http://dataspace.princeton.edu/jspui/handle/88435/dsp01br86b3727

"Court Martial in Iraq: U.S. Army Soldiers Face Court Martial for Actions at Baghdad's Abu Ghraib Prison." 2004. *60 Minutes II*. CBS TV, April 28.

Dagher, Sam. 2009. "2 Blasts Expose Security Flaws in Heart of Iraq." *The New York Times*, August 19.

Datablog. 2011. "War in Iraq: The Cost in American Lives an Dollars." *The Guardian*, December 15. https://www.theguardian.com/news/datablog/2011/dec/15/war-iraq-costs-us-lives

Faint, Charles, and Michael Harris. 2012. "F3EAD: Ops/Intel Fusion 'Feeds' the SOF Targeting Process." *Small Wars Journal*, January 31.

Felter, Joseph, and Brian Fishman. 2008. *Iranian Strategy in Iraq: Politics and Other Means*. West Point, NY: Combatting Terrorism Center, October 13. https://ctc.usma.edu/v2/wp-content/uploads/2010/06/Iranian-Strategy-in-Iraq.pdf.

Fisher, Ian. 2006. "Italy to Withdraw Its Troops from Iraq by End of the Year." *New York Times*, January 20. http://www.nytimes.com/2006/01/20/world/europe/italy-to-withdraw-its-troops-from-iraq-by-end-of-the-year.html?mcubz=0

Flynn, Michael T., Rich Juergens, and Thomas L. Cantrell. "Employing SOF ISR Best Practices." *Joint Force* 50, no. 3 (2008): 56–61.

Fontenot, Colonel Gregory, Lieutenant Colonel E.J. Degen, and Lieutenant Colonel David Tohn. *On Point: The United States Army in Operation IRAQI FREEDOM*. Fort Leavenworth, KS: Combat Studies Institute Press, 2004.

Franks, Tommy. *American Soldier*. New York: HarperCollins, 2004.

Garamone, Jim. 2003. "Predictability, Stability at Heart of Rotation Policy." U.S. Department of Defense, November 6. http://archive.defense.gov/news/newsarticle.aspx?id=27835

Godfroy, Jeanne MAJ. "The Other Side of the COIN—Foundations of the Iraq Insurgency." Paper presented at the Society of Military History. Conference, Montgomery, Alabama, April 2015.

Goode, Erica. 2008. "Iraq Passes Election Law, Setting Aside Kirkuk Status." *The New York Times*, September 24. http://www.nytimes.com/2008/09/25/world/middleeast/25iraq.html?mcubz=0

Gordon, Michael, and Bernard E. Trainor. *The Endgame: The inside Story of the Struggle for Iraq*. New York: Vintage Books, 2013.

Gordon, Michael, and Bernard Trainor. *Cobra II: The inside Story of the Invasion and Occupation of Iraq*. New York: Vintage Books, 2007.

Gourevitch, Philip, and Errol Morris. *Standard Operating Procedure: A War Story*. New York: The Penguin Press, 2008.

Guardia, Mike. *US Army and Marine Corps MRAPS*. New York: Osprey Publishing, 2013.

Higginbotham, Adam. 2010. "U.S. Military Learns to Fight Deadliest Weapons." *Wired*, July 28. http://www.wired.com/magazine/2010/07/ff_roadside_bombs/all/

Hull, Jeanne. "Iraq: Strategic Reconciliation, Targeting, and Key Leader Engagement." Letort Paper Series. Carlisle, PA: Strategic Studies Institute, 2009.

Hull, Jeanne. "Civil Warriors: A Study on Military Intervention and Key Leader Engagement." Doctoral dissertation, Princeton University, April 2014. http://dataspace.princeton.edu/jspui/handle/88435/dsp01z603qx56m

International Crisis Group. "Iraq after the Surge I: The New Sunni Landscape." Accessed April 30, 2008. https://www.crisisgroup.org/middle-east-north-africa/gulf-and-arabian-peninsula/iraq/iraq-after-surge-i-new-sunni-landscape

International Crisis Group. "Iraq's Civil War, the Sadrists and the Surge." Accessed February 7, 2008. https://www.crisisgroup.org/middle-east-north-africa/gulf-and-arabian-peninsula/iraq/iraq-s-civil-war-sadrists-and-surge

International Crisis Group. "Governing Iraq." Middle East Report. No. 17. Washington, DC, August 25, 2003.

Iraq Survey Group. "Final Report and Key Findings." 2004. https://www.globalsecurity.org/wmd/library/report/2004/isg-final-report/

Jaffe, Greg, and David Cloud. *The Fourth Star: Four Generals and the Epic Struggle for the Future of the United States Army*. New York: Penguin Random House, 2010.

Jeanne, Hull. *Executive Summaries and Meeting Notes from the Commander of Multi-Security Transition-Command-Iraq*. June 2004–June 2005.

Kagan, Kimberly. "Enforcing the Law: The Baghdad Security Plan Begins." Institute for the Study of War. http://www.understandingwar.org/iraq-project/publications/reports

Knarr, William, Lieutenant Colonel David Graves and Mary Hawkins. *Interview with Mullah Nadhim Al Jabouri*. Institute for Defense Analysis, February 12 and 14, 2011.

Malkasian, Carter. "Counterinsurgency in Iraq: May 2003-January 2010." In *Counterinsurgency in Modern Warfare*, edited by Daniel Marston and Carter Malkasian, 289–301. Oxford: Osprey Publishing, 2010.

Mansoor, Peter. "Army." In *Understanding Counterinsurgency Doctrine, Operations, and Challenges*, edited by Thomas Rid and Thomas Kearney, 75–86. New York: Routledge, 2010.

McChrystal, Stanley A. "It Takes a Network." *Foreign Policy*, March-April 2011

McChrystal, Stanley A. *My Share of the Task*. New York: Penguin Group Inc, 2013.

McGriff, Roy, III. *Mine Resistant Ambush Protected Vehicles*. Quantico, VA: Marine Corps University, 2004. May 3.

Myers, Steven Lee, and Marc Santora. "Election Date Set in Iraq as Bombs Kill Scores." *The New York Times*, December 8, 2009.

National Security Council. "National Strategy for Victory in Iraq." November 2005. http://graphics8.nytimes.com/packages/pdf/international/20051130military-text.pdf

Obama, Barack. "Responsibly Ending the War in Iraq." Remarks– as Prepared for Delivery: Whitehouse.gov, February 27, 2009. https://obamawhitehouse.archives.gov/blog/2009/02/27/responsibly-ending-war-iraq

Partlow, Joshua, and Michael Abramowitz. "Iraq Passes Bill on Ba'athists." *The Washington Post*, January 13, 2008. http://www.washingtonpost.com/wp-dyn/content/article/2008/01/12/AR2008011201122.html

Phillips, Stephen. "The Birth of the Combined Explosives Exploitation Cell." *Small Wars Journal* (2008). https://smallwarsjournal.com/jrnl/art/the-birth-of-the-combined-explosives-exploitation-cell

Priest, Dana, and William M. Arkin. *Top Secret America: The Rise of the New American Security State*. New York: Little, Brown, and Company, 2011.

Rayburn, Joel. *Iraq After America: Strongmen, Sectarians, Resistance*. Stanford, CA: Hoover Institute Press, 2014.

Rayburn, Joel. *Discussion with a Senior United States Diplomat*. April 2015.

Rayburn, Joel, Frank Sobchak, Jeanne Godfroy, Matthew Morton, James Powell, and Matthew Zais. *The U.S. Army in the Iraq War, Volume I*. Strategic Studies Institute in Carlisle, PA, 2019.

Ricks, Thomas E. *Fiasco: The American Military Adventure in Iraq, 2003 to 2005*. New York: The Penguin Press, 2006.

Rubin, Alissa J. 2008. "Ending Impasse, Iraq Parliament Backs Measures." *The New York Times*, February 14. http://www.nytimes.com/2008/02/14/world/middleeast/14iraq.html?mcubz=0

Rudd, Gordon. *Reconstructing Iraq: Regime Change, Jay Garner, and the ORHA Story*. Lawrence: University Press of Kansas, 2011.

Sanchez, Ricardo. *Wiser in Battle: A Soldier's Story*. New York: HarperCollins, 2008.

Schlesinger, James. "Report to Secretary of Defense Donald Rumsfeld, Independent Panel to Review DoD Detention Operations." August 24, 2004. http://www.antiwar.com/rep2/abughraibrpt.pdf

Sky, Emma. *The Unraveling: High Hopes and Missed Opportunities in Iraq*. New York: PublicAffairs, 2015, Kindle Edition.

Smith, Andrew. "Improvised Explosive Devices in Iraq, 2003-2009: A Case of Operational Surprise and Institutional Response." Letort Papers. Carlisle, PA: Strategic Studies Institute, April 2011.

Sullivan, Marisa. "Maliki's Authoritarian Regime." Washington, DC: Institute for the Study of War, April 2013. http://www.understandingwar.org/sites/default/files/Malikis-Authoritarian-Regime-Web.pdf

Transcript. 2003. "Brian Whitman, W. Hayes Parks, and Ambassador Richard Prosper." Briefing on the Geneva Convention, EPWs, and War Crimes, April 7. http://www.defense.gov/Transcript/Transcript.aspx?TranscriptID=2281

United Kingdom. "Testimony of Sir Richard Sannatt to UK Government's Inquiry." http://www.iraqinquiry.org.uk/media/55290/20100728am-dannatt.pdf

United Nations. 2004. "United Nations Security Council Resolution 1546." June 8. http://unscr/com/en/resolutions/doc/1546

United States Congress, House, Committee on Armed Services, Subcommittee on Oversight and Investigations. *The Joint Improvised Explosive Device Defeat Organization: DoD's Fight against IEDs Today and Tomorrow*. November 2008.

United States Department of Defense. "Update on Force Rotation Plan." November 26, 2003. http://www.defense-aerospace.com/article-view/release/29439/us-sends-extra-troops-tp-iraq-(nov.-27).html

Vanden Brook, Tom. "Armored Vehicles Cut IED Deaths." *USA Today*, September 7, 2010.

Ware, Michael. "Inside Iran's Secret War for Iraq." *Time Magazine* 166, no. 8 (2005): 26–31.

Williams, Timothy. 2009. "Bombings in Iraq, Deadliest since 2007, Raise Security Issue." *The New York Times*, December 8.

Woods, Kevin M. *Saddam and Terrorism*. Alexandria, VA: Institute for Defense Analysis, 2007.

Woodward, Bob, and Dan Balz. 2002. "10 Days in September: At Camp David, Advice and Dissent." *The Washington Post*, January 31. Accessed 17 July 2017. http://www.washingtonpost.com/wp-dyn/politics/news/postseries/tendaysinseptember/

Wright, Donald P., and Colonel Timothy R. Reese. *On Point II: Transition to the New Campaign: The United States Army in Operation IRAQI FREEDOM, May 2003-January 2005*. Fort Leavenworth, KS: Combat Studies Institute Press, 2008.

Zorpette, Glen. 2008. "Countering IEDs." IEEE Spectrum, August 29. http://spectrum.ieee.org/aerospace/military/countering-ieds

7 The American way of war in Africa
The case of Niger

LTC Joseph Guido

ABSTRACT
Increasing attention paid to US casualties in far-flung places such as Tongo Tongo, Niger, and headlines claiming 'secret wars' have fueled discussion about American military's involvement in Africa. Though the continent has been a part of the American way of war since the beginnings of the US – consider the early combat actions of US Marines in Tripoli –, current African conflicts are challenging our understanding of war and approaches to winning it. This article examines the ways America seeks to achieve its ends in Africa with a particular focus upon the last 10 years of US counter-terrorism and stability operations in Niger and the Sahel Region. The author proposes unifying American, Allied, and partner efforts through a strategy of Active Containment.

Introduction

From the Halls of Montezuma
To the shores of Tripoli…

The United States Marines' Hymn

'The shores of Tripoli' above refers to the First Barbary War of 1805, when Lieutenant Presley O'Bannon and his US Marines hoisted the American flag at the Battle of Derne. In fact, it was also in North Africa during World War II that we find the dawn of the US Army we recognize today.[1] More recently, 'Black Hawk Down'[2] and the 1990s US experience in Somalia charted an American policy direction, which lasted for more than two decades in most of the developing world, specifically Africa, a policy that sought to minimize 'boots on ground' and avoid American casualties while limiting intrastate violence and containing conflict. And it was in Sudan that Osama Bin Laden created al-Qaeda in the early 1990s. As we look through time and space, it becomes clear just how considerably Africa has influenced the American military experience and, consequently, our way of war.

Ironically, today as was the case on the Barbary shores, US military posture and presence in Africa has been reactive and lacked unity of effort. US military operations – though frequently successful – are not accomplishing strategic and policy objectives. In the words of one contemporary strategist and war theorist, 'To move from a way of battle to a way of war, Americans must devote more time and energy to thinking about the capabilities needed to turn combat successes into favorable strategic outcomes'.[3] We must look beyond military operations and seek favorable strategic effects.

American ends: policy and strategy in Africa

> This Western mode of attack has been so successful... any potential adversary has now discovered the futility of an open, deliberate struggle on a Western-style battlefield against the firepower and discipline of Western infantry.[4]
>
> Victor Davis Hanson

American grand strategy as concerns Africa has since the Cold War been driven largely by the idea of 'Selective Engagement',[5] a reincarnation of the 'Flexible Response' of the Kennedy administration. Relevant policy architecture focuses upon American 'vital interests' and potential military responses, creating military options with no inherent need for understanding the causes of conflict or belligerents. The Selective Engagement paradigm, which focuses upon themes such as vitality, rationality, and proportionality, affects how the US frames and consequently responds to threats.

Vitality concerns the classification of a particular event or object as a vital interest. But what makes some objectives vital and others not? Who determines what is vital and non-vital? The calculation of vital versus non-vital interests is implied in Selective Engagement and its Cold War predecessor, Flexible Response, but the explicit methodology remains undetermined. It is virtually impossible to identify and distinguish vital interests from other interests, no arithmetic to classify, delineate, or arrange options and alternatives. In Africa, the enormous size, incredible diversity, dizzying complexity, and forceful dynamism of the continent have further frustrated American efforts to rationalize vital interests in order to craft a coherent African strategy. Selective Engagement has substituted process for strategy; in other words, the American way of war approaches violence in Africa as a series of discrete conflicts to be systematically engaged based upon a process of rational cost-benefit analysis. Predetermined problem-solving structures and paradigms distance military 'courses of action' from reality, separating operational success and strategic impact.

African wars also challenge American calculations of proportionality. How can proportional military force be used when conditions are evolving too quickly for calculation, and reliable and timely information is absent? What would have been a proportional response in the case of 'Black Hawk Down'? Or, the Rwandan genocide? Minimally, the US would need a military force available to be deployed on a short notice while understanding the situation sufficiently to provide coherent rules of engagement and a chain of command in remote and austere locations. What forces would the US bring to bear? What would be their mission, under whose command; and how is success defined? These are just some of the challenging questions that theater and operational commanders must answer to successfully employ military power as a component of national power. The architect of Flexible Response, US Secretary of Defense Robert McNamara, ironically noted much later, in a series of interviews after the 9/11 attacks, that 'rationality will not save us'.[6] McNamara concluded in retrospect after his experience with the Vietnam War that leaders never have adequate information and should seek to better understand the limitations of American military power, broaden decision-makers' understanding of the elements of strategic formulation, and search for greater empathy instead of more data when making decisions.[7]

It hardly surprises then, despite much effort and research, that the realities of African wars are confounding many of the existing approaches and theories of conflict. Kenneth Waltz's neorealism classic, *Theory of International Politics*,[8] for example, views actors and power through the current international states system but does not comment on the role of non-state actors in war. James D. Fearon has concluded that wars are fought by rational actors because of private information, incentives to misrepresent, commitment problems, and issue indivisibilities.[9] Both of these neo-realist or rationalist explanations of war require an operative conceptualization largely dependent upon the role of the modern state.[10] Yet, the nation-state and the international states system are largely irrelevant in discussions about conflicts in Somalia, the Central African Republic, or the Congo.[11] R. Harrison Wagner postulates, 'Wars do not require states; they merely require armies. Armies can exist without states, and states are among the possible by-products of conflicts among armies'.[12] He continues, 'A world of independent states is not a world without global order – the independent states are the global order'.[13] D. Scott Bennett and Allan C. Stam call for a more holistic approach to explain war by using multiple theories or analytical lenses: 'A large number of factors suggested by multiple perspectives appear to influence the relative risk of international conflict, thereby simultaneously giving support to many conjectures of international conflict'.[14] These competing theories offer few useful insights for practitioners to better understand and win wars and conflicts in Africa.

On the other hand, The Centre for the Study of Civil War at the International Peace Research Institute in Oslo has analyzed conflict since World War II and concluded it is decreasing globally. The Institute has noted that intrastate conflict has dominated since World War II and proportionally continues to increase even as conflicts globally have declined in number.[15] However, conflicts in Africa and Asia have been increasing, concentrated largely in Central Africa and a band stretching from Central Asia to Southeast Asia. This trend is supported by other research, which indicates more than 60 percent of Demobilization, Disarmament, and Reintegration (DDR) programs have been in Africa.[16] Finally, this research notes that the number of casualties from conflict is decreasing, a trend attributed to the decrease in number of total conflicts, specifically the decreasing number of interstate conflicts, and a 'concentration of intrastate conflicts in non-democratic and very poor countries with limited military capabilities'.[17]

These conclusions about war in Africa offer more questions than answers. For example, this analysis does not account for civilian casualties. It is often said that one civilian died for every eight combatants in World War I; but, by the 1990s, eight civilians died for every combatant killed. Recent research suggests that such statistics may be overstated as civilian casualty statistics are difficult to verify.[18] Regardless, non-combatant casualties are ignored by studies from the Centre for the Study of Civil War despite their importance as a measure in intrastate conflicts. The specific delineations of intrastate war are not provided by the researchers, so it is difficult to know the boundaries of conflict included in their study. This necessarily raises further questions regarding the quantitative analysis of conflict: what is war and who are combatants? What are the boundaries of intrastate conflict: civil war, rebellions, terrorism, insurgencies, narcotics and weapons trafficking, organized crime, or cyber warfare? The very definition and history of the nation-state is in question[19] and the challenge looms: 'How can the US Army be more effective in complex operating environments?'[20]

This 'Volatile, Uncertain, Complex, and Ambiguous' nature of African conflict – while certainly not unique to the continent – has created a de facto American policy to choose military interventions while minimizing costs, particularly American casualties. The current AFRICOM Commanding General, Thomas D. Waldhauser, energized American media during his nomination hearing before the Senate Armed Services Committee when asked if the US had a strategy in Libya or was 'just acting in an ad hoc fashion'. Responding to Senator John McCain, General Waldhauser observed that he was 'not aware of any overall grand strategy at this point'. Unsurprisingly, this generated headlines such as, 'Even AFRICOM's Own

Commander Admits Its Strategy Is Not Working',[21] and, 'Marine General Says U.S. Lacks "Overall Grand Strategy" for Libya'.[22]

Though not necessarily accurate, the exchange highlights the fundamental reality that the appropriate military strategy must spring from an overall policy for Africa. The 2012 (White House) *US Strategy for Sub-Saharan Africa*[23] outlines six overarching actions to guide US regional goals: counter al-Qaeda and other terrorist groups; advance regional security cooperation and security sector reforms; prevent transnational criminal threats; prevent a conflict; mitigate mass atrocities and hold perpetrators accountable; and support initiatives to promote peace and security. These goals are intended to contribute to security, prevent major wars, and enable access to markets while maintaining economic stability and promoting democracy. However, these goals are really a statement of American values instead of a coherent policy or calculated and integrated strategy for Africa. For example, is security cooperation and security sector reform an end unto itself or the ways, or even means, to achieve an end? Are supporting institutions an objective, or is the peace and security resulting from those institutions the objective? Is there a difference? In conclusion, a 'Marshall Plan' for Africa remains elusive.[24]

This absence cannot be attributed solely to a lack of initiative in Washington. A good slice of the problem, as implied above, results from the fundamental characteristics of Africa itself: size, diversity, complexity, and dynamism. Africa is the second largest continent with a complex social and ethnic diversity, more than 2,200 languages in 54 different countries. Africans, almost a billion people, the vast majority under the age of 18, have myriad and competing challenges, which defy simple explanation. There is, therefore, no single or simple US policy and strategy toward Africa but instead an ever-changing and competing kaleidoscope of different policies, objectives, authorities, and strategies to speak to the divergent American political, social, economic, and military objectives in Africa. Yet, it cannot be overstated that American military planners and strategists must have policy guidance to formulate their own constructions: planners must have a sense of direction. Strategy is that direction.

An insightful feature of the *US Strategy for Sub-Saharan Africa* is that the US seeks to work by, with, and through African partners.[25] This indirect approach to peace and security underscores the collective and cooperative security aspects of how America formulates strategy: we are better off together. The US does not seek to fight alone, and the American military creates 'Theater Campaign Plans' to calculate the various ways to use available means in order to achieve military objectives.[26] The American Theater for Africa – the Geographic Combatant Command, US Africa Command (AFRICOM) – articulates in its campaign plan that the main, or decisive, effort is 'building African Partner capacity and strengthening partnerships...through Security Force Assistance'.[27] Security Force Assistance (SFA) and Security Cooperation (SC), therefore, comprise the principle ways and means, which AFRICOM uses to achieve strategic objectives and are central to the logic of the existing American military strategy in Africa.[28]

American ways and means: security force assistance and security cooperation

> If you want to go fast, go alone.
> If you want to go far, go together.
>
> African Proverb

American ways and means in Africa today are a direct result of the 9/11 attacks, when subsequently the US found itself simultaneously engaged in combat operations and state-building activities to deny terrorist sanctuary in Iraq and Afghanistan while monitoring threats in volatile areas ranging from Pakistan to the Philippines, Somalia to West Africa. Security cooperation was regarded as the principal tool to deny sanctuary to violent extremist organizations,[29] promote regional security, and improve regional stability. Security cooperation activities were promoted as a cost-efficient, policy-effective alternative to military interventions in the context of scrutinized budgets, a history of failed interventions in the developing world, and popular sensitivity to direct military interventions.

The *2006 Quadrennial Defense Review* (QDR) outlined the use of security cooperation in 'the new strategic environment' as a proactive measure to address international security threats while preventing fragile states from becoming failed states.[30] The *QDR Execution Roadmap*,[31] in turn, posited that the right security cooperation activities with the right partners would 'reduce the drivers of instability, prevent terrorist attacks or disrupt their networks' as well as 'deny sanctuary to terrorists' and 'separate terrorists from host populations'[32] The US Department of Defense published the *Military Contribution to Cooperative Security Joint Operating Concept* in 2008, which argued that 'cooperative security' should increase partner capacity[33] to meet internal and external threats, as well as enhance their ability to manage security institutions in order to promote good governance, maintain influence and access, and deny terrorist sanctuary.[34]

The Obama administration incorporated many of these concepts in its 2010 *National Security Strategy* (NSS)[35] and the 2011 *National Military Strategy* (NMS).[36] The 2010 NSS sought to 'undertake long-term sustained efforts to strengthen the capacity of security forces to guarantee internal stability, defend against internal threats, and promote regional security and respect human rights and the rule of law'[37] by building 'capacity for responsible governance and security through development and security force assistance'.[38] This NSS harnessed the logic of the preventative hypothesis[39] and cooperative security to conclude that 'preventing wars is as important as wining them, and far less costly'.[40]

Nevertheless, security cooperation activities under these new authorities fell short of commanders' needs and expectations. The time required for implementation, complex fiscal authorities, and legalistic language of the Foreign Assistance Act often made security cooperation authorities, processes, and activities unintelligible to commanders and their staffs.[41] In response, DoD shifted attention from 'Security Cooperation' to 'Cooperative Security' to 'Building Partner Capacity' and finally to 'Security Force Assistance', moving from traditional security cooperation activities under the Foreign Assistance Act toward combat operations under operational command authorities.

The US established the Joint Center for International Security Force Assistance (JCISFA) in response to this shift. In 2008, JSCIFA published the *Commander's Handbook for Security Force Assistance*, which defined security force assistance as 'unified action to generate, employ, and sustain local, host nation or regional security forces in support of a legitimate authority'.[42] The creation of a new literature on security force assistance has largely overlooked the existing literature on Foreign Internal Defense as well as security cooperation. For example, JCISFA concepts of conflict prevention, internal stability promotion, and institutional development[43] are nearly identical to foreign internal defense activities, which encompass the 'participation by civilian and military agencies of a government in any of the action programs taken by another government or other designated organization, to free and protect its society from subversion, lawlessness, insurgency, terrorism, and other threats to their security'.[44]

This divergence of terminology and doctrine has resulted in miscommunication and confusion in ways and means.[45] For example, a RAND study on security force assistance never once mentioned security cooperation.[46] A 2011 Congressional Research Service report on Building Partner Capacity acknowledged that security force assistance 'is an overarching concept that ties into several interests of Congress, including security assistance, security cooperation, foreign military financing, foreign military sales, foreign affairs, foreign aid, overseas contingency operations, and legislative authorities associated with training foreign forces'[47] without clarifying the relationship between security force assistance and security cooperation. A 2012 Government Accounting Office report concluded that the 'Department of Defense needs to do more to define its intent for security force assistance, including the level of effort that geographic combatant commands should devote to security force assistance, how that intent should influence the geographic combatant command's strategies, and what additional actions are required by the geographic combatant commands to plan for and conduct security force assistance beyond their existing security cooperation efforts'.⁴⁸ Those recommendations largely still need to be implemented.

In response, the Joint Staff in 2013 published Joint Doctrine Note 1–13 'Security Force Assistance', which states, 'Security Cooperation has an overarching functional relationship with Security Assistance, Foreign Internal Defense, Security Force Assistance, Security Sector Reform, and all Department of Defense security related activities', and, 'Security Force Assistance is a subset of Security Cooperation activities that develop and sustain Host Nation Foreign Security Forces capabilities'.⁴⁹ Meanwhile, the US Army in 2013 published *FM 3–22 Army Support to Security Cooperation*, which defines security force assistance as security cooperation activities but focuses not on concepts but upon tactical tasks to Army units at or below the Brigade level.⁵⁰

JCISFA has also issued a series of publications to articulate the roles and responsibilities of security force assistance which ultimately define SFA by what it does.⁵¹ Unfortunately, 'Security Force Assistance is synonymous with train, advise, and assist. Security Force Assistance and Partner Capacity Building are virtually identical',⁵² while 'no single proponent integrates all activities to provide a common overarching direction and can justify/prioritize requirements for engagement and stability operations'.⁵³ This underscores the need for greater clarity about roles and responsibilities, unity of effort, and unity of command in security cooperation and security assistance activities. The four US Army Special Operations personnel who were killed in Niger on 4 October 2017 were conducting security force assistance operations. This event has significantly raised the profile of the ways the American military seeks to promote peace and security in Africa as well as the strategic objectives they were working toward.

It is also appropriate to note what any perusal of the aforementioned materials produces: the realization that the focus remains upon tactics at the near-complete expense of what business might term human capital development. In fact, absent institutional capacity and capability, all external input will likely be poorly absorbed and recommendations have not progressed to the logical conclusion to develop professional and, in particular, strategic thinking. The numbers of officers attending appropriate higher-level Joint Professional Military Education as well as technical schools remains inadequate in the extreme, particularly when compared to Chinese efforts in this area.

Niger: application of American ends, ways, and means in conflict

> Porous borders, ample routes for smuggling drugs, weapons, explosives, and other contraband, and corruptible police and security forces make Sub-

Saharan Africa an inviting operational environment for international criminals, drug traffickers, and terrorists. Major Sub-Saharan cities with extensive commercial, financial, and sea and air transportation links to Europe, the Middle East, and Asia are hubs for international criminal activity.[54]

US government document

Niger, one of several countries in the region known as the Sahel, is a sub-Saharan country larger than the state of Texas and possessing the world's second largest uranium reserves. Its population of around 20 million is characterized by ethnic divisions and an agrarian economy. Despite its vast mineral resources, a recent United Nations (UN) index ranks Niger second to last globally in development.[55] As the principal supplier of uranium to France – a nuclear and energy exporting country – Niger is clearly important to France's strategic interests and also becoming increasingly important for other international actors. It is playing a larger role in American military operations in the region,[56] and China has purchased significant resource rights in order to fuel its nuclear ambitions.[57]

The most recent civil war in Niger, often referred to as the Tuareg rebellion of 2007–2009, concluded with a cease-fire signed in May 2009, followed by a peace-agreement later that month.[58] This conflict had erupted in early 2007, when various groups of dissatisfied Tuaregs formed the *Mouvement* Des *Nigériens pour La justice* (MNJ) and launched an insurgency against the government. The MNJ rebellion was motivated by ethnic differences between the nomadic Tuareg of northern Niger and the more sedentary southern people who form the majority of the government, by unequal resource distribution, and by the failure of the state to redress Tuareg grievances such as land rights and access to public health. It was, though, only the most recent conflict in a pattern of rebellions and ethnic tensions.[59] Several countries in the region, such as Mali, have similar socioeconomic security concerns.[60]

Michael T. Klare has argued that conflict over valuable resources will dominate 'the landscape of conflict' in the future. He projects, 'Africa – especially sub-Saharan Africa – will acquire increased strategic importance in the decades ahead, because it houses vast reserves of untapped resources that are sought by a growing array of local and international interests'.[61] This conclusion is consistent with many studies of conflict in West Africa and Niger specifically. For example, Muna A. Abdalla explores the social consequences of underdevelopment in the Sahel. The Tuareg, who bear the cost of industrialized mineral extraction such as disease and environmental degradation, realize few of its benefits. Abdalla concludes that the inequitable distribution of resources has and will continue to lead to conflict in the Sahel as well as attracting significant external attention for resources, particularly from China.[62] Wenran Jeng suggests that 'a major structural requirement for China's continuous industrialization drive is to enter Africa aggressively and extract energy and resources'.⁶³ For China today already consumes more than 30 percent of the world's coal and iron, 27 percent of the steel, 40 percent of the cement, 20 percent of the copper, 19 percent of the aluminum, and 10 percent of the world's energy – and those numbers are rising.⁶⁴

China's transactional approach to politics in conflict areas contributes to instability, because it promotes authoritarian regimes even as it exacerbates existing grievances. Beijing understands that energy 'in areas other than oil is critical for the future evolution of China's energy sector'⁶⁵ and consequently is investing in nuclear energy. It is estimated that China will be the world's largest producer of nuclear energy by 2050.⁶⁶ Niger offers an important supply of uranium for this growing energy demand, where prices are rising due to global demand for energy.⁶⁷ As such, China has been working 'hard to improve its ties with Africa, with frequent visits by top Chinese leaders, increasing the Chinese profile in United Nations peacekeeping operations, launching a cooperation forum, and offering debt reduction to African states'.⁶⁸ Yet, Chinese leaders consistently ignore human rights issues, democracy shortcomings, international law compliance, and even nuclear proliferation. For example, China's Deputy Foreign Minister Zhou Wenzhong remarked in summer 2004, 'Business is business. We try to separate politics from business'.⁶⁹

Beijing's grand strategic component for Africa, neo-mercantilism, may separate politics from business, but China does not separate its national policy and strategy from revenue generation. To the contrary, they are equal.⁷⁰ All organs of Chinese government and business are aligned to maximize resource extraction in Africa. The Chinese consider the social, economic, political, and conflict costs resulting from their programs as largely inconsequential in light of their demand for raw materials.

While natural resources provide incredible growth and development opportunities for countries such as Niger, the 'resource curse' posits an imbalance between resource wealth and government policies that can lead to poor-quality growth, inefficient markets, inequality, and often conflict.⁷¹ The resource curse has even became a focal point in foreign policy debates in the US.⁷² Yvan Guichaoua has noted that government corruption in uranium revenue was 'instrumental in perpetuating elites' survival through a process of "extraversion"; that is, a deliberate relation of dependency on the outside, and specifically, on the former colonial tutor [France]'.⁷³ France supports an authoritarian regime to protect its access to uranium – a mineral which has been of great strategic importance to France's national defense and energy security. That China may substitute for France is of little matter to the equation on the African end. To Guichaoua, the Niger government must increasingly resort to authoritarian measures to ensure untrammeled foreign access to natural resources. In turn, the only way for affected members of the populace to seek redress of grievances is increasingly through extrajudicial and militarized pathways.

After one year of armed rebellion by the MNJ, then-Niger President Mamadou Tandja ordered the Niger military, *Forces Armées Nigériennes* (FAN), to implement a military solution to the conflict. The FAN offensive, launched in the summer 2008, crushed the MNJ fighters and effectively ended the rebellion, setting the conditions for the peace accords in late spring 2009.[74] The peace strategy in Niger intended to establish legal processes to account for crimes committed during the rebellion, amnesty for leaders and groups who agreed to the settlement, and restoration efforts whereby the government would rebuild and develop infrastructure in the affected areas as well as incorporate rebel elements into the government. Several key metrics for stability and continued peace seemed at hand: a clear military victory by government forces over rebel militias, international support for non-violent solutions to the conflict, a transitional justice program which promised reparations and increased development, and a DDR process.

Unfortunately, the state has poorly implemented critical components of the program.[75] The DDR process included surrendering weapons, the formal disbanding of militia or paramilitary elements, incorporation of MNJ fighters into the FAN, and increased representation of Tuareg elements in the Niger government.[76] While calm and peace followed the armistice, the recent increase of violence calls into question long-term prospects for peace as demonstrated by the history of Tuareg recidivism throughout the 20th Century. These elements offer opportunities to terrorists which they are willing to exploit – as American casualties testify.

The US has used security cooperation instruments such as the Trans-Sahara Counter Terrorism Partnership[77] to provide security training and equipment to the FAN in order to deter terrorists as part of what one authority termed 'a pretty broad mission with the government of Niger in order to increase their capability to stand alone and to prosecute violent extremists'.[78] These efforts have also included intelligence and logistical support to US allies such as France in their efforts against violent extremists in the region.[79] Niger is the second-ranking beneficiary of such American assistance in Africa, receiving more than USD 165 million in counterterrorism equipment and training since 2006, not including other State Department initiatives to build the capacity of Niger's security forces for counterterrorism and peacekeeping under Peacekeeping Operations (PKO) funding. As part of this military assistance and support, Niger hosts one of the largest numbers of American military forces in Africa, the White House reporting in 2017 that 645 US military personnel were stationed in the country to support counterterrorism operations with African partners.[80] This figure, according to the US Department of Defense, grew to more than 800 Americans operating in Niger as part of the French-led counterterrorism efforts in the Sahel.[81]

Distinctions between international criminals, drug traffickers, rebels, and terrorists are subtle albeit significant. Mohamed Mokeddem, in his study about al-Qaeda in the Lands of the Islamic Maghrib (AQIM), concludes that the transnational terrorism elements in North and West Africa are little more than criminal and smuggling networks which thrive in the 'ungoverned spaces' of the Saharan desert.[82] Wolfram Lacher has argued that criminal and terrorism problems in the Sahel and Sahara regions result from the lack of effective government institutions to include police and security forces.[83] Both these studies, however, conflate terrorists with criminals. In reality, all terrorists are criminals, but not all criminals are terrorists. These are important distinctions.

Any plan for long-term stability and peace in Niger will need to address the underlying causes of the MNJ rebellion, including the inadequate distribution of mineral wealth from the Tuareg region, underrepresentation of Tuaregs in the Niger government, health concerns and land use conflicts resulting from large-scale mining operations, and lack of justice and law enforcement in northern Niger. As one Niger official involved in implementing the peace agreement has expressed:

> The causes of the revolt remain. The enforcement of the peace agreement is far from successful... [but] If we were always to get into the details regarding the government's attitude... [and] if we were always to get involved in recriminations, [then] there would be no peace. You must at one point stop to give peace a chance and reconstruct bit by bit because it is a long-term endeavor.[84]

The Niger government's poor implementation of post-conflict transitional justice mechanisms and inability to finance multi-billion-dollar development projects seriously questions the government's willingness, interest, and capability to promote peace in its ethnic minority regions.[85] Paul Collier has concluded that real and measurable differences in conflict areas can be made even though there are large requirements for positive development and sustainable growth in post-conflict economies.[86] The time-span required for external support is closer to decades than years, and any stabilization forces will have long-term horizons. The most significant development gains can be made in the first 5 years after conflict so the development emphasis in Niger should come sooner rather than later. These projects must be a component of a comprehensive security and stability effort which places a premium on accountability and justice. State institutions, particularly justice and law enforcement, with a focus upon anti-corruption, must, therefore, feature prominently in any development planning.

Michael W. Doyle and Nicholas Sambanis have posited that the risk of returning to conflict in places like Niger is high. More than half the conflicts they studied are initially peacefully resolved but later see a return to violence.[87] Other studies have demonstrated that international support often departs conflict areas too soon after implementation, leaving a security vacuum.[88] Furthermore, African military or security forces are generally inadequately trained and equipped to handle the complex and interrelated tasks involved with peacekeeping operations.[89] This evidence indicates that external support will be essential to maintain peace, and countries such as China should include supporting these aspects in their development projects.

Uncomfortably for the American military establishment, this places the partner and not the US at the center of the strategy. American success is partner success. Additionally, Africa offers unique opportunities for the US to work with key allies, such as France, as well as competitors, such as China. Although the Chinese claim they are focused solely on business and not politics in Africa, they will likely realize that peace and stability are inseparable from the ability to engage in business. Africa offers opportunities to support allies, support democratic and open market governments, and engage great power competitors.

American soldiers are in Niger as part of the large and continuing commitment of the US to build partner nation capacity, but this begs the question of consistency between available means, strategic objectives, and American values. The nonlinearity and indirectness of security cooperation have uneven results and are exceptionally difficult to quantify.[90] Failing to address underlying causes, festering grievances, and the social elements of conflict will likely undermine American security assistance efforts and decouple American military ends from prescribed ways and means. Not helpful is that US military doctrine has become increasingly doctrinaire without becoming more useful. Finally, conventional wisdom and political science studies or models are unlikely to aid crafting and implementing a strategy for Africa. These studies provide context and insight into what has worked or not, but they cannot predict the future – even more so, in a region as large, diverse, complex, and dynamic as Africa.

A way forward: active containment

There are no American 'secret wars' in Africa. Building Partner Capacity and increasing the capabilities of African states to police themselves is the principal American modus operandi in Africa today. Building Partner Capacity is an instrument derived from ideas underpinning the strategy of Selective Engagement and the imperative to seek reductionist and simplistic decision-making methodologies focused on processes rather than outcomes.[91] Selective Engagement is not a strategy but rather its absence, implying one can pick the right war with the right enemy at the right time in the right place and bring to bear the right kind of combat power to win. Its predecessor, Flexible Response, compelled the Johnson administration to gradually escalate the American war in Southeast Asia in the 1960s without clear objectives or aims. Wars cannot be 'selected', and we will find ourselves in combat at times and places we did not expect. As Leon Trotsky remarked: 'You may not be interested in war, but war is interested in you'.[92]

General Waldhauser's response to Senator McCain was succinctly profound. A 'Grand Strategy' for Libya, and by extension Africa – a misuse of the term 'grand strategy' but useful nonetheless – would require a coherent foreign policy from which to craft military strategy. War is politics, the political, and the application of policy through other means. War and military strategy are subordinate to grand strategy, and American military objectives in Africa need to fit into a wider vision of American grand strategy. This requires an understanding of both war and Africa.

Wars are fought by people. To understand and be successful in war, one must understand the war as well as the people fighting it. Regional knowledge and understanding are inseparable from successful strategy. Additionally, ends and means are never equivalent but must connect: successful partner nation capacity building is not strategy; decapitation strikes on terrorist leaders are not strategy. Those are simply ways and means to achieve ends. Unfortunately, the signature elements of the American Way of War in Africa are the conflation of means with ends and the confusion of strategic locations with strategic partners.

The ends for American military strategy for Africa must be to contain terrorist groups wanting to harm the US, which operate and seek sanctuary in Africa, in order to contribute to achieving the end-state, a viable system at peace within and without. This enemy is cunning, ruthless, and adaptive. The recent attacks upon US Special Forces in Niger and the UN 'Super Camp' at Timbuktu in Mali are testaments to the enemy's ability to adapt to changing circumstances. Terrorist groups such as AQIM are likely running short of cash, effectively targeted by MINUSMA and French forces, and probably frustrated that the world has not yet seen the light that their version of Islam is supposed to illuminate. This pressure has forced these sanctuary-seeking terrorists to make friends, win influence, and build allies with local groups to include rebels like the former MNJ in Niger. The Tongo Tongo ambush was a product of the enemy digging itself deeper into the social structures and fabric of the Sahara for protection and survival as well as teaming up with other militants and violent groups for strength.

A loose alliance of local rebel groups and terrorists successfully operating in the Sahel has been seen before. In early 2012, Malian Rebels including the National Movement for the Liberation of Azawad (MNLA), AQIM terrorists, and fighters trained and equipped from Libya overwhelmed the state security forces of Mali. Several attacks in that period, notably at the Battle of Kidal, where a combined force of these groups demonstrated a level of sophistication far beyond what AQIM alone achieved previously. These attacks were characterized by combined arms operations, complex tactics, and operational planning. The ambush of American Special Forces in Niger and the later deliberate attack upon UN forces at the Timbuktu Super Camp are indicators of a dangerous new alliance between rebels, smugglers, and terrorists. These groups can only achieve this level of sophistication from mutually supporting alliances as they are normally in competition with one another for local support and resources.

It was such an alliance which rapidly broke down in Mali in 2012. By the time Timbuktu was seized by French forces in 2012, AQIM leaders Mokhtar bel Mokhtar and Abu Zaid were fighting one another and with their MNLA allies and Libyan-trained friends. What had been a sophisticated and orchestrated attack against Malian security forces by these violent organizations in Kidal degenerated into internecine warfare. The point is that these groups do not make good neighbors, friends, partners, or allies; this is an important and critical weakness.

Sun Tzu, in *The Art of War*, proposes strategy based upon the principle of economy of force; that is, to preserve one's strength while allowing, enabling, and seeking opportunities to weaken your enemies' strengths and exploit their weaknesses. Master Sun summarizes that economy of force is achieved by attacking the enemy's alliances instead of his forces. The question thus is how to enable the enemy to defeat himself. In the case of northern Mali and Niger, this means we should enable and encourage the enemy to gain ground; let the enemy try to manage 'uncontrollable border areas'. We should very closely monitor the enemy to assist our allies and partners to contain him in the large space he seeks to occupy. Let the enemy respond to the population's reaction to his violence and depravity. The force of such a strategy is to focus our efforts and energy to fragment the enemy instead of attacking him directly. Defeat the enemy by allowing him to defeat himself. Endless decapitation strikes or building partner capacity to attack the enemy only enables the enemy to further reconstitute, reinvigorate, or reincarnate themselves.

We cannot deny all terrorist sanctuary in all places at all times. Similarly, occasional successes in some places are not victory for terrorists in all places for all time. The US should seek to fight and win an economy of force effort based upon the maximization of enemy suffering and minimization of friendly costs incurred. This is a bold divergence from the endless delusory battles invoked by the rubric of Selective Engagement. It advances instead a strategy of Active Containment with an objective to contain terrorists and enemy forces or prevent attacks against Americans and the US, using economy of force efforts across a very broad geographic area. The goal of Active Containment is to allow the enemy forces to fail of their own accord, and later to reestablish a recognizable form of governance. Winning peace is more important than winning battles. This strategy is active, because while 'containing' may seem passive, it will require a great deal of effort and continued investment which should not be underestimated or undervalued. Economy of force should not be confused with the absence of force.

Notes

1. Atkinson, *An Army at Dawn*.
2. Bowden, *Black Hawk Down*. 'Black Hawk Down' also refers to the movie of the same name co-produced and directed by Ridley Scott, from a screenplay by Ken Nolan and released in December, 2001. It dealt with the 'Black Hawk Down' incident, referred to at the time as the Battle of Mogadishu and codenamed Operation Gothic Serpent.
3. Echevarria, *An American Way of War or Way of Battle?* 2. Accessed November 1, 2017. http://www.au.af.mil/au/awc/awcgate/ssi/ssi_op_ed_jan04.pdf
4. Hanson, *The Western Way of War*, 13.
5. Art, "Geopolitics Updated,'", 79–113.
6. Morris, "The Fog of War."
7. McNamara and VanDeMark, *In Retrospect*.
8. Waltz, *Theory of International Politics* (reprint, 2010).
9. Fearon, "Rationalist Explanations for War',", 380–2.
10. Spruyt, "The Origins, Development, and Possible Decline of the Modern State'," 127–149.
11. Kissinger, *World Order*.
12. Wagner, *War and the State* (reprint, 2010), x.
13. Ibid.
14. Bennett and Stam, *The Behavioral Origins of War*, 203.
15. Buhaug et al., *Global Trends in Armed Conflict*. Accessed November 15, 2017. https://www.hbuhaug.com/wp-content/uploads/2014/02/Global-Trends_final.pdf
16. Muggah and Krause, "Closing the Gap between Peace Operations and Post-Conflict Insecurity."',
17. Buhaug et al., *Global Trends in Armed Conflict*.
18. Seybolt, Aronson, and Fischhoff, *Counting Civilian Casualties*.
19. Spruyt, "The Origins, Development, and Possible Decline of the Modern State."
20. *Key Strategic Issues List 2017–2018* (Carlisle Barrack, PA: Strategic Studies Institute, 7 August 2017). Accessed May 1, 2018. https://ssi.armywarcollege.edu/pubs/display.cfm?pubID=1363
21. Turse, "Even AFRICOM's Own Commander Admits its Strategy is Not Working.'," Accessed October 15, 2017. https://www.thenation.com/article/even-africoms-own-commander-admits-their-strategy-is-not-working/
22. McIntyre, "Marine General Says U.S. Lacks "Overall Grand Strategy" for Libya.'," Accessed October 15, 2017. http://www.washingtonexaminer.com/marine-general-says-us-lacks-overall-grand-strategy-for-libya/article/2594496
23. The White House, *U.S. Strategy toward Sub-Saharan Africa*.
24. Which foreign aid, it must be noted, was but only one component of the overarching and far-reaching concept. See Kennan, *An American Life*, 276–336.
25. 'By, through, with' is a term of art used by the U.S. military that connotes working closely with partners to achieve military objectives instead of American-led or unilateral military operations. Linda Robinson, 'SOF's Evolving Role: Warfare "By, With, and Through" Local Forces' (Santa Monica,

CA: RAND, 9 May 2017), Accessed November 15, 2017. https://www.rand.org/blog/2017/05/sofs-evolving-role-warfare-by-with-and-through-local.html
26. Office of the Deputy Assistant Secretary of Defense for Plans, *Theater Campaign Planning Planner's Handbook Version 1.0*, 1–2.
27. United States Africa Command, *Theater Campaign Plan 2000–16'*, 18.
28. United States Africa Command, *United States Africa Command 2017 Posture Statement*. Accessed November 17, 2017. https://www.google.it/url?sa=t&rct=j&q=&esrc=s&source=web&cd=1&cad=rja&uact=8&ved=0ahUKEwiSr4yJrcrXAhWRDuwKHZGZCl4QFggmMAA&url=https%3A%2F%2Fwww.africom.mil%2Fmedia-room%2Fdocument%2F28720%2Fafricom-2017-posture-satement&usg=AOvVaw3wIZ0BmMJEY6A4u2O04H58
29. For discussion, Guido, *Terrorist Sanctuary in the Sahara*. Accessed November 1, 2017. https://ssi.armywarcollege.edu/pubs/people.cfm?authorID=2066
30. Department of Defense, *Quadrennial Defense Review Report*, 13.
31. Department of Defense, *QDR Execution Roadmap*.
32. Ibid., 5–6.
33. 'Increase partner capacity' is now referred to as 'Building Partner Capacity' or BPC. McInnis and Lucas *What is "Building Partner Capacity?"*; and Livingston, *Building the Capacity of Partner States Through Security Force Assistance*.
34. Department of Defense, *Military Contribution to Cooperative Security Joint Operating Concept Version 1.0*, 5–20.
35. The White House, *National Security Strategy*.
36. Department of Defense, *The National Military Strategy of the United States of America 2011*.
37. The White House, *National Security Strategy*, 27.
38. Ibid., 21.
39. McNerney et al., *Assessing Security Cooperation as a Preventative Tool*. This study examines the Preventative Hypothesis, concluding (p.2), 'Although the preventative hypothesis is now an important assumption for U.S. defense policy, data in support of the hypothesis have not been examined thoroughly, and the logic underlying it remains unspecified. For instance, various DoD sources offer different interpretations, many of which are not fully described in terms of casual linkages, essential assumptions, and necessary conditions'.
40. Department of Defense, *The National Military Strategy of the United States of America 2011*, 7.
41. Paul et al., *What Works Best When Building Partner Capacity and Under What Circumstances?*; and Paul et al., *What Works Best When Building Partner Capacity in Challenging Contexts?*
42. Joint Center for International Security Force Assistance, *Commander's Handbook for Security Force Assistance*, 1.
43. 'Institutional Development' from FID is now being referred to by BPC and SFA as 'DIB', Defense Institution Building. McNerney et al., *Defense Institution Building in Africa*.
44. United States Joint Staff, *Joint Publication 3–22*, ix.
45. For example, the Department of Defense published DoD Instruction Number 5000.68 on 27 October 2010 'Security Force Assistance', to establish policy and assign 'responsibilities regarding the preparation of DoD personnel and operational planning for, as well as the conduct of, SFA'. However, this instruction includes no references or mention of SC other than the Joint Doctrine Note definition of SFA 'as a subset of DoD overall SC initiatives', 2.

46. Kelly, Bensahel, and Oliker, *Security Force Assistance in Afghanistan*.
47. Livingston, *Building the Capacity of Partner States Through Security Force Assistance*, 1.
48. Government Accountability Office, "Security Force Assistance," 29.
49. United States Joint Staff, *Joint Doctrine Note 1–13*, I-2.
50. Headquarters, Department of the Army, *FM 3–22*, 1–1. Unfortunately, FM 3–22 does not provide much help in understanding SC and SFA, defining SC as 'all Department of Defense interactions with foreign defense establishments to build defense relationships... a common Service function that supports combatant commands.... [and] a key element of global and theater shaping operations', 1–1.
51. Joint Center for International Security Force Assistance, *Security Force Assistance Planner's Guide*; also, Joint Center for International Security Force Assistance, *SFA Assessment Handbook*; and Joint Center for International Security Force Assistance, *Operational Force Development*.
52. Wuestner, *Building Partner Capacity / Security Force Assistance*, 30.
53. Ibid., 31–32.
54. United States Government, *International Crime Assessment*. Accessed December 2, 2013. https://www.cia.gov/library/readingroom/docs/DOC_0000497956.pdf
55. United Nations, *United Nations Human Development Report 2016'*. Accessed October 15, 2017. http://hdr.undp.org/sites/default/files/HDR2016_EN_Overview_Web.pdf
56. Schmitt, "Drones in Niger Reflect New U.S. Tack on Terrorism.'," Accessed March 5, 2017. http://www.nytimes.com/2013/07/11/world/africa/drones-in-niger-reflect-new-us-approach-in-terror-fight.html
57. Armin Rosen, "One Uranium Mine in Niger Says a Lot About China's Huge Nuclear-power Ambitions.'," Accessed October 21, 2017. http://www.businessinsider.com/niger-uranium-mine-and-nuclear-china-2015-10?IR=T
58. UPI, "Cease-Fire Truce Reached with Niger Rebels'," Accessed November 14, 2013. http://www.upi.com/Top_News/2009/05/15/Cease-fire-truce-reached-with-Niger-rebels/UPI-99581242403588/
59. Saint Girons, *Les Rébellions Touarègues* [The Tuareg Rebellions].
60. Boilley, *Les Touaregs Kel Adagh, Dépendances Et Révoltes*: Du *Soudan Français Au Mali Contemporain* [The Kel Adagh Tuaregs, dependencies and revolts: From French West Africa to contemporary Mali].
61. Klare, *Resource Wars*, 217.
62. Abdalla, "Understanding of the Natural Resource Conflict Dynamics." Accessed October 21, 2013. https://issafrica.s3.amazonaws.com/site/uploads/Paper194.pdf
63. Jian, "Fuelling the Dragon,'", 588. Accessed April 4, 2018. http://gpepsm.paginas.ufsc.br/files/2014/11/JIANG-2009.-China%E2%80%99s-Rise-and-Its-Energy-and-Resources-Extraction-in-Africa.pdf
64. Ibid., 587.
65. Daojiong, "China's Energy Security,'", 186.
66. Zweig and Jianhai, "China's Global Hunt for Energy'," 36.
67. World Nuclear Association, "Uranium Markets'." Accessed December 12, 2013. http://world-nuclear.org/info/Nuclear-Fuel-Cycle/Uranium-Resources/Uranium-Markets/
68. Daojiong, "China's Energy Security,'", 185.
69. Zweig and Jianhai, "China's Global Hunt for Energy'," 32.

70. French, *China's Second Continent*.
71. Shaffer and Ziyadov, *Beyond the Resource Curse*.
72. United States Congress, "Senate Committee on Foreign Relations, Subcommittee on African Affairs."
73. Thorp et al., *The Developmental Challenges of Mining and Oil*, 132.
74. UPI, "Cease-Fire Truce Reached with Niger Rebels."
75. It is significant to note that the comments about the peace accords are circumstantial as the actual document is not publicly available for review.
76. See note 74 above.
77. The Trans-Sahara Counterterrorism Partnership (TSCTP) was stablished in 2005 with partners including Algeria, Burkina Faso, Cameroon, Chad, Mali, Mauritania, Morocco, Niger, Nigeria, Senegal, and Tunisia. TSCTP is a multi-faceted, multi-year strategy implemented jointly by the Department of State, the U.S. Agency for International Development, and the Department of Defense to assist partners in West and North Africa increase their immediate and long-term capabilities to address terrorist threats and prevent the spread of violent extremism. Key areas the U.S. provides support under TSCTP include: enabling and enhancing the capacity of North and West African militaries and law enforcement to conduct counterterrorism operations; integrating the ability of North and West African militaries and law enforcement, as well as other supporting partners, to operate regionally and collaboratively on counterterrorism efforts; enhancing border security capacity to monitor, restrain, and interdict terrorist movements; strengthening the rule of law, including access to justice and law enforcement's ability to detect, disrupt, respond to, investigate, and prosecute terrorist activity; monitoring and countering the financing of terrorism (such as that related to kidnapping for ransom); and reducing the limited sympathy and support among communities for violent extremism. See United States Department of State, 'Programs and Initiatives.', Accessed November 2, 2017 https://www.state.gov/j/ct/programs/
78. Lewis and Bavier, citing Lieutenant General Kenneth McKenzie in "U.S. Deaths in Niger Highlight Africa Military Mission Creep.'," Accessed October 10, 2017. https://www.reuters.com/article/us-usa-africa-security/u-s-deaths-in-niger-highlight-africa-military-mission-creep-idUSKBN1CB2J1
79. Arieff, *Attack on U.S. Soldiers in Niger*. Accessed October 22, 2017. https://fas.org/sgp/crs/natsec/IN10797.pdf
80. Ibid.
81. Associated Press, "Top U.S. General.'", Accessed November 11, 2017. http://www.businessinsider.com/ap-top-us-general-families-americans-deserve-answers-on-niger-2017-10?IR=T
82. Mokeddem, *Al Qaida Au Maghreb Islamique: Contrebande Au Nom* de *L'islam* [Al Qaida in the Islamic Maghreb: Smuggling in the name of Islam].
83. Lacher, "Organized Crime and Terrorism in the Sahel.'," Accessed December 2, 2013. https://www.files.ethz.ch/isn/126014/2011C01_lac_ks.pdf
84. IRIN, "Can Niger Offer Mali Lessons on the Tuareg?" Accessed November 14, 2013. http://www.irinnews.org/report/97823/can-niger-offer-mali-lessons-tuareg
85. Thurston, "With Eye on Mali, Niger Adopts New Strategy for Tuareg North'," Accessed November 15, 2013. http://www.worldpoliticsreview.com/articles/12400/with-eye-on-mali-niger-adopts-new-strategy-for-tuareg-north

86. Collier and Hoeffler, "Aid, Policy, and Growth in Post-Conflict Countries"; and Collier, "Post-Conflict Economic Recovery."', http://graduateinstitute.ch/files/live/sites/iheid/files/sites/international_law/users/vessier9/public/Collier%20-%20Post-conflict%20Recovery.pdf
87. Doyle and Sambanis, "International Peacebuilding."',
88. Chand and Coffman, "How Soon Can Donors Exit from Post-Conflict States?"
89. Mazimba, *Challenges of the African Military in Peacekeeping Missions in Africa*. Accessed December 2, 2013. https://www.google.it/url?sa=t&rct=j&q=&esrc=s&source=web&cd=1&ved=0ahUKEwj5tfS9x8bXAhWNYIAKHWTkDmQQFggmMAA&url=http%3A%2F%2Fwww.dtic.mil%2Fget-tr-doc%2Fpdf%3FAD%3DADA561378&usg=AOvVaw3LQqQHcwc4eH6ulV2QpdBC
90. McNerney et al., *Assessing Security Cooperation as a Preventive Tool*.
91. Varhola, "Foreigners in a Foreign Land."', Accessed November 3, 2015. http://smallwarsjournal.com/jrnl/art/foreigners-in-a-foreign-land-complexity-and-reductionist-staff-approaches-in-stability-oper; also, Moyo, *Dead Aid*.
92. Widely available; see e.g. Accessed June 5, 2018. https://www.goodreads.com/quotes/152853-you-may-not-be-interested-in-war-but-war-is

Disclosure statement

No potential conflict of interest was reported by the author.

Bibliography

Abdalla, Muna A. 2009. "Understanding of the Natural Resource Conflict Dynamics: The Case of the Tuareg in North Africa and the Sahel." *ISS Paper No. 194*. Preotoria, South Africa: Institute for Security Studies. https://issafrica.s3.amazonaws.com/site/uploads/Paper194.pdf

Arieff, Alexis. *Attack on U.S. Soldiers in Niger: Context and Issues for Congress*. IN10797. Washington, DC: Congressional Research Service, October 5, 2017. https://fas.org/sgp/crs/natsec/IN10797.pdf

Art, Robert J. "Geopolitics Updated: The Strategy of Selective Engagement." *International Security* 23, no. 3 (Winter 1998–1999): 79. (Boston, MA: MIT Press). doi:10.2307/2539339.

Associated Press. "Top U.S. General: Families, Americans Deserve Answers on Niger." October 23, 2017. http://www.businessinsider.com/ap-top-us-general-families-americans-deserve-answers-on-niger-2017-10?IR=T

Atkinson, Rick. *An Army at Dawn: The War in North Africa, 1942–1943*. New York: Henry Holt & Co., 2002.

Bennett, D. Scott, and Allan C. Stam. *The Behavioral Origins of War*. Ann Arbor, MI: University of Michigan Press, 2004.

Boilley, Pierre. *Les Touaregs Kel Adagh, Dépendances Et Révoltes: Du Soudan Français Au Mali Contemporain* [The Kel Adagh Tuaregs, dependencies and revolts: From French West Africa to contemporary Mali]. Paris: Éditions Karthala, 1999.

Bowden, Mark. *Black Hawk Down: A Story of Modern War*. New York: Signet Books, 1999.

Buhaug, Halvard, Havard Hegre, and Havard Strand. *Global Trends in Armed Conflict*. Oslo: Peace Research Institute Oslo, 2007. https://www.hbuhaug.com/wp-content/uploads/2014/02/Global-Trends_final.pdf

Callwell, C.E. *Small Wars: Their Principles and Practice*. London: Harrison & Sons, 1906.

Chand, Satish, and Ruth Coffman. 2008. "How Soon Can Donors Exit from Post-Conflict States?" *Center for Global Development Working Paper No. 141*, February 25.

Collier, Paul. 2009. "Post-Conflict Economic Recovery." *Journal of African Economies* 18. AERC Suppliment 1. doi:10.1093/jae/ejp006.

Collier, Paul, and Anke Hoeffler. 2002. "Aid, Policy, and Growth in Post-Conflict Countries." *World Bank Policy Research Working Paper 2902*. New York: World Bank. doi:10.1044/1059-0889(2002/er01).

Daojiong, Zao. "China's Energy Security: Domestic and International Issues." *Survival: Global Politics and Strategy* 48, no. 1 (July 19, 2006): doi:10.1080/00396330600594322.

Department of Defense. *QDR Execution Roadmap: Building Partnership Capacity*. Washington, DC: US Government Publishing Office, May 22, 2006a.

Department of Defense. *Quadrennial Defense Review Report*. Washington, DC: US Government Publishing Office, February, 2006b.

Department of Defense. *Military Contribution to Cooperative Security Joint Operating Concept Version 1.0*. Washington, DC: US Government Publishing Office, September 19, 2008.

Department of Defense. *DoD Instruction 5000.68, Security Force Assistance*. Washington, DC: US Government Publishing Office, October 27, 2010.

Department of Defense. *The National Military Strategy of the United States of America 2011: Redefining America's Military Leadership*. Washington, DC: US Government Publishing Office, February, 2011.

Doyle, Michael W., and Nicholas Sambanis. "International Peacebuilding: A Theoretical and Quantitative Analysis." *The American Political Science Review* 94, no. 4 (December, 2000): doi:10.2307/2586208.

Echevarria, Antulio J., II. *An American Way of War or Way of Battle?* Carlisle, PA: Strategic Studies Institute, January, 2004. http://www.au.af.mil/au/awc/awcgate/ssi/ssi_op_ed_jan04.pdf

Fearon, James D. "Rationalist Explanations for War." *International Organization* 49, no. 3 (1995): (Boston, MA: MIT Press). doi:10.1017/S0020818300033324.

French, Howard. *China's Second Continent: How a Million Migrants are Building a New Empire in Africa*. New York: Alfred A. Knopf, 2014.

Saint Girons, Anne. *Les Rébellions Touarègues* [The Tuareg rebellions]. Paris: Ibis Press, 2008.

Government Accountability Office. "Security Force Assistance: Additional Actions Needed to Guide Geographic Combatant Command and Service Efforts." *Report GAO-12-556*. Washington, DC, May, 2012.

Guido, Joseph. 2017. *Terrorist Sanctuary in the Sahara: A Case Study*. Carlisle, PA: Strategic Studies Institute, November 1. https://ssi.armywarcollege.edu/pubs/people.cfm?authorID=2066

Hanson, Victor Davis. *The Western Way of War: Infantry Battle in Classical Greece*. Los Angeles, CA: University of California Press, 1994.

Headquarters, Department of the Army. *FM 3-22: Army Support to Security Cooperation*. Washington, DC: US Government Publishing Office, January, 2013.

IRIN. "Can Niger Offer Mali Lessons on the Tuareg?" April 11, 2013. http://www.irinnews.org/report/97823/can-niger-offer-mali-lessons-tuareg

Jian, Wenran. "Fuelling the Dragon: China's Rise and Its Energy and Resources Extraction in Africa." *The China Quarterly* 199, (2009). doi:10.1017/S0305741009990117.

Joint Center for International Security Force Assistance. *Commander's Handbook for Security Force Assistance*. Fort Leavenworth, KA: US Government Publishing Office, July 14, 2008.

Joint Center for International Security Force Assistance. *Operational Force Development.* Fort Leavenworth, KA: US Government Publishing Office, December, 2015a.

Joint Center for International Security Force Assistance. *SFA Assessment Handbook.* Fort Leavenworth, KA: US Government Publishing Office, July 1, 2015b.

Joint Center for International Security Force Assistance. *Security Force Assistance Planner's Guide.* Fort Leavenworth, KA: US Government Publishing Office, January 1, 2016.

Kelly, Terrence K., Nora Bensahel, and Olga Oliker. *Security Force Assistance in Afghanistan: Identifying Lessons for Future Efforts.* Santa Monica, CA: RAND Corporation, 2011.

Kennan, George. *An American Life.* New York: Penguin, 2011.

Kissinger, Henry. *World Order.* New York: Penguin Press, 2014.

Klare, Michael T. *Resource Wars: The New Landscape of Global Conflict.* New York: Metropolitan Books, 2001.

Lacher, Wolfram. 2011. "Organized Crime and Terrorism in the Sahel; Drivers, Actors, Options." *Stiftung Wissenschaft und Polik*, January. Accessed December 2, 2013. https://www.files.ethz.ch/isn/126014/2011C01_lac_ks.pdf

Lewis, David, and Joe Bavier. 2017. "U.S. Deaths in Niger Highlight Africa Military Mission Creep." *Reuters News*, October 6. https://www.reuters.com/article/us-usa-africa-security/u-s-deaths-in-niger-highlight-africa-military-mission-creep-idUSKBN1CB2J1

Livingston, Thomas K. *Building the Capacity of Partner States through Security Force Assistance.* Washington, DC: Congressional Research Service, May 5, 2011.

Mazimba, James N. 2012. *Challenges of the African Military in Peacekeeping Missions in Africa.* Carlisle, PA: U.S. Army War College, March 20. https://www.google.it/url?sa=t&rct=j&q=&esrc=s&source=web&cd=1&ved=0ahUKEwj5tfS9x8bXAhWNYIAKHWTkDmQQFggmMAA&url=http%3A%2F%2Fwww.dtic.mil%2Fget-tr-doc%2Fpdf%3FAD%3DADA561378&usg=AOvVaw3LQqQHcwc4eH6ulV2QpdBC

McInnis, Kathleen J., and Nathan J. Lucas. *What Is "Building Partner Capacity?" Issues for Congress.* Washington, DC: Congressional Research Service, December 18, 2015.

McIntyre, Julie. 2016. "Marine General Says U.S. Lacks 'Overall Grand Strategy' for Libya." *Washington Examiner*, June 21. http://www.washingtonexaminer.com/marine-general-says-us-lacks-overall-grand-strategy-for-libya/article/2594496

McNamara, Robert S., and Brian VanDeMark. *Retrospect: The Tragedy and Lessons of Vietnam.* New York: Vintage Books, 1996.

McNerney, Michael J., Stuart E. Johnson, Stephanie Pezard, David Stebbins, Renanah Miles, Angelo O'Mahony, Chaoling Feng, and Time Oliver. *Defense Institution Building in Africa: An Assessment.* Santa Monica, CA: RAND Corporation, 2016.

McNerney, Michael J., Angela O'Mahony, Thomas S. Szayna, Derek Eaton, Caroline Baxter, Colin P. Clarke, Emma Cutrufello, et al. *Assessing Security Cooperation as a Preventative Tool.* Santa Monica, CA: RAND Corporation, 2014.

Mokeddem, Mohamed. *Al Qaida Au Maghreb Islamique: Contrebande Au Nom De L'islam* [Al Qaida in the Islamic Maghreb: Smuggling in the name of Islam]. Algers: Casbah-Editions, 2010.

Morris, Errol. 2004. "The Fog of War." *Sony Pictures.* DVD.

Moyo, Dambisa. *Dead Aid: Why Aid Is Not Working and How There Is a Better Way for Africa.* New York: Farrar, Straus and Giroux, 2010.

Muggah, Robert, and Keith Krause. "Closing the Gap between Peace Operations and Post-Conflict Insecurity: Towards a Violence Reduction Agenda." *International Peacekeeping* 16, no. 1 January 26 (2009): doi:10.1080/13533310802485617.

Nicholson, Jason. 2017. *Balancing Force Modernization and the Most Likely Future Wars We'll Be Fighting*. West Point: Modern War Institute, March 22. https://mwi.usma.edu/balancing-force-modernization-likely-future-wars-well-fighting/

Office of the Deputy Assistant Secretary of Defense for Plans. *Theater Campaign Planning Planner's Handbook Version 1.0*. Washington, DC: Office of the Under Secretary of Defense for Policy, February, 2012.

Paul, Christopher, Colin P. Clarke, Beth Grill, Stephanie Young, Jennifer D. P. Moroney, Joe Hogler, and Christine Leah. *What Works Best When Building Partner Capacity and under What Circumstances?* Santa Monica, CA: RAND Corporation, 2013.

Paul, Christopher, Jennifer D.P. Moronrey, Beth Grill, Colin P. Clarke, Lisa Saum-Manning, Heather Peterson, and Brian Gordon. *What Works Best When Building Partner Capacity in Challenging Contexts?* Santa Monica, CA: RAND Corporation, 2015.

Robinson, Linda. "SOF's Evolving Role: Warfare 'By, With, and Through' Local Forces." May 9, 2017. https://www.rand.org/blog/2017/05/sofs-evolving-role-warfare-by-with-and-through-local.html

Rosen, Armin. 2015. "One Uranium Mine in Niger Says a Lot about China's Huge Nuclear-Power Ambitions." *Business Insider*, October 24. http://www.businessinsider.com/niger-uranium-mine-and-nuclear-china-2015-10?IR=T

Schmitt, Eric. 2013. "Drones in Niger Reflect New U.S. Tack on Terrorism." *New York Times*, New York. July 10. http://www.nytimes.com/2013/07/11/world/africa/drones-in-niger-reflect-new-us-approach-in-terror-fight.html

Seybolt, Taylor B., Jay D. Aronson, and Baruch Fischhoff. *Counting Civilian Casualties: An Introduction to Recording and Estimating Nonmilitary Deaths in Conflict*. Oxford: Oxford University Press, 2013.

Shaffer, Brenda, and Taleh Ziyadov. *Beyond the Resource Curse*. Philadelphia, PA: University of Pennsylvania Press, 2011.

Spruyt, Hendrik. "The Origins, Development, and Possible Decline of the Modern State." *Annual Review of Political Science* 5, June, (2002): 127–149. doi:10.1146/annurev.polisci.5.101501.145837.

Thorp, Rosemary, S. Battistelli, Y. Guichaoua, J. Orihuela, and M. Paredes. *The Developmental Challenges of Mining and Oil: Lessons from Africa and Latin America*. New York: Palgrave Macmillan, 2012.

Thurston, Alex. 2012. "With Eye on Mali, Niger Adopts New Strategy for Tuareg North." *World Politics Review*, October 9. http://www.worldpoliticsreview.com/articles/12400/with-eye-on-mali-niger-adopts-new-strategy-for-tuareg-north

Turse, Nick. 2016. "Even AFRICOM's Own Commander Admits its Strategy is Not Working." *The Nation*, August 2. https://www.thenation.com/article/even-africoms-own-commander-admits-their-strategy-is-not-working/

United Nations. *United Nations Human Development Report 2016*. http://hdr.undp.org/sites/default/files/HDR2016_EN_Overview_Web.pdf

United States Africa Command. *Theater Campaign Plan 2000–16*. Stuttgart, Germany, August 18, 2015.

United States Africa Command. *United States Africa Command 2017 Posture Statement*. Stuttgart, Germany, March 15, 2017. https://www.google.it/url?sa=t&rct=j&q=&esrc=s&source=web&cd=1&cad=rja&uact=8&ved=0ahUKEwiSr4yJrcrXAhWRDuwKHZGZCl4QFggmMAA&url=https%3A%2F%2Fwww.

africom.mil%2Fmedia-room%2Fdocument%2F28720%2Fafricom-2017-posture-satement&usg=AOvVaw3wIZ0BmMJEY6A4u2O04H58

United States Congress. "Senate Committee on Foreign Relations. Subcommittee on African Affairs." *Resource Curse or Blessing? Africa's Management of Its Extractive Industries: Hearing before the Subcommittee on African Affairs of the Committee on Foreign Relations, United States Senate, One Hundred Tenth Congress, Second Session*, September 24, 2008. S Hrg. Washington, DC: U.S. GPO, 2009.

United States Department of State. "Programs and Initiatives." https://www.state.gov/j/ct/programs/

United States Government. *International Crime Assessment*. Washington, DC: National Criminal Justice Reference Service, 2000. https://www.cia.gov/library/readingroom/docs/DOC_0000497956.pdf

United States Joint Staff. *Joint Publication 3–22: Foreign Internal Defense*. Washington, DC: US Government Publishing Office, July 12, 2010.

United States Joint Staff. *Joint Doctrine Note 1–13: Security Force Assistance*. Washington, DC: US Government Publishing Office, April 29, 2013.

United States Marine Corps. *Small Wars Manual*. Washington, DC: Government Printing Office, 1940.

UPI. "Cease-Fire Truce Reached with Niger Rebels." May 15, 2009. http://www.upi.com/Top_News/2009/05/15/Cease-fire-truce-reached-with-Niger-rebels/UPI-99581242403588/

Varhola, Christopher. "Foreigners in a Foreign Land: Complexity and Reductionist Staff Approaches in Stability Operations." *Small Wars Journal*, November 5, (2014). http://smallwarsjournal.com/jrnl/art/foreigners-in-a-foreign-land-complexity-and-reductionist-staff-approaches-in-stability-oper

Von Clausewitz, Carl. *On War*. Translated and edited by Michael Howard and Peter Paret. Princeton, NJ: Princeton University Press, 1976.

Wagner, R. Harrison. *War and the State: TheTheory of International Politics*. Ann Arbor, MI: University of Michigan Press, 2007.

Waltz, Kenneth Neal. *Theory of International Politics*. Reading, MA: Addison-Wesley Publishing Company, 1979.

The White House. *National Security Strategy*. Washington, DC, May, 2010.

The White House. *U.S. Strategy Toward Sub-Saharan Africa*. Washington, DC, June 14, 2017.

World Nuclear Association. "Uranium Markets." http://world-nuclear.org/info/Nuclear-Fuel-Cycle/Uranium-Resources/Uranium-Markets/

Wuestner, Scott G. *Building Partner Capacity / Security Force Assistance: A New Structural Paradigm*. Carlisle, PA: Strategic Studies Institute, February, 2009.

Zweig, David, and Bi Jianhai. "China's Global Hunt for Energy." *Foreign Affairs* 84, no. 5 (September-October, 2005): (). doi:10.2307/20031703.

8 Too little, too late
Protecting American soft networks in COIN/CT

Steve Miska and Samuel Romano

ABSTRACT

Assistance of local-national partners is necessary to the USA in order to protect its national security interests throughout the world. These partners, typically individuals who support USA diplomats, service members, and non-governmental organizations (NGOs) in non-combatant roles, form USA soft networks. Due to the nature of their work, many of these individuals associated with the policy and actions of the USA become vulnerable to violent threats from adversaries. In fact, adversaries have grasped that attacking USA soft networks is a logical approach for enemies fighting from positions of weakness. As a result, examination of other domains may yield best practices that build resiliency in USA soft networks, thereby cementing national security interests. Further, agency theory illuminates critical principles in the relationships between local-national partners and field practitioners, and informs policy development efforts as a result.

Introduction

Before the war, they had both longed for the arrival of the Americans, expecting them to change their lives. They had told each other that they would try to work with the foreigners.[1]

Soft networks refer to the interpreters, local business contractors, politicians, teachers, intellectuals, religious leaders, interpreters, and others deemed vital to USA national interests, as well as their families; in short, the USA's indigenous partners in diplomatic, military, intelligence, and law enforcement operations. These partners are integral to USA counterterrorism (CT) and counterinsurgency (COIN) missions and provide invaluable support to USA diplomatic and military efforts in conflict zones – often in spite of tremendous danger from adversaries.[2]

Threats and attacks against soft networks existed as a facet of irregular warfare long before the wars in Iraq and Afghanistan; indeed, USA patriots often intimidated and attacked British Loyalists during the Revolutionary War. The strategy of attacking soft targets (i.e. soft networks) constitutes a primary method of classic insurgency. Current attack levels against soft networks indicate that these threats will persist, yet USA policy remains woefully inadequate to accomplish the task of strategically insulating local-national partners.

After the onset of the wars in Iraq and Afghanistan, the USA required protective measures to ensure a collaborative effort between USA forces and local-national allies. In Iraq, al-Qaeda, Shia militias, and Sunni insurgents often sought to deliver retribution against those who supported Coalition Forces and the Iraqi government, and violently attacked interpreters and other local-national support staff. Moreover, Iraqi government officials often aided or ignored insurgent and militia attacks against USA local-national allies. As a result of these hindrances and the lack of active protective measures, local-national allies became easy targets for non-conventional adversaries, such as insurgents and militias.

Threats against soft networks represent a viable impediment to USA foreign policy objectives. More than merely supporting operations, soft networks are often integral to successful missions abroad. Utilizing soft networks demonstrably increases the efficiency of counterinsurgency operations for the USA military[3] and naturally improves USA military engagement with the population. Conversely, passively allowing soft networks to come under attack weakens local-national confidence in ongoing USA military and diplomatic efforts, damages host-nation military relationships with USA forces, undermines law enforcement and intelligence investigations, and dilutes USA narratives regarding objectives in conflict zones.[4]

From early on in the Iraq War, diplomats and service members realized that insurgents and militia were attempting to undermine USA objectives by threatening key local allies who supported the USA mission in Iraq. In 2006, 3 years after the beginning of Operation Iraqi Freedom, and 5 years after the beginning of the war in Afghanistan, the USA instituted a special immigration visa (SIV) aimed at assisting interpreters (an important subset of soft networks) who required relocation to the USA. Yet, the program initially only accepted 50 interpreters (from the combined Iraqi and Afghan support staff) to immigrate to the USA.[5] Not only did the number of SIVs fall well below the level of interpreters actively participating in USA operations in Iraq and Afghanistan, but the government failed to efficiently complete the SIV cases for those who were lucky enough to participate.[6]

Although the various departments within the USA government struggle to appropriately protect soft networks, other sectors developed adaptable methods to protect individuals who suffer from similar risks. Non-governmental organizations (NGOs), the media, and the USA Marshal's Service developed methods of identity protection and relocation that insulate at-risk assets. This article examines two cases, NGOs in Somalia and federal-/state-level witness security (commonly referred to as witness protection), that demonstrate effective soft network insulation.

Further, utilizing agency theory, the authors scrutinize micro-level relationships to inform macro-level policy.[7] Stephen A. Ross's agency theory can explain organizational challenges between local-national allies and their handlers. Agency theory outlines the nature of a relationship that has 'arisen between two (or more) parties when one, designated as the agent, acts for, on behalf of, or as representative for the other, designated the principal, in a particular domain of decision problems.'[8] As a result, the authors identify principles adapted by NGOs and witness security professionals to protect soft networks.

This article seeks to examine effective insulation measures to protect at-risk local-national allies and, in doing so, recommends practical policy measures to improve the USA soft network protection. First, the authors examine the value of soft networks to foreign policy missions, as well as the threat to soft networks in recent conflict environments. Second, we outline recent USA policy measures to insulate soft networks, focusing on the SIV, and demonstrate the inadequacy of a single option. We then examine similar at-risk cases in foreign NGO activities and domestic witness security programs, highlighting methods used by NGOs and domestic law enforcement to insulate at-risk assets, specifically identity protection and relocation. The authors then apply agency theory to the practitioner-soft network relationship, in an effort to inform policy development and strengthen soft network protection. Finally, the authors recommend policy measures to improve the USA soft network resilience in both current and future conflict environments.

Threats to soft networks

Despite the active role soft networks play in USA foreign policy, many devalue their contributions, believing these allies serve as mere foreign labor to offset unnecessary burdens on USA forces. In actuality, soft networks serve a crucial role in USA foreign policy efforts, especially as global conflicts have progressively focused more on COIN and CT operations.

When the USA initiated its engagements in Afghanistan and Iraq, many of the military's tactics involved conventional military approaches to countering insurgent and militia violence, such as creating large forward operating bases (FOBs) well outside of population centers, carrying out daily search-and-destroy raids, and relying heavily on airpower and artillery.[9] While intended to deter negative sentiment against the occupying foreign military force, many of these methods instead alienated USA forces from the local population, which prevented effective COIN operations. Moreover, because USA forces were so disengaged from the local populace and could not effectively protect urban areas, attacks against civilians drastically increased. By December 2006, over 125 civilians were killed every night in Iraq.[10] As a result of the rise of rampant violence and local resentment against USA forces, the USA military increasingly recognized the need to pivot away from conventional military methods and adopt COIN doctrine which emphasizes that mission success often relies on protecting the population and indigenous subject matter experts.[11]

Units throughout the USA military adapted their methods to include collaboration with local-national allies. For example, in Iraq, many units expanded their local integration and conducted censuses that increased their awareness of local population dynamics, lending valuable information to intelligence and combat missions.[12] Other units worked closely with local police forces and the Iraqi military during combat operations, and abandoned FOBs in favor of local joint security stations within the city of Baghdad and elsewhere throughout Iraq.[13]

As collaboration between the USA military and local-national allies increased, many USA service members began to realize the dire security situation of USA soft networks. Insurgents and militia sought out local-national allies as a means of indirectly attacking USA efforts in Iraq and Afghanistan, and often threatened, maimed, or killed those assisting USA forces.[14] While the military possessed few policy options to protect local-national allies, an impetus for action emerged from those who worked closely with them. Many professionals – diplomats, journalists, and military leaders – developed close working relationships with Iraqi and Afghani subject matter experts, and felt compelled to assist their counterparts, not only for humanitarian reasons, but, more so, to accomplish USA missions. Yet, despite valuable local-national contributions, the USA policy response was noncommittal. The majority of soft networks remained in danger, forcing many local-national allies to develop individual protection methods.

Initially, these methods were relegated to ensuring the local-national was not exposed to an environment that could compromise his or her identity. Many COIN practitioners were receptive to allowing local-national allies to indicate where he or she would prefer to work and what types of duties they prefer to conduct. For example, while firms used bonuses to encourage interpreters to go on patrol, if the local-national elected not to patrol, they would not have to accompany a unit; the interpreter could simply forfeit the bonus. Further, many local-nationals who accompanied combat units on patrols used face masks to shield their identity, decreasing the likelihood of discovery.

In 2007, the facemask precaution was rendered moot when the Iraq-allied command directed all local-national interpreters to remove their face masks while on patrol, in an attempt to demonstrate a purported decrease in violence. Despite these assertions by the Iraq-allied command, many interpreters did not believe the situation in Iraq had become safe enough. As a result, many resigned, while others refused to participate in combat patrols, particularly patrols that required interpreters to visit their home neighborhood. Those who elected to remain in dangerous combat situations, though, sought out alternative identity protection solutions.

Most local-national allies used nicknames and alibis to shield their identity. In fact, most units accepted an interpreter's nickname as part of the Iraqi psyche, either as an attempt to show loyalty by devising a 'western' style name or as a mechanism to make pronunciation easier. Some interpreters refused to share personal information with other linguists, or even their own families, fearing inadvertent, or intentional identity disclosure to militia, insurgents, or the local government. Interpreters would often tell family members they were attending the Baghdad Police Academy or college to explain lengthy absences.

Additionally, local-national allies would take measures to decrease the amount of visible transit, or utilize multiple taxis to conceal their affiliations from potential adversaries. Many interpreters lived full-time on USA bases, minimizing their transit to and from their neighborhoods, and limiting their interactions with community members who could expose their identity. Even so, when leaving base, some local-national allies would be forced to take multiple taxis to ensure they were not followed, or they would only have trusted friends come pick them up. For instance, a woman returning from her father's funeral in Syria described taking a taxi from Baghdad International Airport to a Shia neighborhood, and only then, after walking through a building and across several blocks, being able to hail a separate cab to complete her journey.[15]

The extent to which soft networks aid USA missions abroad, particularly in light of the increasing necessity of COIN/CT tactics, cannot be overstated. Collaboration with local-national allies increases awareness in conflict zones, improves the likelihood of mission success, and upholds the USA reputation. The wars in Iraq and Afghanistan exposed glaring deficiencies in the USA ability to protect local-national allies. In an attempt to remedy the situation, Congress authorized the first policy measure aimed at protecting soft networks: the special immigrant visa.

The Special Immigrant Visa

Although many local-national allies were promised a better life in return for assisting the USA missions in Iraq and Afghanistan, the USA was unable to effectively protect its soft networks. Individuals were often killed when insurgents learned of their USA affiliation. As a result, in 2006, Congress recognized the threat to interpreters (a specific subset of soft networks).

The National Defense Authorization Act (NDAA) for Fiscal Year 2006 and the Immigration and Nationality Act (INA) included important provisions that classified military interpreters as special immigrants. This legal classification made local-national interpreters eligible for permanent residency in the USA. Interpreters were able to qualify for the program if they had been employed for at least 1 year after 20 March 2003, received a recommendation from a supervisor about the nature of their service, and had encountered a serious threat stemming from their employment. Further, the special immigrant classification demarcated two specific employment groups of Iraqi and Afghan local-nationals who could apply for SIVs: interpreters who worked directly with combat units as interpreters, and interpreters who worked for the USA in non-combatant capacities. Eligible non-combatant personnel included individuals who worked on USA military installations as support personnel, as well as local-national translators who worked with the International Security Assistance Force.[16] Despite the number of local-national allies working in various capacities with USA forces in Iraq and Afghanistan, the initial authorization made only 50 visas available each year for interpreters. Due to calls from many USA officials, including Ambassador to Iraq, Ryan Crocker, this number was amended in 2007 to allow 500 additional visas for local-national interpreters.[17]

Local-national allies who worked with the USA in other capacities finally began to receive assistance in 2008, when Section 1244 of the 2008 NDAA made 5,000 visas available to Iraqi nationals who worked with the USA in any non-combatant service role.[18] This program initially expired in 2013, but was immediately extended to allow 4,500 new visa applications. However, the program for Afghan nationals was permitted to only accept applications from 1,500 individuals between 2009 and 2013.[19] Even after being amended in 2013, the Congressional Research Service noted that despite the State Department's 8,000 requested visas (and an estimated 13,000 applicants), only 4,000 SIVs were made available.[20] Thus, in spite of its efforts to insulate soft networks, the USA was unprepared to manage the number of applications and remained unable to adequately protect valuable local-national allies. Further, the USA failed to develop viable alternatives to immigration, and, as a result, the SIV became the only option to protect at-risk local-national partners.

Shortcomings Within the SIV

Since its creation, critical flaws within the SIV application process limited its effectiveness. When provisions were passed in the 2006 NDAA, the bill failed to include language that limited the maximum processing time for an SIV application. As a result, a single application often took multiple years to reach the approval stage, and once approved, local-national allies faced incredible hurdles, which prevented efficient immigration to the USA. For example, because the USA embassy in Iraq had been shuttered, Task Force Justice (a special unit organized by the Dagger Brigade Combat Team) was forced to develop an 'Underground Railroad' that safely transported Iraqi interpreters from Baghdad to Amman, Jordan, and onward to the USA. Moreover, interpreters were often forced to create alibis to cross the Jordanian border illegally, putting their lives in further danger.[21] Many applicants required extensive background checks and remained in the system even longer as a result, contributing to an overall backlog of SIV applications. For translators operating in active conflict zones, and who often needed urgent extraction from their environments, the SIV process became simply too lengthy. Consequently, the failure to process SIV applications in a timely manner resulted in the deaths of many innocent local-national allies.[22]

In 2013, Congress addressed this processing delay, mandating a 9-month maximum processing time for applications in the 2014 NDAA.[23] Unfortunately, this law did nothing to address the situations of applicants who had spent years waiting for admission to the USA while their applications were in-process. Visa application processing speed increased, but the small number of visas issued each year failed to eliminate the existing backlog and effectively insulate local-national allies.

Beyond the application backlog, policy gaps that further disadvantaged at-risk local-national allies existed within the application process itself. A 2010 analysis of the SIV application process by Northeastern University revealed that in addition to extensive processing delays, 'the application is less a process than a series of procedural impediments that are nearly insuperable without experienced, English-speaking, legal counsel.'[24] The application process for an SIV required local-nationals to seek assistance to navigate 14 discrete steps including direct communication between the applicant and the USA embassy, an onerous, and often dangerous, imposition.

In 2016, the Congressional Research Service issued a report addressing these complications in the Special Immigrant Visa Program, stating that many applicants encountered 'difficulties obtaining a recommendation from a supervisor and a copy of the work contract.'[25] For instance, when the SIV was first introduced for Afghan applicants, the visa application required approval from the USA Chief of Mission in Kabul, which presented a significant barrier for many applicants who were typically unable to reach the Chief of Mission.[26]

Additionally, applicants applying through the SIV program and Direct Access Programs (DAP) struggled to acquire the appropriate documentation from the contracting companies that employed them – hindering any chance that their application would be expediently processed. Since the USA does not require contractors and other language service providers to share proof of employment with interpreters, it became nearly impossible for applicants to produce the required documentation to support their applications. Moreover, a report from the International Refugee Assistance Project (IRAP) indicated that 'U.S. military contractors...have refused to provide former employees with such documentation,'[27] and while applicants struggled to acquire the documentation to complete their application, they received no guarantee of protection from the USA or their contractor.

As a result, despite its intentions, the SIV process was heavily criticized for its inability to protect at-risk local-national allies. A Yale law student and director for IRAP stated in 2010 that the SIV program 'treats applicants—many of whom are on the run and often facing death threats—as if they were being audited by the Internal Revenue Service.'[28] A senior State Department official described the SIV process as 'more difficult for applicants to navigate than the refugee process it was supposed to bypass.'[29]

Congressional attempts to address the problems in the SIV program were typically met with heavy resistance. Senator John McCain of Arizona and Senator Jeanne Shaheen of New Hampshire, consistent champions of the SIV, advocated for increasing the number of available visas based upon the danger to local-national allies. A bipartisan effort in 2016 advanced legislation that would have added an additional 2,500 visas, but was blocked by Senator Mike Lee of Utah, who said his quarrel was not with the visa program but rather with the fact that this measure was getting a vote while one of his own, unrelated measures was not.[30] Additionally, Senator Grassley of Iowa expressed concerns about the cost of the additional visas, arguing that they would be a significant expense of $446 million over 10 years,[31] despite the federal government's current budget of $4.407 trillion.[32] As a result of these challenges, congressional measures failed to address the government's struggle to streamline regulations regarding visa eligibility and applications, leaving local-national partners in jeopardy.

The consequences of the SIV's ineffectiveness contributed to the larger issue of inadequate soft network protection. A report from ProPublica documents 667 cases of USA contracted Iraqi nationals who were killed or injured between 2003 and 2008.[33] In 2014, the violence against Afghan translator soft networks was so severe that IRAP estimated that an Afghan was killed every 36 hours due to their affiliation with the USA.[34] A congressional report on the Afghan SIV program noted that there were 9,701 principal applicants and 1,551 family members with applications pending in when the program ended in 2016.[35] No One Left Behind (NOLB) estimates in their 2017 Annual Report that as many as 50,000 individuals in Iraq and Afghanistan remain eligible for some form of assistance.[36] These figures are not inconsequential. They demonstrate a glaring shortcoming in USA foreign policy, and an inability to protect those who sacrifice their lives to contribute to USA missions.

Yet, the experience of at-risk local-nationals is not unique to the wars in Iraq and Afghanistan. NGOs abroad, particularly in dangerous environments, rely heavily on local-nationals to operate effectively. Similarly, USA witness protection programs rely on at-risk witnesses and informants to provide critical information in legal cases. Local-nationals who aid NGOs in conflict zones and critical witnesses operate at the risk of being attacked by nefarious actors. Consequently, NGOs and state and federal USA witness protection programs have developed measures to protect assets, specifically: (1) identity protection and (2) relocation. In order to demonstrate the effectiveness of these measures, as well as the potential to incorporate best practices into future USA policy, this article highlights the case studies of NGOs in Somalia, and domestic witness security programs in the USA.

Non-Governmental Organizations in Somalia

Local-national NGO staffers suffer from threats similar to those USA government soft networks encounter in conflict zones. This section examines NGOs' strategies for protecting local-national allies in Somalia. Studying the methods NGOs use to protect local-national allies may yield more effective protection practices to be shared with policymakers in other domains. Further, in cases of methodology that cannot scale to requirements within USA government departments, certain practices may still yield positive results in select cases.

The Somali terrorist organization al-Shabaab often threatens individuals known to associate with NGOs, focusing especially on local-nationals who aid western organizations. Al-Shabaab controls much of south and central Somalia, and attempts to establish a shadow government that regulates the activities of NGOs and other organizations within al-Shabaab-controlled territory. Local-national staffers often feel the brunt of anti-NGO sentiment and experience 'threatening phone calls and visits by armed men.'[37] As a result, NGOs in Somalia have developed risk mitigation tactics for local-national staff, typically consisting of identity protection. In cases when threats prove imminent and identity protection fails, NGOs seek to relocate individuals and/or their family members.

In order to ensure the safety of local-national staff in dangerous environments, NGOs in Somalia attempt to hide the identity of local staff and provide avenues to mask staffer affiliation with western organizations. For example, many NGOs in Somalia explicitly prevent western staff from traveling to Mogadishu, and rely on local-national staff to execute projects and programs in dangerous areas. This policy preemptively incorporates a level of identity protection for local-national staffers by placing degrees of separation between local-national staffers and western practitioners. Instead of direct contact, email and telephone calls become the primary means of coordination, effectively insulating local-national NGO networks from insurgent threats.[38]

The ability to decrease direct contact between international staff and local staff often enables NGO utilization of subcontracting projects. These projects allow for further degrees of separation for local-national staff. Despite the potential moral hazards inherent in subcontracting, such as an inability to confirm the status and quality of work, NGOs develop measures that verify effective progress by subcontractors while ensuring local-national staff safety. For example, one NGO found that weekly situation reports and photos (submitted using indirect contact methods) helped ensure compliance and effective operation, while still maintaining distance between the NGO and the local-national partner.[39] Other NGOs hire Somali expatriates as international staff, a measure that allows international staff to operate with local-national partners without drawing al-Shabaab's suspicion. NGO use of subcontracting introduces a local solution to threats against local-national partners affiliated with western NGOs, thereby avoiding the necessity to resort to extreme relocation.

In order to best protect local-national staff identities, some NGO hiring processes involve collaborating with local government officials. For instance, international staff coordinate directly with local authorities to ensure local participation, and use measures such as '[leaving] a lock box with the local authorities [so] applicants [could] put their submissions in there,'[40] and not be identified.

Despite the effectiveness of identity protection measures, in select situations where local staff are in grave danger, NGOs seek to relocate their staffers within the same locality, either permanently or temporarily. If local relocation is unable to alleviate the threats, some NGOs resort to regional relocation measures (that is, relocate the individual to a neighboring country). NGOs ability to use local and regional relocation measures that successfully insulate at-risk local-national partners further demonstrates the viability of alternative practices in comparison with extreme relocation methods like the SIV.

In comparison with the USA military, NGOs in Somalia are able to more easily relocate local-national staff due to a lack of bureaucratic and organizational challenges. For example, in an interview with the author, one international staffer mentioned that he relocated Somali staffers from Mogadishu to Nairobi and Somaliland for a month to allow threats to die down.[41] This move involved few coordinating measures for the NGO, as it already had offices established in Puntland, Somaliland, Ethiopia, Kenya, and elsewhere throughout the region. Moreover, the process of relocation involved relatively few documentation hurdles (such as those often found in the SIV program), and required no interaction with the USA Department of State, as the local staffer was able to easily handle the visa requirements himself. Conversely, If a USA military officer made the recommendation to relocate an interpreter (e.g. from Iraq to Jordan), he or she would need to coordinate with multiple agencies and seek approval from the Jordanian government. Failing that, the officer would need to seek an alibi to sneak the interpreter across the border. Since NGOs in Somalia are less hindered by layers of bureaucracy, they are able to devise flexible solutions to offset credible threats against local-national allies, and are therefore able to ensure local-national staff security without necessitating extreme relocation.

In summary, NGOs in Somalia benefit from the ability to flexibly utilize measures that insulate local agents. Lacking bureaucratic challenges, they adapt methods to specific threats, local cultures, and opportunities to collaborate with local government. These NGOs actively prevent international staff from making overt contact with local staff, function without an obvious presence in conflict zones, and hire local-national subcontractors to complete projects. These practices create degrees of separation between local staff and international practitioners, and insulate local-national partners. When relocation is required, NGOs in Somalia resort to temporary relocation first, whether local or regional. In light of their ability to protect soft networks more effectively than most USA government departments and agencies, NGOs in Somalia offer best practices that can be creatively adapted by interagency operators in military, intelligence, and diplomatic operations to more effectively protect USA local-national allies in conflict zones.

USA Domestic Protection Programs

Similar to Iraqi and Somali at-risk local-nationals, critical witnesses, informants, and victims in the USA face threats from domestic criminals. In order to protect these individuals, the USA maintains domestic protection programs that safeguard key individuals and their families from organized criminals, gangs, and other malign actors. Given the success of these programs at the national and state level in the USA, adapting these methods to function in a conflict zone abroad could yield significant benefits to soft network protection.

Since 1971, the USA has operated a federal USA Witness Security program (commonly referred to as witness protection) to insulate at-risk USA Department of Justice witnesses. Many protected witnesses have inside information due to personal engagement in criminal enterprises or relationships with actors inside the network.[42] As a result, criminal ability to identify, threaten, and attack these witnesses increases. The witness security program (in a similar fashion to NGOs in Somalia) utilizes local identity protection and relocation measures to insulate agents. Witnesses and their families receive new identities, full documentation, and new housing to ensure adversaries are unable to attack them.[43]

The motivation for these protective measures is clear: 'with enhanced security measures, witnesses [are] more likely to cooperate with police and prosecutors in identifying criminals and testifying against them.'[44] Similar to local-national allies in conflict zones, the USA Department of Justice understands the value of effectively insulating critical partners, and, is successful in doing so: 'The Witness Security Program has successfully protected approximately 18,865 participants from intimidation and retribution since the program began in 1971,'[45] a figure clearly demonstrating the program's ability to insulate at-risk partners.

Complementing the federal program, many states operate their own programs to protect the identities of at-risk individuals. New Hampshire, for example, maintains a victim services division which helps protect victims of domestic violence, sexual assault, and stalking.[46] While the program does not use measures to the same extent as federal witness protection programs, it does provide substitute addresses for all forms of identification including driver's license, healthcare, and other government services, and, in doing so, effectively protects at-risk individuals.

The success of USA domestic protection programs reveals the fundamental benefits of relocation and identity protection measures. The ability to successfully protect at-risk individuals, particularly witnesses and informants, greatly aids USA law enforcement efforts. Protecting these partners increases the likelihood that individuals will cooperate with law enforcement and testify against dangerous actors. Moreover, the methods used by New Hampshire's victim services division are examples of creative identity protection techniques that do not necessitate relocation, and could be applied in other circumstances, particularly protecting local-national allies in COIN/CT operations. USA efforts to protect its soft networks abroad would greatly benefit from selective application of similar methods.

Considering the nontraditional cases of NGOs in Somalia and USA domestic protection programs, agency theory can be a lens to evaluate relationships between actors. By extension, the theory helps inform relationships between USA government practitioners and local-national allies at the micro-level. Through that examination, we are better able to imagine creative policy options to apply in COIN, CT, and other situations in conflict zones.

Agency Theory and Understanding Soft Network Risk

Although developed as an economic framework to study the effects of business relationships, agency theory can be used to examine any environment where human beings routinely interact. Stephen A. Ross began the modern development of agency theory by stating that 'the relationship of agency is one of the oldest codified modes of social interaction.'[47] Ross goes on to define the theory as '[a] relationship [that] has arisen between two (or more) parties when one, designated as the agent, acts for, on behalf of, or as representative for the other, designated the principal, in a particular domain of decision problems.'[48] Policymakers can utilize agency theory to better understand motivation and incentives in the relationship between the USA (the principal) and the local-nationals (agents) who make up USA soft networks. Similarly, the theory illuminates relationships and challenges with NGOs, witness security, and many other actors. By understanding agency problems at the micro-level, leaders can more effectively shape macro-level USA foreign policy for conflict zones.

More specifically, adverse selection and moral hazard, two aspects of agency theory, can help explain the principal–agent relationship that arises with soft networks. First, adverse selection occurs as a result of asymmetric information that the agent possesses prior to engaging in a contract, which makes the principal unable to 'completely verify [the agent's] skills or abilities either at the time of hiring or while the agent is working.'[49] For example, an Iraqi interpreter may claim he understands tribal mores and Iraqi Security Force (ISF) protocol while interviewing for a position with a commander. However, the commander has no absolute method of verifying the interpreter's claim until the interpreter interacts with sheiks or ISF leaders. The commander may be unable to identify a deficiency unless the sheiks or ISF leaders provide him with feedback on the interpreter's performance. Second, moral hazard occurs when an agent shirks duties or behaves in a way not necessarily aligned with the principal's interest. For example, since NGOs have few mechanisms to confirm local-national staff reports, a staffer may provide false updates on the status of a project. Summarizing these two issues, Kathleen Eisenhardt, an agency theory scholar, suggests that 'the agency problem arises because a) the principal and the agent have different goals and b) the principal cannot determine if the agent has behaved appropriately.'[50]

These challenges can negatively affect both parties' ability to successfully conduct their duties. For example, a local-national staffer working for an NGO in Somalia possesses better information about the risks and culture in a given locale, while the principal possesses a better understanding of the international community's pressures. Therefore, each party's motivation and requirements differ, and, if unchecked, can lead to negative results throughout the relationship. As a result, dangerous operating environments, like Somalia, require principals to operate with focus and determination in an attempt to align interests and compensate for high levels of information asymmetry and unequal risk sharing. This is similar to COIN and CT environments.

By framing the motives and experiences of actors in various contexts, agency theory illuminates the relationships that exist across multiple principal–agent relationships involving at-risk partners. Specifically, when applied to the previously discussed cases of NGOs and domestic protection programs, agency theory clarifies the multi-faceted relationships that exist between practitioners (principals) and soft networks, and can inform future insulation methods.

Examining NGO relationships, principals typically assume the contractual and bureaucratic responsibilities of managing systems and staffers. Unlike the military and other government organizations, many NGOs conduct local-national hiring internally (rather than using contracting firms who assume functions like interviewing, hiring, paying salaries, and supervising). When NGOs assume the functions of a contracting firm within the organization, NGO practitioners develop a close managerial relationship with agents similar to a military commander's more personal relationship with his or her agents.

However, as a result of direct hiring, NGO principals recognize the risk differential inherent during operations in dangerous environments. Moreover, since they cannot force their way in similar to a military operation, NGOs that operate in conflict environments like Somalia are forced to more flexibly adapt to the requirements and experiences of at-risk local-national agents. For example, as mentioned earlier, NGOs operating in Somalia rely heavily on local-national partners, since international workers would incur significant danger if found working in insurgent territory. Due to this dependency on local-national workers, NGOs must ensure the viability of indigenous networks or suffer negative organizational outcomes. This awareness differs from the case of the USA military, where principals often fail to acknowledge the threat to interpreters and other partners until it is too late because they do not understand implications of unequal risk sharing and asymmetric information.

In the case of domestic protection programs, witness protection relationships align divergent interests between prosecutors (principal) and protected witnesses (agent), while simultaneously establishing the principal's control over the agent, thereby reducing moral hazard. Further, the witness protection program displays many cases of asymmetric information between principal and agent, since witnesses have valuable information that prosecutors require for a criminal indictment.

Accordingly, prosecutors often attempt to enter into a contract with protected witnesses. The contract, essentially an agreement to testify in exchange for insulation from retribution, serves two purposes. First, the contract provides the prosecutor reasonable assurance that the witness will help the investigation to indict criminal actors. Second, the contract provides a measure of assurance to the witness that he or she will be protected from potential attack.

As a result, the contract better aligns the interests of the principal and agent, reducing both asymmetric information and risk imbalance.

Applying agency theory to NGO practitioners in Somalia and domestic protection programs yields similar conclusions. In both cases, challenges relating to the contextual environment, asymmetric information concerns, and divergent interests between principals and agents are present, unless corrected by policies that align interests. Although divergence in interests can never be fully eliminated, steps can be taken to help principals better understand an agent's risk, and as a result, develop proactive measures to ensure their agents' insulation from harm. Thus, in addition to utilizing identity protection and relocation measures, ensuring that USA practitioners (principals) more adequately understand local-national allies' risks (agents) can facilitate more effective protection of soft networks.

Agency theory yields a better understanding of the principal–agent relationship in various contexts. The theory illuminates the dual challenges of moral hazard and adverse selection, which are characterized by asymmetric information and unequal risk sharing between agents and principals. As a result, both examined cases provide opportunities to add policy options to the COIN or CT operator's menu to more effectively insulate soft networks. Specifically, the cases of NGOs in Somalia and domestic witness security employ the principles of identity protection and relocation to mitigate the risks inherent in the principal–agent relationship. As a result, those principles inform new, creative options for government policy makers.

While it would be far-fetched to assume all government practitioners will develop an in-depth understanding of agency theory, incorporating major themes found in an agency theory analysis of the US soft network relationship could greatly aid policy development. A fundamental understanding of the principles of asymmetric information and unequal risk sharing, and how the principles impact relationships in conflict zones, would increase US ability to properly insulate soft networks. This goal could be accomplished by ensuring principles like identity protection and relocation are incorporated into redeployment training for US staff (both military and diplomatic), as well as into the formation of principal–agent relationships in conflict zones.

Recommendations

In light of the national security imperative to protect USA soft networks, this article recommends a variety of policy initiatives to protect existing soft networks, as well as preemptive measures to protect local allies in future conflicts. These recommendations outlay potential practical policy measures for governmental consideration, specifically sourcing best insulation practices from other sectors' protection programs, and pre-deployment training to increase USA practitioners' awareness of soft network risks. Additionally, this article recommends organizational steps aimed at increasing the USA government's ability to ensure that soft network protection programs are effective.

From this article's case studies, two principles to ensure soft network insulation are apparent: (1) the need to safeguard agent identities and (2) the need to relocate those agents if identity protection is insufficient. Based on these principles, the USA should pursue identity protection and local/regional relocation as practical policies to insulate soft networks. In cases where identity protection and local or regional relocation will not succeed, the USA should retain an international relocation policy similar to the SIV for Iraqi and Afghan interpreters. These policies will strengthen USA protection of soft networks, and, in doing so, contribute to USA mission success in conflict zones.

Policies that ensure identity protection for local allies are integral to insulating soft networks. The case studies from Somalia and the USA revealed multiple examples of identity protection policies, such as programs to alter identities using substitute addresses and alternate forms of identification, degrees of separation, and local relocation possibilities. In the future, policymakers should ensure the presence of multiple options, and allow both principals and agents the creative flexibility to devise identity protection solutions for their given operational context.

In cases where identity protection measures are insufficient, the USA should develop strategies to relocate agents. Agents should be relocated if they become compromised, or exposed to undue risks which inhibit their ability to affect the mission. Relocation could be temporary or permanent, depending on the circumstances involved, and, ideally, within the agent's indigenous country in order to minimize disruption to his/her employer and the agent's personal life. Temporal relocation should always be considered first, in order to minimize agent social/cultural disruption and the impact to operational effectiveness.

If relocation becomes necessary, local/regional relocation options are far more viable than extreme relocation measures (such as the SIV), and it is important to limit the extent of social and physical displacement. As some researchers point out, a move can be 'a profoundly disorienting and destabilizing personal experience, which leaves a legacy of people trying to come to terms with their displaced lives.'[51] Thus, the USA should seek to minimize the disruption to the extent possible, while balancing the risks of exposure to the local agent.

Despite the additional benefits of local/regional relocation, the USA should develop a breadth of potential relocation options to minimize disruption to local-national lives and ensure appropriate protection. The following guidelines elucidate three general options for geographic relocation. The first option is local relocation. By relocating agents within a country, rather than internationally, logistics remain relatively simple, minimizing social disruption. Depending on the nature of the environment, the agent could potentially maintain their identity. However, if the context is too dangerous, a local solution should include altering the informant's identity, while seeking to protect their family and employment options.

The second relocation option is to relocate the agent regionally. If the operating environment carries extreme risk, an adjacent country may provide the necessary insulation to protect the agent and his or her family. Regional relocation destinations should be carefully evaluated in order to fully understand the legal status of the relocated agent. Furthermore, principals should attempt to relocate agents to a country with similar culture and language in order to decrease assimilation challenges. During a regional relocation, principals should remain cognizant of the agent's physical safety from enemy threats, familial presence, and employment opportunities.[52] Most importantly, the USA must ensure the thoroughness of relocation evaluations, specifically with regard to regional complications that could undermine soft network protection, as well as regional support for USA missions.

For example, when Iraqi nationals were endangered by militia and terrorist threats, many Iraqis migrated to Jordan, Syria, Egypt, Turkey, Lebanon, or Iran. In cases of such large-scale relocation, particularly within the Middle East, the USA must consider many host-countries' fear of receiving large amounts of refugees. Jordan, for example, fears that 'the displacement of Iraqis could be a protracted one with the potential of destabilizing governments,'[53] particularly in the wake of the 70-year experience of hosting Palestinian refugees.

Given many Middle Eastern governments' reluctance to accept refugees, USA policymakers must prepare for the possibility of a third relocation option: extreme relocation like the SIV. That is, in the case that neither local nor regional relocation options are viable, the agent may require international relocation to an allied country, such as Australia, European countries, or the USA.

Both the principal and agent must be aware that international relocation carries noteworthy assimilation costs and psychological ramifications, particularly in comparison with local or regional relocation. Specifically, this type of relocation often involves significant social upheaval, which could create high friction from assimilation, similar to the plight of many relocated witnesses in the USA program. Moreover, many Iraqi refugees who relocate to the USA face substantial assimilation challenges and are forced to rely heavily upon a sponsor to help their acculturation.[54] These potential ramifications should be considered during relocation policy development.

Despite the necessity to develop thoughtful local, regional, and international relocation options to protect the USA soft networks, any relocation option should be a last resort strategy. Former USA relocation policies, such as the SIV, have underscored an inability to preemptively insulate soft networks. Although it was formulated with the intent to insulate soft networks, the SIV was ultimately a reactionary strategy. The USA failed to enact policy that would have proactively protected local-national allies from the outset, and instead used the SIV to ineffectively counteract the damage that was already done. Given continued USA participation in operations and conflicts around the world, as well as the likelihood that the USA will be involved in future conflicts, it is important to enact preemptive policy options that strengthen vital soft networks.

Therefore, government agencies should consider best practices culled from other domains and lessons learned from an agency theory evaluation of relationships with soft networks to proactively insulate indigenous partners. As mentioned, awareness of local agent risk on behalf of principals remains a serious issue for policymakers and USA COIN/CT practitioners. Utilizing agency theory's framework for soft network relationships, the USA should implement pre-deployment training that addresses protection issues. This training should instruct appropriate identity protection methods, tools for soft network risk assessment and, in worst-case scenarios, options for relocation. By allowing practitioners to understand risks and asymmetric information challenges from the agent perspective in advance, creative leaders can imagine ways to counter adversary's attempts to undermine soft networks and adopt new policy options to build resiliency into those networks.

In addition to pre-deployment training, government agencies should take specific organizational steps to ensure identity protection policy of soft networks. These steps include: (1) designating Deputy Assistant-level Secretaries for Soft Network Protection (or assigning a current DAS-level official with this responsibility), to ensure that departments and agencies prioritize soft network protection; (2) appointing a congressional commission to investigate losses (i.e. agents killed/threatened, leaked intel, lost opportunities, scarce human resources etc.) on the ground in conflict zones; and (3) Department of Defense cooperation with the Department of State to engage other countries of asylum in an international relocation program. In order to achieve these steps, legislation must be passed that ensures the resources and authority to protect indigenous partners. This legislation will require concerted political will on behalf of those in government, but such steps are necessary to ensure the protection of local-national allies, and by extension, USA interests.

Conclusion

The U.S. should expect its enemies to continue using age-old methods of coercion to threaten soft networks and counter USA influence in foreign environments. As a result, the national security community must increase its awareness and develop strategic responses to threats. Beyond the moral responsibility of safeguarding those who sacrifice life and limb, implementing protection policies will enhance mission success and counter enemy efforts to undermine USA foreign policy. A strong protection policy would indicate USA commitment to engaging and protecting local allies. By protecting soft networks abroad, the USA maintains its ability to counter insurgent, terrorist, and criminal networks, enhancing current operations, law enforcement investigations, and other real national security interests. If the USA does not devise creative policy measures to protect its own interests and its most trusted partners, it will be unable to counter the developing and dynamic threats present in current geopolitical contests.

The USA will never be able to wholly eliminate threats to soft networks, yet it can take assertive, concrete measures to mitigate and manage them, and in doing so, apply pressure to the next generation of malign actors. In this vein, it is in the USA national interest to protect critical indigenous actors who demonstrate a willingness to cooperate with USA operatives during COIN and CT operations.

In addition to protecting existing local-national partners, future protections for soft networks should factor into policy development. The USA must mold an operational culture that looks beyond the mission of the moment and incorporates an understanding of the long-term strategic implications of building networks with lasting potential. The USA should generate awareness amongst interagency teams of the risk imbalances between principals and agents in the field. Moreover, principals should seek to understand agent risk in order to mitigate them and better align interests, as well as reduce information asymmetries. However, education will only aid soft network protection if our field operatives have the necessary policy tools to respond in the field.

Options must be proactively implemented to insulate soft networks abroad. Implementing the recommended policy measures discussed above will allow governmental agencies and departments to utilize measures that most apply to strategic challenges facing soft networks. Moreover, the ability to choose from a broad range of policy options will protect USA soft networks far more effectively, as the current portfolio only has one tool– the SIV–which does not meet the strategic needs of many stakeholders. Soft networks are managed most effectively with a mixed-method approach, using proactive policies in-country, and resorting to relocation measures as a last resort.

If the USA does not provide its operators with flexible options to protect soft networks, it will continue to leave its closest allies at the mercy of malign actors. Abandoning these networks endangers USA legitimacy in conflict zones, and risks the success of future operations – operations that are increasingly characterized by enemies' ability to effectively employ a strategy of intimidation and extermination against USA allies. Regardless of contemporary strategic setbacks, such as those witnessed in Iraq, policies that demonstrate USA commitment to protecting its soft networks will reinforce USA narratives and aid successful COIN and CT operations.

Soft Networks are a valuable, and necessary, asset to the pursuance of USA interests. An inability to secure these networks hinders current and future interests. Therefore, the USA must ensure its local-national allies feel secure, and in cases when they do not, reassure local-national allies of USA protection. To this end, the USA must commit to effectuating substantive policy that provides soft networks with viable security and relocation options. If the USA fails to do so, it risks the success of vital national security operations, and will likely face a more difficult operational environment in future conflicts. Finally, aside from the practical reasons for protecting our agents abroad, protecting soft networks clearly aligns with American values. As a country that prioritizes patriotism, hard work, and freedom, we can, and must, do more to support our most trusted partners.

Notes

1. Packer, "Betrayed," 31.
2. Warren and Miska, "Soft Networks," 3.
3. Russell, "Innovation in War," 601-3.
4. Miska, presentation to the Pacific Council on International Policy, 2 February 2017.
5. Under section 1059 of the National Defense Authorization Act for Fiscal Year 2006, Public Law 109-163, up to 50 Iraqi and Afghan translators working for the U.S. military have been eligible for special immigrant visas (SIVs) each fiscal year (FY). Public Law 110-36, which President Bush signed into law on 15 June 2007, amended section 1059 by expanding the total number of beneficiaries to 500 a year for FY 2007 and FY 2008 only. In FY 2009, the number of visas available for this category reverted to 50 annually. However, on 30 September 2014, the Iraqi SIV program ended, leaving thousands without an option for relocation to the USA.
6. Hsu and Wright, "Crocker Blasts Refugee Process."
7. Agency theory dictates 'an agency relationship has arisen between two (or more) parties when one, designated as the agent, acts for, on behalf of, or as representative for the other, designated the principal, in a particular domain of decision problems.' For more see Ross, "The Economic Theory of Agency."
8. Ibid, 134.
9. Kilcullen, *The Accidental Guerrilla*, 124.
10. Ibid, 126.
11. FM 3-24/MCWP 3-33.5 *Counterinsurgency*, Headquarters USA Army.
12. Russell, "Innovation in War," 601.
13. Kilcullen, *The Accidental Guerrilla*, 135.
14. The List Project Policy Proposal, May 2010.
15. Conversation with Steve Miska, Baghdad, Iraq, October, 2007. Identity of individual protected.

16. Bruno, "Iraqi and Afghan Special Immigrant Visa Programs," 4.
17. Ibid, 4.
18. Ibid, 4.
19. Ibid, 5.
20. La Corte, "Our Immigration System Is Killing Our Allies."
21. During the latter half of 2007, Task Force Justice would process up to three dozen SIV participants, six of whom would enter the U.S. military as 09L interpreters. The Underground Railroad continued from Baghdad to Amman to the U.S. until the U.S. Baghdad Embassy finally allowed interviews at their location in the Green Zone in late 2007.
22. See note 20 above.
23. Public Law 113–66, "National Defense Authorization Act for Fiscal Year 2014."
24. Rigby, *University Honors Junior/Senior Projects*.
25. Bruno, 12-13.
26. Ibid, 12.
27. International Refugee Assistance Project, *Fifteen Years On*, 10.
28. Sanghiva, "Abandoned in Baghdad."
29. Ibid.
30. Huetteman, "'They Will Kill Us."
31. Ibid.
32. Amadeo, "U.S. Federal Budget Breakdown."
33. Miller, "Chart: Iraqi Translators, a Casualty List."
34. See note 20 above.
35. Department of State, *Joint Department of State/Department of Homeland Security Report*, 1-6.
36. No One Left Behind Annual Report, *No One Left Behind*, 3.
37. Email correspondence with Steve Miska, 10 April 2011. Identity of individual and NGO protected by nondisclosure agreement.
38. Interview with Steve Miska, 3 February 2011. Identity of individual and NGO protected by nondisclosure agreement.
39. See note 37 above.
40. See note 38 above.
41. Ibid.
42. The Massachusetts cases found that '87% of witnesses stated that they knew the perpetrator,' and that 'approximately half (50%) of all critical witnesses had a past conviction, 40% had an open case, and 19% of critical witnesses were on probation at the time the petition was filed.' Deval L. Patrick, 'An Overview of Cases in Fiscal Year 2007,' The Commonwealth of Massachusetts Witness Protection Program, (October 2007), 14.
43. U.S. Marshals Service, "Witness Security Program brief."
44. Ibid.
45. USA Marshals Service, *Witness Security Division Fact Sheet*.
46. Department of Justice, New Hampshire, Address Confidentiality Program brief.
47. See note 8 above.
48. Ibid.
49. Eisenhardt, "Agency Theory: An Assessment and Review," 61.
50. Ibid, 58.
51. Fyfe, and McKay, "Witness Intimidation, Forced Migration and Resettlement," 77-90.
52. Ibid, 35-36.

53. Ferris, "The Looming Crisis."
54. See The International Rescue Committee, "Iraqi Refugees in the United States."; Semple, "Iraqi Immigrants Face Lonely Struggle in U.S." and author firsthand experience with Iraqi immigrant families in the U.S.

Disclosure statement

No potential conflict of interest was reported by the authors.

Bibliography

Amadeo, Kimberley. "U.S. Federal Budget Breakdown." *The Balance*, July 10, 2018.
Bruno, Andorro. "Iraqi and Afghan Special Immigrant Visa Programs." *Congressional Research Service*, February 26, 2016
Department of Justice, New Hampshire, Address Confidentiality Program. Accessed November 23, 2010. http://www.doj.nh.gov/victim/addressfaq.html
Department of State. *Joint Department of State/Department of Homeland Security Report: Status of the Afghan Special Immigrant Visa Program*. April 2017
Eisenhardt, Kathleen. "Agency Theory: An Assessment and Review." *The Academy of Management Review* 14, (January 1989): 57–74.
Ferris, Elizabeth. "The Looming Crisis: Displacement and Security in Iraq." Foreign Policy at Brookings, Policy Paper Number 5, August 2008.
Field Manual 3-24/MCWP 3-33.5 Counterinsurgency. *Headquarters USA Army*, December 15, 2006.
Fyfe, Nicholas R., and Heather McKay. "Witness Intimidation, Forced Migration and Resettlement: A British Case Study." *Transactions of the Institute of British Geographers* 25(New Series), no. 1 (2000): 35–36.
Hsu, Spencer S., and Robin Wright. "Crocker Blasts Refugee Process." The Washington Post, September 17, 2007.
Huetteman, Emmarie. "'They Will Kill Us': Afghan Translators Plead for Delayed U.S. Visas." *The New York Times*, August 9, 2016.
International Refugee Assistance Project. *Fifteen Years On: Protecting Iraqi Wartime Partners*. New York, NY: Urban Justice Center, March 20, 2018.
International Rescue Committee. "Iraqi Refugees in the United States: In Dire Straits." *A Report of the IRC Commission on Iraqi Refugees*, June 2009.
Kilcullen, David. *The Accidental Guerrilla: Fighting Small Wars in the Midst of a Big One*. Oxford: Oxford University Press, 2009.
La Corte, Matthew. "Our Immigration System Is Killing Our Allies." *Foundation for Economic Education*. (August 4, 2015).
The List Project Policy Proposal, May 2010.
Miller, T. Christian. "Chart: Iraqi Translators, a Casualty List." *ProPublica*, December 18, 2009.
Miska, Steve, and Roslyn Warren. "Soft Networks: Time to Counter the Enemy's Logical Strategy." *Combating Terrorism Exchange* 3, (November 2013): 4.
No One Left Behind Annual Report. *No One Left Behind*, 2017.
Patrick, Deval L. "An Overview of Cases in Fiscal Year 2007." The Commonwealth of Massachusetts Witness Protection Program, October 2007.
Public Law 113-66. *National Defense Authorization Act For Fiscal Year 2014*. December 26, 2013.

Rigby, Brendan. "Mission Impossible: An Assessment of the Iraqi Special Immigrant Visa." *Northeastern University Honors Junior/Senior Projects*, Boston, MA, May 1, 2010.

Ross, Stephen A. "The Economic Theory of Agency: The Principal's Problem." *The American Economic Review* 63, no. 2 (May 1973): 134. Papers and Proceedings of the Eighty-fifth Annual Meeting of American Economic Association.

Russell, James A. "Innovation in War: Counterinsurgency Operations in Anbar and Ninewa Provinces, Iraq, 2005–2007." *The Journal of Strategic Studies* 33, no. 4 (2010): 601.

Sanghiva, Saurabh. "Abandoned in Baghdad." *The New York Times*, August 30, 2010.

Semple, Kirk. "Iraqi Immigrants Face Lonely Struggle in U.S." *The New York Times*, August 13, 2009.

U.S. Marshals Service. "Witness Security Program Brief." Accessed July 11, 2018. https://www.usmarshals.gov/witsec/index.html

USA Marshals Service. *Witness Security Division Fact Sheet*. Department of Justice, Office of Public Affairs, April 13, 2018. https://www.usmarshals.gov/duties/fact sheets/witsec.pdf

9 Systems failure
The US way of irregular warfare

David H. Ucko

ABSTRACT
Since 9/11, the United States has achieved notable gains against al Qaeda, and also Islamic State (IS), all while avoiding another mass-casualty attack at home. Yet, institutionally, culturally, and in its capabilities, the US government remains seriously ill-equipped for the task of countering irregular threats. Partly as a result, Islamist extremism shows no sign of being defeated, having instead metastasized since 9/11 and spread. Why, given the importance accorded to counterterrorism, has the US approach remained inadequate? What is impeding more fundamental reforms? The article evaluates the United States' way of irregular warfare: its troubled engagement with counter-insurgency and its problematic search for lower cost and lower risk ways of combating terrorism. It suggests needed reforms but acknowledges also the unlikelihood of change.

Since 9/11, the United States has developed the military capability of targeting and eliminating individual terrorist leaders and operatives. It has maintained a powerful conventional combat capability, which helped it overthrow the Taliban regime in Afghanistan and Islamic State (IS) in Iraq. It has amassed substantial operational experience in counterinsurgency in several theatres and, at times, achieved impressive results at the tactical and operational levels. It has also developed and fielded materiel and structures relevant to counterinsurgency and stability operations. And yet, despite these advances, nearly two decades since the mass-casualty terrorist attacks of September 2011, the US government's ability to counter irregular actors remains underdeveloped and deeply inadequate.

The US national security community does not recognize this deficiency as such. Instead, most see the confrontation against non-state armed groups as manageable through drones, special operations forces, and proxies. At any rate, following the bruising campaigns in Iraq and Afghanistan, and with apparently escalating tensions with China and Russia, there is currently no appetite to invest further and reorient instruments of national power for irregular warfare. And yet, the threat that awoke the United States to this challenge in 2001 has if anything gotten worse, taking advantage of political instability in the Middle East, Africa, and Central and South-Southeast Asia. The ideology behind the 9/11 attacks, then limited to a small group of extremists based in Afghanistan, has also spread, globally, as seen with the flow of fighters volunteering to join Islamic State (IS) and the continued mobilization and attacks that occur in its name. Though the US homeland has so far been spared another major attack, the threat of mass-casualty terrorism has not significantly diminished. More than that, counterterrorism is badly straining the West's cosmopolitan fabric and liberal values, which, at a deeper level, are what it is fighting to uphold.

Against this backdrop, this article examines two questions. Why, given the importance accorded to combatting terrorism and defeating insurgency, has the US investment in the required capabilities been so inadequate? And why, despite failure, have we not seen greater rates of change? The article addresses these two questions by evaluating, first, the limitations of America's direct engagement with counterinsurgency, as attempted in Iraq and Afghanistan, and then the indirect strategies formulated to counter irregular threats 'on-the-cheap', through drones, special operations forces, and partnership capacity-building. By way of conclusion, the piece comments on the possible future trajectory of US engagement with irregular warfare.

America's brief counterinsurgency era

In both the Iraq and Afghanistan wars, initial gains by US forces unleashed new waves of instability, prompting more protracted engagements. To combat rising levels of insecurity, the US Department of Defense (DoD) gradually adopted the tasks of stabilization and counterinsurgency. A military more adept at such tasks, it was reasoned, could hasten a propitious US withdrawal from these troubled campaigns. In the aftermath of the 11 September attacks, some also perceived an enhanced military ability to reverse 'state failure' as necessary to deprive terrorist organizations of sanctuary.[1]

Mainly from 2005 onward, US military priorities shifted from a near-exclusive focus on major combat operations to a greater emphasis on the types of missions encountered in theatre, be they termed 'counterinsurgencies', 'stability operations', or, rather perversely, 'small wars'. In 2005, the DoD issued a directive that positioned stability operations on the same level of importance as major combat operations.[2] The US Army, together with the Marine Corps, published new doctrine on counterinsurgency that would greatly influence the treatment of the topic across NATO.[3] And with its massive resources, particularly in times of war, the US military reoriented training and built new hardware to meet the challenges of operating in urban, contested environments.

The rate of learning was at times impressive, particularly given the supposedly sclerotic nature of change within military organizations.[4] For this very reason, the reforms also challenged the US military's orthodoxy and culture. Historically, despite repeated engagement in stability operations, occupation, and even counterinsurgency, the US military has defined strength in terms of the capabilities needed to fight a 'conventional' adversary shaped, sized, and operating very much like itself.[5] Given this metric, investments to counter different enemies have been difficult to justify. For reasons that remain under-examined, the US military regards non-state, untraditional, or unconventional adversaries as less sophisticated, less lethal, and therefore, as less worthy of preparation. Of course, it does not help that irregular campaigns – really campaigns in which one side shuns the norms and laws of war – sit so badly with military institutions: victory is often ambiguous, success is political rather than military, and casualties must be expected as part of a long-haul effort likely to span years if not decades.[6]

When nonetheless engaged in counterinsurgency, the US military tends to compensate for its lack of preparation by adapting more or less effectively, but it always forgets what it has learned soon after the campaign is over. This is, one might say, a 'US counterinsurgency syndrome', though it is by no means the only state to engage with the challenge of insurgency in this infelicitous manner.[7] To do better, it would be necessary to prioritize counterinsurgency and stability operations as an integral slice in the spectrum of operations, prepare and train accordingly, and, most importantly, tackle the challenge without miscasting it as more manageable than what it really is. So far, this test has proved beyond US capacity. It is not only the case that the United States failed to adapt sufficiently during the highpoint of operations in Iraq and Afghanistan, or that it will now 'no longer be sized to conduct large-scale prolonged stability operations', as stated in the 2014 DoD quadrennial defense review (QDR), but rather that it has also failed to understand and build the capabilities to conduct irregular warfare even on a lower scale. The problem, in other words, is not only quantitative but qualitative.[8]

How can one measure the extent of learning – or lack thereof? Some studies of military learning have sought to isolate *one* specific metric – often published doctrine – as a yardstick for institutional change.[9] Yet, the value of published doctrine is overstated: although 'doctrine can serve as evidence of institutional learning', it is less certain that it is 'central to how militaries execute their missions'.[10] As Sarah Sewell put it in her foreword to the University of Chicago edition of the FM 3–24 field manual, 'In theory doctrine jumpstarts the other "engines of change". But each engine is in a separate car with its own driver, already headed toward an important destination'.[11] To ascertain the full significance of doctrine, it is necessary to go beyond the publication of field manuals and consider the change elsewhere: education, training, organizational structures, technology (or resourcing), and culture. On these fronts, change has been far less formidable, plausibly because whereas there is no immediate limit to how many field manuals can be printed, actual programmatic change must come at the expense of preexisting priorities.

In terms of training and education, despite some changes in curriculum and exercises, the US military was never able to overhaul a system that, particularly in the classroom, remained devoted to Cold War-era concepts and case studies. Training exercises were more easily adapted to mirror the conditions of Iraq or Afghanistan and no doubt flattened the learning curve for those units involved. However, equipping junior leaders with the broad knowledge and analytical skills required for counterinsurgency proved beyond the reach of the US armed services. Gen. (ret.) Sir John Kiszely, former head of the British Defence Academy, captures some of the bewildering demands: they must possess the ability to

> apply soft power as well as hard ... work in partnership with multinational, multiagency organizations, civilian as well as military ... master information operations and engage successfully with the media; conduct persuasive dialogue with local leaders ... mentally out-manoeuvre a wily and ruthless enemy; and, perhaps most often overlooked, measure progress appropriately.

As Kiszely adds, these competences require an understanding of 'the political context; the legal, moral and ethical complexities; culture and religion; how societies work; what constitutes good governance; the relationship between one's own armed forces and society; the notion of human security; the concept of legitimacy; the limitations on the utility of force; the psychology of one's opponents and the rest of the population'.[12]

Meeting these demands is almost impossible in the best of circumstances, let alone when the US military considers them ancillary to those 'traditional' skills required for 'real' wars. Yet, the problem is only partially one of ambition – it relates also to the lack of interest displayed by US institutions of professional military education in boosting language proficiency, social scientific skills, and acumen in the humanities. In many of these institutions, faculty are not encouraged to be academically trained or active and so syllabi are rarely updated or sufficiently rigorous. The entire academic experience in war colleges is too often thought of as a year off.[13] This expectation rests on a military-educational culture that does not value broader academic achievement. Thus, despite various plans and roadmaps, most of the officers seeking to go further academically have had to do so on their own time. Also, in educating senior leadership, the focus has remained overwhelmingly conventional, with scant attention paid to critical topics such as military governance, political economy, or counterinsurgency campaign planning.[14]

In terms of organizational structures, the US Army – the main military actor in counterinsurgency – showed no desire to reorient its force structure to augment seriously its suitability for counterinsurgency. Incidentally, America's reengagement with counterinsurgency coincided with what the Army termed 'the most ambitious restructuring of its forces since World War II', namely, their modularization into brigade combat teams (BCTs) of 3500–4000 soldiers each.[15] The fluidity resulting from such flux might have been exploited to incorporate some of the urgent lessons drawn from ongoing campaigns, such as the need for military police, engineers, medical units, civil affairs, linguists, psychological operations (PSYOPS), and explosive ordnance disposal teams, to name but a few of the assets commonly called for but available in far too short supply. Instead, the BCT units, though marketed as flexible, remain near-exclusively configured for major combat operations.[16] Despite stability operations having been designated by the DoD as equal in importance to conventional combat, no part of the force structure was specifically oriented toward the tasks of such operations: the establishment of civil security and control, the restoration of essential services, and support to governance and to economic and infrastructure development.[17]

Absent more convincing reforms to the Army's force structure, ad hoc solutions were devised to address enduring capability gaps. One such 'solution' was the Human Terrain Teams (HTT), groups of anthropologists and social scientists with relevant knowledge or skills. Forming part of the brigade staff, HTTs were to provide deployed units with insight and methodologies to better understand the local population. Stood up hastily and with uneven training, the teams received mixed reviews, but insofar as they answered a need felt by troops in theatre, they also pointed to enduring capability caps within the military itself. Though US intelligence adapted quickly post-9/11 to locate and strike targets, it has 'neglected "white" information about the population that was necessary for success in population-centric campaigns such as counterinsurgency (COIN) operations'.[18] Thus, despite deploying with civil affairs, PSYOPS, intelligence, and other similar units, the US military remained 'deaf, dumb, and stupid' as it engaged with the world.[19] For future interventions, it is worth asking whether improvised organizational fixes such as HTTs can compensate for the lack of institutionalized capabilities within the force structure or whether the latter should in fact be developed to meet the requirements of modern operations.

In terms of technology, there have been impressive advances as a result of the ongoing information revolution and in the areas of drones and counter-improvised explosive device (IED) measures. More fundamentally, however, the system opposed remodeling itself for the new operations of the 21st century. Indeed, in its budget requests, DoD continued to pour money into costly programs of questionable relevance in the given strategic environment. Released at the height of the US counterinsurgency campaign in Iraq, the budget request for FY08 'move[d] ahead with the vast majority of the acquisition programs included in the Services' long-range plans – most of which were also projected in the last, pre-9/11, Clinton Administration defense plan'.[20] The Army sunk its funds into the Future Combat Systems, whereas more relevant platforms, such as the troop-carrying MRAP (Mine-Resistant, Ambush Protected), received attention only following Congressional intervention.[21] The Marine Corps invested in concepts and programs for over-the-horizon amphibious assaults, with the V-22 Osprey, the Joint Strike Fighter, and the Expeditionary Fighting Vehicle – a floating tank of sorts – accounting for almost all of its spending. All 'would be more useful for refighting the island-hopping campaign of World War II than for policing western Iraq'.[22]

This continuity in priorities stems in part from the dynamics of the Iron Triangle – the 'special relationship' between the Pentagon, Congress, and the private defense industry – but it also reflects the armed services' culture and self-understanding. The Army sees itself as a force designed to 'fight and win the nation's wars', and these are not taken to include what once were actually termed 'military operations *other than war*'.[23] The Marines, meanwhile, are primarily concerned with not being seen as or actually becoming a 'second land army' and therefore tend to promote their identity-furnishing role in amphibious attack – from the ship to shore – all the while taking for granted supposed proficiency in small wars. As a result, the Marine Corps also actively resisted the call to fund and field mine-resistant MRAP vehicles. Intended to deal with the murderous threat of IEDs in Iraq, the vehicle was too heavy for helicopter transport and therefore ran counter to the Marines' desire of mobility and quick deployment.

If the culture of the armed services is to blame, so is the bureaucratic culture of the US military and its active resistance to needed change. In terms of working practices, centralized management and the reliance on outdated career templates have stunted the institution's shift from a peacetime military that deployed infrequently and briefly to one engaged in several protracted wars.[24] Inflexible, process-driven, and laden with regulations, the personnel system of DoD and the armed services consistently fails to track or nurture needed skills and assets and prefers to promote according to decades-old career paths. As a result, as per a 2011 poll, a mere 7% of junior officers agreed that the Army 'does a good job retaining the best leaders' and only 30% agreed that the military personnel system 'promotes the right officers to general'.[25] In part, the problem is one of risk-aversion, as the Army has institutionalized a zero-defects culture in which any transgression of existing operating procedures is likely to harm a career and is therefore discouraged. The outcome, however, is the smothering of creativity, initiative, and adaptation.[26]

The rotational system by which the American armed forces fights wars, with formed units transitioning in and out of the battlefield, has also been found wanting – yet refuses to change. When the US Army won the Second World War, it replaced the system whereby units stayed together for the duration of the war in favor of a rotational policy that remained in place throughout Korea, Vietnam, and more recent conflicts.[27] Though this approach is germane for a peacetime operational tempo, it staunches the continuity needed to retain awareness, maintain contacts, and achieve operational effectiveness over the longer term.[28] John Paul Vann famously quipped that 'the United States has not been in Vietnam for nine years, but for one year nine times', and the problem has not been adequately addressed since then.[29] The solution is not necessarily to enforce longer tours – though they were extended to 15 months during the surge in Iraq (and it is worth noting that soldiers deploying to Malaya – that canonical case of counterinsurgency – did so for periods of 24 months).[30] A more plausible solution would be to ameliorate transitions between deployments, so as to enable the required continuity, or to structure rotations so that sections of the same unit return to the same area until the war is over. Nothing like this has happened, because, even at the height of the wars in Iraq and Afghanistan, it was deemed more important to service bureaucratic procedure than to win the war.

On one level, the US government is fully aware of these weaknesses. The Joint-Staff-commissioned capstone study into past operations, *A Decade of War*, noted 'a failure to recognize, acknowledge, and accurately define the operational environment', a 'conventional warfare paradigm ... ineffective when applied to operations other than major combat', a 'failure to adequately plan and resource strategic and operational transitions', and 'uneven' inter-agency coordination due to 'inconsistent participation in planning, training, and operations'.[31] The issue, however, is that whereas little of the above analysis will strike reform-oriented leaders and thinkers as new, it has been impossible – despite vigorous attempts by senior proponents – to reform the vast bureaucracy.[32] This is not merely due to institutional inertia but also the willed resistance of those who view counterinsurgency and engagement against irregular threats as a misuse of military resources. To this group, nation-building, counterinsurgency, and stability operations offer no return on what is a significant investment and do not relate to US national security. On the basis of steps taken (and not taken) and investments made (and not made), it would seem that this is a camp with serious sway.

The argument against counterinsurgency capabilities rests on a presumed bifurcation and, therefore, a choice between *irregular* scenarios such as those seen in Iraq or Afghanistan and *conventional* operations, such as those seen in the first 3 weeks of the Iraq War in 2003 or in the 1991 Operation Desert Storm. The US military has long touted the need to be ready for 'full-spectrum' operations, to wit, for irregular, conventional, and a host of other possible contingencies.[33] Yet, decisions about resource allocation still operate on an implicit dichotomy between the high- and the low-end of the conflict spectrum, and, as seen, the former wins out. It is true that – *operationally* – the Army and Marine Corps, for several years after 9/11, were almost exclusively committed to counterinsurgency, or at least to operations *called* counter-insurgency, but *institutionally*, force structure and resource-allocation only adapted superficially to the demands of the contemporary operating environment. To the degree that reform occurred – in training, education, and doctrine – changes were brought in from the margins so as to disrupt minimally preexisting investments. This is a very problematic way of achieving meaningful change.

More helpful would be an unlikely bottom-up review intended to build a capability that truly reflects current and prospective needs. Rather than bifurcate and pick and choose, irregular and regular challenges must be understood as overlapping. The theoretical distinctions can be a helpful heuristic; yet, as reflected by the rise of 'hybridity' and 'unrestricted warfare' to describe the mingling of conventional and unconventional approaches – also by states – the reality on the battlefield seldom fits our preexisting conceptual categories.[34] Nor is such hybridity in any way new or likely to go away.[35] Current trends point to a need, even in conventional campaigns, for skills and capabilities such as those called for in the Iraq and Afghanistan efforts. When territory is seized, engagement with the population will be unavoidable. Urbanization suggests operations in built-up areas as the norm, where people and politics cannot be ignored. The military is also engaging with adversaries that will blend regular and unregulated forms of violence, exploit a mediatized battleground, and combine the use of force with subversion, politics, and information operations. The aim of the institutional learning is therefore not narrowly 'to learn counter-insurgency', rather to learn how to conduct *modern wars*, the complexity of which simply cannot be wished away.

Yet this is exactly what is now happening. Though the wars in Iraq and Afghanistan are not yet over, American ground forces have sought to retrain on conventional combat capabilities lost or weakened since 9/11. Some of this re-familiarization is fully justified. US Army soldiers should be able to conduct combined arms manoeuver. Worryingly, though, the rebalancing is based on the supposition of having *already perfected* counterinsurgency. The 2014 QDR, for example, spoke tellingly about the '*expertise* gained during the last ten years of counterinsurgency and stability operations in Iraq and Afghanistan'.[36] This confidence does not reflect the mixed operational experiences of the US military in either case nor the basic (legacy) continuity in how the force was structured, trained, educated, and equipped. Certainly, the track record is not one that justifies the closing of the Army Irregular Warfare Center, which was shuttered in 2014, the phasing out of the HTT without any equivalent replacement, or the cuts to the counter-IED organization stood up during the Iraq War.[37] As to DoD's expectation that it can 'protect the ability to regenerate capabilities that might be needed' in future counterinsurgencies, the lessons emerging from Iraq and Afghanistan do not offer much hope.[38]

The moment is now upon the US military when it needs to learn from its past experiences and question what type of military force is needed for 21st-century security threats. For the Navy and Air Force, the quest for relevance is less pressing, given the rise of near-peer rivals in Russia and China. For the Army in particular (and to a lesser degree the Marine Corps), questions of what makes a relevant ground force have been pushed aside. Instead, the Army faces an identity crisis, unable to compete with the Air Force and Navy in terms of stand-off weapons yet unwilling to embrace the one area where it is truly king – the occupation of territory, its cities, people, politics, and all. Its plea for relevance now involves the jargon of 'multidomain battle'. The attempted explanation of the general commanding the US Army Training and Doctrine Command is unintentionally revealing:

> Put simply, Army forces will maneuver to positions of relative advantage and project power across all domains to ensure joint force freedom of action. We will do this by integrating joint, interorganizational and multinational capabilities to create windows of domain superiority to enable joint force freedom of maneuver. Joint commanders will then exploit those windows of superiority by synchronizing cross-domain fires and maneuver to achieve physical, temporal, positional and psychological advantages.[39]

Seldom has so much jargon been deployed to say so little, but one thing is clear: counterinsurgency is out.[40]

Moon without a planet: where is the policy?

Beyond the continuity within the US military, a second fundamental limitation to US effectiveness in counterinsurgency is the lack of a deployable and capable civilian component that could direct military operations to serve a political policy. Within the Western context, counterinsurgency finds its heyday in the colonial era or during the wars of national liberation that marked imperial retreat. As such, they were prosecuted by states with a quasi-permanent civilian and military presence abroad, as in Malaya, Algeria, or the Philippines. These resources and structures are no more. This limitation matters, because counterinsurgency, so the texts tell us, is 80% political and 20% military. The main aim is not to kill and capture insurgents but to address the causative factors of violence.[41] This task is undeniably political, which is why counterinsurgency must be understood not as a military activity but as 'armed politics' or 'armed reform'. Much like political campaigns, counterinsurgency seeks mobilization and popular empowerment, yet all while shots are being fired.[42]

As any student of government will know, the requirements of reform are daunting, as they challenge the entrenched privileges of the elite. Inspirational leadership, the threat of imminent defeat, or accommodation of bottom-up pressures may compel some elites to change course, but in many cases, the very deficiencies that brought on insurgency preclude the measures required to address it, resulting in a tailspin of instability leading to chronic civil war or outright regime change. Such outcomes occurred also during the colonial times, in which theorization about counterinsurgency was born.[43] And yet, as a practical matter, it was easier for imperial governments to ensure reform over structures that they controlled or where they had semi-permanent advisors on hand (as in Malaya) than it is today for Western states to prod, push, and entice sovereign and quite independent governments, be it in Kabul or Baghdad, to follow the advice on offer. It certainly does not help that these regimes were themselves weak, having been freshly imposed through Western actions – in some ways *they* are the revolutionaries – and that the West's diplomatic skills appear so very limited.[44]

Looking specifically at the latest US engagements with counterinsurgency, it quickly becomes clear that it lacks the deployable civilian capabilities necessary to plan and guide an expeditionary campaign of 'armed reform'. Instead of colonial administrators, the United States engaged in Iraq via two organizations – the Coalition Provisional Authority and the Organization of Reconstruction and Humanitarian Assistance – neither of which 'had the right people or assets to make their presence felt throughout the country.... Few among them had any detailed knowledge of the Iraqi milieu'.[45] By 2006, in Afghanistan, the United States had recognized the need for a 'Comprehensive Approach', but this rhetorical innovation could not link a massive inter-departmental bureaucracy, much of which was domestically focused, for the purpose of coordinated campaigns abroad. Even when ambassadors and joint force commanders worked well together, civil–military coordination was hampered by the respective agencies' different assessment of the situation, priorities, and cultures.[46]

Funding and resourcing of the 'Comprehensive Approach' also remained lackluster, even for the State Department and the US Agency for International Development (USAID), the most expeditionary of American civilian government bodies. USAID had downsized following the Vietnam War, in which it was heavily involved, and abandoned the prospect of again playing a similar role. As a result, USAID's deployment to Vietnam was itself larger than the agency's entire staff in 2006. Despite some structural reforms following 9/11, it lacked, much like the State Department itself, a sizeable operational capability and a standing deployable corps. These two organizations could 'send a few people quickly, but for such substantial operations ... both have to recruit staff, write and sign contracts, and conduct training – a time-consuming process for which the situation on the ground can't wait'.[47] It is also the case that sections within USAID continued to resist a role in stability operations and alongside DoD.[48] Instead, USAID has evolved into a contracting organization for various NGOs and development agencies – entities that, on their part, are eager to maintain impartiality and honor the 'humanitarian space' and therefore resist coordination and cooperation with the armed forces of the state.[49]

As to State, its main effort to stand up a suitable structure – the Office of the Coordinator for Reconstruction and Stabilization (S/CRS) – was undercut by inadequate funding. Attempts to establish a Response Readiness Reserve or a Civilian Reserve Corps failed to replicate the expeditionary civilian structures of historical campaigns. Within the appropriations committees on the Hill, there was no interest in funding civilian expeditionary capabilities, which were seen as peripheral to national security and irrelevant to congressional districts (unlike military spending, which can bring jobs and investment).[50] Meanwhile, turf battles within the State Department meant S/CRS struggled to establish itself. Its transformation, 6 years in, into a Bureau of Conflict and Stabilization Operations signaled lowered ambition for the body. Despite serving as a clearing-house for niche expertise, 'its interagency role has remained marginal rather than central'.[51] More broadly, the State Department never succeeded in changing the culture, career paths, risk tolerance, or personnel procedures to enable this type of expeditionary work.[52] As a result, and given the huge resource imbalance between defense and diplomacy, the US response to irregular threats remained predominantly military. Even when the military made gains, it was a 'moon without a planet to orbit'.[53]

The dysfunctional relationship between political direction and military effort can be addressed – and it begins by changing the cultural reliance and unquestioned faith in the military as a strategic problem solver. To enable political solutions to political problems, the State Department would need to be put in charge over regional policy and thereby direct the military combatant commands (Central Command [CENTCOM], Indo-Pacific Command [INDOPACOM], etc.) in line with political objectives.[54] This would require a regional viceroy position held by an ambassador with the requisite regional linguistic and political acumen and effectively end the tendency whereby ambassadorial posts are given as political favors to unqualified candidates.[55] The State Department would then need to be reorganized and resourced to man the major regional commands (along with its other core functions), resulting in a deployed civilian diplomatic corps executing policy with military support.[56] Others suggest a 'hybrid civil/military capacity' that would be deployable and capable of seamless planning and execution of politico-military missions, with politics driving the use of force rather than vice-versa.[57] So far, nothing of the sort has materialized.

Send in the drones

The disappointing results of counterinsurgency combined with the onerous demands of preparing for other such challenges have encouraged the emergence of more indirect means of exerting influence. Under the administration of President Barack Obama, particularly in his first term, drones came to characterize this approach, with unmanned aerial vehicles being used to launch missiles on suspected al-Qaeda operatives in Pakistan, Libya, Yemen, Somalia, and elsewhere.[58] These drone strikes have eliminated key operatives, disrupted al-Qaeda activities, and forced the group and its affiliates to adopt cumbersome precautions to avoid the 'eye in the sky'.[59] Framed this way, the institutional and political support for drone strikes is easy to see. For one, Obama credited the drone policy with preventing terrorist plots that would have targeted 'international aviation, US transit systems, European cities and our troops in Afghanistan'.[60] Furthermore, drones also reached areas where, for practical or political reasons, ground forces could not operate.

Still, US reliance on drones is far from unproblematic. The most pressing challenge is that the effectiveness of drones appears intertwined with perceptions of legitimacy – of the strikes themselves, of course, but more deeply also of the United States and all that it represents. Irregular warfare is commonly seen as a competition over a relevant population's perception of legitimacy, and the concern with the drone strikes is whether they are in fact contributing toward or eating away at American legitimacy around the world. If that legitimacy, as commonly thought, is in some way related to the number of individuals motivated to take up arms against America, it suddenly becomes difficult to know whether the drones strikes create more terrorists than they eliminate.

The legitimacy crisis of the drone program has three roots.

First, it is assumed that the civilian casualties caused by drone strikes anger not only the victims' families and friends but also entire communities, driving some of them toward anti-American ideologies. There is substantial anecdotal evidence to suggest such a process.[61] Proponents of the drones claim that the number of civilian casualties is low and meets the Just War criteria of proportionality and military necessity.[62] Yet, the total body count is contested and arriving at a clear assessment of the human cost of drone strikes, for many reasons, is difficult. What is undeniable is that civilians, in significant numbers even, have died. As one indication, the London-based Bureau of Investigative Journalism claims that by 24 May 2016, between 493 and 1168 civilians had been killed in US drone strikes in Pakistan, Yemen, and Somalia combined. In a sense, the numbers are almost beside the point. It is the very fact of civilian deaths and the perceived transfer of risk from US security personnel to civilians on the ground that angers the world, particularly when incidents of collateral damage, however isolated, are spread instantly and widely through social media.

Second, the perceived illegitimacy of the drone strikes stems also from their dubious legality, which relies on the application of international humanitarian norms outside a declared conflict. When the program first started, it was classified and so wrapped in secrecy that members of the US national security community would not even acknowledge its existence in unclassified fora.[63] Perversely, this practice persisted even as a public debate on drones raged. The secrecy was counterproductive as it delayed an official US government narrative as to when drone strikes were permitted and why. In response to growing concern, the Obama administration in 2013 shared the legal criteria for the strikes with lawmakers in Congress but, fatefully, not with the public, and so, the legitimizing effects of the increased transparency were minimal at best.[64] In public, the defense 'oscillate[d] between putting forward a law of armed conflict framework and a self-defense framework'.[65]

It was not until December 2016, a month prior to leaving office, that the Obama administration made public the legal case for drone strikes, which it based on the just war principles and the legal authority to target al-Qaeda operatives provided by the 2001 Authorization for Use of Military Force.[66] It is not clear whether, from a public relations standpoint, this explication made the drone strikes any less toxic. Missing, so far, is a concerted effort to 'make the case' – to achieve the buy-in both internationally and domestically. Instead, under the Donald Trump administration, the United States has not only increased its use of drone strikes but also foregone any effort to invest in public diplomacy, legitimacy, or multilateral agreement.[67] In such circumstances, the tangible benefits of this program may easily be outweighed, or at least greatly compromised, by its intangible negative symbolism and political payload.

Third, the US drone program denotes several moral hazards: the pilots face no risk (beyond the psychological), outrage about dead foreigners seems far too easy to brush aside, and the threshold for legal authorization appears, even if it is not, much too low, with the US government acting as judge, jury, and executioner. This asymmetry between the mightiest superpower operating with impunity in the territory of failing states is likely to inflame tensions and evoke strong passions. An active effort to address this reaction would require establishing a more convincing narrative, collaborating *internationally* with the host-nation states where strikes take place, and explaining more explicitly and transparently why each strike was necessary, the case for which must be strong enough to convince even in the eventuality of collateral damage. If a compelling case cannot be made so that Americans *and others* are swayed, the net gain of the strike must be carefully reassessed, both in terms of its tangible and intangible effects.

In place of transparency and clarity, the US drone program remains shrouded in confusion and ambiguity. It is at present questioned whether the United States is 'at war' or simply 'in a war' in which it plays a supportive role for others. Are the drone strikes an instrument of counterterrorism to protect America from attack or an attempt to aid partner governments in their own counterinsurgency efforts? The distinction is critical, as it speaks to the strategic utility of the tactic. The elimination of individual operatives would be appropriate against a terrorist group, because they are unrepresentative of the society they seek to change and must therefore rely heavily on the limited manpower that they can recruit. An *insurgency*, meanwhile, claims a broader basis of legitimacy, mobilizes not a handful but hundreds, even thousands, of followers, and feeds off of local grievances. In such settings, isolated strikes have limited value absent consolidation or follow-up.[68] The White House claims that the drone attacks are launched exclusively to protect American lives, yet given the sheer number of strikes involved, and the fact that with so-called signature strikes, the target's identity is not necessarily known, it would appear as if the criteria and purpose are far broader.[69] The drones, in other words, have become a military response to a political problem, a counterinsurgency air force operating by itself.[70]

For the strikes to gain strategic meaning against insurgent or proto-insurgent outfits such as Al-Qaeda in the Arabian Peninsula, al-Shabaab, or Tehrik-i-Taliban Pakistan, this armed campaign would need to be complemented by a broader military effort to control territory, which in turn must be guided and shaped by a political strategy that addresses the reasons for mobilization into violence. Though the US drone strikes have at times enjoyed the closed-door support of local governments – in Yemen and Pakistan[71] – there is no sign of a coordinated strategy that would integrate the strikes within a combined campaign plan.[72] Instead, regardless of purpose, enemy, and context, the strikes are underpinned by a fatal assumption that 'if only we can get enough of these bastards, we'll win the war'.[73] Meanwhile, the local population wherefrom the violent extremist organization stems is left with few options, with armed radicals on the one hand and the threat of American drone strikes on the other. Who in such a context will support the United States? Who could afford to do so, when the group still holds the ground?[74]

With these complications, it is perhaps not surprising that while drone strikes have weakened al-Qaeda core and forced other groups to adapt, the movement that executed the 11 September 2001 attacks and the ideology that fueled it have assumed new shapes and forms – in Syria, Iraq, North Africa – all the while Pakistan, Yemen, and Somalia are still torn apart by jihadist violence.[75] The drone program is a tactic posing as a strategy, yet because it seems so tantalizingly decisive and denotes such minimal risk, comparatively speaking, it 'has taken on a life of its own, to the point where tactics are driving strategy rather than the other way around'.[76]

Building partnership capacity: proxies

Besides drones, the US approach to countering irregular warfare also relies heavily on 'building partnership capacity' – advice and assistance rendered to partner nations to augment their abilities to combat irregular threats within their territory. From 2009–15, DoD disbursed almost USD 256 million to Yemen under various security assistance programs, all while the State Department committed USD 34 million in Foreign Military Financing.[77] In fiscal year 2015, almost USD 320 million were allocated to Somalia as security force assistance, most of it to support the African Union peacekeeping force in the country. In April 2017, the Trump administration decided to deploy a few dozen soldiers from the 101st Airborne Division to train and equip Somalia's army 'to better fight al-Shabab'.[78] Indirect engagements such as these have become a hallmark of the US strategy to counter irregular threats, with 148 countries now involved in US-led building partnership capacity efforts.[79] Despite a proliferation of activity, the overall approach lacks strategic coherence and the results are therefore mixed.

The multiplicity of programs designed to boost the capabilities of friendly governments springs *in part* from the negative experiences in Iraq and Afghanistan. Due to the costs, duration, and modest gains of these *direct* engagements, the US national security community has shifted to emphasize supporting roles. In some regard, the shift echoes the Nixon Doctrine, adopted following the Vietnam War, which sought to limit US involvement to advice and assistance and held host-nation governments responsible for their own defense.[80] The approach also rests, at least with respect to counterinsurgency, on a handful of cases, wherein the United States has supported counterinsurgency efforts that have been deemed largely successful: the Colombian fight against FARC, the El Salvadoran war on Farabundo Martí National Liberation Front (FMLN), and the US Special Operations Forces effort, alongside the armed forces of the Philippines, to combat the al-Qaeda-linked Abu Sayyaf.[81]

Proponents of building partnership capacity point to five key advantages. First, the indirect approach puts local forces in the lead and thereby obviates the linguistic and cultural hurdles encountered by foreign troops. Second, by keeping the response local, the counterinsurgency campaign remains untarnished by the stigma of foreign occupation. Third, putting local forces in the lead also reduces the political costs for the intervening government. Fourth, these interventions are also commonly less financially costly – a corollary of the smaller footprint.[82] Fifth, and most fundamentally, the indirect approach puts the local government in charge for solving what is, after all, its problem. In other words, it rightly recognizes the limits on what external powers can achieve by themselves in a foreign land, particularly one they scarcely understand. The focus on partnerships also touches on the essence of expeditionary counterinsurgency: the imperative of maintaining host-nation legitimacy, building capacity, and engaging in a sustainable manner.

While the notion that 'small is beautiful' – that indirect deployments make more sense – is largely correct, the analysis cannot stop at this point. Indeed, the indirect approach, like counterinsurgency or interventions of any type, comprises severe challenges. It should be recognized, for example, that while it may be cheaper or lower in risk, the building of partnership capacity has not to date helped the United States achieve its strategic objectives.[83] In Iraq, Syria, Afghanistan, Libya, Mali, and elsewhere, US attempts to stand up a local defense against insurgency have often faltered, with forces either collapsing, proving wholly inadequate, or switching sides. Where the approach is said to have worked – in Colombia, El Salvador, or the Philippines – outcomes have been less impressive than commonly recognized and/or were conditional on key factors that are not easily reproduced.

One such condition is close familiarity with the recipient military – its needs and culture – and an ability to build on its capabilities. In the fight against FARC, US assistance to Colombia was greatly aided by the two countries' long history of cooperation, stretching back to the Korean War, and to the integration of their respective militaries in education and other parallel institutions. Against such a backdrop, US advisors not only understood their partner but also benefited from a basic foundation of familiarity that could be sustained through more episodic touch-ups. Hence, it was possible to build on existing needs and abilities, with the US providing precisely those niche capabilities that the Colombian armed forces needed: communications and tactical mobility, special forces training, medics, and human rights training.[84]

In contrast, in most of the places where the aim has been to counter al-Qaeda-related groups, familiarity and integration with the host-nation have been limited. Unaware of local institutions, culture, and needs, US efforts to build a military end up mirror-imaging its own military institution and result in assistance that is meaningless or, even, counterproductive. As T.X. Hammes points out, 'In both Iraq and Afghanistan ... trying to impose a merit-based, technologically savvy, equipment-intensive approach onto societies where relationships and social standing have a heavy bearing on organizational behavior proved a bridge too far.'[85] One particular problem, reflecting US military culture, is the reliance on providing high-technological capabilities as silver bullets to irregular warfare challenges. As Philip Carter has argued, 'In American hands, sophisticated weapons work because they are supported by a complex U.S. military machine, one that includes global supply chains, advanced maintenance systems, and millions of well-educated and trained military, civilian and contractor personnel. That machine is impossible to replicate, especially during a short-term or crisis mission like that in Syria'.[86]

In contrast with the effort in Colombia, which was centralized initially under the Plan Colombia program, efforts in countries threatened by al-Qaeda are far more fragmented, less coordinated, and therefore less effective. As an example, the United States is engaged in at least seven initiatives of security-force assistance in Mali, where local forces, with French support, are combating al-Qaeda in the Islamic Maghreb (AQIM).[87] While the scale of the initiative is on aggregate significant, overall engagement is split between different authorities, budgets, and structures, resulting in dispersed and irregular contact with the intended beneficiaries. Within the recipient force, a limited number of companies received training twice a year, but as their members rotated, no capable units were produced. Where equipment was provided, it was not matched to the needs and abilities of the local forces, whose proficiency at desert warfighting remained inferior to that of AQIM. Lacking was a comprehensive DoD-wide, or even special operations forces-run, program to augment the Malian army.[88] Also, missing were broader efforts to address the institutional or logistical capacity of the Malian armed forces, its mobility, or the longer term transfer of needed skills through train-the-trainer programs.

Another key constraint on US efforts at building partnership capability is the limited appetite of policy-makers and politicians to insert US advisors on the frontlines. The purpose of the indirect approach is in part to avoid risk and exposure, and for that reason, US forces are shielded from the more immediate of battlefield dangers. However, such risk-aversion runs counter to the established best practices of advisory work. In the oft-cited case of El Salvador, celebrated as a model small-footprint intervention, the cap on advisors – only 55 were allowed in country at any one time – and the prohibition on their joining the El Salvadoran armed forces (ESAF) on operations greatly limited oversight and leverage over how the local force performed. It also reduced opportunities for US forces to conduct advising 'on the job', where quick learning could have an immediate impact. Whereas US military aid protected the El Salvadoran regime during the campaign's early phase, it proved impossible to optimize ESAF for counterinsurgency, sufficiently reduce human-rights abuses, or defeat FMLN either politically or militarily.[89]

What the US and UK militaries found in Iraq and Afghanistan, and what historical cases also make clear, is that the effectiveness of training, the accountability of those trained, and their gradual accumulation of confidence and skills are best enabled through 'partnering' with local security forces: by living and operating with them, day and night, from the same base, and on the same streets. Curiously, the US approach to advisory work tends to follow the same restrictive rules of engagement as seen in El Salvador, again to limit risk. According to reporting in 2016, US advisors in Syria were barred from engaging in offensive missions other than in self-defense.[90] Until April 2016, 2 years after the ISIS advance across Iraq, US advisors in that country were restricted to division headquarters, creating significant space between them and the frontline. President Obama then authorized deployments at the brigade and battalion level, but only 'for critical missions'.[91] Donald Trump has since relaxed these rules of engagement, yet the scandal that erupted, when four US advisers were killed in Niger on 4 October 2017, also illustrates the political costs in blurring the supposed Rubicon between adviser and participant to a war.

It is this imaged Rubicon that has shaped US engagement in advisory efforts around the world. In the effort to combat AQIM, US advisors have been sent to Libya, Sudan, Algeria, and Niger, but they remain at headquarters and are not authorized to engage in combat operations.[92] In other, less high-value campaigns, such as the US effort to advise and assist in the search for the Lord's Resistance Army, a mere 100 US military advisors were 'dispersed among four nations in Central and East Africa', a ratio of advisor to advisee that forces serious questions about overall effectiveness and commitment to the cause.[93]

The reluctance to get involved on the frontlines also stems from a qualitative problem, namely, the limited number of advisors that the US military can provide. Traditionally, advisory work has been a special operations mission, meaning that there are limited numbers of troops available for such work. This specialization speaks partly to the linguistic and cultural skills needed to partner with host-nation forces but also to the regular (general-purpose) forces' resistance to advisory work in favor of traditional combat operations. When the need for advisory work expanded post-9/11, to combat a transnational and dispersed threat operating in weak states, many reform-minded officers and academics urged the Army and Marine Corps to prioritize this type of work. Nevertheless, proposals for change never really got off the ground.[94] The notion of singling-out specialized forces for advisory work cut against the ground services' culture and self-perception as war-fighters. Indeed, until mid-2008, the US Army did not recognize advisory positions as command experience, meaning that a soldier's involvement in such teams would not appear on career records.[95]

The lack of preparation and interest in advisory work helps to explain the mixed success record when these forces were nonetheless told to partake and were forced to adapt. Problems with mirror-imaging or the excessive reliance on technological fixes are, for example, well known, but as Greentree notes, 'It is hard to get around the fact that militaries can only attempt to transfer what they know'.[96] It is in this context noteworthy that in 2017 the Army finally announced the creation of six permanent Security Force Assistance Brigades dedicated to advising foreign forces. This announcement, 16 years after 9/11, signaled a 'marked departure' from earlier ad hoc attempts to achieve strategic effect.[97] For supporters of the military's role in countering irregular threats, this was good news, though it remains to be seen how these troops will be prepared adequately for this mission and if they will operate at anything beyond the tactical level. As discussed above, reliance on indirect engagement does not simplify counterinsurgency; in some ways, it even makes it harder.[98] It requires key skills that, history suggests, cannot readily be mass-produced.

There is, of course, one final, fundamental condition for the effectiveness of advisory work – one that looks likely to haunt US efforts of this type for the foreseeable future, to wit the need for a viable strategy toward which security operations can contribute. In the quest to defeat an insurgency, the professionalization of a country's armed forces or security sector is but one part of a broader puzzle. Much depends on the *political objectives* that the security operations serve. Where this strategy is misguided or altogether absent, security operations have little or no meaning. By analogy, it serves no purpose sharpening the scalpel if the surgeon operating is drunk.

A political strategy is critical, as it is typically at the *political* level that partnerships with host-nation governments fray. Partners are willing to accept military aid, but to undergo the political or social reforms deemed necessary for success is another matter. El Salvador's government gladly accepted assistance but inducing it to curb its military or reform politically proved far more fraught. In Vietnam, it was precisely US dissatisfaction with the Diem regime's unwillingness to comply with American guidance that led to his overthrow and the introduction of US combat troops. Even in the Philippines, in the lauded struggle against Abu Sayyaf, it is worth noting that despite almost two decades of operations, the group is still alive and a threat. Uniformed members of the Philippines armed forces blame the lack of progress on the absence of a national strategy capable of giving political meaning to the military gains at the tactical level, as well as the continued problems of corruption, poor governance, and economic underdevelopment that haunt the areas affected by subversion.[99]

The issue here is that governments facing insurgency almost by definition suffer from a legitimacy deficit – hence the armed resistance – and it is not uncommon that they are more concerned with retaining power and privilege than with undercutting dissent through effective reform. This dilemma obtains whether the United States intervenes directly, indirectly, or not at all. The predicament for counterinsurgency advisors is therefore formidable. Regrettably, for all its interest in the indirect approach, the United States has not confronted the limits of its own diplomatic powers, a problem that looks set to worsen given the Trump administration's cuts to the State Department and other civilian instruments of power.

Conclusion

The US government has since 9/11 developed a host of new organizations, technologies, and efforts to combat irregular, non-state armed groups. Almost two decades in, the United States can congratulate itself for having avoided another mass-casualty attack on its homeland, for having averted the greatest possible terrorist threat, namely, the combination of terrorism with weapons of mass destruction, and for having imposed ways of destabilizing and targeting murky, clandestine networks in a wide variety of countries, resulting in the killing of a number of senior-level terrorist operatives. At the same time, the threat of al-Qaeda has not been defeated. Instead, it has metastasized, all the while fostering a slew of related and affiliated organizations across most of the globe. Perhaps the most obvious sign of America's limited progress in its fight against political Islam was the rise of IS and the apparent cachet of its brand and ideology, not just in the Muslim-majority world but among volunteers from across the globe.

Poor strategy, contingency, and the complexity of the task help explain the lackluster scoresheet, but it is also true that the American state was badly prepared for this challenge and has refused, through a combination of inertia and resistance, to evolve. Within the military, the long, grinding campaigns in Iraq and Afghanistan required a form of adaptation that was unanticipated and incompatible with institutional orthodoxies and preexisting plans. Though adaptation in the field was at times impressive, rather than internalize the few positive and many negative lessons of these campaigns, the US armed forces have tended to revert to status quo ante, with the challenge of countering irregular warfare sidelined in force structure and budget allocation. Within the broader US government, wherein interest in irregular warfare was always limited, there is today very little to indicate a preparedness to understand and counter the threat as more than a set of targets to be serviced.

Underpinning the underdeveloped capabilities is a lack of strategy – and even of strategic competence. Put simply, despite many years of engagement ostensibly against al-Qaeda, there is very little consensus in the United States about the importance of this struggle, what it is meant to achieve, or when it ends. The rise of IS further clouded this discussion, with the political class in Washington DC undecided on the level of attention to be devoted to this brutal and fiercely anti-American threat. Despite rhetorical commitment, the US government has been unwilling, after two exhausting campaigns in Iraq and Afghanistan, to invest substantially to fight terrorism around the world. The tendency under Obama was to put terrorism back in its box, yet politicians also know that they cannot afford to appear blasé about this threat, something that Donald Trump deftly exploited on the campaign trail. Once in office, he has not deviated from the Obama approach save to approve military engagement that has been but a version of what has gone before. In fact, if the administration's domestic policies and actions are factored into the equation, the situation is possibly worse than under Obama, given the willingness of both the Justice Department and the Department of Homeland Security to set aside fidelity of reporting and integrity in analysis in favor of the president's partisan political concerns.

This fundamental uncertainty as to terrorism – never mind its relation to insurgency – and the meaning of either for US national security helps explain the inconsistent effort to pursue this threat. On the one hand, the United States has spent extraordinary fiscal and political capital to reach and eliminate key operatives; on the other, it refuses to realign or restructure its instruments of national power to deal more holistically with irregular challenges. Thus, on the one hand, terrorism is headline news and appears to consume the American people more than most other threats and perils;[100] on the other, it has also been difficult to tie convincingly the threat of Islamist terrorism, responsible for approximately six American deaths per year since 9/11, to the imperatives of national security. The outcome has been a reliance on approaches thought to be low in cost – the use of drones, of proxies – which even when combined do not amount to a strategy and may be causing more harm than good.

A better way forward would involve three fundamental steps.

First, the United States must do what it can to prevent terrorist attacks domestically but also establish the resilience necessary not to over-react when one nonetheless occurs. So long as another mass-casualty attack is prevented – and efforts to that end cannot be allowed to lapse – the American media and public must learn to frame and react proportionally to lower yield attacks. Terrorism is not principally about taking lives but sending a message, and on this front, it relies upon the receptiveness and defenselessness of those targeted. For the sake of rational policy-making and a healthy society, the temptation to politicize and fear-monger must be avoided, as it only plays into the hands of the adversary.

Second, the United States must refocus internationally, not just on eliminating key terrorist leaders – though this may at times be necessary – but on creating the conditions where insurgent groups cannot thrive. This effort will require establishing a narrative not of what the US is fighting against but rather of the values and principles that it is fighting for. Such a narrative has been sorely lacking since the 9/11 attacks – or at the very least it has been inconsistently broadcast and contrasted with practice. With the right leadership, a reboot is not impossible. The United States can play on its traditional standing as a symbol of freedom, values, and human rights, though clearly mending burned bridges will not occur overnight. Still, a continued failure to inspire and failure to compel will continue to increase the cost of strategic effectiveness on the global stage. Without its values, the United States loses its best argument in the global competition for influence and power.

Third, it is necessary for Washington, if it wishes to pursue its role as superpower, to create the wherewithal and acumen required for global leadership. The instruments of state with which the United States, and indeed most states, seek to create strategic effects abroad have been found inappropriate and counterproductive for the task at hand. Though deep-rooted reform is unlikely, a better configuration would decentralize policymaking and execution away from Washington, establish regional commands led by civilians rather than the military, and produce hybrid civil–military teams that can operate seamlessly in insecure theatres under one command. In short, how much longer, and to what end, can we accept organizations and structures that patently fail to achieve their mission?

Notes

1. For a critique of this concept, see Call, "The Fallacy of the 'Failed State'," 1491–1507. Also Aidan Hehir, "The Myth of the Failed State and the War on Terror," 307–32.
2. US Department of Defense, "Directive 3000.05: Military Support for Stability, Security, Transition, and Reconstruction (SSTR) Operations" (2005).
3. US Department of the Army and United States Marine Corps, *FM 3–24/MCWP 3–33.5. Counterinsurgency* (Washington DC: US Army, 2006).
4. See Ucko, *The New Counterinsurgency Era*; Serena, *A Revolution in Military Adaptation*.
5. Schadlow, *War and the Art of Governance*.
6. Weigley, *The American Way of War*.
7. Blaufarb, *The Counterinsurgency Era*; Downie, *Learning from Conflict*. The British Army has also, and despite repeated engagement in counterinsurgency, struggled to institutionalize the lessons of campaigns, necessitating quick adaptation on the ground with each new engagement. See Ucko and Egnell, *Counterinsurgency in Crisis*.
8. US Department of Defense, "Quadrennial Defense Review" (Washington DC, 2014). 19.
9. This is the metric employed in Cassidy, *Peacekeeping in the Abyss*; Downie, *Learning from Conflict*; Deborah Denise Avant, *Political Institutions and Military Change*.
10. Downie, *Learning from Conflict.*, 23; Cassidy, *Peacekeeping in the Abyss*.
11. Sewell, "Introduction to the University of Chicago Press Edition," xxxv.
12. Kiszely, "Post-Modern Challenges for Modern Warriors."
13. Observation based on author's employment at the US National Defense University, 2011–2017. The one exception to this rule is the College of International Security Affairs (CISA), the DoD flagship for the study of irregular warfare. Its faculty, however, is 34 strong compared to e.g. National War College's faculty of 66. See also Stiehm, *The U.S. Army War College*; Maj. Gen. Robert Scales (USA, Ret.), "Slightly 'Steamed,' Gen. Scales Explains His Criticism of the Military's War Colleges," Foreign Policy (blog), 11 May 2012, https://foreignpolicy.com/2012/05/11/slightly-steamed-gen-scales-explains-his-criticism-of-the-militarys-war-colleges/.
14. Burke, "Sorry, Pentathlete Wasn't on the Syllabus." See also, Ucko, *The New Counterinsurgency Era*, 143–44.
15. *Association of the United States Army. The U.S. Army: A Modular Force for the 21st Century. Torchbearer Issue* (Arlington, VA: AUSA: Institute of Land Warfare, 2005).
16. For more on this point, and for proposals on how to reform the units to reflect the challenges of irregular operations, see Burgess, "Transformation and the Irregular Gap," 25–34.
17. Flournoy and Schultz, *Shaping U.S. Ground Forces for the Future*, 20.
18. Joint and Coalition Operational Analysis, "Decade of War, Volume I: Enduring Lessons from the Past Decade of Operations" (Suffolk, VA: Joint Staff J7, 15 June 2012).

19. Gen. Stanley McChrystal, as cited in Lamb and Franco, "National-Level Coordination and Implementation," 227.
20. Kosiak, *Analysis of the FY 2008 Defense Budget Request*, 20. The budget request sought "$27 billion for aircraft programs, up $4.1 billion or 18 percent from this year; $14.4 billion for ship programs, up $3.2 billion or 29 percent; and $6 billion for space programs, an increase of $1.2 billion or 25 percent more than Congress authorized this year."
21. Towell, Daggett, and Belasco, "Defense: FY2008 Authorization and Appropriations," 29.
22. See "Fiscal Year 2009 Budget Request: Summary Justification" (Arlington, VA: Department of Defense, 4 February 2008), 164–65. See also Boot, "The Corps Should Look to Its Small-Wars Past." While extra-budgetary supplemental appropriations helped pay for operations, they were not intended for general capability-building, the bulk of it being, by force, allocated toward pay and benefits, as well as on resetting worn-out equipment. Disturbingly, however, even these extra-budgetary bills were used to fund conventional weapons platforms, supplementing, quite literally, the allocations made for such systems in the base budget. Towell, Daggett, and Belasco, "Defense: FY2008 Authorization and Appropriations," 15.
23. OOTW includes 'strikes, raids, peace enforcement, counterterrorism, enforcement of sanctions, support to insurgency and counterinsurgency, and evacuation of noncombatants'. See Joint Chiefs of Staff, *JP 3–07 Joint Doctrine for Military Operations Other than War* (Washington DC, 1995), vii, http://oai.dtic.mil/oai/oai?verb=getRecord&metadataPrefix=html&identifier=ADA327558.
24. Ricks, "Our Generals Failed in Afghanistan."
25. Kane, "Why Our Best Officers Are Leaving."
26. Mansoor, *Baghdad at Sunrise*, 350.
27. Palmer, *The 25-Year War*, 204–5.
28. Aswell, *Calming the Churn*.
29. As cited in Krepinevich, *The Army and Vietnam*, 206.
30. Yet as William Stothard Tee, chief instructor at the Jungle Warfare School from 1948 to 1951, explains, even "two years in Malaya ... is not really a sufficient time to become acclimatised, to become trained and become used to the circumstances and the enemy." See Stothard Tee, Imperial War Museum Sound Archive, Accession no. 16 January 6397, 1996.
31. Joint and Coalition Operational Analysis, "Decade of War, Volume I: Enduring Lessons from the Past Decade of Operations", 2, 3, 15, 25.
32. Some key advocates of reform, whose efforts have in singular moments overcome the system, include Robert Gates as Secretary of Defense, Gen. David Petraeus as Commanding General of Ft. Leavenworth, and Gen. H. R. McMaster as Director of the Army Capabilities Integration Center, and Deputy Commanding General, Futures of the US Army Training and Doctrine Command.
33. Full-spectrum operations feature as a theme in US Army doctrine going back to the 1960s, though these have at different times been called "full-dimensional" operations.
34. "Hybrid threats" is defined by Frank Hoffman, intellectual progenitor of the term, as incorporating "a full range of different modes of warfare including conventional capabilities, irregular tactics and formations, terrorist acts including indiscriminate violence and coercion, and criminal disorder." Hybrid wars, Hoffman adds, "can be conducted by both states and a variety of non-state

actors." Hoffman, *Conflict in the 21st Century*. See also Qiao, Santoli, and Wang, *Unrestricted Warfare*.
35. Murray and Mansoor, *Hybrid Warfare*.
36. US Department of Defense, "Quadrennial Defense Review." 19. My emphasis.
37. McGarry, *Pentagon's New Role for JIEDDO Counter-IED Agency*.
38. See US Department of Defense, "Quadrennial Defense Review." 19.
39. Perkins, "U.S. Army Training and Doctrine Command" (Arlington, VA: Association of the United States Army, 16 September 2016), https://www.ausa.org/articles/us-army-training-and-doctrine-command-%E2%80%98army%E2%80%99s-architect%E2%80%99-adapts-current-and-future-success.
40. It really is: it has been replaced by the term 'wide area security', defined thus: 'Wide area security is the application of the elements of combat power in unified action to protect populations, forces, infrastructure, and activities; to deny the enemy positions of advantage; and to consolidate gains in order to retain the initiative'. US Department of the Army, "Unified Land Operations" (Arlington, VA, October 2011), 6.
41. Galula, *Counterinsurgency Warfare*, 63.
42. For the phrase, 'insurgency is armed politics', and complete discussion, see Marks, 'Insurgency in a Time of Terrorism', 33–43.
43. In Malaya, for example, Britain struggled to maintain congenial relations, first, with the sultans and rulers, then with the emerging class of national politicians via which the counterinsurgency was run. In Dhofar, the solution to Said bin Taimur's refusal to accede to British reforms was a military coup carried out by his own son and with the support of the British government.
44. See Egnell, "A Western Insurgency in Afghanistan."
45. Collins, "Initial Planning and Execution in Afghanistan and Iraq."
46. Lamb and Franco, "National-Level Coordination and Implementation: How Systems Attributes Trumped Leadership," 208.
47. Hegland, "Pentagon, State Struggle to Define-Nation Building Roles."
48. Indicative of this tendency were the bureaucratic maneuverings necessary for the creation of the Office of Military Affairs within USAID.
49. It has also proved difficult for the US military to incorporate said organizations in its military planning, and so, at best, their presence, contribution, and effectiveness are simply assumed to obtain.
50. Ucko, *The New Counterinsurgency Era*, 97.
51. Greentree, "Bureaucracy Does Its Thing," 341.
52. Those who volunteer leave not only their career path but also a billet now to be filled, temporarily, by their agency. Civilians who deploy are hampered by rapid rotation schedules and risk-averse security protocols, greatly limiting their effectiveness. For more detail, see Paul Fishstein and Andrew Wilder, "Winning Hearts and Minds? *50*. See also Greentree, "Bureaucracy Does Its Thing," 338–442. It may be further noted that the first actual courses for personnel did not commence until early 2009.
53. Sewell, "Introduction to the University of Chicago Press Edition," xl.
54. I am grateful to Michael Davies for this idea.
55. Oakley and Casey, "The Country Team."
56. Marks, "Next Generation' Department of State."
57. Keith Mackiggan, *Oral Testimony given at the Iraq Inquiry*, 2010, iraqinquiry.org.uk/transcripts/oralevidence-bydate/100107.aspx., 52.

58. According to New America, President Bush oversaw 48 drone strikes in Pakistan, killing 399–540 people, whereas President Obama oversaw 353 strikes, killing 1934–3094 people. See "Drone Strikes: Pakistan," New America, accessed 18 May 2017, /in-depth/americas-counterterrorism-wars/pakistan/.
59. Prior to being killed in a drone strike, Atiyah Abd al-Rahman, al-Qaeda's second-in-command, wrote a message to bin Laden complaining that his fighters "were getting killed faster than they could be replaced." See Miller and Tate, "Al-Qaeda's No. 2 Leader Is Killed in Pakistan, U.S. Officials Say." Letters recovered from Osama bin Laden's Abbottabad compound also reveal the al-Qaeda leader's deep concern about drones and the burdensome countermeasures they imposed on his organization. See Burke, "Bin Laden Letters Reveal Al-Qaida's Fears of Drone Strikes and Infiltration"; Williams, "The CIA's Covert Predator Drone War in Pakistan, 2004–2010," 871–92
60. "Obama's Speech on Drone Policy," *The New York Times*, 23 April 2013, http://www.nytimes.com/2013/05/24/us/politics/transcript-of-obamas-speech-on-drone-policy.html.
61. See Sudarsan Raghavan, "When U.S. Drones Kill Civilians, Yemen's Government Tries to Conceal It," *The Washington Post*, 24 December 2012; "Did a 13-Year-Old Boy Join Al-Qaeda?" Yemen Times, accessed 19 May 2017, http://www.yementimes.com/en/1855/report/4851/Did-a-13-year-old-boy-join-Al-Qaeda.htm.
62. This was the defense alluded to by President Obama. See "Obama's Speech on Drone Policy." See also, for example, Steven Groves, "Drone Strikes: The Legality of U.S. Targeting Terrorists Abroad," Backgrounder (The Heritage Foundation, 9 April 2013), /terrorism/report/drone-strikes-the-legality-us-targeting-terrorists-abroad.
63. Author's personal experience operating within this community.
64. Shane, "John Brennan, C.I.A. Nominee, Clears Committee Vote."
65. Brooks, "Drones and the International Rule of Law."
66. See The White House, "Report on the Legal and Policy Frameworks Guiding the United States' Use of Military Force and Related National Security Operations," December 2016, http://apps.washingtonpost.com/g/documents/national/read-the-obama-administrations-memo-outlining-use-of-force-rules/2234/.
67. Penney et al., "C.I.A. Drone Mission, Curtailed by Obama, Is Expanded in Africa Under Trump."
68. For the crucial distinction between terrorism and insurgency, and by extension between counterterrorism and counterinsurgency, see chapter 1 of Marks, *Maoist People's War in Post-Vietnam Asia*.
69. On this point, see the lax interpretation of imminence developed under the Obama administration to authorize drone strikes on US-citizens within the senior rungs of al-Qaeda. Presumably, the threshold for non-US citizens is lower still. Ackerman, "How Obama Transformed an Old Military Concept."
70. Micah Zenko, cited in Elliott, "Have U.S. Drones Become a 'Counterinsurgency Air Force' for Our Allies?" See also Plaw and Fricker, *The Drone Debate*, 67–69.
71. See, respectively, Booth and Black, "WikiLeaks Cables"; "Secret Memos 'Show Pakistan Endorsed US Drone Strikes'," *BBC News*, 24 October 2013, http://www.bbc.com/news/world-asia-24649840.
72. A helpful contrast is provided by the use of British military force in Sierra Leone, which was integrated within a local Sierra Leonean campaign plan to defeat the Revolutionary United Front (RUF). See Ucko, "Can Limited Intervention Work?" 847–77.

73. New York University law professor Philip Alston, as cited in Coll, "Obama's Drone War."
74. The 2015 film, *Eye in the Sky*, though fictional, superbly portrays this dilemma.
75. Coll, "Obama's Drone War."
76. Cronin, "Why Drones Fail."
77. Government Accountability Organization, "Yemen: DOD Should Improve Accuracy of Its Data on Congressional Clearance of Projects as It Reevaluates Counterterrorism Assistance," Report to Congressional Committees (Government Accountability Organization, 2015), 6. http://oai.dtic.mil/oai/oai?verb=getRecord&metadataPrefix=html&identifier=ADA617200.
78. "US Deploys 'a Few Dozen' Troops to Somalia: Pentagon," *Al-Jazeera*, 16 April 2017, http://www.aljazeera.com/news/2017/04/deploys-dozen-troops-somalia-pentagon-170416033127155.html.
79. Crotty, "The FY 2016 Budget," 7. Stephen Biddle et al. put it, 'this idea of using "small footprint" SFA [security force assistance] to secure US interests without large ground-force deployments is now at the very forefront of the US defense debate'. See Biddle, Macdonald, and Baker, "Small Footprint, Small Payoff," 2.
80. Nixon, "Address to the Nation on the War in Vietnam," 4-1.
81. See Marks, "Colombian Army Adaptation to FARC"; Ucko, "Counterinsurgency in El Salvador," 669–95; Wilson, "Anatomy of a Successful COIN Operation," 2–12.
82. As Fernando Luján points out, "Since the approval of Plan Colombia in 1999, the cost to run the entire program – including all military and civilian assistance – has roughly equaled the cost of running the Iraq or Afghanistan war for a single month during the surge." See Luján, "Light Footprints," 8.
83. 'Within the case studies explored, BPC [building partnership capacity] was least effective as a tool for allowing the United States to extract itself from conflict (victory in war/war termination). However, it was most effective as a tool for building interpersonal and institutional linkages, and for alliance building'. See McInnis and Lucas, *What Is 'Building Partner Capacity?'* i.
84. Interview with General Carlos Ospina, former Commander of the Colombian Armed Forces, Washington DC, October 2014.
85. Hammes, "Raising and Mentoring Security Forces in Afghanistan and Iraq," 332.
86. Carter, "Why Foreign Troops Can't Fight Our Fights."
87. Pan Sahel Initiative (PSI), African Crisis Response Initiative (ACRI), African Contingency Operations and Training Assistance (ACOTA), International Military Education and Training (IMET), Counterterrorism Fellowship Program (CTFP), Flintlock exercise, and the Global Peace Operations Initiative (GPOI).
88. Shurkin, Pezard, and Zimmerman, *Mali's Next Battle*, 16–25. See also Powerlson, "Enduring Engagement Yes, Episodic Engagement No: Lessons for SOF from Mali."
89. Ucko, "Counterinsurgency in El Salvador"; Ramsay III, "Advising Indigenous Forces."
90. Lake, "Orders for US Forces in Syria."
91. Tilghman, "U.S. Combat Adviser Mission in Iraq Expands to Battalion Level." One such critical case was the liberation of Mosul, where U.S. advisors, while still officially behind, operated very close, to a constantly shifting frontline of troops. See Sisk, "US Doubles Number of Advisors in Iraq as Forces Push into Mosul."
92. "U.S. Army to Train Africa Forces in Anti-Terror," *CBS News*, 24 December 2012, http://www.cbsnews.com/news/us-army-to-train-africa-forces-in-anti-terror/.

93. "The Nature of the U.S. Military Presence in Africa, An Exchange between Colonel Tom Davis and Nick Turse," *Mother Jones*, 26 July 2012, http://www.motherjones.com/politics/2012/07/nature-us-military-presence-africa.
94. Flournoy and Schultz, "Shaping U.S. Ground Forces for the Future," 31; Nagl, "Institutionalizing Adaptation."
95. Sheik, "Army Opposes Permanent Advisor Corps to Train Foreign Forces."
96. Greentree, "Bureaucracy Does Its Thing," 336.
97. Freedberg, "Army Builds Advisor Brigades."
98. As Biddle et al. find, "For the foreseeable future, small footprints mean small payoffs for the US – where limited US interests preclude large deployments, major results will rarely be possible from minor investments in SFA." Biddle, Macdonald, and Baker, "Small Footprint, Small Payoff," 7.
99. Observations gleaned through continuous engagement with members of the Philippines armed forces, Washington, DC, 2011–2017.
100. Anderson, "The Psychology of Why 94 Deaths from Terrorism."

Acknowledgement

This article draws on a shorter and earlier version of the same text. See David H. Ucko, "Learning Difficulties: The US Way of Irregular Warfare," *S&F Sicherheit und Frieden* 36, no.1 (2018).

Disclosure statement

No potential conflict of interest was reported by the author.

Bibliography

Ackerman, Spencer. 2013. "How Obama Transformed an Old Military Concept so He Can Drone Americans." *Wired*, February 5, 2013. https://www.wired.com/2013/02/obama-imminence/

Anderson, Jenny. "The Psychology of Why 94 Deaths from Terrorism are Scarier than 301,797 Deaths from Guns." *Quartz* (blog). Accessed May 19, 2017. https://qz.com/898207/the-psychology-of-why-americans-are-more-scared-of-terrorism-than-guns-though-guns-are-3210-times-likelier-to-kill-them/

Association of the United States Army. *The U.S. Army: A Modular Force for the 21st Century. Torchbearer Issue*. Arlington, VA: AUSA: Institute of Land Warfare, 2005.

Aswell, Andrew P. "Calming the Churn: Resolving the Dilemma of Rotational Warfare in Counterinsurgency." Naval: Postgraduate School, Monterey, California, 2013.

Avant, Deborah Denise. *Political Institutions and Military Change: Lessons from Peripheral Wars*. Ithica: Cornell University Press, 1994.

Biddle, Stephen, Julia Macdonald, and Ryan Baker. "Small Footprint, Small Payoff: The Military Effectiveness of Security Force Assistance." *Journal of Strategic Studies* (12 April 2017): 1–54. doi:10.1080/01402390.2017.1307745.

Blaufarb, Douglas S. *The Counterinsurgency Era: U.S. Doctrine and Performance— 1950 to Present*. New York: The Free Press, 1977.

Boot, Max. "The Corps Should Look to Its Small-Wars Past." *Armed Forces Journal*, March 2006.

Booth, Robert, and Ian Black. "WikiLeaks Cables: Yemen Offered US 'Open Door' to Attack Al-Qaida on Its Soil." *The Guardian*, December 3, 2010. sec. World news. https://www.theguardian.com/world/2010/dec/03/wikileaks-yemen-us-attack-al-qaida

Brooks, Rosa. "Drones and the International Rule of Law." *Ethics & International Affairs* 28, no. 01 (2014): 83–103. doi:10.1017/S0892679414000070.

Burgess, Kenneth. "Transformation and the Irregular Gap." *Military Review*, December 25–34, 2010.

Burke, Crispin. "Sorry, Pentathlete Wasn't on the Syllabus." *Small Wars Journal*, January 29, 2009. www.smallwarsjournal.com/mag/docs-temp/169-burke.pdf.

Burke, Jason. "Bin Laden Letters Reveal Al-Qaida's Fears of Drone Strikes and Infiltration." *The Guardian*, March 1, 2016. https://www.theguardian.com/world/2016/mar/01/bin-laden-letters-reveal-al-qaidas-fears-of-drone-strikes-and-infiltration.

Call, Charles T. "The Fallacy of the 'Failed State'." *Third World Quarterly* 29, no. 8 (December, 2008): 1491–1507. doi:10.1080/01436590802544207.

Carter, Phillip. "Why Foreign Troops Can't Fight Our Fights." *The Washington Post*, October 2, 2015. 2015–10.

Cassidy, Robert M. *Peacekeeping in the Abyss: British and American Peacekeeping Doctrine and Practice after the Cold War*. Westport, CT and London: Greenwood Publishing Group, 2004.

Coll, Steve. "Obama's Drone War." *The New Yorker*, November 24, 2014. http://www.newyorker.com/magazine/2014/11/24/unblinking-stare.

Collins, Joseph J. "Initial Planning and Execution in Afghanistan and Iraq." In *Lessons Encountered: Learning from the Long War*, edited by Richard D Hooker and Joseph J Collins, 21–88. Washington DC: NDU Press, 2015. http://purl.fdlp.gov/GPO/gpo63576.

Cronin, Audrey Kurth. "Why Drones Fail." *Foreign Affairs*, July 1, 2013.

Crotty, Ryan. "The FY 2016 Budget: The Defense Impact." Washington DC: Center for Strategic & International Studies, February 3, 2015. https://csis-prod.s3.amazonaws.com/s3fs-public/legacy_files/files/publication/150203_FY16_Budget_Analysis.pdf.

"Did a 13-Year-Old Boy Join Al-Qaeda?" *Yemen Times*, May 19, 2017. http://www.yementimes.com/en/1855/report/4851/Did-a-13-year-old-boy-join-Al-Qaeda.htm.

Downie, Richard Duncan. *Learning from Conflict: The U.S. Military in Vietnam, El Salvador, and the Drug War*. Westport, CT: Praeger, 1998.

"Drone Strikes: Pakistan." New America. Accessed May 18, 2017. http://www.newamerica.org/in-depth/americas-counterterrorism-wars/pakistan/

Egnell, Robert. "A Western Insurgency in Afghanistan." *Joint Force Quarterly*, no. 70 (2013). http://ndupress.ndu.edu/Portals/68/Documents/jfq/jfq-70/JFQ-70_8-14_Egnell.pdf

Elliott, Justin. "Have U.S. Drones Become a 'Counterinsurgency Air Force' for Our Allies?" ProPublica. Accessed November 27, 2012. http://www.propublica.org/article/have-u.s.-drones-become-a-counterinsurgency-air-force-for-our-allies

"Fiscal Year 2009 Budget Request: Summary Justification." Arlington, VA: Department of Defense, February 4, 2008.

Fishstein, Paul, and Andrew Wilder. "Winning Hearts and Minds? Examining the Relationship between Aid and Security in Afghanistan." Medford, MA: Feinstein International Center, Tufts University. January 2012. http://fic.tufts.edu/assets/WinningHearts-Final.pdf

Flournoy, Michele, and Tammy Schultz. *Shaping U.S. Ground Forces for the Future: Getting Expansion Right*. Washington DC: Center for a New American Security, 2007.

Freedberg, Sydney J. "Army Builds Advisor Brigades: Counterinsurgency Is Here To Stay." *Breaking Defense*. 2017. http://breakingdefense.com/2017/02/army-builds-advisor-brigades-counterinsurgency-is-here-to-stay/

Galula, David. *Counterinsurgency Warfare: Theory and Practice*. New York: Praeger, 1964.

Government Accountability Organization. "Yemen: DOD Should Improve Accuracy of Its Data on Congressional Clearance of Projects as It Reevaluates Counterterrorism Assistance." *Report to Congressional Committees*. Washington DC: Government Accountability Organization, 2015. http://oai.dtic.mil/oai/oai?verb=getRecord&metadataPrefix=html&identifier=ADA617200.

Greentree, Todd. "Bureaucracy Does Its Thing: US Performance and the Institutional Dimension of Strategy in Afghanistan." *Journal of Strategic Studies* 36, no. 3 June 1 (2013): 325–356. doi:10.1080/01402390.2013.764518.

Groves, Steven. "Drone Strikes: The Legality of U.S. Targeting Terrorists Abroad." Backgrounder. The Heritage Foundation. April 9, 2013. http://www.heritage.org/terrorism/report/drone-strikes-the-legality-us-targeting-terrorists-abroad.

Hammes, T.X. "Raising and Mentoring Security Forces in Afghanistan and Iraq." In *Lessons Encountered: Learning from the Long War*, edited by Richard D Hooker and Joseph J Collins, 227–344. Washington, D.C.: National Defense University Press, 2015.

Hegland, Corine. "Pentagon, State Struggle to Define-Nation Building Roles." *The National Journal*, April 30, 2007.

Hehir, Aidan. "The Myth of the Failed State and the War on Terror: A Challenge to the Conventional Wisdom." *Journal of Intervention and Statebuilding* 1, no. 3 (November, 2007): 307–332. doi:10.1080/17502970701592256.

Hoffman, Frank G. *Conflict in the 21st Century: The Rise of Hybrid Wars*. Arlington, VA: Potomac Institute for Policy Studies, 2007.

House, The White. "Report on the Legal and Policy Frameworks Guiding the United States' Use of Military Force and Related National Security Operations." December 2016. http://apps.washingtonpost.com/g/documents/national/read-the-obama-administrations-memo-outlining-use-of-force-rules/2234/

Joint and Coalition Operational Analysis. *Decade of War, Volume I: Enduring Lessons from the past Decade of Operations*. Suffolk, VA: Joint Staff J7, June 15, 2012.

Joint Chiefs of Staff. 1995. *JP 3-07 Joint Doctrine for Military Operations Other than War*. Washington DC. http://oai.dtic.mil/oai/oai?verb=getRecord&metadataPrefix=html&identifier=ADA327558.

Kane, Tim. "Why Our Best Officers Are Leaving." *The Atlantic*, February 2011. https://www.theatlantic.com/magazine/archive/2011/01/why-our-best-officers-are-leaving/308346/.

Kiszely, John. 2007. "Post-Modern Challenges for Modern Warriors." *The Shrivenham Paper*. Defence Academy of the United Kingdom, December.

Kosiak, Steven M. *Analysis of the FY 2008 Defense Budget Request*. Washington DC: Center for Strategic and Budgetary Assessment, 2007.

Krepinevich, Andrew F., Jr. *The Army and Vietnam*. Baltimore, MD: JHU Press, 2009.

Lake, Eli. 2016. "Orders for US Forces in Syria: 'Don't Get Shot'." *Bloomberg*, August 11, 2016–08.

Lamb, Christopher J., and Megan Franco. "National-Level Coordination and Implementation: How Systems Attributes Trumped Leadership." In *Lessons*

Encountered: Learning from the Long War, edited by Richard Jr Hooker and Joseph J. Collins, 165–276. Washington DC: National University Press, 2015.

Luján, Major Fernando. "Light Footprints: The Future of American Military Intervention." *Voices from the Field*. Washington DC: Center for a New American Security, March, 2013.

Mackiggan, Keith. Oral Testimony given at the Iraq Inquiry. Accessed 2010. http://iraqinquiry.org.uk/transcripts/oralevidence-bydate/100107.aspx

Mansoor, Peter R. *Baghdad at Sunrise: A Brigade Commander's War in Iraq*. New Haven, Conn.; London: Yale University Press, 2009.

Marks, Edward. 2010. "Next Generation' Department of State." *American Diplomacy*, January 3, 2010. http://www.unc.edu/depts/diplomat/item/2010/0103/oped/op_marks.html.

Marks, Thomas A. *Colombian Army Adaptation to FARC*. Carlisle, PA: The Strategic Studies Institute, 2002.

Marks, Thomas A. "Insurgency in a Time of Terrorism." *Joint Center for Operational Analysis and Lessons Learned (JCOA-LL) Bulletin* VIII, no. 3 (September, 2006): 33–43.

Marks, Thomas A. *Maoist People's War in Post-Vietnam Asia*. Bangkok: White Lotus, 2007.

McGarry, Brendan. "Pentagon's New Role for JIEDDO Counter-IED Agency." n.d. http://www.military.com/daily-news/2015/03/14/pentagon-dismantles-jieddo-counter-ied-agency.html

McInnis, Kathleen J., and Nathan J. Lucas. "What Is 'Building Partner Capacity?' Issues for Congress." *CRS Report*. Washington DC: Congressional Research Service, December 18, 2015.

Miller, Greg, and Julie Tate. "Al-Qaeda's No. 2 Leader Is Killed in Pakistan, U.S. Officials Say." *The Washington Post*, August 27, 2011.

Murray, Williamson, and Peter R. Mansoor, eds. *Hybrid Warfare: Fighting Complex Opponents from the Ancient World to the Present*. New York: Cambridge University Press, 2012.

Nagl, John A. *Institutionalizing Adaptation: It's Time for a Permanent Army Advisor Corps*. Washington, DC: Center for a New American Security, 2007.

"The Nature of the U.S. Military Presence in Africa, an Exchange between Colonel Tom Davis and Nick Turse." *Mother Jones*, July 26, 2012. http://www.motherjones.com/politics/2012/07/nature-us-military-presence-africa

Nixon, Richard. "Address to the Nation on the War in Vietnam." *See Department of the Army, FM 100-20, Internal Defense and Development*, November 3, 1969. 4–1.

Oakley, Robert B., and Michael Casey Jr. "The Country Team: Restructuring America's First Line of Engagement." Strategic Forum. Institute for National Strategic Studies. Accessed 2007. http://oai.dtic.mil/oai/oai?verb=getRecord&metadataPrefix=html&identifier=ADA473212

"Obama's Speech on Drone Policy." *The New York Times*, April 23, 2013. http://www.nytimes.com/2013/05/24/us/politics/transcript-of-obamas-speech-on-drone-policy.html

Palmer, Bruce. *The 25-Year War: America's Military Role in Vietnam*. Lexington: The University Press of Kentucky, 2014. http://public.eblib.com/choice/publicfullrecord.aspx?p=1634048.

Penney, Joe, Eric Schmitt, Rukmini Callimachi, and Christoph Koettl. "C.I.A. Drone Mission, Curtailed by Obama, Is Expanded in Africa under Trump." *The New York Times*, October 9, 2018. sec. World. https://www.nytimes.com/2018/09/09/world/africa/cia-drones-africa-military.html

Perkins, Gen. David G. "U.S. Army Training and Doctrine Command: 'Army's Architect' Adapts for Current and Future Success." Arlington, VA: Association of the United States Army. Accessed September 16, 2016. https://www.ausa.org/articles/us-army-training-and-doctrine-command-%E2%80%98army%E2%80%99s-architect%E2%80%99-adapts-current-and-future-success

Plaw, Avery, and Matthew S. Fricker. *The Drone Debate: A Primer on the U.S. Use of Unmanned Aircraft outside Conventional Battlefields*. Lanham; Boulder; New York; London: Rowman & Littlefield, 2016.

Powerlson, Simon J. "Enduring Engagement Yes, Episodic Engagement No: Lessons for SOF from Mali." MA thesis, Naval Postgraduate School, 2013. http://calhoun.nps.edu/bitstream/handle/10945/38996/13Dec_Powelson_Simon.pdf?sequence=1

Qiao, Liang, Al Santoli, and Xiangsui Wang. *Unrestricted Warfare: China's Master Plan to Destroy America*. Panama City, Panama: Pan American Publishing, 2002.

Raghavan, Sudarsan. 2012. "When U.S. Drones Kill Civilians, Yemen's Government Tries to Conceal It." *The Washington Post*, December 24.

Ramsay, Robert D., III. "Advising Indigenous Forces: American Advisors in Korea, Vietnam, and El Salvador." *Global War on Terrorism, Occasional Paper*. Ft. Leavenworth, KS: Combat Studies Institute Press, 2006.

Ricks, Thomas E. 2016. "Our Generals Failed in Afghanistan." *Foreign Policy*, October 18. https://foreignpolicy.com/2016/10/18/our-generals-failed-in-afghanistan/

Scales, Robert, Maj. Gen. (USA, Ret.). "Slightly 'Steamed,' Gen. Scales Explains His Criticism of the Military's War Colleges." Foreign Policy (blog). Accessed May 11, 2012. https://foreignpolicy.com/2012/05/11/slightly-steamed-gen-scales-explains-his-criticism-of-the-militarys-war-colleges/

Schadlow, Nadia. *War and the Art of Governance: Consolidating Combat Success into Political Victory*. Washington DC: Georgetown University Press, 2017.

"Secret Memos 'Show Pakistan Endorsed US Drone Strikes'." *BBC News*, October 24, 2013. sec. Asia. http://www.bbc.com/news/world-asia-24649840

Serena, Chad C. *A Revolution in Military Adaptation: The US Army in the Iraq War*. Washington, D.C: Georgetown University Press, 2011.

Sewell, Sarah. "Introduction to the University of Chicago Press Edition: A Radical Field Manual." In *The US Army/Marine Corps Counterinsurgency Field Manual*, edited by The United States Army and Marine Corps. Chicago: University of Chicago, 2007.

Shane, Scott. "John Brennan, C.I.A. Nominee, Clears Committee Vote." *The New York Times*, March 5, 2013. http://www.nytimes.com/2013/03/06/us/politics/brennan-vote-by-senate-intelligence-panel.html

Sheik, Fawzia. "Army Opposes Permanent Advisor Corps to Train Foreign Forces." *Inside the Pentagon*, September 13, 2007.

Shurkin, Michael, Stephanie Pezard, and S. Rebecca Zimmerman. *Mali's Next Battle: Improving Counterterrorism Capabilities*. Santa Monica, CA: RAND Corporation, 2017.

Sisk, Richard. "US Doubles Number of Advisors in Iraq as Forces Push into Mosul." *Military.Com*, January 4, 2017. http://www.military.com/daily-news/2017/01/04/us-doubles-number-advisors-in-iraq-forces-push-mosul.html.

Stiehm, Judith. *The U.S. Army War College: Military Education in a Democracy*. Philadelphia, PA: Temple University Press, 2002.

Tilghman, Andrew. "U.S. Combat Adviser Mission in Iraq Expands to Battalion Level." *Military Times 4*, July 27, 2016. http://www.militarytimes.com/story/military/2016/07/27/us-combat-advisor-mission-iraq-expands-battalion-level/87625432/.

Towell, Pat, Stephen Daggett, and Amy Belasco. "Defense: FY2008 Authorization and Appropriations." *CRS Report for Congress. Congressional Research Service*, May 11, 2007.

"U.S. Army to Train Africa Forces in Anti-Terror." *CBS News*, December 24, 2012. http://www.cbsnews.com/news/us-army-to-train-africa-forces-in-anti-terror/

U.S. Department of the Army. "Unified Land Operations." Arlington, VA, October 2011.

U.S. Department of the Army and United States Marine Corps. *FM 3-24/MCWP 3-33.5. Counterinsurgency*. Washington DC: U.S. Army, 2006.

Ucko, David H. *The New Counterinsurgency Era: Transforming the U.S. Military for Modern Wars*. Washington DC: Georgetown University Press, 2009.

Ucko, David H. "Counterinsurgency in El Salvador: The Lessons and Limits of the Indirect Approach." *Small Wars & Insurgencies* 24, no. 4, October 1 (2013): 669–695. doi:10.1080/09592318.2013.857938.

Ucko, David H. "Can Limited Intervention Work? Lessons from Britain's Success Story in Sierra Leone." *Journal of Strategic Studies* 39, no. 5–6, September 18 (2016): 847–877. doi:10.1080/01402390.2015.1110695.

Ucko, David H., and Robert Egnell. *Counterinsurgency in Crisis: Britain and the Challenges of Modern Warfare*. New York: Columbia University Press, 2013.

US Department of Defense. Directive 3000.05: Military Support for Stability, Security, Transition, and Reconstruction (SSTR) Operations, 2005.

US Department of Defense. "Quadrennial Defense Review." Washington DC, 2014.

"US Deploys 'A Few Dozen' Troops to Somalia: Pentagon." *Al-Jazeera*, April 16, 2017. http://www.aljazeera.com/news/2017/04/deploys-dozen-troops-somalia-pentagon-170416033127155.html.

Weigley, Russell. *The American Way of War: A History of United States Military Strategy and Policy*. Bloomington, IN: Indiana University Press, 1977.

Williams, Brian Glyn. "The CIA's Covert Predator Drone War in Pakistan, 2004–2010: The History of an Assassination Campaign." *Studies in Conflict & Terrorism* 33, no. 10 September 20 (2010): 871–892. doi:10.1080/1057610X.2010.508483.

Wilson, Gregory. "Anatomy of a Successful COIN Operation: OEF-Philippines and the Indirect Approach 2–12." *Military Review* 86, no. 6 (December, 2006): 2–12.

Index

4th of August Regime, Greece 36
9/11 terrorist attack 120, 124, 141, 181; impact on US policy 163, 223–44

A Decade of War (Joint and Coalition Operational Analysis) 229
Abdalla, M.A. 184
Abizaid, J.P. 146, 149, 151–7, 162
Abrams, C. 81, 92, 93
Abu Ghraib prison 150–1
Abu Sayyaf 241
Abu Zaid 190
Acheson, D. 47
Active Containment 188–91
Adams, J. 16
Afghan Local Police *see* ALP
Afghan National Army *see* ANA
Afghan National Police *see* ANP
Afghan New Beginnings Program *see* ANBP
Afghanistan 101–25, 223–6, 230–4, 237–9, 242; and 9/11 141; adjacent countries and 94; clientelism 102–12; Disarmament, Demobilization, and Reintegration (DDR) program 107; factionalization 105; Interim Administration 106; land parcelling 108; militias 102, 103, 105–17, 118, 121, 123–5; North Atlantic Treaty Organization (NATO) 108; paramilitary groups 101–4, 107, 109, 112, 113, 116–20, 124–5; soft networks 201–5, 206, 207–8, 215; US success 143
Afghanistan Independent Human Rights Commission 123
Africa 176–91; 9/11 and 181–3; active containment 188–91; Niger 183–8; policy 177–81
AFRICOM (US Africa Command) 179, 180–1
Ahl Asaib al Haqq (Leagues of the Righteous, Iraq) 148
Alam, Mir 109, 115–17, 129n55, 131n82
The Alamo 21
Albania 33, 37, 50, 51
Algeria 3, 4
Allawi, Ayad 154, 155, 159
ALP (Afghan Local Police) 111, 114–15, 117–18, 123, 130n62
al Qaeda: Afghanistan and 104–5, 120, 141–3; Africa and 176, 180, 187; Iraq and 142, 156, 158, 161, 164, 201; use of drones by US 234, 235, 236; use of proxies 237–9
al Qaeda in the Islamic Maghreb *see* AQIM
American Revolution 2–3, 15
ANA (Afghan National Army) 117
Anbar, Iraq 147, 154
Anbar Awakening 159, 160
ANBP (Afghan New Beginnings Program) 107–8
ANP (Afghan National Police) 117, 122
Ansar al-Islam 142
Ap Bac, Battle of 87
AQIM (al Qaeda in the Islamic Maghreb) 187, 189–190, 239–240
Arista, M. 23
Army Irregular Warfare Center 230
ARVN (Vietnamese Army) 85, 86, 87, 91
Athens, Greece 42
Austin, M. 19

Ba'ath Party, Iraq 142–3, 146, 149, 151, 159
Badr Corps 147–8, 159
Baghdad, Iraq 145, 157, 158, 159
Baghlani, Ghulam Sakhi 116
Baker, J. 157
Balkans 32, 40, 52
Balkh, Afghanistan 106, 110–11, 115, 118, 122
Banana Wars 7
Basrah, Iraq 159

Bay of Pigs invasion 72
BCTs (Brigade Combat Teams), Iraq 158, 227
Bennett, D.S. 178
Biddle, S. et al. (2017) 249n98
Bissell, R. 71–2
Black Hawk Down 176
Bohannon, C. 88
Bolshevik Revolution 34
Bonn Process 106
Boot, M. 5
Bravo, N. 21, 26–7
Bremer, L.P. 146, 149, 152, 154
Brigade Combat Teams see BCTs
Britain 2–3; colonialism 3–4, 14, 15, 31, 246n43; and Greece 31–2, 37–8, 39, 40, 42–6, 48, 54; and Middle Eastern oil 33; Sierra Leone 247n72
Bulgaria 33, 34, 37, 40, 41, 50
Bundy, M. 71
Bush, G.W. 104, 125n1, 141–2, 145, 157, 160
Bustamante, A. 21

Cairo, Egypt 37
Camau, Vietnam 83
Carlos IV, King of Spain 15
Carter, P. 238
Casey, G. Jr. 154, 155–7
Cecchinel, L. 114, 117, 118
CENTCOM (US Central Command) 142, 143, 146, 152
Central Intelligence Agency see CIA
Central Intelligence Group see CIG
CERP (Commander's Emergency Response Funds), Afghanistan 113
CFLCC (Coalition Forces Land Component Command), Iraq 144, 146
Chahardara, Afghanistan 113, 114, 115, 117–18, 123
Chapultepec Castle 26
'Charge of the Knights' operation, Iraq 159, 160
Cheney, D. 142
Chieu Hoi program, Vietnam 88, 91
China: and Africa 188; colonialism 3–4; communism 32; and Niger 184–5; People's Republic of 53
Churchill, W. 40, 42, 57n41
Churubusco, Mexico 26
CIA (Central Intelligence Agency) 7, 50, 51, 62–73, 120
CIG (Central Intelligence Group) 65–67
CIP (Critical Infrastructure Protection), Afghanistan 112–14, 115, 118

CISA (College of International Security Affairs) 244n13
Civil Guard, South Vietnam 84, 88
Civil Operations and Revolutionary Development Support see CORDS
CJTF-7 (Command Joint Task Force), Iraq 146, 153, 154
clientelism 102–12, 113, 115, 118–21, 125
Close, D. 39, 45, 46n77, 48n58, 50, 54
CMATT (Coalition Military Assistance Training Team) 153, 155
Coalition Police Assistance Training Team see CPATT
Coalition Provincial Authority see CPA
Colby, W. 93
Cold War 38, 46, 62–73, 144, 149, 177; Central Intelligence Agency (CIA) and 63–4, 67–73
College of International Security Affairs see CISA
Collier, P. 187
Collins, J.J. 232n45
Colombia 1, 104, 238
colonialism: British 3–4, 14, 15, 246n43; Chinese 3–4; French 3, 4, 14, 15; Japanese 3, 4, 32; Netherlands 3, 4; Portuguese 3; Russian 4; Spanish 4, 6–7, 14, 15, 16, 19
Combat Studies Institute 132n98
Combined Joint Special Operations Task Force, Afghanistan 123
COMINFORM (Communist Information Bureau) 63
Comintern (Communist International) 34
Command Joint Task Force Iraq see CJTF-7
Commander's Emergency Response Funds, Afghanistan see CERP
Commander's Handbook for Security Force Assistance 182
communism: China 53; and Greece 32, 33–56; global 53–4; see also Cold War; Soviet Union; Vietnam War
Communist Information Bureau see COMINFORM
Communist International see Comintern
Communist Party of Greece see KKE
'Comprehensive Approach' 232
Constantine I, King of Greece 34–5, 36
Constantine II, King of Greece 53
Contreras, Battle of 25
CORDS (Civil Operations and Revolutionary Development Support) 81, 91, 93
Cortés, H. 15
Cós, M. P. de 20

Counter-Guerrilla Warfare Task Force 71
CPA (Coalition Provincial Authority), Iraq 146, 149, 152, 153, 154
CPATT (Coalition Police Assistance Training Team), Iraq 153, 155
Critical Infrastructure Protection, Afghanistan *see* CIP
Crocker, R. 152, 157, 158
Cyprus, invasion of 53

DAP (Direct Access Programs) 206
Dasht-e-Archi, Afghanistan 117, 130n62
Dashti Leili massacre, Afghanistan 118–21
Daud, Mohammad 109
Dawa party, Iraq 157, 161
DDR (Demobilization, Disarmament, and Reintegration) programs 107–8, 112, 123, 179, 186
de Gaulle, C. 3
Dekemvriana ('December Events'), Greece 43, 55
Demertzis, K. 36
Demobilization, Disarmament, and Reintegration *see* DDR
Democratic Army of Greece *see* DSE
Democratic Party, US 16, 17, 18, 22, 23, 24
Department of Defense *see* DoD
DIAG (Disbandment of Illegal Armed groups), Afghanistan 123
Dimitrov, G. 41
Direct Access Programs *see* DAP
DoD (Department of Defense) 68, 142, 162, 182, 224, 227–8, 237
domestic protection programs 210–11
Donovan, W. 64–5, 67
Doolittle, J. 71
Dostum, Abdur Rashid 103, 104, 105, 106–7, 119–22, 124, 133n112
Downie, R.D. 255n10
Doyle, M.W. 187
drones 234–6
drug trafficking 111, 183
DSE (Democratic Army of Greece) 46, 50–1, 53, 55
Dulles, A. 69, 70, 71

EAM (Greek Liberation Front) 38, 39, 42, 43, 44
Eaton, P. 153
ECLIPSE II 144
EDES (National Democratic Greek League) 38, 39
EEPs (Explosive Formed Projectiles) 162
Eikenberry, K. 155
Eisenhardt, K. 212

Eisenhower, D. 53, 71
EKKA (National and Social Liberation), Greece 41
El Salvador 10, 239, 241
ELAS (National Popular Liberation Army), Greece 38, 39–43, 44, 45
ELD (Socialist Union of People's Democracy), Greece 43
ESAF (El Salvadoran Armed Forces) 239
Ewell, J. 93
Explosive Formed Projectiles *see* EEPs

F3EAD process, Iraq 164
Fahim, Marshall 106, 117
Fallujah, Iraq 150, 154, 155, 158
FAN (*Forces Armées Nigériennes*) 186
FARC (Revolutionary Armed Forces of Colombia) 1
Fardh al Qanoon ('Enforcing the Law'), Iraq 158
Faryab, Afghanistan 124
fascism 36, 37, 38, 39, 44
Fearon, J.D. 178
Ferdinand, King of Spain 15
Filisola, V. 21
First Barbary War 176
'Flexible Response' 177, 188–9
FM 3–22 Army Support to Security Cooperation (US Army) 183
FOBs (Forward Operating Bases), Iraq 155, 156, 158
Forces Armées Nigériennes see FAN
Foreign Assistance Act 182
Fortier, L.J. 66
Forward Operating Bases *see* FOBs
Fraleigh, B. 86, 90
France: and Africa 189–90; colonialism 3, 4, 14, 15; and Mexico 21; and Niger 184, 185; Revolution 15; and Southeast Asia 32
Franks, T.R. 126n11, 142, 146
Future Combat Systems 228
Future of Iraq project 144

Gallieni, J. 4
Gandhi, M. 11n8
Garner, J. 144, 146
Gates, R. 157
Gechi, Nabi 109, 113–14, 122
General Popular Radical Union, Greece 36
Geneva Accords 82, 83
George, King of England 15
Germany: Provincial Reconstruction Team, Afghanistan 109; occupation of Greece 37, 38–43; U.S. Army and 32
'Ghafiki Project' 147

Giustozzi, A. 108, 123, 124, 126n13, 128n35
Global War on Terror *see* GWOT
Golden Dome Mosque, Samarra 156
Goodhand, J. 109
Gramsci, A. 10n3
'Grand Strategy' 189
Grassley, C. 207
Great Depression 35, 52
Great Idea 34, 35
Greco-Italian War 52
Greco-Turkish War 52
Greece 7, 31–56; agriculture and occupation 37; Allied blockade 38; Axis occupation 52; Communism 34–7, 40–1; drought 45; ethnic minorities 38; First World War 52; GDP growth 52; hyperinflation 37; invasion and occupation 37–9; Junta 53; militia 42; monarchy 46; nationalism 33; refugees 52; refugees 35; resistance movement 37–9; social engineering attempts 36–7; strategic importance of 47; strikes 36; youth organization 36
Greek Communist Party 33
Greek Democratic Army 55
Greek Liberation Front *see* EAM
Greentree, T. 240
Griswold, D. 48, 50, 54
Guadalupe Hidalgo, Treaty of 27
Guichaoua, Y. 185
Gulf War 143
GWOT (Global War on Terror) 104, 153

Habsburgs 15
Hakimi, A. 109
Hamilton, L. 157
Hanson, V.D. 177
Harkins, P. 85, 88, 90
hate crime, anti-Muslim 133n106
Al Hawza (newspaper) 154
Hazaras, Afghanistan 105–6
Henderson, L. 49–50
Herrera, J.J. 22
Hezbi Islami party, Afghanistan 117, 127n21, 132n92
High Mobility Multipurpose Wheeled Vehicles *see* HUMMWVs
Hill, C. 161
Hillenkotter, R. 68
Hoffman, F. 5, 245n34
Hoover Commission 71
Hoxha, E. 51
HTTs (Human Terrain Teams) 227, 230
Huk (Hukbalahap) movement, Philippines 82, 88; Rebellion 4, 5
Hull, C. 38
Human Rights Watch 105, 110–11, 116
Human Terrain Teams *see* HTTs
HUMMWVs (High Mobility Multipurpose Wheeled Vehicles) 163

Iatrides, J.O. 46n72
ICA (International Cooperation Administration) 84
ICDC (Iraqi Civil Defense Corps) 153
IEDs (Improvised Explosive Devices) 147, 158, 162–3, 227, 228, 231
IIS (Iraqi Intelligence Service) 147
Immerman, R. 64
Improvised Explosive Devices *see* IEDs
INA (Immigration and Nationality Act) 205
India 3, 4, 46
Indochina 4
ING (Iraq National Guard) 155
Intelligence, Surveillance, and Reconnaissance, Iraq *see* ISR
International Cooperation Administration *see* ICA
International Refugee Assistance Project *see* IRAP
International Security Assistance Force *see* ISAF
interpreters 200–1, 203–6, 207, 210, 212, 213
Iran 32, 66, 145, 160
IRAP (International Refugee Assistance Project) 207
Iraq War 72, 140–66; civilian casualties 203; cost of 166; detentions 150–1; ethnic cleansing 148; intelligence failures 144–5, 149–50; Interim Iraqi Government (IIG) 154, 155; invasion 145–6; militia 147–8, 149, 154, 155, 156, 158–61, 201; national elections 156, 157; paramilitary groups 145–7; post-war strategy 152–3; relocation program 216; soft networks 201, 202–8, 212, 216; Surge policy 157–8, 160, 161, 162, 163; US withdrawal 153
Iraq National Guard *see* ING
Iraq Study Group 157
Iraqi Civil Defense Corps *see* ICDC
Iraqi Governing Council 149, 154
Iraqi Intelligence Service *see* IIS
Iraqi Security Forces *see* ISF
IS (Islamic State) 5, 223–4

ISAF (International Security Assistance Force) 118
ISF (Iraqi Security Forces) 155–6, 212
ISR (Intelligence, Surveillance, and Reconnaissance), Iraq 164
Italy 37, 39
Iturbide, A.C.D. de 15, 21
Iturrigaray, J. 15

al Ja'afari, Ibrahim 152
Jackson, A. 16–17
Jamiat-I Islami party, Afghanistan 103, 105–8, 115, 116, 117–18, 122–3
Jamshidi, Ismail 110
Japan, colonialism 3, 4, 32
Jaysh al Mahdi, Iraq 148, 154, 159
JCISFA (Joint Center for International Security Force Assistance) 182, 183
JCS Strategic Survey Committee *see* JSSC
Jefferson, T. 16
JIATFs (Joint Inter-Agency Task Forces), Iraq 164
Johnson, L.B. 53, 188–9
Joint Center for International Security Force Assistance *see* JCIFSA
Joint Inter-Agency Task Forces, Iraq *see* JIATFs
Joint Special Operations Command, Iraq *see* JSOC
Joint US Military Advisory and Planning Group *see* JUSMAPG
Jombesh-I Milli party, Afghanistan 103, 105–6, 108, 115, 118, 119, 122
JSOC (Joint Special Operations Command), Iraq 164
JSSC (JCS Strategic Survey Committee) 65
JUSMAPG (Joint US Military Advisory and Planning Group) 49

Kabul, Afghanistan 105, 106
Karbala, Iraq 147, 154, 159
Karzai, Hamid 127n19, 130n65
KDP (Kurdistan Democratic Party), Iraq 148
Kearney, S. 24, 25
Kennan, G. 50, 54, 66, 68, 69
Kennedy, J.F. 71, 72, 85, 90
Kerik, B. 153
Khaliq, Enaytullah 123
Khanabad, Afghanistan 110, 116
Kidal, Battle of 189
Kieu Cong Cung 84
Kirkuk, Iraq 148, 159
Kiszely, J. 226
KKE (Communist Party of Greece) 34, 35, 38, 40–1, 45, 48, 51, 55

Klare, M.T. 184
Komer, R. 8
Koliopoulos, J.S. 46n75
Korea 4, 32
Krulak, V. 90
Krushchev, N. 72
Kunduz, Afghanistan 106, 109, 110–11, 113–16
Kurdistan Democratic Party *see* KDP
Kurds 142, 147, 148, 156, 157, 158
Kuwait 145

Lacher, W. 187
Lambe, G. 159
Lansdale, E.G. 5, 7, 82, 85, 90, 92
Latin America 6
Lausanne, Treaty of 35
Lee, M. 207
Lee, R.E. 25
Lenin, V. 34
Liberal Party, Greece 36
Libya 179–80
Long An, Vietnam 90
Loy Kanam, Afghanistan 129n55
Luján, F. 248n82
Lyautey, H. 4

MAAG (Military Assistance Advisory Group), Vietnam 85, 88
Macmillan, H. 44
MACV (Military Assistance Command), Vietnam 81, 85, 86, 88–9
MacVeagh, L. 44, 48, 49
Magruder, J. 65, 66
Magsaysay, R. 82
Maiksii, I. 40
Malaya 4, 229, 246n43
Maley, W. 128n36
Mali 189–90, 239
al Maliki, Nuri 120, 157, 158, 159, 160, 161
Maniadakis, K. 36
Manifest Destiny doctrine 16, 22
Mao Zedong 53
Margh ('Death') group, Afghanistan 134n118
Markos Vafiades 49
'Markos Junta' 50
Marks, T.A. 1
Marshall, G.C. 68
Marshall Plan 47, 52, 53, 68
Marxism 10n3
Matamoros, Mexico 19, 23
Mazar-e Sharif, Afghanistan 104, 106–7, 120, 121, 122
Mazower, M. 46n74
McCain, J. 179, 207

McChrystal, S. 164
McCloy, J. 65
McKiernan, D. 144, 146
McNamara, R. 85, 90, 178
Meligalas, Greece 41–2
Mendenhall, J. 90
Metaxas, I. 36–7, 52
Metz, T. 154
Mexican War 6–7, 14–29; campaigns 23; Constitution 20; first 'overseas deployment' of U.S. forces 23; Mexican surrender 27; *las Siete Leyes* (the Seven Laws) 21; volunteers 24
Mexico City 19, 25–6
Military Assistance Advisory Group *see* MAAG
Military Assistance Command, Vietnam *see* MACV
Military Contribution to Cooperative Security Joint Operating Concept (DoD) 181
militias: Afghanistan 102, 103, 105–17, 118, 121, 123–5; Greece 42; Iraq 147–8, 149, 154, 155, 156, 158–61, 201; Niger 186; US 24; Vietnam 88, 91, 94
Mine Resistant Ambush Protected fleet *see* MRAP
'Mini-Tet' 92
MNC-I (Multi-National Corps-Iraq) 154, 155–7, 159
MNJ (*Mouvement des Nigériens pour la justice*) 184, 186, 187
MNLA (National Movement for the Liberation of Azawad) 189–90
MNSTC-I (Multi-National Security Transition Command-Iraq) 154, 155–6
Mogadishu, Battle of 191n2
Mohseni, Ghulam Mustafa 117
Mokeddem, M. 187
Mokhtar bel Mokhtar 190
Molino del Rey, Battle of 26
Mosul, Iraq 148, 248n91
MRAP (Mine Resistant Ambush Protected) fleet 163
Mukhopadhyay, D. 122
Multi-National Corps-Iraq *see* MNC-I
Multi-National Security Transition Command-Iraq *see* MNSTC-I
Murad, Sayed 123
Mussolini, B. 37

Najaf, Iraq 147, 154, 155
Napoleon Bonaparte 6, 15
Nashir, Nizamuddin 110
National and Social Liberation, Greece *see* EKKA
National Democratic Greek League *see* EDES
National Directorate of Security, Afghanistan *see* NDS
National Guard, Greece 42
National Intelligence Authority *see* NIA
National Liberation Front, Greece 38
National Military Strategy *see* NMS
National Movement for the Liberation of Azawad *see* MNLA
National Popular Liberation Army, Greece *see* ELAS
National Security Act 66, 67
National Security Council *see* NSC
National Security Strategy see NSS
nationalism 33, 38, 39, 45, 50, 143, 160
NATO (North Atlantic Treaty Organization) 47, 53, 108, 112, 113, 224
natural resources 33, 147, 184–5, 187
NDAA (National Defense Authorization Act) 205, 206
NDS (National Directorate of Security), Afghanistan 109, 110, 115, 116
Negroponte, J. 154
Netherlands, colonialism 3, 4
New Spain 15
Ngo Dinh Diem 83, 85, 86, 89, 90, 91
NGOs (non-governmental organizations) 202, 208–14, 233
NIA (National Intelligence Authority) 66
Niger 183–91; costs to US 183, 186, 240; militia 186; mineral resources 184–5; Tuareg rebellion 184
Nitze, P. 69
Nixon Doctrine 237
NMS (National Military Strategy) 181
NOLB (No One Left Behind) 207
Nolting, F. 88, 89
non-governmental organizations *see* NGOs
Noor, Atta Mohammad 103, 104, 106–7, 108, 110–111, 118, 121–2, 129n59, 132n88
North Korea 53, 153
Northern Alliance, Afghanistan 104–5, 109, 119–21, 143
Northern No-Fly Zone, Iraq 142, 148
Novo, A. 7
NSC (National Security Council) 67, 68, 69, 69–70, 142, 144
NSS (*National Security Strategy*) 181–2

Obama, B. 160, 181, 234–5, 239
O'Ballance, E. 50n99
O'Bannon, P. 176

ODAs (Operational Detachment Alphas) 120, 121
Odierno, R. 158, 159, 160, 161
Office of Humanitarian Reconstruction and Assistance 144, 146
Office of the Coordinator for Reconstruction and Stabilization see S/CRS
Office of Rural Affairs, Vietnam 86, 88–91
Office of the Secretary of Defense see OSD
Office of Special Operations see OSO
Office of Strategic Services see OSS
Omar, Mohammad 109, 116
OPC (Office of Policy Coordination) 69, 70
Operation Enduring Freedom 118
Operation Gothic Serpent 191n2
Operational Detachment Alphas see ODAs
OPLA (Organization for the Protection of the People's Struggle), Greece 41
Osama bin Laden 120, 141, 176
OSD (Office of the Secretary of Defense) 143
OSO (Office of Special Operations) 67, 70
OSS (Office of Strategic Services) 64–5
Ottoman Empire 34, 35

Packer, G. 200n1
Palestine 46
Palo Alto, Battle of 23
Papandreou, G. 53
paramilitary groups 64, 67; Afghanistan 101–4, 107, 109, 112, 113, 116–20, 124–5; Iraq 145–7
Paredes y Arillaga, M. 22, 23
Partsalides, D. 43, 44
Pashtuns, Afghanistan 105, 108, 109, 113, 117, 121, 124–5, 132n88
Pastry War 21
Patras, Greece 43
Patrick, D.L. 220n42
Patriotic Union of Kurdistan, Iraq see PUQ
Patterson, R. 65
Peace Research Institute, Oslo 179
Pearl Harbor attack 63
People's Party, Greece 36
People's Republic of China 53
Perkins, D. 145, 231n39
Petraeus, D. 8, 154, 155–6, 157, 158, 159, 162
Philippines 4, 5, 7, 82, 88, 241
Phoenix program, Vietnam 91
PIC (Provincial Iraqi Control) 154–5
Pillow, G.J. 25
Plan Colombia program 238

political systems 10n3
Polk, J.K. 16, 17–19, 22–5, 27, 29
Portugal, colonialism 3
Powell, C. 142
Preventative Hypothesis 192n39
Provincial Iraqi Control see PIC
proxies 237–41
Psarros, D. 41
PUK (Patriotic Union of Kurdistan), Iraq 148

Qala Jangi prison 119, 121
Qala Zeini prison 119
Qala-e Zal, Afghanistan 113
QDR (Quadrennial Defense Review) (DoD) 181
Quirino, E.R. 82
Quitman, J.A. 25

al-Rahman, Atiyah Abd 247n59
Ramadi, Iraq 158
Republican Guard, Iraq 145
Requests For Forces, Iraq see RFFs
Resaca de la Palma, Battle of 23
Revolutionary Armed Forces of Colombia see FARC
Revolutionary Development, Vietnam 81, 91, 92, 93
Revolutionary United Front, Sierra Leone see RUF
RFFs (Requests For Forces), Iraq 143
Roosevelt, F. 47, 64–5
Ross, S.A. 202, 211–12
Rostow, W. 71
RUF (Revolutionary United Front), Sierra Leone 247n72
Rumania 50
Rumsfeld, D. 126n11, 141–2, 143, 146, 149, 153, 157
Russia, colonialism 4

al-Sadr, Muqtada 148
al-Shabaab 208
Saddam Hussein 142, 143, 144–7, 151, 153
al-Sadr, Muqtada 154, 155, 159
Sadr City 154, 155
Sadrists 154, 159
Said bin Taimur 246n43
Samarra, Iraq 155, 156
Sambanis, N. 187
San Antonio, Mexico 20, 21
San Jacinto, Battle of 21
SANACC (State-Army-Navy-Air Force Coordinating Committee) 68
Sanchez, R. 146

Santa Anna, A.L. de 20–1, 25, 28
Sayedkhaili, Abdul Rahman 110
SC (Security Cooperation) 180
SCIRI (Supreme Council for Islamic Revolution in Iraq) 147–8
Scobie, R. 42–3
Scott, W. 6, 17, 18, 23–9, 29
Scotton, F. 92
S/CRS (Office of the Coordinator for Reconstruction and Stabilization) 233
SDC (self-defense corps), Vietnam 84, 88
Security Cooperation see SC
Security Force Assistance see SFA
Selective Engagement 177, 188, 190
self-defense corps see SDC
Selective Engagement 177, 188, 190
Seminole War 18
Senate CIA Torture Report 2014 125
Sewell, S. 225
SFA (Security Force Assistance) 180, 183, 240
Shaheen, J. 207
Sheberghan, A. 118
Shi'as, Iraq 147–9, 152, 154, 156–61
Shiberghan Prison 132n98
Shrine of Hazrat Ali 122
Siantos, G. 43, 44
Sierra Leone 247n72
Singletary, O. 28
al Sistani, Ali 147
SIV (special immigration visa) 201, 204–8
Slidell, J. 19
Smith, W. B. 70
Smyrna, Greece 35
Socialist Union of People's Democracy, Greece see ELD
Socialist Workers Party of Greece 34
SOFA (Status of Forces Agreement), Iraq 160–1
soft networks 200–19; and agency theory 211–14
Somalia 176, 208–11
'Sons of Iraq' see Anbar Awakening
Souers, S. 66
Soviet Union: Cold War 62–73; and Greece 32–5, 40–2, 45–6, 47, 48, 49, 54–5
Spain, colonialism 4, 6–7, 14, 15, 16, 19
special immigration visa see SIV
Special Operations Executive, Britain 38
SSU (Strategic Services Unit) 65, 66–7
Stalin, J. 33, 35, 40–6, 48, 50, 54–5, 57n41, 63, 65–6
Stam, A.C. 178
State-Army-Navy-Air Force Coordinating Committee see SANACC

Status of Forces Agreement, Iraq see SOFA
Stothard Tee, W. 245n30
Strategic Framework Agreement, Iraq 160
Strategic Hamlet Program, Vietnam 86, 90, 91
Strategic Services Unit see SSU
Stuart, D. 64
Sudan 176
Sun Tzu 190
Sunnis, Iraq 146, 147–9, 154–61, 166
Sunni Awakening see Anbar Awakening
Supreme Council for Islamic Revolution in Iraq see SCIRI
Surge policy, Iraq 157–8, 160, 161, 162, 163
Syria 145

Taiwan 85
Taliban 101, 103–6, 108–10, 112–21, 124, 143, 223
Tandja, M. 186
Task Force Justice, Iraq 206
Taylor, M. 72, 90, 92
Taylor, Z. 17, 18–19, 23, 24, 25
technology, use of 227–8, 234–6
Tet Offensive, Vietnam 81, 91
Texas 16, 19, 20–3, 27
Thessaloniki, Greece 35, 36, 42, 43
Thurman, J. 145
Tibet 3
Timbuktu, Mali 189–90
Tito, J.B. 33, 46, 50
TOGETHER FORWARD I and II, Iraq 157
Tongo Tongo ambush 189
TPFDL (Time Phased Force Deployment List), Iraq 143
Tran Ngoc Chau 91
Trans-Sahara Counterterrorism Partnership see TSCTP
Tratados de Velasco 21
Truman, H.S. 47–8, 53, 54, 65–6, 67, 71, 74n29
Truman Doctrine 47, 53
Trump, D. 237, 239–40
Tsaldaris, K. 48
TSCTP (Trans-Sahara Counterterrorism Partnership) 194n77
Tsirimokos, I. 43, 44
Tuaregs 184, 186–7
Turkey 35, 47, 48, 52, 53, 66, 160
Twiggs, D.E. 25

UN (United Nations) 108, 121, 156, 189
UNAMA (United Nations Assistance Mission Afghanistan) 106, 111

United Agrarian Party, Greece 44
United Alignment of Nationalists, Greece 45–6
United Nations Assistance Mission Afghanistan see UNAMA
UNSCR (UN Security Council Resolution) 154
U.S. National Defense Strategy 2018 5
US Strategy for Sub-Saharan Africa 180
USAID (US Agency for International Development) 232–3
USIS (US Information Service) 92
USOM (United States Operations Mission), Vietnam 84, 86, 91
Uzbeks, Afghanistan 105, 106, 109, 122

Van Buren, M. 17, 22
Van Fleet, J. 49
Van Wagenen, M.S. 28
Vann, J.P. 229
Vaphiades, M. 46, 51
Varkiza, Greece 43–6
Velouchiotis, A. 38, 41, 44
Venizelos, E. 34–5
La Venta de La Mesilla (Gadsden Purchase) 28
Veracruz, Mexico 19, 21, 25
Veremis, T.M. 46n75, 46n77
Viet Minh 82, 83, 84
Vietcong 85, 86–7, 89, 90–2
Vietnam War 7–8, 53, 81–96; armed capacity 88–8; Census-Grievance process 91; counterinsurgency factors 94–6; Central Intelligence Agency (CIA) and 72; Free Fire Zones 89; militia 88, 91, 94; US policy 84–5, 229, 241; USAID 232
Vietnamese Army see ARVN
Village Stability Operations, Afghanistan 118

Wagner, R.H. 178
Wahab, Ghafar 123
Waldhauser, T.D. 179–80
Wali, Amruddin 113
Wallace, W. 145, 146
Waltz, K. 178
Washington, G. 16
Weapons of Mass Destruction, Iraq see WMD
Weigley, R. 18, 24
Wenran J. 184
West Point Military Academy 24
Westmoreland, W, 81, 92
Whig Party, US 16, 17, 2, 23, 24
White Terror, Greece 44, 46
Williams, T.H. 19
Winders, R.B. 17, 25
Wisner, F. 69–70
Witness Security program 202, 210–11, 213, 215–16
WMD (Weapons of Mass Destruction), Iraq 142, 145, 151
Wolfowitz, Paul 120, 141–2
Wool, J.E. 24
Worth, W.J. 25
World War I 34–5, 52, 179
World War II 31, 37, 39, 65–7, 144, 148–9, 176, 228

'X' 42
Xinjiang 4

Yerganak, Afghanistan 119
Yugoslavia 50–1, 55

Zachariades, N. 35, 37, 43–4, 46, 48, 51, 55
Zargar, Haji Gul Ahmad 110
al Zarqawi, Abu Mus'ab 142, 156, 158, 164
Zegart, A. 64
Zhou Wenzhong 185